THE MAKING OF MODERN THEOLOGY

19TH AND 20TH CENTURY THEOLOGICAL TEXTS

This series of theological texts is designed to introduce a new generation of readers — theological students, students of religion, ordained ministers and the interested general reader — to the writings of some of those Christian theologians who, since the beginning of the 19th century, have had a formative influence on the development of Christian theology. Each volume in the series is intended to introduce the theologian, to trace the emergence of key or seminal ideas and insights, particularly within their social and historical context, and to show how they have contributed to the making of modern theology. The primary way in which this is done is by allowing the theologians chosen to address us in their own words.

There are three sections to each volume. The Introduction includes a short biography of the theologian, and an overview of his or her theology in relation to the texts which have been selected for study. The Selected Texts, the bulk of each volume, consist largely of substantial edited selections from the theologian's writings. Each text is also introduced with information about its origin and its significance. The guiding rule in making the selection of texts has been the question: in what way has this particular theologian contributed to the shaping of contemporary theology? A Select Bibliography provides guidance for those who wish to read further both in the primary literature and in secondary sources.

Available in this series

1 Friedrich Schleiermacher: Pioneer of modern theology
2 Rudolf Bultmann: Interpreting faith for the modern era
3 Paul Tillich: Theologian of the boundaries
4 Dietrich Bonhoeffer: Witness to Jesus Christ

THE MAKING OF MODERN THEOLOGY

19th and 20th Century Texts
General Editor: John de Gruchy

DIETRICH BONHOEFFER

Witness to Jesus Christ

JOHN DE GRUCHY

COLLINS

Collins Liturgical Publications
8 Grafton Street, London W1X 3LA

Collins San Francisco
Icehouse One — 401
151 Union Street, San Francisco, CA 94111-1299

Collins Liturgical in Canada
c/o Novalis, Box 9700, Terminal,
375 Rideau St, Ottawa, Ontario K1G 4B4

Distributed in Ireland by
Educational Company of Ireland
21 Talbot Street, Dublin 1

Collins Liturgical Australia
PO Box 316, Blackburn, Victoria 3130

Collins Liturgical New Zealand
PO Box 1, Auckland

Library of Congress Cataloging-in-Publication Data

De Gruchy, John W.
  Dietrich Bonhoeffer: witness to Jesus Christ.

  (The Making of modern theology)
  Bibliography: p.
  Includes index.
  1. Bonhoeffer, Dietrich, 1906-1945.   I. Title.
II. Series.
BX8080.B645D4   1987   230′.044′0924   87—18264

ISBN 0-00-599058-0 (cased)
ISBN 0-00-599979-0 (paperback)

First published 1988

Typographical design Colin Reed
Typeset by Swains (Glasgow) Limited
Printed in Great Britain by
Richard Clay Ltd, Bungay, Suffolk

CONTENTS

ABBREVIATIONS

AB	*Act and Being*
C	*Christology* (revised edition)
CD	Karl Barth, *Church Dogmatics*
CF	*Creation and Fall*
DB	Eberhard Bethge, *Dietrich Bonhoeffer: Theologian, Christian, Contemporary*
DWK	*Das Wesen der Kirche*
E	*Ethics*
FFP	*Fiction from Prison*
GS	*Gesammelte Schriften*
LPP	*Letters and Papers from Prison*
LT	*Life Together*
NRS	*No Rusty Swords* (revised edition)
SC	*Sanctorum Communio*
TP	*True Patriotism*
USQR	*Union Seminary Quarterly Review*
WF	*The Way to Freedom*
ET	*English translation*

ACKNOWLEDGEMENTS

The publishers acknowledge with thanks permission to reproduce the following copyright texts from works by Dietrich Bonhoeffer:

by permission of Wm Collins Sons & Co:

pp. 102-113, *Christology*, trans. Edwin Robertson. Wm Collins, 1978

pp. 153-169, 217-225, 284-287, 321-339, 302-312, 88-113 from *No Rusty Swords*. Revised by John Bowden. Fontana, 1970

pp.75-96 passim from *The Way to Freedom*. Edited and introduced by Edwin H. Robertson. Wm Collins, 1973

pp. 28-33 from *True Patriotism*. Edited and introduced by Edwin H. Robertson. Wm Collins, 1973

by permission of Wm Collins Sons & Co and Harper and Row, Publishers, Inc.:

pp. 79-141 passim from *Act and Being*, trans. Bernard Noble. Copyright © 1956 by Christian Kaiser Verlag. Copyright © 1961 in the English translation by Wm Collins and Harper and Row

pp. 20-119 passim from *Sanctorum Communio (Communion of Saints)*, trans. R. Gregor Smith. Copyright © 1960 by Christian Kaiser Verlag. Copyright © 1963 in the English translation by Wm Collins and Harper and Row

by permission of Christian Kaiser Verlag:

pp. 110-126, *Gesammelte Schriften*, III, ed. E. Bethge

by permission of Fortress Press:

pp. 30-44 from *Spiritual Care*, trans. Jay Rochelle. English translation copyright © 1985 Fortress Press by permission of Harper and Row, Publishers, Inc.:

pp. 17-39 from *Life Together*, trans. John Doberstein. Copyright © 1954 by Harper and Row

by permission of Macmillan Publishing Co:

pp. 74-77 from *Fiction from Prison*, trans. Ursula Hoffmann, ed. and introduced by Clifford Green. Copyright © 1981 Macmillan

by permission of SCM Press and Macmillan Publishing Co:

pp. 33-38, from *Creation and Fall*, trans. John C. Fletcher. SCM Press and Macmillan, 1959

pp. 64-88 passim, pp. 188-201 passim, pp. 224-254 passim, from *Ethics*. Copyright © in the English translation SCM Press 1955, and Macmillan, 1955

'After Ten Years', pp. 380-383, pp. 278-362 passim from *Letters and Papers from Prison*. Copyright in The Enlarged Edition SCM Press 1971, and Macmillan Paperbacks, 1972

pp. 35-60, from *The Cost of Discipleship*, trans. Reginald Fuller. Second edition © SCM Press 1959, and Macmillan Paperbacks, 1963

AUTHOR'S NOTE

There are several collections of Bonhoeffer's writings available for the English reader. This volume differs from them in two major respects. Firstly, it traces the chronological development of Bonhoeffer's theology from its early beginnings in Tübingen and Berlin to its sudden, untimely ending in Tegel prison. Secondly, instead of offering snippets from many sources within the Bonhoeffer corpus, it provides substantial extracts, and often the full text, of those writings which document his development. For this reason there are extensive extracts from his two earliest books, presently out of print in English, *Sanctorum Communio* and *Act and Being*. The selected texts also demonstrate the various ways in which Bonhoeffer has contributed to the shaping of contemporary Christian thought and practice, and they provide an interesting and pertinent commentary on the period and locations in which they were written.

In editing the texts I have not attempted to make Bonhoeffer's language inclusive, except that where he uses *Menscheit* I have generally used 'humanity' rather than 'mankind'. His use of *Mensch* (i.e. human being) is invariably followed by masculine pronouns, so I have left the translation as 'man'. Although I have used the standard, and, where available, the revised English translations, I have, on occasion, taken the liberty of making some changes in the interests of clarity or accuracy. But these have been kept to a minimum.

It would be remiss of me not to express thanks to all the authors who are participating in the 'Making of Modern Theology' series, and also to thank Sue and Geoffrey Chapman and all at Collins Liturgical Publications for their keen interest and commitment to the project. I am also grateful to Clifford Green and Keith Clements for their helpful comments on the penultimate text of this particular volume, and to Nan Oosthuizen for her enthusiasm and secretarial help.

John de Gruchy
University of Cape Town
September, 1987

INTRODUCTION
THE DEVELOPMENT OF BONHOEFFER'S THEOLOGY

THE MAKING OF A THEOLOGIAN

On 9 April, 1945, Dietrich Bonhoeffer, aged thirty-nine, died at the hands of a Gestapo hangman in the concentration camp at Flossenbürg. Bonhoeffer's theological legacy is remarkably rich and extensive, despite the unsettled character of his life and his untimely death. Some of his books, notably *The Cost of Discipleship*, and his *Letters and Papers from Prison*, have become theological classics. But these well-known writings are part of a much larger corpus of books, essays, lectures and sermons[1]* which have had a profound influence on the development of modern theology and the church. Had he lived longer he might have dominated the theological scene in the second half of the twentieth century in succession to Karl Barth, Rudolf Bultmann, and Paul Tillich. As it was, he became a paradigmatic martyr-theologian for the twentieth century.[2]

In his definitive biography, *Dietrich Bonhoeffer: Theologian, Christian, Contemporary*, Eberhard Bethge, his friend and confidant, has shown the extent to which Bonhoeffer's life and theology were bound together. More recently, in his introduction to the English edition of Bonhoeffer's *Fiction from Prison*, Clifford Green refers to Bonhoeffer himself as being 'a highly autobiographical thinker'. But significantly, Bonhoeffer's autobiography 'was not the experience of an isolated individualist but, like the basic pattern of his thinking, intrinsically social' (FFP: ix). With this in mind I have chosen to describe his theological development in tandem with his biography and social context; hence the chronological structure of this introductory essay and the selected texts. This will enable the reader to locate the texts and discern some of the ways in which Bonhoeffer contributed to the making of modern theology.

Born in Breslau, Germany, on 4 February 1906, Dietrich moved to Berlin in 1912 when his father Karl Bonhoeffer became professor of psychiatry at the University. His family was well-educated, gifted,

---

* Numbered footnotes are on pp. 302-303.

closely-knit, part of upper-middle class, privileged society. Bethge, a later member of the family by marriage to Bonhoeffer's niece Renate, tells us that Dietrich 'grew up in a family that derived its real education, not from school, but from a deeply-rooted sense of being guardians of a great historical heritage and intellectual tradition' (DB: 4).

The fact that Bonhoeffer became a theologian was surprising. His family were disenchanted members of the Church of the Old Prussian Union (Lutheran and Reformed) and seldom participated in Sunday worship. They perceived the church as an extension of bourgeois culture, closed to intellectual challenge, and incapable of addressing the urgent issues facing society. Dietrich's initial sense of vocation at age fourteen had little to do with the church. He chose to become a theologian in order to excel at something of his own choice and different from the careers of his brothers, despite paternal reservations and the puzzled queries of the family. In 1923 at age seventeen, having completed his high-schooling in the thorough classical German tradition, Dietrich left home and began his theological studies at the University of Tübingen.

During his year at Tübingen (1923/4) Bonhoeffer delved deeply into philosophy, studied the New Testament under Adolf Schlatter, who had a lasting influence upon his understanding and interpretation of Scripture, and was introduced to the great liberal theologians Friedrich Schleiermacher and Albrecht Ritschl by the systematic theologian, Karl Heim, though Heim himself did not particularly impress him. Given Bonhoeffer's ability as a pianist and his interest in music, it is not surprising that he also managed to include amongst his seminars one on Beethoven's symphonies.[3]

Together with his older brother Klaus, Dietrich journeyed to Rome in the Spring of 1924. Having explored the ruins of the ancient imperial city, they went on to Sicily and North Africa. But Bonhoeffer was glad to get back to Italy, and in the weeks that remained of his vacation, his interest shifted from imperial to ecclesiastical Rome. He attended lectures on church history and worshipped in St Peters. While unhappy about some Catholic dogmas, it was in Rome that Bonhoeffer discovered for the first time the reality of the church as a living, worshipping, and universal community.

On returning to Germany, Bonhoeffer enrolled at the University of Berlin, where he stayed until the completion of his studies. During his four years of study he obtained a thorough grounding in all the disciplines necessary for a German pastor and theologian. The Berlin theological faculty included several renowned scholars. Numbered amongst them was Karl Holl, whose knowledge of Luther contributed to the shaping of Bonhoeffer's theology, and Reinhold Seeberg, the conservative systematic theologian whose neo-Hegelianism exerted an influence on Bonhoeffer's early theological endeavours. The most distinguished member of the faculty was the doyen of liberal theologians, Adolf von Harnack, who had succeeded Ritschl in 1886. Regarded with grave suspicion by Berlin's conservative church leaders, his scientific studies in the history of Christianity made a considerable impression on Bonhoeffer. Harnack deeply regretted, however, that this young promising student came under the spell of the 'unscientific' Karl Barth then teaching at Münster.

While he never formally studied under Barth, Bonhoeffer avidly read his writings, and Barth undoubtedly became his most influential teacher. Bonhoeffer was attracted to Barth because he found the theology of his Berlin professors inadequate for what he was seeking to do. As Thomas Day has aptly said, 'He tried to use his professors' conceptual tools to articulate his real concerns, and the weight of their system-inherent questions almost sank his argument.'[4] Yet, in one of his last letters from prison, on 3 August 1944, Bonhoeffer made the revealing comment that although he was a 'modern theologian', that is, one influenced by Barth, he was 'still aware of the debt' he owed to 'liberal theology. There will not be many of the younger men' he added, 'in whom these two trends are combined' (LPP: 378).

THEOLOGICAL FOUNDATIONS*
A THEOLOGY OF SOCIALITY

Bonhoeffer's theological studies reached their fulfilment in his doctoral dissertation *Sanctorum Communio*, written under the supervision of Seeberg. Few doctoral theses make exciting reading, and Bonhoeffer's is no exception. One sympathetic commentator calls it dense, involuted and clumsy![5] Yet no less than Karl Barth wrote about its 'broad and deep vision' which 'is to this very day more instructive, more stimulating, more enlightening and more truly "edifying" to read than a great deal of the better-known writing that has since been published on the problem

* For texts, see below pp. 43-97.

of the church'.[6] Whatever the verdict, no serious student of Bonhoeffer's theology can avoid grappling with *Sanctorum Communio*, for it is here that we discover some of the foundations for all that follows.

Sanctorum Communio was a pioneering theological work, described in its subtitle as 'A Dogmatic Enquiry into the Sociology of the Church'. No one had previously attempted to relate systematic theology and sociology in this way. Neo-orthodox theologians would have been suspicious of the very idea, and sociologists would have questioned the legitimacy of dogmatics entering their domain. Nevertheless Bonhoeffer went a long way to achieve his stated aim 'to understand the structure, from the standpoint of social philosophy and sociology, of the reality of the church of Christ which is given in the revelation of Christ' (SC: 20).

Bonhoeffer's dissertation was not a study in ecclesiology narrowly conceived, but an exploration of the sociality of Christianity. In the Preface, he wrote:

> The more theologians have considered the significance of the sociological category for theology, the more clearly the social intention of all the basic Christian concepts has emerged. 'Person,' 'primal state,' 'sin' and 'revelation' are fully understandable only in relation to sociality. *(SC: 6)*

Seeberg and the Hegelian tradition more generally, influenced Bonhoeffer's theology of sociality. This understanding of Christianity, which shapes Bonhoeffer's early theology, provides a key building block for what follows, and is influential in his thought to the end.[7]

Behind Bonhoeffer's immediate interest in ecclesiology lay a more fundamental concern. He set out to locate theology in the context of human social and ethical relations in history, rather than in the epistemological framework of post-Kantian philosophy or the individualism of existentialism. The individualism of both excluded the possibility of a true knowledge of God. For Bonhoeffer, the empirical existence of the church in history provided the place where such knowledge becomes possible. Hence the use of sociological categories recast in the light of faith.

The fulcrum of the five tightly packed chapters is the second, in which Bonhoeffer discusses 'the Christian concept of the Person'. As John Calvin began his *Institutes of the Christian Religion* by relating 'the knowledge of God and of man', so Bonhoeffer, taking sociality seriously, integrates the indissolubly related concepts of person, community and God. 'It is in relation to persons and community that the concept of God is formed.' But while 'in principle, the nature of the Christian concept of community can be reached as well from the concept of God as from the concept of the person', Bonhoeffer chose to begin with the latter (SC: 22).

Existentialism and personalist philosophies exerted a powerful influence on theology during the 1920's. Although Kierkegaard's influence can be seen in *The Cost of Discipleship*, Bonhoeffer never fell under the Dane's spell in quite the same way as Barth did. And although Bonhoeffer used 'I-Thou' terminology extensively, *Sanctorum Communio* contains no reference to Martin Buber's classic *I and Thou* published in 1923. Bonhoeffer borrowed the terms from the philosopher Eberhard Grisebach, who also introduced him to the key idea that personal existence is constituted by social relations.

Working from a personalist perspective, Bonhoeffer discusses the nature of the person as arising through ethical encounter with 'the other', the 'I' coming into being through being addressed by the 'Thou'. The 'Thou' presents the 'I' with a barrier beyond which the 'I' cannot go. This experience is an acknowledgement of transcendence which evokes ethical responsibility. In this way the 'I' encounters and knows the divine 'Thou' in, with and under the human 'Thou'.

Just as people discover their personal identities through their ethical encounters with others, so Bonhoeffer holds that communities with their distinctive cultures ('Objective spirit [*Geist*]') also have a personal character; so a community can be regarded in a special sense as a 'Collective person'. This does not exist apart from the individual members of the community, but it does make the community an ethically accountable body and makes individual persons responsible for the corporate communities to which they belong. Thus persons in relation to each other and to their communities are intrinsically social-ethical-historical beings. True community is not constituted by like-minded people associating, but by participating in mutual ethical relationships.

The relationship of the person to this community is neither contractual nor one in which the individual is absorbed into a mass, but one in which persons submit to a higher obligation, and, in doing so, find themselves. Indeed,

> God does not desire a history of individual men, but the history of the community of men. Nor does he desire a community which absorbs the individual into itself, but a community of persons. . . . The structures of the individual and the collective unit are the same. Upon

these basic relations rests the concept of the religious community and the church. *(SC: 52)*

Sin destroys human community, however, because it is the will affirming itself and not the other person. All human community is *peccatorum communio*, the old humanity united 'in Adam' and 'subject to endless fragmentation' (SC: 85). But through the vicarious atonement of Christ, humanity is restored, and the 'collective person' (Adam) is superceded by the collective 'Second Adam'. This is nothing less than 'Christ existing as the congregation' (*Christus als Gemeinde existierend*).* Gemeinde is translated 'congregation' understood not as an institution but as a 'community of persons'. With this formulation, central to Bonhoeffer's early theology, we arrive at the *sanctorum communio*.

The concept of 'vicarious action' (*Stellvertretung*), through which Christ realizes the church, is crucial and, in various forms, recurs throughout Bonhoeffer's theology. Christ creates and holds the new humanity together, not through solidarity — that 'is never possible between Christ and man' — but through vicarious action which 'is the life-principle of the new humanity' (SC: 107). This is not, in turn, something which the community can achieve by moral effort. The Holy Spirit actualises what Christ has done, thereby creating the *sanctorum communio* in the midst of the *peccatorum communio*.

The 'I-Thou' relationship is, thus, fulfilled through the love of God, which is the gift of the Holy Spirit subsisting in faith. It is through the surrender of several persons to each other that a 'community of new persons' arises (SC: 125). Indeed, the *sanctorum communio* is a community of love in which there is a structural togetherness, the members 'being for one another'. This is expressed in service of the neighbour, intercession, and the mutual granting of the forgiveness of sins, a mystery which lies at the heart of Christian community. The church is therefore 'a sociologically unique structure', a means to an end, and an end in itself, existing to do God's will, but being in itself a realization of that will.

Bonhoeffer warns against reducing the church to a religious society, or identifying it with the Kingdom of God. The first does not take seriously the reality of revelation as the basis of the church; the second does not take seriously the historical reality of the empirical church, its character as *peccatorum communio*. Thus Bonhoeffer declares that

---

* *Gemeinde* is translated 'congregation' understood not as an institution but as a 'community of persons'.

God established the reality of the church, of mankind pardoned in Jesus Christ. Not religion, but revelation, not a religious community, but the church: that is what the reality of Jesus Christ means. And yet there is a necessary connection between revelation and religion, as there is between religious community and the church.   (*SC: 111*)

Bonhoeffer, as John Phillips observes, 'is perfectly willing to grant his liberal teachers their conception of the church as a "religious community", provided that they have first understood it as a community whose determination is solely from God'.[8]

Although *Sanctorum Communio* posits 'Christ existing as the congregation', Bonhoeffer nowhere really discusses the reality and meaning of Jesus Christ, least of all when he develops his understanding of the person. Even his use of the Pauline 'body of Christ' functions like a formal concept. Indeed, as Ernst Feil observes, 'the issue for him was not so much the concrete Christ who entered history as it was the concept of the church as collective person'.[9] Although Bonhoeffer succeeds in breaking with Kantian idealism, he was, at this stage, too much under the influence of neo-Hegelianism. A healthy dose of empirical sociology, combined with a more adequate Christology, then on the horizon of his thought, would have transformed the dissertation. But this was Bonhoeffer's first, not final project, completed, we must remember, at the age of twenty-one to satisfy his Berlin professors.

A THEOLOGY OF FREEDOM

Bonhoeffer began his vicariate in the German-speaking Lutheran Church in Barcelona at the beginning of 1928. The German community, consisting largely of businessmen and their families, was isolated from political developments in Germany, satisfied with their self-centred existence, and oblivious to the poverty of the surrounding city. Few attended church, and the elderly senior minister did little to challenge their apathy. Bonhoeffer stirred the waters, with some success, but the life and witness of the congregation was far removed from his vision of the church. Nevertheless, the year gave him space in which to develop beyond his family circle and the constraints of the Berlin faculty. His writings show that he was becoming increasingly interested in ethics. When he returned to Berlin in 1929 he began working on *Act and Being*, his *Habilitationsschrift* needed to start a career as an academic theologian.

Act and Being, Bonhoeffer's most difficult book, is a tightly-knit and well-structured attempt to develop a theological anthropology. The theme of sociality remains central but now Bonhoeffer grapples with how two great philosophical traditions — transcendental and ontological — and the theologies drawing upon them, understand human existence. The opening paragraph provides his rationale: 'It seems to me,' Bonhoeffer writes, 'that the latest developments in theology can be interpreted as an attempt to come to grips with the problem of act and being' (AB: 11). The attempts to resolve the problem range from Barth 'with his "critical reservation" ' who 'wishes to maintain the freedom of God's grace, and to establish human existence on that ground', to the Catholic Thomist E. Przywara 'who puts forward his ontology of the *analogia entis* in opposition to dialectical theology's preoccupation with the act' (AB: 12).

All these viewpoints illustrate at bottom a widespread wrestling with the same problem, one which is theology's legacy from Kant and idealism. The problem is one of forming genuine theological concepts and of choosing whether one is to use ontological categories in explaining them or those of transcendental philosophy.
'There has to be' Bonhoeffer continues, 'a theological interpretation of what "the being of God in revelation" means and how it is known, of what may be the interrelation of belief as act and revelation as being, and correspondingly of where man stands when seen from the standpoint of revelation' (AB: 12).

Act and being is divided into three parts. In the first, Bonhoeffer examines the epistemologies of transcendental and ontological philosophies. Both assume that human beings can understand themselves autonomously without any revelation from beyond the self. Genuine transcendentalism recognizes the limits of reason, but the problem remains that 'reason is entangled in itself'. Real belief in God is ruled out since 'there is no possibility of asserting the being of God outside the I' (AB: 32). Ontological systems, various as they are (Husserl, Scheler, Heidegger), in principle exclude the possibility of a God beyond the self, for either God is identified with the 'I' or is left out all together (AB: 58).

Bonhoeffer then examines those theologies whose understanding of God's revelation has been influenced by transcendental or ontological philosophies. Transcendentalism finds its clearest expression in Barth's 'actualism', then still dominant in his theology. For Barth revelation is pure act contingent upon God's freedom; it creates its own response, cannot be bound to anything, and God is free to suspend it at any moment. Revelation as act means that God is beyond human knowledge, evading every human attempt to grasp God cognitively. Insofar as this enabled Barth to overcome the weaknesses of theologies of being, Bonhoeffer concurred. But he raised critical questions about its consequences, and embarked on a far-reaching critique of dialectical theology, including Bultmann's theology of human existence.

Barth, Bonhoeffer argued, did not take sufficient account of what God has actually done in Jesus Christ. He had not broken free from Kantian transcendentalism, so God must always remain beyond human knowledge. But for Bonhoeffer, as for the later Barth, God has placed himself freely before and for human beings in Jesus Christ.

God is not free *of* man but *for* man. Christ is the Word of his freedom. God is *there*, which is to say: not in eternal non-objectivity but 'haveable', graspable in his Word within the Church.   (*AB: 90*)

The paradox of God's freedom is precisely the limitation which he places upon that freedom in the Incarnation. With Luther, Bonhoeffer maintains that God is always *pro me* and *pro nobis*, God *for* us. And in continuity with Luther's 'theology of the cross', another key element in Bonhoeffer's theology, he affirms that the finite is capable of bearing the infinite (*finitum capax infiniti*). Barth, at this point, was closer to Calvin's rejoinder, *finitum incapax infiniti*. This early disagreement provides the clue to the essential difference between their respective theologies.[10]

Unlike theologies of act, theologies of being safeguard the continuity, objectivity, and 'givenness' of revelation. There are three possible forms: revelation identified as doctrine (e.g. Lutheran orthodoxy), religious experience (e.g. Pietism), and religious institution (e.g. Roman Catholicism). But each of these 'understand the revealed God as an entity (*seiendes Sein*)', whereas the being of God transcends entities (AB: 111). Nevertheless Bonhoeffer insisted that a genuine ontology must be affirmed, as long as we do not try to bring revelation under human control.

Bonhoeffer attempted to resolve the problems created by both theologies of act and being by restating his theology of sociality. In the final section of Part B, the heart of *Act and Being*, he returns to his formula 'Christ existing as the congregation'. The problem with all the theologies he had examined was that

they overlooked, in searching for 'reality', that man in reality is never *only* the single unit, not even the *one* 'claimed by the Thou', but invariably finds himself in some community, whether in 'Adam' or in

'Christ'. The Word of God is given to humanity, the gospel to the
congregation of Christ. When the sociological category is thus introduced, the problem of act and being — and also the problem of
knowledge — is presented in a wholly fresh light.   (*AB: 122*)

The church is constituted by the proclamation of Christ's death and
resurrection, whereby the event of the past becomes a present event in
eschatological tension with the future. This maintains the necessary
contingent character of revelation, its character as God's act in
freedom. At the same time, God's very self is given in Christ to this
community which believes and declares the gospel, and it is there that
revelation is structured. God's freedom is expressed in being bound
to men and women in community.

Finally Bonhoeffer examines the act-being problem further in relation to humanity 'in Adam' or 'in Christ'. In the former condition
humanity is in bondage to sin and therefore to self, a state of being
destructive of human sociality. In the latter, humanity is set free from
guilt and sin and genuine sociality is restored. Bonhoeffer's resolution
of the anthropological problem is, therefore, that the self is redeemed
from beyond itself through faith, and that this takes place where the
Word is preached, and where the 'I' is brought into a new relationship
with others 'in Christ'. So Bonhoeffer concludes *Act and Being* in
classical Lutheran style:

In contemplation of Christ, the tormented knowledge of the I's lacer-
ation finds the 'joyful conscience', confidence and courage. The
slave is unbound. He who has grown to the man in exile and wretch-
edness grows to be the child as he finds his home. Home is the congregation (*Gemeinde*) of Christ, which is always 'future', the present
'in faith', because we are always children of the future; always act,
because being; always being, because act. Here in faith becoming a
reality, there in vision perfected, this is the new creation of the new
man of the future, who no longer looks back on himself but only away
from himself to the revelation from God, to Christ; the man who is
born out of the narrowness of the world into the breadth of Heaven,
who becomes what he was or, it may be, never was: a creature of God
— a child.   (*AB: 184*)

A THEOLOGY OF THE WORD

No sooner had Bonhoeffer completed the manuscript of *Act and Being*
than he set sail for New York and a year (1930/1) of studies at Union
Theological Seminary. The experience was very different from his

years as a theological student in Germany. Although the students were very open towards each other, they did 'not see the radical claim of truth on the shaping of their lives'. This made seminars 'very innocuous', crippling 'any radical, pertinent criticism' (NRS: 83). The professors at Union, he wrote

> represent what the enlightened American requires of theology and the church, from the most radical socialising of Christianity — Professors Ward and Niebuhr — and the secularisation of its philosophy and organization — Professor Lyman and Professor Elliot — to a liberal theology oriented on Ritschl — Professor Baillie.

The students, likewise, fell into the same categories.

> Without doubt the most vigorous, though perhaps not the deepest, of them belong to the first group. They have turned their back on all genuine theology and study mainly economic and political problems, often in active collaboration with the relevant organizations.

(NRS: 85)

This resulted, in Bonhoeffer's opinion, in an extraordinarily thin intellectual preparation for the ministry.

Bonhoeffer was particularly concerned about the prevailing misunderstanding of Barth's theology of the Word. In a paper on 'The Theology of Crisis and its Attitude Toward Philosophy and Science', presented to John Baillie's seminar, he sought to remedy the situation. The paper demonstrates Bonhoeffer's grasp of Barth's theology, but even more, his own identification with neo-orthodoxy's theology of the Word of God. Critique of Barth is entirely lacking, probably due to what Bethge calls his 'proselytizing zeal' on behalf of Barth's theology over against the liberal theology and social gospel of North American Protestantism (DB: 117).

Unimpressed as he generally was by American theology, Bonhoeffer grew to appreciate the action-oriented theology of Reinhold Niebuhr and Eugene Lyman who 'confronted him with ethical challenges of this-worldly activity, not allowing an easy retreat into the dichotomy between thought and life, between ideas and decisions'.[11] He was also deeply impressed by the vibrant faith and spirituality of black Christians in the ghetto of Harlem, where he taught Sunday school at the Abyssinian Baptist Church, and discovered how Christianity was related to the struggle for human rights. And then there was Bonhoeffer's transforming friendship with fellow student, Jean Lasserre, a French pastor and deeply committed pacifist. Lasserre's testimony caused Bonhoeffer to regard the Sermon on the Mount not as a theological problem but as a charter for Christian discipleship. Lasserre more than any other person helped Bonhoeffer overcome any residual nationalism, without which it would have been impossible for him to become later such a passionate worker for international peace and friendship through the churches in Europe.

Whether Bonhoeffer was ever a strict pacifist is a matter of debate, but during the next few years he was as near to being one as really makes little difference.[12] Lasserre's example certainly contributed to what Bethge has described as Bonhoeffer's shift from being a theologian to becoming a Christian (DB: 153f). Certainly something decisive happened at this time which reshaped his life and vocation. Later he described it in the following way:

> For the first time I discovered the Bible. . . . I had often preached, I had seen a great deal of the church, and talked and preached about it — but I had never become a Christian. . . . I had never prayed, or prayed only very little. For all my abandonment, I was quite pleased with myself. Then the Bible, and in particular the Sermon on the Mount, freed me from that. Since then everything has changed. I have felt this plainly, and so have other people about me. It was a great liberation. It became clear to me that the life of a servant of Jesus Christ must belong to the church, and step by step it became plainer to me how far that must go.　　　　　　　　　　　　*(DB: 155)*

Later, when imprisoned, Bonhoeffer mentioned that he had not changed a great deal in the course of his life 'except perhaps at the time of my first impressions abroad and under the first conscious influence of father's personality. It was then' he continued, 'that I turned from phraseology to reality' (LPP: 275). Whether this refers to the impact of Bonhoeffer's visit to Rome and North Africa, or to his year in New York, has been debated. But there can be no doubt that the change was an ongoing process, greatly affected by his American experience.

CHRISTOLOGY AND REALITY*

The Germany to which Bonhoeffer returned in July 1931 was in a state of political paralysis and economic crisis. Hitler's ominous rise as a major contender for power filled families like the Bonhoeffers with foreboding. Before settling down in Berlin, Bonhoeffer went to visit Barth who was then teaching at the University in Bonn. This was his first personal encounter with Barth, then aged forty-five, and although historical developments prevented them from ever becoming close friends and colleagues, it marks the beginning of an important relationship.

Bonhoeffer always respected the older theologian's judgment, and at crucial moments he turned to him for advice. Barth also had great respect for his younger friend, and in later years spoke highly of his writings and was influenced by them. Yet it is a mark of their relationship that Bonhoeffer retained his critical independence of Barth, and Barth himself raised some sharp questions in return. Bonhoeffer, of course, was denied the opportunity of knowing the developments in Barth's theology beyond *Church Dogmatics*, volume II, part 2.

In September 1931, Bonhoeffer, as an official German youth delegate, attended the meeting of the World Alliance for Promoting International Friendship through the Churches held in England, at Cambridge. This was his first formal involvement in the ecumenical movement. Given his leadership talents, his theological insight, language skills, and commitment to both the ecumenical and peace causes, it is not surprising that he was elected one of the youth secretaries of the World Alliance. Later in the year, on 15 November, Bonhoeffer, aged twenty-five, was ordained to the Christian ministry in Berlin and became chaplain to the students at the Technical College and a pastor in the economically depressed suburb of Wedding. Bonhoeffer's ministry to the children of the poor demonstrated his concern to serve those less fortunate than himself.

At the same time as he was engaged in these responsibilities, Bonhoeffer was a *Privatdozent*, or unpaid lecturer, at the University. During his two years (1931-33) at the university he became a 'minor sensation', attracting a significant number of students to his lively seminars (DB: 157). Many of the insights which later found expression in *The Cost of*

---

* For texts, see below pp. 98-123.

Discipleship were first explored in the informal discussions which Bonhoeffer had with the circle of students who gathered around him.

Bonhoeffer's formal lectures began with a course on 'The History of Systematic Theology in the 20th century' (GS: V, 181f). Then followed series on the essence of the church (*Das Wesen der Kirche*), Christian ethics, 'Creation and Sin' (published later as *Creation and Fall*), and, finally, Christology. Also of note is his seminar on Hegel in the Summer of 1933. These lectures provide the bridge between his early theology and that which follows in the church struggle and in prison. They demonstrate Bonhoeffer's new commitment to doing theology from the perspective of committed discipleship to Jesus Christ as Lord of the world.

CHURCH AND REALITY

In his lectures on *Das Wesen der Kirche* Bonhoeffer continued to affirm that the church is the place where God's revelation is known. But the stress is now upon the Lordship of Christ over the church and the world. The problem is, however, that the church stands on the periphery of life and not at the centre of the world where the Incarnate Christ is present (DWK: 45). The church is therefore called to be in solidarity with the world, and there represent and confess Christ as Lord. In drawing out the practical consequences of this for the life of the church, Bonhoeffer introduces two themes which recur several times later on and find final expression in his prison letters. He says that 'the first confession of the church before the world is the deed', and in counterpoint, refers to the need for a 'discipline of the secret' or arcane discipline in the life of the church (DWK: 58, 180f).

In July 1932, Bonhoeffer attended a Youth Peace Conference in Czechoslovakia. In his paper on 'A Theological Basis for the World Alliance', Bonhoeffer insisted that the ecumenical movement needed a more adequate theological foundation. One which would enable it to affirm its character as the universal church of Jesus Christ, avoid a misdirected social activism and the meaningless passing of resolutions, and learn to proclaim the Word of God to the world with the authority of Christ 'in the most concrete way possible'. Even Barth's theology, Bonhoeffer argued elsewhere, prevented the church from speaking and acting as concretely as it should (GS: V, 226).

In order to speak and act concretely, the church had to have 'knowledge of the situation', hence Bonhoeffer's important statement that 'reality is the sacrament of command'. Only a knowledge of reality would enable the church to discern God's Word 'for us, today'. Just as the sacrament makes the preaching of the gospel visible, so a knowledge of reality makes the proclamation of the commandment possible. The command of the gospel means obeying Jesus Christ as Lord; it is not a matter of abstract principles, but specific directions related to the context in which the church and the Christian live. This meant speaking out unequivocally against re-armament, and speaking clearly on behalf of world peace in the name of Christ. Failing this, a 'qualified silence' would be more appropriate.

But how are we to know God's commandment in any given situation? Bonhoeffer examined two options. The first was the biblical law expressed in the Sermon on the Mount. Bonhoeffer rejected this because the teaching of Jesus cannot be applied legalistically to the concrete situation facing 'us today'. Although Bonhoeffer had begun to take the challenge of the Sermon on the Mount with new seriousness, he refused to allow it to function in this way. Peace was not an absolute. The second option was the traditional answer of Lutheran orthodoxy based on the doctrine of the 'orders of creation'. Bonhoeffer rejected this option out of hand. Not only did it exalt nationalism, the state and culture to inviolable orders created by God, thereby legitimizing war, it also prevented the church from speaking and acting prophetically within the political arena. As an alternative, Bonhoeffer spoke of a theology of forgiveness, through which justice and truth become possible, as the ground of peace. Such a reconciling message, he argued, would enable the Word Alliance to speak with one voice to the nations of Europe as they prepared, yet again, for war.

CREATION AND CHRIST

The following Winter semester (1932/3) Bonhoeffer began to lecture on 'Creation and Sin'. These lectures show his new interest in the study of the Bible, and the determinative role which Christology now began to play in his theology. Indeed Bonhoeffer's interpretation of the Bible was itself, like that of Barth, Christological. In the Preface to *Creation and Fall*, which he wrote later, Bonhoeffer explained that the subtitle 'A Theological Interpretation of Genesis 1-3', meant regarding the Old Testament as well as the New as the book of the church and therefore reading it in the light of its fulfilment in Christ (CF: 8).

Creation and Fall is an exposition of Bonhoeffer's earlier 'theology of sociality', presented in a more accessible form. For example, in discussing the *imago Dei* (Genesis 1:26f), Bonhoeffer points to human sociality as its central meaning. His discussion of the *analogia relationis* is especially interesting because of the way in which Barth used this understanding of analogy in the development of his own theological anthropology.[13] For Bonhoeffer, however, the stress is on sociality rather than sexuality. Also of importance is Bonhoeffer's emphasis on human freedom in relation to the freedom of God. Men and women have been given the freedom to rule and act responsibly over the created order. This anticipated much of what Bonhoeffer was to write later in the essays which comprise his *Ethics*.

Perhaps the most pertinent example of Bonhoeffer's Christological interpretation is found right near the end of the lectures where, in commenting on Genesis 3:21, he tackles the problem of the 'orders of creation' head on. Creation, he argued, must be interpreted from the perspective of redemption in Christ. In making 'garments of skin' for fallen Adam and Eve, the Creator has become the Preserver. Thus, Bonhoeffer writes:

> All the orders of our fallen world are God's orders of preservation on the way to Christ. They are not orders of creation but preservation. They have no value in themselves. They are accomplished and have purpose only through Christ. God's new action towards man is that he preserves him in his fallen world, in his fallen orders, on the way to death, approaching the resurrection, the new creation, on the way to Christ. *(CF: 91)*

This was a very polemical statement given the way in which theologians sympathetic to National Socialism had used the doctrine of the 'orders of creation'. Bonhoeffer's use of 'orders of preservation' is indicative of his searching for an alternative formulation which would overcome the dangers inherent in the traditional doctrine. Later he moved away from the 'orders of preservation' also, and, in his ethical reflections, wrote, as we shall see, about the mandates.

Although *Creation and Fall* was Bonhoeffer's best-seller thus far, many Old Testament scholars were highly critical of his exegesis. And, of course, it remains a matter of debate today whether it is legitimate to interpret the Hebrew scriptures in the way he did.[14] Be that as it may, Bonhoeffer's theological interpretation enabled him to speak directly and sharply to the situation in which he and his students found themselves.

Several important things regarding Bonhoeffer's use of the Bible are of interest at this point. The first is his growing love for the Old Testament because of its 'earthiness', its focus on creation, the world and history. Here we find the biblical roots of his later reflections on Christianity in a 'world come of age'.[15] The second is his concern to listen to what the Bible has to say about the issues facing the church and the nations, for that meant listening to the word of Christ.[16] But thirdly, it must be remembered that Bonhoeffer's espousal of the Hebrew scriptures as the book of the church occurred at a time when German Christians were, for anti-Semitic reasons, rejecting the Jewish roots of their faith. Bonhoeffer's Christological interpretation was an affirmation that the church dare not surrender its Jewish roots if it is to remain faithful to Jesus Christ.

CHRIST THE CENTRE

Bonhoeffer's 1933 lectures on Christology are pivotal in understanding the development of his theology. Everything had been leading him to ask the fundamental question 'who is Jesus Christ?'. This question now becomes the theme which holds his theology together, providing it with both continuity and a basis for new developments in changing circumstances. Indeed, the Christology of 1933 clearly anticipates that of his prison letters.

For Bonhoeffer, Christology is not about the unanswerable question 'how' did the 'Word become flesh', but the question 'who' is this Word that addresses us in Jesus, and in turn asks us about ourselves. Indeed, the question is about revelation, and can only be answered within the community of faith. Hence Bonhoeffer's insistence, with Martin Kahler, that 'the Christ who is preached is the real Christ', and the rejection of the attempt by liberal theology to discover the authentic 'Jesus of history'.[17] To speak of Jesus Christ is an attempt to express the inexpressible. Yet the church must do so.

> To speak of Christ means to keep silent; to keep silent about Christ means to speak. When the church speaks rightly out of a proper silence, then Christ is proclaimed. And Christology is precisely the study of this proclamation. (C: 27)

Bonhoeffer affirms a classical Chalcedonian Christology (Jesus Christ is 'truly God and truly human'), but also Martin Luther's 'theology of the cross'. In continuity with his discussion on the 'who' and the 'how', he writes: 'The primary question in Christology is not about the possibility of uniting deity and humanity, but rather about the concealment of the God-Man in his humiliation' (C: 54). Christ is present in the world as Word, Sacrament, and as Church, but incognito, hidden in his humiliation. This leads to the question 'where' in the world is Christ to be found? Bonhoeffer's answer is that 'the one who is present in Word, Sacrament and Church is at the centre of human existence, of history and of nature' (C: 60).

Given Bonhoeffer's context, his comments on 'Christ as the Centre of History' are particularly significant:

The promise of a Messiah is everywhere alive in history. History lives in and from this expectation. That is what gives it significance, the coming of the Messiah.

Due to human sin, this promise remains unfulfilled and corrupt, and the world continually creates and glories in its own Messiahs. But, Bonhoeffer continues,

Only at one point does the thought break through that the Messiah cannot be the visible and demonstrated centre of history, but must be the hidden centre appointed by God. This is the point at which there is a stream against the popular movement of corrupted messianism — it is in Israel.

Christ, the Messiah, is therefore 'at one and the same time the destroyer and the fulfiller of all the messianic expectations of history'. And so, 'the meaning of history is tied up with an event which takes place in the depth and hiddenness of a man who ended on the cross. The meaning of history is to found in the humiliated Christ' (C: 62). In so far as Christ is present in the church, the church is then placed at the centre of history and the state.

Bonhoeffer's 'Critical or Negative Christology' follows and sets the parameters within which a constructive restatement of Christology can take place for today. He stresses the need for the church to regain the concept of heresy so that the 'true church' can be distinguished from the 'false church' — a concern for the 'boundaries of the church' which became more critical and urgent as the church struggle in Germany unfolded. And, then, finally, Bonhoeffer took some important steps towards the development of a 'positive Christology'.

Breaking away from Barth, Bonhoeffer once again drew deeply on Luther in his understanding of the 'humiliation of Christ', in insisting on the freedom of God *for* humankind (*pro nobis*), and in his affirmation of *finitum capax infiniti*. For Bonhoeffer as for Luther, 'the child in the manger is wholly God'. Thus the Christological basis is established for Bonhoeffer's prison theology in which he speaks of the weakness and

suffering of God. This provides new depth for Bonhoeffer's understanding of Christ as the 'representative' (*Stellvertretung*), speaking now
of his solidarity with humankind in suffering, and his vicarious action in
redemption. And because there is an intrinsic relationship between
Christ and the church, this development in Christology has enormous
consequences for the church.

> It is with this humiliated one that the church goes its own way of
> humiliation. . . . There is here no law or principle which the church
> has to follow, but simply a fact — put bluntly, it is God's way with the
> church. (*C: 113*)

CONFESSING CHRIST CONCRETELY*

Adolf Hitler became Chancellor of the Third Reich on 30 January
1933. Central to his programme to resolve the 'Jewish Question' was a
series of discriminatory laws which disqualified all people of Jewish
descent from holding any state office. As the Evangelical Church in
Germany (the twenty-eight Provincial churches or *Landeskirchen* comprising Lutheran and Reformed confessions) was a state church, all
pastors within it were state officials. The Aryan Clause meant that all
pastors of Jewish background had to be expelled from office. The
German Christians (*Deutsche Christen*), who were Nazis, supported this
move, though it was strongly opposed by others.

THE STATUS CONFESSIONIS

Bonhoeffer was the first Evangelical theologian to attack the legislation.
In his essay on 'The Church and the Jewish Question', written on 7
May, he stated clearly what options were open to the church in relating
to the state. We now see more precisely what Bonhoeffer meant when he
said in his *Christology* lectures that the church is the centre of the state.
Without the proclamation and witness of the church, the state would
inevitably destroy itself, and, in the process, lose 'its most faithful servant'.[18] Bonhoeffer delineated three ways in which the church should
act towards the state. First of all, it must remind the state of its responsibility, that is its prophetic task; secondly, it must aid the victims of
state action. Clearly Bonhoeffer had the Jews in mind. But the third
possibility 'is not just to bandage the victims under the wheel, but to put

* For texts, see below pp. 124-220.

a spoke in the wheel itself' (NRS: 221). This possibility would arise when the church found itself terrorised by the state, and thus in a *status confessionis* in which it had to confess its faith anew against a serious threat to the integrity of its message.

Part of Hitler's strategy in exercising total control over Germany was to ensure that both the Evangelical and the Roman Catholic churches in Germany would submit to his authority. In the case of Rome, Hitler engineered this through the Concordat with the Papacy signed on 20 July 1933. While some individual Catholics continued to oppose Hitler, the Concordat effectively compromised the resistance of the Catholic church.[19]

In the case of the Evangelical Churches, Hitler initially sought to achieve his ends through supporting the German Christians (*Deutsche Christen*) whom he could depend on to implement his ideological programme. As a means whereby the *Landeskirchen* could be controlled, Hitler appointed Ludwig Müller, an unknown military chaplain, as his special adviser on church affairs. This led to pressure from the German Christians for the restructuring and uniting of the *Landeskirchen* under the leadership of a *Reichsbischof.* There was considerable opposition from within the churches to this move, but the new constitution was adopted. The two contenders for the office of *Reichsbischof* were Ludwig Müller and Friedrich von Bodelschwingh, the elderly church statesman who had the support of the recognized church leadership and other groups opposed to the *Deutsche Christen*, including the Young Reformers, a group to which Bonhoeffer belonged at this time.

Hitler called for the election of church officers to take place on 23 July. Amidst much heated controversy and confusion, von Bodelschwingh withdrew, and the elections, rigged in favour of Ludwig Müller, resulted in his appointment as *Reichsbischof.* On the Sunday on which the election was held, Bonhoeffer preached in Berlin and called upon the church to be a confessing church and not succumb to the attacks being made upon it.

> Church stay a church! But church confess, confess, confess! Christ alone is your Lord, from his grace alone can you live as you are. Christ builds. . . . The Confessing Church is the eternal church because Christ protects her. (*NRS: 212*)

By now it was clear to both Bonhoeffer and Barth that a *status confessionis*, the first since the Reformation, had arrived.[20] Having accepted the fact of the *status confessionis*, the next crucial issue for theologians was to determine the most appropriate action which the church should take.

Bonhoeffer was a leading participant in the formation of the Pastor's Emergency League which Martin Niemöller initiated to assist ministers affected by Nazi action. He also drafted the Bethel Confession, the first confessional attempt to counter the Nazi ideology in the Evangelical Church. However, disappointed by the diluted final version of the Bethel Confession, and the failure of pastors to resign from the state church over the implementation of the Aryan Clause, and generally in need of respite from the stifling atmosphere of Nazi Germany, Bonhoeffer accepted a call to serve two German-speaking Lutheran congregations in London. In October 1933 he crossed the Channel to England.

Bonhoeffer's self-imposed exile in London did not bring tranquillity. He was soon involved in ministering to Jews and other German exiles, and became the main interpreter of the German church situation within Britain. This required frequent visits to Berlin. It also led to a very significant friendship with Bishop George Bell of Chichester, a leading ecumenist, supporter of the emerging Confessing Church, and advocate of Jews seeking a new home in England. In the light of his earlier disappointment, Bonhoeffer was pleasantly surprised by the emergence of the Confessing Church, and soon discerned its significance for the ecumenical movement. On 14 March 1934, he wrote to Bishop Bell:

> The question at stake in the German Church is no longer an internal issue but is the question of the existence of Christianity in Europe. . . . I shall only wish you would see one of the meetings of the Emergency League now — it is always, in spite of all the gravity of the present moments, a real uplift to one's own faith and courage — Please do not be silent now! I beg to ask you once more to consider the possibility of an ecumenic delegation and ultimatum. (NRS: 263)

While Bonhoeffer was not at the First Confessing Synod of the German Evangelical Church held at Barmen in May 1934, he strongly affirmed the Barmen Declaration, and worked hard to ensure that the Confessing Church was regarded as the authentic Evangelical Church in Germany.[21] Thus Bonhoeffer played a vital role in the preparations for and the events of the crucial 'Life and Work' Conference held at Fanö in Denmark, 22-30 August 1934.

While the official German delegation at Fanö came from the pro-establishment leadership of the Reich church and included several *Deutsche Christen*, Bonhoeffer and others ensured that the Confessing

Church was also well represented. Significantly, it was at Fanö that the ecumenical movement came out decisively on the side of the Confessing Church, a stand which later became more ambiguous. Looking back on Fanö a year later, Bonhoeffer wrote:

> With the Fanö conference the ecumenical movement entered on a new era. It caught sight of its commission as a church at a quite definite point, and that is its permanent significance.   (*NRS: 329*)

In an address at Fanö on 'The Church and the Peoples of the World' (NRS: 289f), Bonhoeffer anticipated the contemporary discussion on the need to move beyond 'polite ecumenism', and for the ecumenical movement to speak concretely and decisively as the church of Jesus Christ to the issues facing the modern world.[22] He also made a proposal, recently renewed, that the churches should hold an ecumenical peace convocation to outlaw war.

TRUE AND FALSE CHURCH

Towards the end of 1934 Bonhoeffer was invited by the leaders of the Confessing Church to return to Germany to direct a Preachers' Seminary. Such seminaries had been established to provide a post-university year of pastoral formation in preparation for service within confessing congregations. Bonhoeffer readily accepted the invitation, even though it meant postponing his planned trip to India to see Gandhi, and also leaving London. He was now anxious to share more directly in the Church Struggle.

Bonhoeffer returned to a Germany in which the Confessing Church found itself under increasing pressure. At its second Synod, held in Dahlem in 1935, the Confessing Church had taken a clear stand on church order, rejecting the official church government. Hitler's policy was to divide the leadership by providing pastors with the option of remaining 'neutral'. They could uphold the gospel and confessions freely without state interference, as long as they accepted the official church committees and kept out of politics. This appealed to many Lutheran pastors within the Confessing Church for whom church order was a matter of indifference compared with the pure preaching of the gospel and fidelity to the confessions. But it compromised the opposition of the Confessing Church and rendered it largely ineffective. Bonhoeffer became more resolved to help those students and pastors who would not compromise.

Bonhoeffer's theology of this period was thus shaped by the struggle for a true and faithful church against the insidious inroads of heresy and falsehood. For Bonhoeffer these were matters of life and death. Within the ecumenical Anglo-Saxon world he found that confessing Christ faithfully soon ran up against a liberal indifference to questions of truth. In some ways this was more troublesome than confronting the *Deutsche Christen*. His lectures and essays illustrate the issues then in a way that remains remarkably pertinent for the ecumenical church today.[23]

Bonhoeffer's most significant theological contribution to the ecumenical movement was his article on 'The Confessing Church and the Ecumenical Movement' written at Finkenwalde in July 1935. The article has a two-fold thrust. Bonhoeffer argued that the Confessing Church in Germany presented the ecumenical movement with a unique challenge to confess the gospel with authority and clarity as the church of Jesus Christ. But, at the same time, the ecumenical movement challenged the Confessing Church in Germany to discover the ecumenical implications of its confession, to listen to the voice of the wider church, to recognize its own failures and weaknesses, and not glory in its confession.

Few things Bonhoeffer wrote during the church struggle provoked such controversy as did his lecture to his students at Finkenwalde on 'The Question of the Boundaries of the Church and Church Union' in April 1936. By this stage Bonhoeffer was thoroughly disillusioned by the ineffectiveness of the Confessing Church, which he attributed to its desire to maintain unity at all costs, as reflected at the Synod at Bad Oeyenhausen (1936). It was trying to protect its own space in the world at the expense of bearing a faithful witness to Jesus Christ. In his lecture Bonhoeffer tackled the problem by placing it in the context of the Reformation debate on the boundaries of the church. How does a church exercise discipline, exclude heretics, and retain its character as the church which faithfully confesses Jesus Christ?

Bonhoeffer began by stressing that the Lutheran concept of the church leaves the question of its boundaries open and stresses only the joyful proclamation 'Here is the Gospel!' In other words, unlike the Reformed Church's self-understanding, the Lutheran Church does not draw boundaries between itself and the world, between those who belong and those who do not. The true church cannot legalistically determine its boundaries *a priori* in any situation. The decision about boundaries has to be made in the midst of the struggle, and the unity of the church is a product of its faithful confession of Jesus Christ in that context. The true church recognizes the boundaries which are drawn by the world, and in every situation it declares explicitly what these boundaries are.

Thus, it was not the Confessing Church which initiated the 'status confessionis' but National Socialism and the *Deutsche Christen*; the recognition of the boundaries of the 'true church' came in response to the position adopted by the 'false church'. A more contemporary example of this recognition of boundaries, in many respects influenced by Bonhoeffer's insights, has been the declaration that 'apartheid is a heresy'. The boundaries of the 'true church' have been determined in response to the racism of the 'false church' or the world.

All this led Bonhoeffer to reflect on the authority of the Barmen Declaration and the decisions taken at the Dahlem Synod concerning church order. These, he argued, must be accepted as given. Thus Bonhoeffer made his extremely controversial statement: 'Whoever knowingly cuts himself off from the Confessing Church in Germany cuts himself off from salvation'. This rephrasing and updating of the traditional *extra ecclesian nulla salus* alienated some of his friends and supporters, and led others to rush apologetically to his defence.[24] But it indicates how seriously Bonhoeffer regarded the decisions reached by the Confessing Church. Salvation itself was at stake!

Two years later, Bonhoeffer returned to this theme, clearly unrepentant. In a lecture in October 1938 to young confessing pastors in Pomerania on 'Our Way According to the Testimony of Scripture', he asked whether faithfulness to the gospel impinged on church order. His response was unequivocal.

> To obey the heretical church government is to disobey Christ. For Christ's sake we must disobey the heretical church government, even if it has been appointed by the state. But disobedience to the false church regime must be matched by true obedience to the right church government. The latter must be supported for the sake of the Gospel; in any given form it is an *adiaphoron* (i.e. something indifferent). But where it is to be subjected by outside force to a law which is alien to the church it may not yield, but must bear witness in word and deed to its freedom from the alien law and its sole obedience to Jesus Christ. *In statu confessionis nihil est adiaphoron.* (*WF: 190*)

To confess Christ concretely affects every aspect of the church's life.

COSTLY DISCIPLESHIP

Bonhoeffer had been working on the themes which finally found expression in *The Cost of Discipleship* from at least as early as November 1932. More immediately the book was a compilation drawn from lectures which Bonhoeffer gave to his students at Finkenwalde together with his exegesis of the Sermon on the Mount. Karl Barth expressed hesitancy when he first heard what Bonhoeffer was planning to do, but two decades later, when he himself wrote on sanctification and discipleship, Barth drew on the insights of *The Cost of Discipleship* and acknowledged that it was the best guide on the subject.[25] On looking back in prison, Bonhoeffer admitted there were dangers in his treatment of the subject, but stood by what he had written (LPP: 369).

The structure of the English edition of *The Cost of Discipleship* partly obscures Bonhoeffer's intention. The German original is divided into two, not four parts, the first of which is an exposition of discipleship in the synoptic gospels, and the second which deals with the same theme, but in terms of Pauline theology. Bonhoeffer clearly wanted to show that following Jesus the suffering Messiah (the Synoptics) is an integral part of believing in and obeying Christ as Lord (Paul). In this way he sought to counter the Lutheran tendency to separate justification by faith from costly discipleship both in theology and practice.

Bonhoeffer maintained that the doctrine of justification was being misused by Evangelical Christians in Germany to justify their passive acceptance and even support of the status quo. A living and obedient faith in Jesus Christ had been replaced by belief in a doctrine about faith; the Sermon on the Mount had been conveniently side-stepped by regarding it as law rather than gospel. The result was 'cheap grace' instead of the 'costly grace' of true discipleship. For Bonhoeffer the church in Germany had become a peddlar of cheap grace, a Christianity without real discipleship. This was the real enemy because it undermined evangelical faith and allowed the church to be captured by alien ideologies such as Nazism. Hence Bonhoeffer's insistence that 'only he who believes is obedient, and only he who is obedient believes' (COD: 69).

The ecclesiology of *The Cost of Discipleship* radically separates the church and the world. In joining the church we step out of the world into the fellowship of the body of Christ over which he alone is Lord. But this does not mean that the church is meant to retreat into a ghetto, or that the true church is invisible. The body of Christ is as real to the contemporary disciples as was the Incarnate Christ to the first disciples, and following Christ today means following him bodily into the world. But in the world the church will always be in conflict with the world, for the world is controlled by the anti-Christ. Indeed, the conflict will intensify until the church has been deprived of its last inch of space on earth, and then the end will come. But the true church lives eschatologically, ready to strike tent and move on to meet the coming Lord. It therefore neither conforms to the world nor retreats from it, but in the midst of the world seeks to realize increasingly in its life the form of Christ (*Gestalt Christi*), the suffering Lord. *The Cost of Discipleship* is thus a powerful call to follow Christ in costly obedience. 'When Christ calls a man' Bonhoeffer wrote, 'he bids him come and die.'

AN EXPERIMENT IN COMMUNITY

Bonhoeffer participated in his last ecumenical conference in London in February 1937. In September, the Gestapo closed down the Finkenwalde seminary, and Bonhoeffer and some of his brethren began a clandestine ministry in the collective pastorates in Köslin, Gross-Schlönwitz and Sigurdshof. Early the next year he was forbidden to preach or teach in Berlin. Shortly thereafter, through the influence of his friends and family circle, Bonhoeffer began to make contact with the leaders of the German resistance and conspiracy against Hitler. But all the time he kept working at his exegetical writings, and tried to help those pastors who were struggling to be faithful to their confession of Jesus Christ.

During his ministry in England Bonhoeffer had spent a week (March 1935) at the Anglican Community of the Resurrection in Mirfield. He had long been aware of the need for the church to be a living community of persons rather than a conglomerate of 'justified individuals'. The experience at Mirfield strengthened this conviction, and the invitation to direct the Preachers' Seminary at Finkenwalde provided him with a unique opportunity to put his thoughts into practice. Under Bonhoeffer's leadership, Finkenwalde thus became an experiment in Christian community. This was something unprecedented in the German Evangelical Church with its historic wariness of anything that looked like a Catholic monastery. But Bonhoeffer was convinced that the church and its pastors could not minister to the world, especially a world in crisis, unless the 'body of Christ' became a reality. 'For the Word to be heard in Germany there was needed a community in which it would become audible, one whose life together would call other Christians to responsibility in their own local communities, a community who would stand uncompromisingly apart from the national delirium in solidarity with the victims.'[26]

Bonhoeffer's little classic, *Life Together*, was written in September 1938. By then the seminary had been closed for a year. It therefore represents more Bonhoeffer's reflection on the experiment in community rather than a description of precisely what took place. For Bonhoeffer, Christian community is centred upon worship and the study of the Scriptures and it results in mutual support and strengthening for service in the world. *Life Together* explored this in considerable depth, and has subsequently provided many Christians and communities with practical guidance and theological insight. In a remarkable synthesis, Bonhoeffer combines rich insights on community life derived from Catholic spirituality with a Reformation emphasis on the centrality of the Word.

In order to understand *Life Together*, several things need to be kept in mind. It should be remembered that Bonhoeffer formed a 'community of brothers' at Finkenwalde. The 'brothers' stayed there on a semi-permanent basis, as distinct from the seminarians who came for about six months and then moved on into parish work, or later into the army unless they were arrested and imprisoned. It was primarily within the 'community of brothers' that Bonhoeffer sought to put his idea of Christian community into practice.

Life together at Finkenwalde was not a way of escape from the political and church struggles, but a way of engagement. Finkenwalde was not simply a community of preparation for ministry, but one already engaged in serving others. People in the community were welcomed to its worship on Sundays; groups of seminarians went out week by week to minister in nearby parishes; they worked amongst University students in Greifswald; they attended synods and other meetings of the Confessing Church; and they sought to encourage congregations and pastors to remain faithful to the Barmen Declaration. Bonhoeffer regarded his own theological work at Finkenwalde as a contribution to the life and witness of the Confessing Church. Together with his students, he discussed the issues of the day, and these set the agenda for their prayers and provided the context for their study of the Bible and theological reflection.

As Bonhoeffer understood it, Christian community is very different from those forms of community where the focus of attention is self-fulfilment or where group dynamic techniques are employed to achieve goals. The focus at Finkenwalde was upon the Word of God in Jesus Christ. This Word could only be heard in the context of worship and disciplined study, and it required total dependence on Christ, the confession of sins, and the sharing of goods. The centrality of the Word in the life of the Christian community was, thus, the focus of Bonhoeffer's lectures on pastoral care.[27] Indeed, Bonhoeffer called the 'cure of souls' 'a special sort of proclamation', in strong contrast to other approaches where the minister is more a psychotherapist than a theologian, pastor or priest.

In the light of this emphasis on the Word, it is not surprising that at Finkenwalde Bonhoeffer concentrated his theological reflection on the disciplined study of Scripture, and required the same of his students. At the beginning of the Finkenwalde period he lectured on 'The Presentation of New Testament Texts' (NRS: 302f). He discussed more precisely what he meant by a theological interpretation of the Bible, and how this relates to historical-critical exegesis. In doing so he drew a distinction between that form of presentation in which the New Testament must justify itself to the present age, and that in which the present age must justify itself before the Christian message (NRS: 303). The former, characteristic of the biblical approach of both liberal theology and the *Deutsche Christen*, was firmly rejected. Bonhoeffer likewise attacked those who concentrate on hermeneutics rather than the substance of the biblical message. 'Where the question of *presentation* becomes the *theme of theology*,' he declared, 'we can be certain that the cause has already been betrayed and sold out' (NRS: 305). The study of Scripture together with a knowledge of reality provide the basis for the concrete confession of Jesus Christ the crucified and risen Lord.

PROTESTANTISM WITHOUT REFORMATION

Bonhoeffer was now aware that he would soon be conscripted into the military, an eventuality which he would have resisted to the embarrassment of the Confessing Church which, while anti-Nazi, was anxious not to be regarded as unpatriotic. So Bonhoeffer organized an invitation through Reinhold Niebuhr to return to New York in June 1939 to minister to German refugees and teach at Union Theological Seminary. It was a soul-searching time, indeed it has been argued that during his short stay he underwent an identity-crisis.[28] The fact is that he stayed there only a few weeks (2 June–27 July) before he decided he had to return to Germany to share in the struggles yet to come.

A month later, back in Germany, he wrote an essay on his perceptions of Christianity and the church in the United States. He entitled it 'Protestantism without Reformation'. Few writings describe so well the difference between Protestantism in Europe and that in the New World, and fewer still have analyzed the differences with such theological insight. Bonhoeffer is not content with a phenomenological description and comparison, he is much more concerned with the question of truth: 'What is God doing to and with his church in America?' And, related to that, what challenge does American Christianity present to the church in Germany, and vice versa. In this respect his essay follows closely on his earlier article on 'The Confessing Church and the Ecumenical Movement', and much of his discussion remains of contemporary interest and importance.

Bonhoeffer noted that some important theological developments had taken place in the United States since his first visit almost ten years before. In this regard he referred to the influence of Barth, Emil Brunner, Karl Heim, Paul Tillich and Søren Kierkegaard, and singled out Reinhold and Richard Niebuhr amongst the few American theologians who 'speak in a reformed way'. Bonhoeffer remained as sharp and perceptive in his criticisms of the all-pervasive liberal theology, the neglect of serious Christology, and the failure of the American church to live under the authority of the Word of God. But he responded positively to the practicality and social concern of the North American church. Now he saw the need for dialogue between 'Protestantism without Reformation' with its strong ethical emphasis, and 'the churches of the Reformation', with their dogmatic concentration. To bring these together was the decisive task for theology today.

Germany invaded Poland in September 1939 and the second World War began. At the time Bonhoeffer was back fulfilling his responsibilities with the collective pastorates in Köslin and Sigurdshof. Many of his students, both past and present, were in prison or in military service. In order to keep in touch and continue his ministry to them, Bonhoeffer wrote circular letters. In his Christmas letter in 1939, Bonhoeffer reminded them that they are called to be theologians before all else, and that this required commitment to the Word become flesh. Thus Bonhoeffer brought his contribution to the church struggle to a climax with a powerful Christological statement. Just when we might have assumed that the task of theology had come to an end, Bonhoeffer insists that it was even more urgent. Yet for him, doing theology would now be undertaken incognito amidst political intrigue and action, and in dialogue with secular friends and co-conspirators.

THE LIFE OF FREE RESPONSIBILITY*

THE ETHICS

Writing to Eberhard Bethge from Tegel prison in November 1943, Bonhoeffer reproached himself for not having finished his *Ethics* (LPP: 129). As a student he had been encouraged by Seeberg to concentrate on ethics, and this had increasingly become the focus for his theology. Now it became a passion intensified and directed by the events of the time and the context within which he now found himself as a member of the resistance. Isolated from the church, he found a new community of reference and discourse amongst his secular co-conspirators. He was busy writing a draft chapter of his proposed *Ethics* when, on 5 April 1943, he was arrested at his parents' home.

During these years Bonhoeffer was in the employ of the German military intelligence (*Abwehr*), ironically the centre of German resistance to Hitler. Bonhoeffer was ostensibly employed by the *Abwehr* because, it was argued to the suspicious Gestapo, his ecumenical contacts could help in gathering information useful to the war effort. This enabled Bonhoeffer to travel without much difficulty to Switzerland, where he met Barth, and Sweden, where he met Bishop Bell, his chief ecumenical contact in London. His real purpose was to help Jews escape from Germany, and get the support of the Allies for the German resistance. He largely succeeded in the first, but failed in the second.

The *Ethics* which we now have was edited by Bethge after the war and published posthumously in 1949. In his Preface Bethge acknowledged: 'This book is not the *Ethics* which Dietrich Bonhoeffer intended to have published. It is a compilation of the sections which have been preserved, some of them complete and others not, some already partly rewritten and some which have been committed to writing only as preliminary studies for the work which was planned' (E: 7). Since its first publication it was restructured by Bethge himself in 1963, and is presently being thoroughly revised once again. Clifford Green, one of those involved in this process, has now suggested that the *Ethics* 'must be considered a less fragmentary and much more

---

* For texts, see below pp. 221–268.

coherent text than previously assumed. To be sure, the manuscripts do not constitute a finished and polished book; they retain an experimental character. But there is a purposeful development, both within the manuscripts themselves and from his writings in the later 1930's to the *Letters and Papers from Prison*.[29]

According to an outline of his book that Bonhoeffer made in October 1940, the work was to begin with a chapter on 'Ethics as Formation', which is printed as chapter three in current editions. In this chapter Bonhoeffer categorically rejects the idea that ethics is a set of principles which have to be applied. 'It is not written that God became an idea, a principle, a programme, a universally valid proposition or law, but that God became man' (E: 85). In fact, Christian ethics means being conformed to the incarnate, crucified and risen Christ who longs to take form in all people. The church is 'nothing but a section of humanity in which Christ has really taken form' (E: 83). Thus ethics is defined as 'the bold endeavour to speak about the way in which the form of Jesus Christ takes form in our world' (E: 88).

From this perspective Bonhoeffer analyzed the historical 'inheritance and decay' of the 'Christian west', which has hitherto found its unity and meaning in Christ. This inheritance has been squandered to such an extent that the west has become hostile to Christ, an hostility which reached its nadir in the 'expulsion of the Jews' and therefore 'the expulsion of Christ'. Within that history the church has too often failed to fulfil its task and has contributed to the decay. The way to the renewal of the West begins through an acknowledgement of guilt, and this places upon the church a particular responsibility. As the vicarious representative (*Stellvertreter*) of the world, the church not only acknowledges its own guilt but takes the guilt of the nation upon itself, thereby enabling the rebirth and renewal of human community. Bonhoeffer was clearly struggling to understand the fate of Germany, indeed, of Europe, and to lay a foundation for a truly Christian civilization once the war was over.

THE REALITY OF CHRIST AND THE WORLD

Bonhoeffer continued his reflections on the historical situation of the West in the next chapter of his *Ethics*, entitled 'The Church and the World'. He began by referring to 'one of our most astonishing experiences during the years when everything Christian was sorely oppressed'. Over against the barbarism, irrationality, and dehumanization of the Nazi state, a new alliance had formed between the defenders of endangered human values and Christians.

> Reason, culture, humanity, tolerance and self-determination, all these concepts which until very recently had served as battle slogans against the church, against Christianity, against Jesus Christ himself, had now, suddenly and surprisingly, come very near indeed to the Christian standpoint. (*E: 55*)

These values, which had their origin in Christ, but which had been subsequently squandered by the church, had now returned home.

Bonhoeffer related this process quite concretely to the experience of confessing congregations who in faithfulness to Jesus Christ closed their ranks, and became increasingly smaller. They sought to embody 'the total and exclusive claim of Christ' ('he that is not with me is against me', Matthew 12.30). And yet, this exclusiveness could lead to fanaticism not freedom unless the church is equally open to those 'good people' who 'suffer for the sake of a just cause' ('he that is not against us is for us', Mark 9.40). Such secular men and women were lost to the church since the Enlightenment because of its failure to proclaim the gospel in such a way as to ensure the survival of justice, truth, humanity and freedom. But

> In times which are out of joint, in times when lawlessness and wickedness triumph in complete unrestraint, it is rather in relation to the few remaining just, truthful and human men that the gospel will make itself known. (*E: 61*)

Hence the need for the church to re-think what it means to proclaim the gospel to 'good people', and not just to self-satisfied churchgoers whose sins while formally confessed and forgiven, were in fact justified by the cheapening of grace. Here we have the first intimations of what Bonhoeffer later called the 'unconscious Christianity' of his secular friends and co-conspirators.

True to his Lutheran heritage, Bonhoeffer continued to affirm justification by faith as the final and ultimate word about our relationship to God. But the ultimate is nonetheless integrally related to penultimate concerns. The struggle for humanity and justice, typical of the 'good, secular men' Bonhoeffer knew in the conspiracy, had to become the struggle of the church. Like John the Baptist, the church's task was to prepare the way for the coming of the Messianic kingdom through its participation in the struggle for justice, human rights and peace.

'The problem for Bonhoeffer's ethics', writes Robin Lovin, 'was to retain the fundamental principle that "The Good is simply and solely the will of God", giving that principle normative status without excluding non-Christians from the moral discussion, making decisions about the will of God for a whole society without reducing the principle to a vague theological affirmation that leaves concrete moral decisions untouched.'[30] This is one reason why Bonhoeffer was attracted to Catholic moral theology with its emphasis upon natural law. The loss of the concept of the natural, Bonhoeffer wrote, 'meant a serious and substantial loss to Protestant thought'; for this reason it was unable to handle the penultimate, and was found wanting in preserving those values which safeguard life in society (E: 143f). This was of vital importance in the Third Reich with its wholesale destruction of human rights. But Bonhoeffer did not simply incorporate Catholic moral theology into his ethics, he sought to recover the natural for the sake of the gospel. The penultimate must point towards the ultimate, indeed in Christ they are brought together as one reality (E: 145).

Bonhoeffer's Christological understanding of 'reality' (*Wirklichkeit*) is fundamental to his ethics. In Christ, God has overcome the division of the world into secular and sacred spheres, and brought all of reality under his authority. Hence 'the point of departure for Christian ethics is not the reality of one's self, or the reality of the world; nor is it the reality of standards and values. It is the reality of God as he reveals himself in Jesus Christ' (E: 189). Ethics is about 'participation in the reality of God and of the world in Jesus Christ today' (E: 195). The implication for theology is that it is unbiblical to 'think in two spheres' and act as though the political and secular realm had nothing to do with Christian ethics and obedience. This was the fatal theological error, derived from the Lutheran doctrine of the 'two kingdoms', which prevented Christians in Germany from opposing Hitler.

Closely related to the doctrine of the 'two kingdoms', and equally disastrous for the church in the Third Reich, was the doctrine of the 'orders of creation'. As we have seen, throughout the church struggle Bonhoeffer had sought an alternative, Christological way, of relating the commandment of God to ethical action in the world, and so overcome the dangers of the 'orders of creation' with its tendency to absolutise the state and culture. He now moved away from 'orders of preservation' because this phrase had, by then, been co-opted by supporters of the status quo, and, in its place, spoke of the 'mandates'. 'We speak of divine mandates' he wrote, 'rather than divine orders because the word mandate refers more clearly to a divinely imposed task rather than to a determination of being' (E: 207). Bonhoeffer did not deny that there are spheres such as labour, marriage, government, and the church, but he refused to give them any ultimacy. He restructured them in the light of the Incarnation, and for the sake of the future. God in Jesus Christ calls us to responsible action within them, but action always in accord with the one commandment which comes to us in Christ.

THE ACT OF FREE RESPONSIBILITY

In his discussion of 'The Structure of Responsible Life' Bonhoeffer reached the heart of his ethical reflections. Central to this chapter is his concept of 'Deputyship' (*Stellvertretung*), which he now develops in a way that relates to his own role as a conspirator. In *Sanctorum Communio* it was through the 'vicarious action' of Jesus Christ that the church was established; in the *Ethics* the focus of Christ's 'deputyship' has shifted from the church to the world, because the whole world is now brought under the reign of Christ. But equally deputyship has become central to an ethic which includes both Christians and non-Christians in their life in the world.[31]

There is another important shift. Larry Rasmussen summarizes it as follows:

> In *The Cost of Discipleship* the key word is singleminded obedience. This is what is commanded. But in *Ethics* it is freedom, permission, liberty that are commanded. Bonhoeffer certainly does not drop obedience as a key term for Christian ethics, but now he always adds 'and freedom' when speaking of obedience; too, he now speaks of a real tension between obedience and freedom. They stand in tension with and complement each other.

Related to this is a change with regard to the divine law as an absolute boundary; it is no longer absolute, but open to acts of free responsibility in the boundary situation. This 'is the wedge that opens the way for the exception. In Bonhoeffer's case, the exception was tyrannicide.'[32]

No one involved in a conspiracy, least of all tyrannicide, would discuss the ethical issues openly, and it is not surprising that there is no such discussion in the *Ethics*. But there is a great deal that relates to ethics in the boundary situation, and therefore to situations in which it might become necessary to put 'a spoke in the wheel' of an unjust government. Christian ethics in the boundary situation, Bonhoeffer argued, required the risk of concrete decision. Not to take the risk would be a denial of responsibility. Responsible action is obedience to the command of God, but it is also action which arises out of the freedom to interpret that command in abnormal situations where traditional norms no longer seem to apply.

There was enormous physical risk for the conspirators — that they were prepared to accept; but they were also perplexed about the ethical issues, whether their plans were morally justified. Theologically, the question was whether tyrannicide would place them outside the will of God. The conspirators were, after all, good patriotic Germans of Lutheran background, some of them military officers pledged to serve the state with total loyalty. Hence Bonhoeffer's intense struggle with the question of guilt:

> When a man takes guilt upon himself in responsibility, and no responsible man can avoid this, he imputes this guilt to himself and to no one else; he answers for it; he accepts responsibility for it. He does not do this in the insolent presumptuousness of his own power, but he does it in the knowledge that this liberty is forced upon him and that in this liberty he is dependent upon grace. Before other men the man of free responsibility is justified by necessity; before himself he is acquitted by his conscience; but before God he hopes only for mercy. (*E: 248*)

The act of free responsibility demonstrates precisely that Bonhoeffer's ethics is not about being and doing good, but about discerning God's will in context and, having done everything possible to avoid being deluded by self-interest or seduced by fanaticism, to act accordingly, trusting in God's grace. Bonhoeffer's inner struggle with such issues is poignantly revealed in his essay 'After Ten Years', written as a Christmas gift to some of his co-conspirators a few months before his arrest.

CHRIST IN A WORLD COME OF AGE*

THEOLOGY IN PRISON

After his arrest, Bonhoeffer was placed in Tegel prison in Berlin where he was interrogated and kept until 8 October 1944. He was then incarcerated in the maximum security Gestapo cells at Prinz-Albrecht-Strasse. In February 1945, as the war drew to its climax, he was hurriedly taken to Buchenwald, Regensburg, and, finally to Flossenbürg. He was originally arrested because the Gestapo suspected he was engaged in aiding Jews to escape; but the Gestapo now knew that he was part of the conspiracy which had led to the abortive attempt on Hitler's

---

* For texts, see below pp. 269-297.

life on 20 July the previous year. Together with several other conspirators, he was summarily condemned to death and executed on 9 April.

The letters which contain his seminal theological reflections are from the Tegel period. They are but a few of the many which Bethge and others received. But they were the main reason why Bethge edited and published them in 1951 under the suggestive title *Widerstand und Ergebung*. Literally 'resistance and submission', the title evocatively conveys Bonhoeffer's existential struggle in prison to resist succumbing to fate and, instead, to discern God's purpose in history and maintaining hope. Bethge's main intention in preparing the material for publication, something which Bonhoeffer himself never anticipated, was to share Bonhoeffer's last theological reflections with a wider audience. Little did he foresee the dramatic and profound impact this would have upon the theological world.

Bonhoeffer's provocative explorations and concepts soon created concern amongst the more orthodox, perplexing many who held *The Cost of Discipleship* in high esteem, and at the same time stimulated others in even more radical directions. Bonhoeffer was held responsible for the 'death of God theology' and the secularization of the gospel. The publication of Bishop John Robinson's *Honest to God* in 1963 hastened the process of a 'creative misuse of Bonhoeffer'. At the end of his life Karl Barth confessed that Bonhoeffer's theological fragments from prison remained something of a mystery to him, and cautioned against taking them too seriously.[33] This he said, notwithstanding Bethge's clear and comprehensive discussion of the issues in his biography.[34] Bethge, it must be recalled, was the recipient of the letters containing the theological reflections, and therefore the sounding-board for Bonhoeffer's thoughts.

In prison, Bonhoeffer was busy writing a book with the probable title of *The Essence of Christianity*,[35] a title with an important history in German theology. Ludwig Feuerbach used it for his famous lectures given in Berlin in 1841 in which he turned theology on its head and radically redefined Christianity in humanistic terms. Under the same title Adolf von Harnack, Bonhoeffer's illustrious teacher, in his lectures in Berlin in 1918, redefined Christianity as belief in 'the Fatherhood of God, the brotherhood of man, and the infinite value of the human soul'. Bonhoeffer's title for his lectures on the 'essence of the church', which he gave in Berlin in 1932, was in all probability deliberately and polemically chosen with all this in mind.[36] Focussing on the church as the locus of revelation by implication meant rejecting both Feuerbach's reduction of theology to anthropology, and Harnack's liberalism.

But now, twelve years later in a Berlin prison, Bonhoeffer chose to write about the 'essence of Christianity', fully aware of what such a title would convey to a theologically literate audience. In his lectures in 1931 on the history of systematic theology, he had stated that Feuerbach put two questions to theology which still remained unanswered. The first concerned the truth of its propositions, whether they did not rest on an illusion. The second was about their relevance to real life (GS: V, 187). These are the precise questions which Bonhoeffer now tried to answer.[37]

There has been considerable debate about whether the theological probings expressed in these last writings indicate a radical turning point in Bonhoeffer's theology. With some justification, the proponents of this view argue that the Bonhoeffer of the letters has finally broken with Barth's theology of the Word, and shifted his sights away from the church to the world.[38] However, the majority of commentators claim, rightly in my view, that there is remarkable continuity in Bonhoeffer's theology from beginning to end. This does not mean that there were no important changes; clearly there were. But these were responses to changing reality worked out in relation to the foundations already laid, not radical breaks with previously held positions.

Throughout his theological development, Bonhoeffer had sought to relate a theology of revelation to reality, first focused on the church, but very soon encompassing the world as a whole, whether understood negatively (*Cost of Discipleship*) or more positively as in prison. Yet, while he drank deeply from the well of Barth's theology, he was always critical (except in New York!) of its lack of concreteness, and now, in prison, of its 'revelational positivism'. On the other hand, while he always rejected Kantian idealism, and the liberal theology which built upon it (especially in New York), he always took seriously the questions of nineteenth century theology, posed so sharply by Feuerbach. And these questions now came to the fore in prison. Both his affirmation of a theology of revelation and his struggle with reality found their focus in the question 'Who is Jesus Christ, for us, today?' And it is precisely this question that sparks off his prison reflections:

The question is: Christ and the world come of age. The weakness of liberal theology was that it conceded to the world the right to determine Christ's place in the world; in conflict between the church and the world it accepted the comparatively easy terms of peace that the world dictated. Its strength was that it did not try to put the clock back, and that it genuinely accepted the battle (Troeltsch), even though this ended with its defeat (LPP: 327, Letter of 8 June 1944).

THE ESSENCE OF CHRISTIANITY

In his 'Outline for a Book', Bonhoeffer designated chapter one as 'A Stocktaking of Christianity'. Such an undertaking was necessary because the world had 'come of age', and was now inevitably set along the path of secularization. God had been pushed onto the boundaries of human existence, and was now a 'god of the gaps' or *Deus ex machina* who was called on only when all other resources failed. What remained was individual piety and a church of bourgeois privilege which existed on the peripheries of life. A church, and therefore a Christianity, rejected by both the working class masses and the intelligent elite.

Bonhoeffer's concept of the 'world come of age', borrowed from Kant, was not a moral but a historical judgment. He did not mean that the world had become better, wiser or more just. But in continuity with his essay on 'Inheritance and Decay' (*Ethics*), he was describing the logical consequences of the eighteenth century Enlightenment. He did not mean that God as such was on the boundaries of the world and therefore irrelevant to human existence at the centre. Rather, he was arguing that God as commonly projected by the church had become redundant for secular men and women struggling with reality, and was only a felt need for the weak and the comfortable. This was not the God of the Bible. While few would agree with Bonhoeffer today that we have arrived at a 'time of no religion at all', quite the reverse, it is true that there are many who would like to be Christians and intelligent, socially concerned men and women, followers of Jesus without the trappings of what Bonhoeffer defined as religion or a God who is beyond credibility.

But what precisely did Bonhoeffer mean by religion, a concept notoriously difficult to define? In continuity with Feuerbach's critique that God is a projection made necessary by human weakness, Bonhoeffer regarded religion as human dependence upon God on the boundaries of life. But he gave specific content to this by defining it more precisely as a form of individualism and a metaphysical system. Religion's individualism made human beings abscond from their responsibility for the world, and its attempt to provide a schematic and secure answer to the search for salvation enabled men and women to avoid the direct challenge of the gospel. Indeed, for Bonhoeffer, religion is always partial, turned inward, whereas faith 'is always something whole, an act involving the whole of life'. 'Jesus' Bonhoeffer wrote, 'calls men, not to a new religion, but to life' (LPP: 362).

Affirming Barth's critique of religion (LPP: 286), Bonhoeffer therefore rejected the need for any 'religious *a priori*' (Schleiermacher, Ritschl, Seeberg) in humankind as the presupposition of faith. On the contrary he argued that religion, however helpful in previous ages, was now an obstacle to genuine faith in Jesus Christ, hence the imperative of developing a 'non-religious interpretation of Christianity'. It was this task which he proposed to undertake in the second chapter of his book.

The fundamental issue in the second chapter was clearly the question of God. As in his early theology, Bonhoeffer rejects any idealist metaphysical approach to the question, and focuses on ethical transcendence and sociality, but now understood in terms of his developed Christology. 'Our relation to God is not a "religious" relationship to the highest, most powerful, and best Being imaginable — that is not authentic transcendence, but our relation to God is a new life in "existence for others" through participation in the being of Jesus' (LPP: 381).

Bonhoeffer's proposal is not an apologetic for Christianity, nor a dilution of the Christian message. The purpose of his non-religious interpretation was to allow the gospel to address modern men and women at the centre of their lives, and to do so in such a way that they could respond without having to become 'religious'. There are undoubtedly similarities, as well as differences, between Bonhoeffer and Bultmann's hermeneutical project at this point, though Bonhoeffer distanced himself from Bultmann.[39] Contrary to much popular opinion, by 'non-religious interpretation', Bonhoeffer did not mean the reduction of the Christian faith nor the rejection of the church, worship, prayer, and the creeds, even though he was critical of what he called Barth's 'revelational positivism'. Christian faith and practice had to be re-worked, not rejected, and the clue to the task was more than an intellectual exercise in hermeneutics. What was required was a radical change (*metanoia*) which would transform Christian praxis by relating it to the 'sufferings of God at the hands of a godless world'.

The final chapter of the proposed book was one in which the consequences of the above for the church would be discussed. Bonhoeffer's ecclesiology is not developed in his prison reflections, but it is always implied. For him it was impossible to think of Jesus Christ without also thinking of the church. The church in a world come of age would need to regain its position at the centre of the world, not in a spirit of triumphalism, but in openness to secular people and a willingness to engage with them in the struggles and issues which shape life in society. This meant becoming a 'church for others' in conforming with Jesus Christ, rather than following a path of self-preservation, concrete 'righteous actions' rather than repeating worn-out cliches or enunciating principles.

It is in this context that we can understand Bonhoeffer's cryptic remarks about 'unconscious Christianity' which we find referred to twice in his *Letters and Papers from Prison* and also, interestingly, in the novel which he wrote in prison. In a letter to Bethge, postmarked 27 July 1944, he relates 'unconscious Christianity' to 'natural piety', and in some fragmentary notes dated from the same period, he refers to 'unconscious Christianity' as a possible interpretation of Matthew 25, the parable of the Last Judgment (LPP: 373, 380). This concept, similar in many ways to that of Karl Rahner's 'anonymous Christianity', finds its fullest expression, however, in Bonhoeffer's autobiographical prison novel (FFP: 76f). Here we find continuity between his concern for non-religious 'good people' (*Ethics*), typified by his own family and his friends in the conspiracy, and the development of a 'non-religious interpretation of Christianity'. In Ruth Zerner's words, 'Through the concept of "unconscious Christianity" he fitted the non-religious among his family and friends into his Christian worldview.'[40]

Openness to the world alone would, however, lead to a loss of Christian identity and substance, and 'righteous action' alone could not be sustained for long, unless the church also practised a *disciplina arcanum* or 'discipline of the secret'. This referred, historically, to an ancient practice of the church which became necessary when, having survived persecution and the 'catacombs', it came out into the open as the established religion. It meant that only the baptized could be present for the celebration of the eucharist. In this way the 'mysteries' of the faith were preserved. Bonhoeffer was not suggesting the literal use of this precise practice, but the appropriate equivalent for today. Only in such a way could the faith be preserved from profanation and cheap grace be avoided.

In a remarkable passage of his sermon, written in prison, for the baptism of Dietrich Bethge, Bonhoeffer brought all these thoughts together and pointed forward to the future.

Our church, which has been fighting in these years for its self-preservation, as though that were an end in itself, is incapable of taking the word of reconciliation and redemption to humankind and the world. Our earlier words are therefore bound to lose their force and cease, and our being Christians today will be limited to two things: prayer and righteous action among men. All Christian thinking, speaking, and organizing must be born anew out of this prayer and action. . . . It is not for us to prophesy the day (though the day will come) when men will once more be called so to utter the word of God that the world will be changed and renewed by it. It will be a new language, perhaps quite non-religious, but liberating and redeeming — as was Jesus' language; it will shock people and yet overcome them by its power; it will be the language of a new righteousness and truth, proclaiming God's peace with men and the coming of his kingdom.   (*LPP: 300*)

A POSTSCRIPT

Bonhoeffer did not leave us a carefully worked out systematic theology, though a careful reading of his writings will reveal the coherence of his thought. Bonhoeffer's legacy is rather that of seminal ideas which arose out of his engagement with the realities of his historical context. But it is more than simply a legacy of ideas. What we discern in Bonhoeffer's writings, confirmed in a remarkable way by his life and death, is an authentic witness to Jesus Christ in relation to the situations in which he found himself. He does not provide us with ready-made answers for our time, but he does indicate how we might respond in faithfulness to the gospel. With the proviso that we do not allow his ideas to become 'rusty swords' in our hands, he provides us with insights and concepts which can help us in our task of bearing witness to the gospel in different contexts.

A glance at the bibliography (p. 298ff.) will indicate some of the ways in which Bonhoeffer's life and thought have enabled theologians to respond to contemporary issues. The bibliography is not, however, exhaustive. It excludes many works which, while not directly related to Bonhoeffer's theology, have been profoundly influenced by it, for example, the debate about religion and 'secular Christianity', and the Marxist-Christian dialogue. Most of these are listed in the new *Bonhoeffer Bibliography* edited by Clifford Green and Wayne Floyd. It is appropriate, however, to mention some of the literature which relates more specifically to areas where Bonhoeffer's ideas have been particularly seminal during the last decade.

Christians and Jews after the Holocaust   Eberhard Bethge has written several essays on this theme, notably 'Dietrich Bonhoeffer and the Jews' (in Godsey and Kelly eds., *Ethical Responsibility: Bonhoeffer's Legacy to the Churches*, and 'The Holocaust and Christian Anti-Semitism: Perspectives of a Christian Survivor' (*USQR*, xxxii, 3-4, 1977). Also of importance is the essay by William Peck, 'From Cain to the Death Camps: An Essay on Bonhoeffer and Judaism' (*USQR*, xxviii, 2, 1973).

Contextual and Liberation Theology   Julio Santa Ana's article on 'The Influence of Bonhoeffer on the Theology of Liberation' (*Ecumenical Review*, 28, 2, April 1976) was the first essay to explore this theme. See also G. Clarke Chapman, 'Bonhoeffer and Liberation Theology' (in Godsey and Kelly eds., *Ethical Responsibility*).

Confessing Christ Today   Many articles and papers related to the fiftieth anniversary of the Barmen Declaration in 1984 deal with Bonhoeffer's significance today for the church's witness. See in particular Bethge, 'The Confessing Church Then and Now: The Barmen Declaration, 1934 and 1984' (The International Bonhoeffer Society, English Language Section, *Newsletter*, 31, May 1986). On the significance of Bonhoeffer for the church struggle in South Africa, see John W. de Gruchy, *Bonhoeffer and South Africa*, and for the task of the church in Britain see Keith Clements, *A Patriotism for Today*.

Spirituality and Community   Amongst the many articles two will have to suffice: Burton Nelson's 'Bonhoeffer and the Spiritual Life: Some Reflections' (in *Journal of Theology for Southern Africa*, 30, March 1980), and Kelly, 'Freedom and Discipline: Rhythms of a Christocentric Spirituality' (in Godsey and Kelly eds., *Ethical Responsibility*).

One of the remarkable facts about Bonhoeffer is the way in which he has not only contributed ideas to so many different areas of theological reflection and church life, but done so in many different cultural contexts throughout the world from Japan to Latin America, Europe to South Africa. The fact is, as Geffrey Kelly has indicated, Bonhoeffer is 'a transitional figure in the history of theology'. By this Kelly means that Bonhoeffer 'pointed to a new phase in Christian thinking that would involve a realistic questioning of all the traditional presuppositions of religion and faith'. And, indeed, 'the re-thinking of all the theological concepts that we have more or less taken for granted and the renewal of the church in a more human direction through the witness of unselfish service are an effort to cope with the challenge posed by his theological-pastoral legacy'.[41]

SELECTED TEXTS

1

THEOLOGICAL FOUNDATIONS[*]

SANCTORUM COMMUNIO

Sanctorum Communio *was Bonhoeffer's doctoral dissertation originally written when he was twenty-one years old under the supervision of Professor Reinhold Seeberg, and presented to the Faculty of Theology at Berlin University in 1927. After some rigorous editing it was published in 1930. The English edition (translated by R. Gregor Smith, Collins, London, and Harper & Row, New York, 1963) from which our extracts are taken, was based on the third German edition of 1960 and, while well translated, it 'confusingly and erroneously conflates material from the various texts' (Green,* Bonhoeffer: the Sociality of Christ and Humanity, *Missoula, Scholars Press, 1975, p. 89, n. 3). It has also long been out of print. The latest German edition published as volume 1 in the new definitive series* Dietrich Bonhoeffer Werke, *Chr. Kaiser Verlag, München, 1986), is a critical edition of the first German edition of 1930.* Sanctorum Communio *is a lengthy theological treatise comprising five tightly-knit chapters:*

Chapter 1 *Towards a Definition of Social Philosophy and Sociology*
Chapter 2 *The Christian Concept of the Person and the Concepts of Social Basic Relations*
Chapter 3 *The Primal State and the Problem of Community*
Chapter 4 *Sin and the Broken Community*
Chapter 5 *Sanctorum Communio*

Our selections need to be read in relation to this table of contents, but are not intended as a substitute for reading the work as a whole. They serve as an introduction to some of the significant themes within Sanctorum Communio *which are important for understanding Bonhoeffer's theological development. In editing the extracts, care has been taken to overcome some of the translation problems in the English text. Page numbers refer to the English edition.*

---

[*] See also above, pp. 3-12.

CHAPTER I

TOWARDS A DEFINITION OF SOCIAL PHILOSOPHY AND SOCIOLOGY

The sociology of religion is a phenomenological study of the structural characteristics of religious communities. But to avoid misunderstanding it should be noted that the present work on *sanctorum communio* is theological rather than sociological. Its place is within Christian dogmatics, and the insights of social philosophy and sociology are drawn into the service of dogmatics. We wish to understand the structure, from the standpoint of social philosophy and sociology, of the reality of the church of Christ which is given in the revelation in Christ. But the nature of the church can be understood only from within, *cum ira et studio*, and never from a disinterested standpoint. Only by taking the claim of the church seriously, without relativising it alongside other claims or alongside one's own reason, but understanding it on the basis of the gospel, can we hope to see it in its essential nature. So our problem has to be attacked from two, or even from three, sides: that of dogmatics, of social philosophy, and sociology.

In the next chapter we shall show that the Christian concept of the person is real only in sociality. Then we shall show, in a social-philosophical section, how man's spiritual being is likewise possible and real only in sociality. Then in a purely sociological section we shall consider the structures of empirical communities, being by that time in a position to refute the atomist view of society. Only then, through the insight we have acquired into the nature of community, shall we be able to come near to a conceptional understanding of Christian community, of the *sanctorum communio*.

(SC: 20-21)

*

CHAPTER II

THE CHRISTIAN CONCEPT OF THE PERSON AND THE CONCEPTS OF SOCIAL BASIC-RELATIONS

Every concept of community is related to a concept of the person. The question about what constitutes community can only be answered by asking what constitutes a person. Since the aim of our inquiry is to understand a particular community, namely, the *sanctorum communio*, we must investigate its particular concept of the person. Concretely this means that we must study the Christian concept of the person. In understanding the meaning of person and community, we shall also have said something decisive about the concept of God. For the concepts of person, community and God have an essential and indissoluble relation to one another. It is in relation to persons and personal community that the concept of God is formed. In principle, the nature of the Christian concept of community can be reached as well from the concept of God as from the concept of the person. In choosing the latter as our starting-point, we cannot reach a soundly based view of it, or of community, without constant reference to the concept of God. (*SC: 22*)

*

The Christian concept of the person may now be defined as constitutive of, and presupposed in, the concept of Christian community; that is, in theological terms, the concept of the person as found in primal man (*Mensch*), but in man after the Fall, and that means, not in man living in unbroken communion with God and his fellow-men, but in man who knows good and evil. This concept necessarily builds upon the fact of man's spiritual nature, upon its structural and individual personal nature. In this general concept, too, the Idealist concept must be overcome by a concept which preserves the concrete individual concept of the person as ultimate and willed by God. (*SC: 28*)

*

From our concept of time there follows an idea which is quite meaningless for the idealist: the person is continually arising and passing in time. It is not something timelessly existing, it has a dynamic and not a static character; it exists only when a man is morally responsible; it is continually recreated in the perpetual change inherent in all life. Every other concept of person cuts through the abundance of life of the actual person. The ultimate reason for the inadequacy of idealist philosophy to grasp the concept of the person lies in its having no voluntarist concept of God, and in its lack of a profound concept of sin; and joined to these defects is its attitude to the problem of history. The idealist conception of the person does not indicate an accidental logical defect, but is inherent in the system. Idealism has no conception of movement. The movement of the dialectic of mind is abstract and metaphysical, whereas the movement of ethics is concrete. Further, idealism has no understanding of the moment in which the person is threatened by the absolute demand. The idealist moralist knows what he ought to do, and, what is more, he is always in principle able to do it, just because he ought. Where is there room for distress of conscience, for infinite *Angst* in face of a decision?

This brings us close to the problem of reality, of the real barrier, and thus of social basic-relations. It is a Christian recognition that the person, as a conscious person, is created in the moment when a man is moved, when he is faced with responsibility, when he is passionately involved in a moral struggle, and confronted by a claim which overwhelms him. Concrete personal being arises from the concrete situation. Here too, as in idealism, the encounter lies wholly in the mind [*Geist*]. But mind means something different in each case. For Christian philosophy the human person comes into being only in relation to the divine person which transcends it, opposing and subjugating it. The autonomy of the mind, in the idealist individualist sense, is unchristian, since it involves the human mind being filled with absolute value, which can only be ascribed to the divine mind. The Christian person arises solely from the absolute distinction between God and man; only from the experience of the barrier does the self-knowledge of the moral person arise. The more clearly the barrier is recognized, the more deeply the person enters into responsibility. The Christian person is not the bearer of the highest values, but the concept of value is to be related to his being as a person, that is, to his creatureliness.   (*SC: 30 f*)

*

Moreover, the individual exists only through the 'other'. The individual is not solitary. For the individual to exist, 'others' must also exist. But what is this 'other'? If I call the individual the concrete I, then the other is the concrete Thou. But what is the philosophical status of 'Thou'? First, every Thou seems to presuppose an I, which is immanent in the Thou, and without which a Thou could not be distinguished from objects. Thus Thou would seem to be equal to the 'other I'. But this is only correct within limits. Beyond the limit set to epistemology there is a further limit, set to ethical and social knowledge, or discernment. The other may be experienced by the I simply as Thou, but not himself as I, that is, in the sense of the I that has become I by the claim of a Thou. In the sphere of moral reality the Thou-form is fundamentally different from the I-form.   (*SC: 32*)

*

The transcendence of the Thou has nothing to do with epistemological transcendence. This is a purely moral transcendence, which is experienced only by the man who makes a decision, which can never be demonstrated to someone standing outside. Thus all that is to be said about the Christian concept of the person can only be grasped by one who is himself involved in responsibility.

(SC: 33)

*

The important question arises, how the I-Thou relationship may be thought of along with the concept of God. Is the idea of God to be included in the category of the Thou?

We know God as the absolute, that is, however, also as self-conscious and spontaneously active will. This expresses formally and metaphysically the personal nature of God as pure mind, whose image is present in every man, as the remnant of God's likeness. Now it does not conflict with such a concept of God that he may be experienced by us as a Thou, that is, as an ethical barrier; further, this experience of God as Thou has *a priori* no effect on his I, either as being individually limited or as itself ethically addressed. If God is a Thou for us — that is, is active will over against us — this does not mean that we are a barrier for God. This has its application for the concept of God. God is impenetrable Thou, and his metaphysical personality, conceived of as absolute self-consciousness and self-activity, does not affect what we have said about his being as I.

(SC: 34)

*

The problem is the relation between the person, God, and social being. The I arises only with the Thou; responsibility follows on the claim. 'Thou' says nothing about its own being, but only about its demand. This demand is absolute. What does this mean? It claims the whole man in his claimlessness. But this seems to make a man the creator of the other's moral person, which is an intolerable thought. Can it be avoided? The person-forming activity of the Thou is independent of its personal being. Now we add that it is also independent of the will of the human Thou. No man can of himself make the other into an I, into a moral person conscious of responsibility. God, or the Holy Spirit, comes to the concrete Thou, only by his action does the other become a Thou for me, from which my I arises. In other words, every human

Thou is an image of the divine Thou. The character of a Thou is in fact the form in which the divine is experienced; every human Thou has its character from the divine Thou. This is not to say that it is not a Thou, but a quality derived from God. But the divine Thou creates the human Thou, and because God wills and makes it this human Thou is real, absolute and holy, like the divine Thou. Here we might speak of man as God's image in virtue of his effect upon the other man. But since one man's becoming Thou for another does not in principle alter anything about the Thou as a person, it is not his person as an I that is holy, but the Thou of God, which here becomes visible in the concrete Thou of social life. The other man is Thou only in so far as God makes him this. It is only in God that the claim of the other resides; but for this very reason it is the claim of the other.

To sum up: the person in his concrete life, wholeness and uniqueness, is willed by God as the ultimate unity. Social relations must therefore be understood as built up interpersonally upon the uniqueness and separateness of persons. The person cannot be surpassed by an a-personal mind, or by any 'unity' which might abolish the multiplicity of persons. The basic social category is the I-Thou relation. The Thou of the other man is the divine Thou. So the way to the other man is also the way to the divine Thou, a way of recognition or rejection. In the 'moment' the individual again and again becomes a person through the 'other'. The other man presents us with the same problem of cognition as does God himself. My real relation to the other man is oriented on my relation to God. But since I first know God's 'I' in the revelation of his love, so too with the other man: here the concept of the church finds its place. Then it will become clear that the Christian person achieves his true nature when God does not confront him as Thou, but 'enters into' him as I.

Hence the individual belongs essentially and absolutely with the other, according to the will of God, even though, or even because, each is completely separate from the other. (*SC: 36*)

*

CHAPTER III

THE PRIMAL STATE AND THE PROBLEM OF COMMUNITY

A. THE METHODOLOGICAL PROBLEM: THE ORIGINAL UNBROKEN COMMUNITY

Our aim is to present the concept of the person which holds true within history, that is, after the Fall. This aim is justified because (1) in a real sense history only begins with sin, in that the factor that makes history possible, namely death, is bound up with sin, and (2) if our chief question concerns real Christian community then the metaphysical concept of the person yields nothing; we need a definition of the person which has a Christian content. The whole of idealism is unaware of any cleft between the primal state and the Fall, or of the significance of this cleft for the person and the view of community. It is this recognition of the inner history of the concept from the primal state to sin, that is, in the depths where we ascribe to sin a qualitative reality in connection with history, that we make a fundamental separation from idealism. Origin and *telos* are an unbroken continuum for idealism, and are synthesized in the concept of 'essence'. All that interferes with this, on the one hand sin, on the other hand Christ, cannot disturb this essential and necessary continuum. This straight-line conception of the history of the spirit abolishes anything specifically Christian. Neither sin nor salvation can alter the essence of this history.

To return: if the metaphysical concept of person is taken in a positive Christian sense, that is, in the direction of God, then we have the concept of person which belongs to the primal state. Is there any connection with a concept of community? Undoubtedly man in the primal state must be thought of as being in immediate community of service with God, as we find in Genesis 1 and 2. It is the concept of the church which first makes it clear that this immediate community means something more than the ontic I-Thou relation. This community is a real connection of love between an I and an I. In the Christian concept of God, known to us from the revelation in Christ, but also from the church of Christ, the community of God and social community belong together. So we maintain that the immediate community of God demands also the immediate community of man, that the latter is a necessary correlate of the former, and that it is no accident that we read in Genesis 2.18: 'It is not good that the man should be alone'. The immediate community of

49

God is documented in the immediate community of man. But what does immediate community mean? In the community of God it clearly means, first, the absolute identity of purpose of the divine and the human will, within the relation of the creative to the created, that is, the obedient will. In other words, within the relation of ruling and serving. The idea of a community of love and of this connection of ruling and serving appear together here, in this image of the primal state, anticipating their connection and distinction in the ideas of the kingdom of God and the rule of God. In religious language, certainly, this community is built upon immediate and mutual love; but because love rules when it serves we have the problem here of a pure association of authority: by limitless serving God rules limitlessly over men. In that God establishes this law for community, man serves him limitlessly in fulfilling it, and God rules over men. Among men, therefore, immediate love must take other forms, since the absolute ruling character of a creative will over a created will falls away, and mutual service is a common service under the rule of God. But since all persons are created unique, even in the community of love the tension between wills is not abolished. This means that conflict as such is not the consequence of the Fall, but arises on the basis of common love for God, in that every individual will strives to reach the one goal of serving the divine will, that is, serving the community, in its own way. (*SC: 40 f*)

*

B. THE SOCIO-PHILOSOPHICAL PROBLEM: HUMAN SPIRITUALITY AND SOCIALITY

The problem of this section is the relation between man's spirituality and sociality. We shall show that man, as spirit, is necessarily created in a community, and that his general spirituality is woven into the net of sociality. This is extremely important in providing a clarification of the relation between the individual and the community, and the right background for the typology of community; on this basis we can clarify the problem of the religious community and the church. (*SC: 44*)

*

1. *Personal being as structurally open*

Man is embedded in an infinite abundance of possibilities of expression and understanding. By a million arteries a stream of spirituality has entered him, before he was aware of it, and he can only notice it when he is in the midst of it.

He knows that he understands, expresses, and is understood. The three experiences go together. They are present, potentially at least, in every spiritual act, and all spiritual acts are thus potentially bound up with sociality. In the life of feeling, too, where man thinks he is most isolated, he is certain of being able to express — if not fully, at least to some degree, which provides the limit to any expression — what he feels. This means that he is also certain that he can be understood and can understand the feelings of others. Thus sociality is involved here too.

At this point the concept of basic relations, and the supplementary concept of interaction, are in danger of being confused with empirical theories. It is only in interaction with other spirits that self-conscious thinking and willing are possible and meaningful. This we shall have to verify. First, the social phenomenon of speech, which is so closely connected with thought that it may well be said that it largely makes thinking possible, and has been given precedence over thought, the word over mind.

(SC: 45)

*

The will, too, as an activity arising from self-consciousness, is possible only in sociality. Further, it is of the nature of the will as an activity that it is effective in community. Will arises where there are 'oppositions'. And strictly only another will can be an opposition of this kind. When it is a matter of removing a natural obstacle, it is not really the will which experiences opposition, but one's natural strength (or the will's means of organization). The will itself experiences opposition only in the will of a person who wills something different. It is only in the struggle with other wills, in overcoming them and making them part of one's own will, or in being oneself overcome, that the strength and wealth of the will are deployed. Such a struggle takes place in miniature wherever man lives in the community of the I-Thou relation. For where person meets person, will clashes with will, and each struggles to subdue the other. Only in such encounters does the will reach its essential determination. As an isolated phenomenon the will is without meaning. Here again we come upon the basic significance of sociality for human spirituality (*Geistigkeit*).

(SC: 47)

*

To sum up, man's entire spirituality is interwoven with sociality, and rests upon the basic relation of I and Thou. 'Man's whole spirituality becomes evident only along with others: the essence of spirit is that the self is through being in the other' (Othmar Spann). The I and the Thou are fitted into one another in infinite nearness, in mutual penetration, for ever inseparable, resting on one another, in inmost mutual participation, feeling and experiencing together, and sustaining the general stream of spiritual interaction. Here the openness of personal being is evident. But the question arises: is there any point in still speaking of I and Thou, if everything is now apparently one? Is not every apparently individual phenomenon just a participation in the one supra-individual work of the spirit? (*SC: 48*)

*

2. *Personal being as structurally closed*

The idea of personal openness threatens to turn into that of an a-personal spirit. With the beginnings of spirituality the I plunges into a sea of spirituality. It awakens and finds itself existing in the midst of this sea. It can only live in this context, and it knows that every Thou it meets is borne along by the same stream. But the characteristic form in which all this takes place is the form of the Thou. That is, man knows that his I is real only in the relation with the Thou. Clearly, then, he is not just the reservoir for a certain amount of objective spirit, a receptive organ, but an active bearer and member in this whole context of relations. Otherwise there would be no I-Thou relation, and no spirituality. The more the individual spirit grows the more it plunges into the stream of objective spirit, sustaining it; and out of this movement the power for individual spiritual life is increased.

Thus the person's openness requires closedness as its correlate, if we are to be able to speak of openness at all. So the question whether there is an individual being which is untouched by social links must in a certain sense be answered affirmatively, if the idea of the I-Thou relation is not to be abandoned. On the other hand there is a danger that in trying to save the idea of an a-social core of personal being we might be thinking atomistically. A basic change of this kind would matter a great deal for our view of the church.

The tragedy of all idealist philosophy was that it failed to break through to personal spirit. But its tremendous merit (and that of Hegel in particular) was its recognition that the principle of spirit was something objective, reaching beyond everything individual, and that there was an objective spirit, the spirit of sociality, which was something in itself as opposed to all individual spirit. It is our task to affirm the one without denying the other, to keep the insight without joining in the error.

(*SC: 48*)

*

The individual personal spirit lives solely by virtue of sociality, and the 'social spirit' becomes real only in individual embodiment. Thus genuine sociality leads to personal unity. One cannot speak of the priority either of personal or of social being. We must hold firmly to the fact that alongside those acts which are real only in sociality there are also purely introversive acts. It is clear that the latter are also possible only in a person living in full sociality — than which there is indeed no other kind of person. So far as experience is concerned these acts isolate the I from the Thou completely; but on the other hand it is not the intimate act which constitutes the person as structurally closed. Rather, no social intention is conceivable without this structural closedness, just as no intimate act is conceivable without the corresponding openness. On the other hand, the social intention is directed towards openness of the person, and the intimate act towards his closedness. But it is wrong to distinguish in the person an inaccessible, completely isolated core and a completely open layer surrounding it. The unity and the closedness of the whole person are presupposed together with sociality.

(*SC: 49*)

*

If the equilibrium between social and personal being is to be maintained, what meaning does the community acquire as a metaphysical unity in relation to the individual? We maintain that the community can be understood as a collective person, with the same structure as the individual person.

(*SC: 50*)

*

A community is a concrete unity. Its members must not be thought of as individual: the centre of action does not lie in each member, but in all together. This unity is the starting-point for our thought, for one does not reach the one from the many, and an individualist starting-point precludes understanding of the situation. It is not that many persons, coming together, add up to a collective person, but the person arises only through being embedded in sociality. And when this happens, simultaneously the collective person arises, not before, yet not as a consequence of the arising of the individual. That is, the collective person exists only where individual persons exist. But since the collective person as a centre of acts is possible only as a concrete purposive community, it can only be possible where the individual person is a real part of the concrete community. (*SC: 51*)

*

I-Thou relations are also possible between a collective person and an individual person. For the collective person is in fact also an individual person. It is only when collective persons are included in social intercourse that the richness of this can be properly grasped. To grant the collective person, then, does not limit the basic sociological category of I-Thou relations; rather, in the eyes of God, the all-embracing Person, collective and individual persons have the same structure, both closed and open, with mutual completion, and social and introversive intentions within a structural unity. (*SC: 51*)

*

What is the theological significance of these observations? Man is not conceived of by God, the all-embracing Person, as an isolated, individual being, but as in natural communication with other men, and in his relation with them not satisfying just one side of his otherwise closed spiritual existence, but rather discovering in this relation his reality, that is, his life as an I. God created man and woman, each dependent on the other. God does not desire a history of individual men, but the history of a community (*Gemeinschaft*) of men. Nor does he desire a community which absorbs the individual into itself, but a community of men. In his sight the community and the individual are present at the same moment, and rest in one another. The structures of the individual and the collective unit are the same. Upon these basic relations rests the concept of the religious community and the church. (*SC: 52*)

*

C. THE SOCIOLOGICAL PROBLEM

1. *Social community as community of will*

Where men are brought together by sheer impulses it is not possible to speak of human society. The impulses of imitation, subordination, sociability, and in particular of hunger and sexuality, man has in common with the animals. Specifically human community is present only when conscious human spirit is at work, that is, when community is based on purposive acts of will. Human community does not necessarily arise from such acts of will, but it has its being in them. Human community is by nature a community of will, and as such it gives meaning to its own natural form. *(SC: 53)*

*

One must never conclude, however, from the unity of will, whatever its nature, that there is some kind of unity of persons, that is, some fusion of persons. Community of will and unity of will are built upon the inner separateness of I and Thou. We have already rejected the idealist argument that the identity of what is willed demands the homogeneity and unity of persons. The man who is united with me in what we intend is structurally just as separate from me as the man who is not so united with me. Between us there is the boundary of those who have been created as individual persons. Only with this conception of community is the Christian idea of a divine community possible. Otherwise such a communion with God becomes unification in the sense of overstepping the boundary of the I-Thou relation, a mystical fusion.

To see the individual person as an ultimate unit, created by God's will, but as real only in sociality, is to see the relations of one with another, built upon difference, as also willed by God. This means that strife is the basic sociological law. Concretely this means that in every social relation there must be an element of partisanship. Only in the conflict of wills does genuine life arise, only in strife does power unfold. *(SC: 54)*

*

2. *Typology of social communities*

Bonds between wills can be regarded from the standpoint of the relation between the goal that is willed and the will to community, that is, the direction of the wills. This analysis provides us with an understanding both of the closeness and the looseness of the bond. The other way of looking at the matter is to study the relative strength of the wills. From these two approaches it seems to me that we can get at the nature of every bond between wills, even though in any particular case the analysis may be made more difficult by the presence of a combination of several types.

We begin with the first approach. Every will strives to reach a goal. There are two possibilities for the relation between this goal and the will to community, and in each the will has a different form. (*SC: 55 f*)

*

According to modern terminology — in Tönnies's creative definitions — the first would be called 'community' (*Gemeinschaft*)in a special sense, and the second 'society' (*Gesellschaft*, ie an association). We shall keep his terminology. It would be easy to identify this distinction with the genetic one of associations which have 'grown' and those which have been 'made', between those already existing and those which are willed. The family, the nation and the church would be among the first, limited liability companies, clubs, and perhaps sects (as in Weber and Troeltsch) among the second. But this identification is basically false. A nation is a community in the special sense, but it has not grown, but has been willed, moreover as an end in itself, having its own value, for every community is a community of will. (*SC: 55 f*)

*

The directness of the bond between persons is expressed in a community by closeness, and in a society by looseness, both in the form of their life and in their psychological attitude. It must, however, be emphasized that no pure type actually exists. There is no community without acts of will which are those of a society, and no society without acts of will which are those of a community, because society is by nature based on community.

So far we have spoken of the way in which the direction of the will is determined, about its purposive intention and its intention of meaning. The question now arises of the relative strength of wills. This can appear as a relation of power and as a relation of authority. In the former the dominated will is activated mechanically by the will in power, whereas in the latter there is presupposed an understanding of the command by the one who obeys. This is sociologically significant in so far as in an association of power there can be no community, whereas in one of genuine authority community is not only present, but for the most part realized. This is most important for the concept of the church.

(SC: 58 f)

*

We have distinguished between a will for meaning and purposive will, a structure of meaning and a structure of purpose, between community and society. The meaning of society is clear. But why should we speak, in connection with community, of 'a will for meaning' and 'a structure of meaning'? Because in this kind of bond the will is not self-establishing, but recognizes something established, it is not related to a purpose but to value, because what demands acknowledgement is a structure of values which cannot be grasped rationally or teleologically. Or, to put it from another angle, because community by its nature does not point purposively beyond itself. Unlike many sociologists, we do not consider that it is possible to elaborate the *telos* of a community, a family or a nation, however delicate our insights. A community may have a rational *telos*, but it is not contained within it, the community itself is not this *telos*. It is its very nature that this should be so. Rather, community is permeated with value, as history is, and as value itself lies beyond intramundane limitations. As history by its nature finds its *telos* at the boundary of history (regarded as the end of time, and beyond time), that is, in God, so community is founded in God, and willed by him. History has no rationally perceptible purpose, it comes from God and goes to God, it has meaning and value as such, however broken its origin and its destiny may be. So, too, genuine community, in marriage, the family, the nation, is from God to God, and its *telos* lies on the boundaries of history.

(SC: 61)

*

In contrast, a society as a structure of purpose is purely within history. For the realization of its purpose it is constituted in history. Its purpose can be the purely personal desire of each individual (earning money, or connections), and with the satisfaction of the individuals the duration of the society is, ideally, at an end. If a society's purpose goes beyond the individual, say over a whole generation, then the duration corresponds to this purpose. If the purpose of the society is the dream of many people to establish the kingdom of God on earth, then its purpose lies at the end of history, which is thought of as the end of time. The category of 'development' appears, which is not found in a community. But the idea of society never goes beyond the idea of the purpose which constitutes it. A puposive association which tries to reach beyond what is temporarily possible for it, ceases to be an association. Here the end of history is the end and not a boundary. Thus the idea of a concrete society as purely teleological is necessarily intra-historical, and temporally conditioned.   (*SC: 61 f*)

*

3. *Objective spirit*

Without being aware of it, people speak of objective spirit in a double sense: (1) in the sense in which the spiritual is objectivized in contrast to unformed spirit, and (2) in the sense in which the spiritual is social in contrast to subjective. The basis for both is the recognition that where wills unite, a 'structure', that is, a third thing, previously unknown, arises, independent of its being willed or not willed by the persons joining with one another. This general recognition of the nature of objective spirit was a discovery of qualitative thinking, which arose in Romanticism and Idealism. It is only here that concrete totality arises; it is not a question of numbers, but depends on the way people think of it, and experience it as a phenomenon. Two wills encountering one another form a 'structure'. A third man joining them does not see just the two men joined together, but rather a third thing, the structure itself, opposes his will with a resistance which is not identical with the will of the two individuals, but can be greater than the resistance of the individuals, or — if such an idea were possible — of the sum of all individuals. It is this 'structure' which is objective spirit. Not only does it confront the third man, who is seeking admittance to a society of friendship, as something independent and autonomous, but it also intrudes as a third thing between the two who are bound together in however primitive a structure. The persons thus experience their community as something real outside themselves, disengaging itself from them, and rising above them.   (*SC: 65*)

*

From all this it follows that society and community have a different view of time. In a community the intention reaches to the bounds of time, in a society it is bounded by time. This eschatological character, which a community shares with history, contains its deepest meaning, as being given 'from God to God'. This is the basis of the 'holiness' of human life in community, whether it is a physical community of blood and race, or a historical community like the nation, or a community of destiny like marriage or friendship. It is in virtue of this holiness that all such human structures are in principle indissoluble. The idea of society, on the other hand, does not go beyond the idea of the goal which constitutes it; it is temporal, and intra-historical. For a society the end of history is really an end, and not just a boundary. That is why only a community, and not a society, can become a 'church'.

The most profound difference between the two social forms lies in the fact that we can attribute personal character to the objective spirit of the community, but not to that of the society. (*SC: 67*)

*

There is a centre of action which is proper to the experience of community (love, sympathy, rejoicing, etc.) and a particular way of acting in community, alongside other individuals, in the sense of social equilibrium and the image of the monad.

Thus we do not have here the conception of a being of the spirit, called the spirit of a people, rising up with power from metaphysical depths. But in the dialectical movement, in which persons arise, there also arise individual collective persons, and only when this is seen does the richness of the monadic image of social life become clear. Collective persons are self-conscious and self-active.

But it is also clear why no personal character can be ascribed to a society. Objective spirit is regarded only as a means to an end, whereas a person can never be only a means to an end. (*SC: 68*)

*

In relation to the doctrine of the primal state, we may now say that theologically all the relationships in community which we have discussed can be represented in the integral state, that is, within the community of love, both social and religious, which was originally given, and that therefore the spiritual form (this community of love) and the natural form (the empirical community) are so created that they rest in one another. From this it is easy to draw conclusions about the character of the empirical community.

We have now to show how, with the coming of sin, the spiritual form takes a new shape, and how these altered ethical relationships are related to the unchanged natural forms. The idea of the collective person can then be fully elaborated. *(SC: 69 f)*

*

CHAPTER IV

SIN AND THE BROKEN COMMUNITY

The world of sin is the world of 'Adam', the old humanity; but the world of Adam is the world for which Christ atoned and which he turned into a new humanity, into his church. This did not happen, however, in such a way that Adam was completely overcome, but in such a way that the humanity of Adam still lives on in the humanity of Christ. Thus a discussion of the problem of sin is indispensable to an understanding of the *sanctorum communio.*

Our essential task in this chapter is to reveal the new basic social relationships, between the I and the Thou and equally between the I and humanity, which are postulated by the concept of sin.

Whereas the previous spiritual form had grown up upon the basis of love, the Fall changed this to selfishness. This gave rise to the break in immediate communion with God, as it did to that in immediate communion with man. This alteration in direction brought about a change in man's whole spiritual attitude. Morality and religion in their true sense are lost to his nature; they are still visible only as forms in legal order and natural religion.

Whereas the primal relationship of man to man is a giving one, in the state of sin it is purely demanding. Every man exists in a state of complete voluntary isolation; each man lives his own life, instead of all living the same God-life. Each man now has his own conscience. Conscience did not exist in the primal state; it was only after the Fall that Adam knew what good and evil were. Conscience can just as well be the ultimate prop for self-justification as the point at which Christ strikes home at man through the law. Hearing the divine law in solitude and recognising his own sinfulness man comes to life again as an ethical person, though in ethical isolation. With sin ethical atomism enters into history. This is essentially applicable to the spiritual form. All the natural forms of community remain, but are corrupt in their innermost core. *(SC: 70 f)*

*

A. ORIGINAL SIN

Every act is at once an individual act, and one in which humankind's general sin is brought to life again. In this way we have established the universality of sin as necessarily given along with and in individual sin.

From this recognition of the bond between the individual and the race there emerges what has been called the experience of common sinfulness. 'I am a man of unclean lips, and I dwell in the midst of a people of unclean lips', Isaiah cries, as, in the utmost loneliness, he confronts the holiness of God. In speaking thus he is not divesting himself of his personal guilt, but rather positing it together with the awareness that in him the sin of the whole people comes to life, and that his sin stands in the closest connection with it. The experience of ethical solidarity and the recognition that one is the *peccator pessimus* belong together. But the experience does not in any way constitute sociality; but sociality is present before and apart from it. It is necessary to bear this carefully in mind. The experience of ethical solidarity is built upon the uncompromising singularity of the person, so that even in the awareness of the closest belonging together the ontic and ethical separateness of individual persons on account of sin can never cease, nor fade from the consciousness. There is no over-leaping the limits of the I. Here we once again meet the I-Thou relation presented above (realized in the guilty sense), the 'abolition' of which is possible only in the concept of the church. We now add, however, to complete the picture, that it is not only the Thou which is essential to the I, but the race too. The 'experience' of the *peccatorum communio* in its relation to the basic ontic relationships paves the way for the experience of the church. (*SC: 79 f*)

*

B. ETHICAL COLLECTIVE PERSONS

If the subject of sin is at once the individual and the race, what is the form of sociological unity suitable for the humanity of Adam? This reintroduces the question of the ethical personality of collective persons which we previously left open and which determines whether there is any meaning in the idea of a collective person. Is it possible to regard the collective person as an ethical person, that is, place it in the concrete situation of being addressed by a Thou? If so, then we shall have proved that it is a centre of action.

The meaning and reality of such a call can be comprehended only by one who, as a part of an empirical community, has experienced it. It is

61

the Israelite concept of the people of God, which arose solely through being thus challenged by God, by the prophets, by the course of political history and by alien peoples. The call is to the collective person, and not to the individual. It is the people that is to do penance as the people of God. It was the people, and not the individuals, who had sinned. So it was also the people who must be comforted (Isa. 40.1). When peoples are called, God's will is seen shaping history, just as when the individual is called, he experiences his history. There is a will of God for the people, just as there is for the individual. When a people conscientiously submits to God's will and goes to war, to fulfil its history, its mission in the world, thus entering completely into the ambiguity of human sinful action, it knows that it is summoned by God, that history is to be made; here war is no longer murder. God does not only have eyes for the nation; he has a purpose for every smallest community, for every friendship, every marriage, every family. And in this same sense he has a purpose for the church too. It is not only individual Germans and individual Christians who are guilty; Germany and the church are guilty too. Here the contrition and justification of individuals is of no avail; Germany and the church themselves must repent and be justified. The community which is from God to God, which bears within it an eschatological meaning — this community stands in God's sight, and does not dissolve into the fate of the many. It has been willed and created, and has fallen into guilt; it must seek repentance, it must believe in and experience grace at the limits of time. It is clear that this can happen only 'in' the individual. Only thus can the hearing of the call be concretely comprehended, and yet it is not the individuals, but the collective person (*Gesamtheit*) who, in the individuals, hears, repents and believes. The centre of action lies in the collective person. Thus the collective guilt of a community is something else than guilt as a social phenomenon in the community. The 'people' is to repent, but it is not a question of the number who repent, and in practice it will never be the whole people, the whole church, but God can so regard it 'as if' the whole people has repented. 'For the sake of ten I will not destroy it' (Gen. 18.32). He can see the whole people in a few individuals, just as he saw and reconciled the whole of humanity in one man. Here the problem of vicarious action arises, which we deal with later. When the collective person is addressed ('He who has an ear, let him hear what the Spirit says to the churches' — Rev. 2 and 3), the conscience of each individual person is addressed. Each person, however, has only one conscience, which is valid for him both as a member of the collective person, and as an individual. For there are not two strata in man, one social and one private; a man is structurally a unity, and it is only the directional intentions which can be in conflict in him. He must know himself and make decisions as an inner unity, must not therefore blindly subject himself to the concrete claims of the collective person, but struggle through to an integrated decision of the will. Only upon such integrated persons is the ethical community built. Our conception of collective guilt is thus not that of a fault deriving from certain contents or parts of the soul; but the concrete form of collective guilt is the total guilt of the integrated person.

These insights now have to be applied to the concept of humanity. Humanity is the universal community comprising all communities. The participation in its life as a community is authenticated by the affirmation of life lived in fellowship with others. For this always exists within the collective human person. It too, like every person, is capable of receiving the ethical call, as it can be heard for the whole of humanity in the story of Jesus Christ. The collective human person has a heart. The individual authenticates his participation in this in its ethical aspect, that is, by every act of repentance and recognition of guilt. The collective person's heart beats at the point where the individual recognizes himself both as an individual and as the race, and bows to God's demand. Here is the seat of its moral unity; it has in reality one conscience, in so far as every man is Adam. It is a structural peculiarity of the humanity of Adam that it breaks up into many isolated individuals, even though it is united as humanity, which has sinned as a whole; it is 'Adam', a collective person, which can be superseded only by the collective person, 'Christ existing as the congregation' (*Gemeinde*). The sign of belonging to the old humanity, to the first Adam, lies in sin, and the individual's awareness of guilt reveals to him his connection with all those who have sinned; in recognizing that he belongs to the humanity of Adam, the individual places himself within the *peccatorum communio*. 'The humanity of sin' is one, even though it consists throughout of individuals; it is a collective person and yet subject to endless fragmentation; it is Adam, as every individual is both himself and Adam. This duality is its nature, annulled only by the unity of the new humanity in Christ.

(*SC: 82-85*)

*

CHAPTER V

SANCTORUM COMMUNIO

A. BASIC PRINCIPLES

Until now we have been pursuing two, or rather three, different lines of thought, which we now have to bring together in our minds; or better, whose union, which is already present in the reality of the church, we now have to explore. On the one hand there was the line of thought about men being basically related to one another by ontic personal relationships. On the other hand there was the discovery of the human spirit's pre-volitional sociality, and the consequent investigation of the forms of empirical real community relationships, which always require volitional social acts to authenticate themselves as personal social relationships. The ontic-ethical basic relationships in the state of sin not only form the basis for all personal social relationships, but are requisite, even, for their empirical formation. When they are changed, or re-created, in the concept of the church, the concrete form of the community must also change; indeed it is this which makes the development of a special empirical form of community possible and necessary. We recognize certain basic forms as in accordance with creation, and consequently the question now arises, to what extent the form of the church enters into them, and whether in it we shall be able to find the synthesis of them all.

Since even when the ethical basic relationships are changed sin remains, which means that the old ontic relationships are not radically annulled, every empirical formation will necessarily be subject to the ambiguity inherent in all human actions. What is unprecedently new, however, is that the new basic relationships have their own form; that the meaning of these relationships is that they produce such a form. In this we can perceive a special will of God which it is not open to us to belie by condemning everything that has taken on a form as the handiwork of man. It is in the necessary bond between the basic relationships and the empirical form of community as a special form that the nature of the church, formally speaking, resides.

There are basically two ways of misunderstanding the church, one historicising and the other religious. In the first, the church is confused with the religious community; in the second, with the kingdom of God. In the first, the character of reality which is possessed by the new fundamental relationships based on God is overlooked in favour of the 'religious motives' which in fact lead to empirical community (the urge to do missionary work, the need to impart one's faith, etc.). This outlook, however, receives its plain judgment in the words of John: 'You did not choose me, but I chose you' (John 15.16). The second misunderstanding springs from not taking seriously the fact that man is bound by history; that is, historicity is either deified as an object, as in Roman Catholicism, or it is simply evaluated as accidental, subject to the law of sin and death. This, however, is not to accept but to circumvent God's will, which is to reveal in the church as he did in Christ everything which he reveals by concealing it in the guise of historical events. To put it differently: the 'seriousness' which is so much talked about is carried so far that it loses its real character and becomes formalistic. The first misunderstanding is almost unavoidable in the study of the church from the historical or sociological point of view; but it is equally at home in the religio-romantic circles of the Youth Movement. The second is met with in theology. Both are dangerous, for both can be nourished by solemn and earnest religious feeling. In neither, however, is there any grasp of the reality of the church, which is at once a historical community and established by God.

(SC: 87-88)

*

The concept of the church is possible only in the sphere of reality based on God; that is, it is not deducible. The reality of the church is a reality of revelation, part of whose nature it is to be either believed or denied. So if we want to find an adequate criterion for justifying the church's claim that it is the church of God, this is possible only if we place ourselves within it, if we submit in faith to its claim. Belief, of course, is not a possible method of arriving at scientific knowledge, but as the belief which accepts the claim made in revelation, it is the given premise for positive theological knowledge. It would be completely wrong, too, to 'establish' from the belief in Christ the belief in the church as a conceptual necessity. What is conceptually necessary is not for that reason real. Rather there is no relation to Christ in which the relation to the church is not necessarily presupposed.

(SC: 89)

*

In recognizing that we can understand what a community is only from a study of the concrete religious form, we are thrown back upon the problem of the church. It is possible to discern certain communal intentions from a study of the actual contents of Christian faith, as these are found in empirical groupings. But in this way we cannot reach the concept of the church. (Schleiermacher even thought that he could reach the concept of the church from the general concept of religion). This can only be done when the Christian revelation is believed, that is, taken seriously. The Christian concept of the church is reached only by way of the concept of revelation. But once the claim of the church has been accepted, it is as superfluous as it is impossible to prove its general necessity. The situation is the same as with the Christological attempts to prove the necessity of redemption, after its reality has been comprehended. Only by first believingly making the meaning of redemption one's own can one clearly see what makes this reality necessary. Only from reality can we deduce necessity in dogmatics. This is basic to the concept of revelation. *(SC: 96)*

*

B. POSITIVE PRESENTATION
LEADING TO THE BASIC PROBLEMS AND THEIR DEVELOPMENT

The church is God's new purpose for men. His will is always directed towards actual historical man, and therefore has its beginning in history. At some point in history it must become visible and comprehensible. But since the primal community, in which God speaks and the Word becomes deed and history through men, is rent asunder, now God himself must speak and act, and because his Word is always deed this means that he simultaneously accomplishes a new creation of men. Thus his will is at the same time fulfilled, that is, revealed. So just as the church has its beginning in Christ, so it is fulfilled in him. He is the corner-stone and foundation of the building, and the fullness of the church is his body. He is the first-born among many brethren, and yet all are one in him — Eph. 1.4 f. . . . If we, the members of the Christian church, are to believe that God in Christ has reconciled us, the Christian church, with himself, then in the Mediator of our reconciliation there must be combined not merely the love of God that reconciles, but at the same time the humanity that is to be reconciled, the humanity of the new Adam.

If the church consummated in Christ is to build itself up in time, the will of God must constantly be realized anew, no longer acting as a general principle for all men, but in the personal appropriation of individual men; and this appropriation is possible only upon the ground of

God's action in Christ, and pre-supposes both the being of humanity in the church (which is consummated in Christ) and the bringing of the individual into the church, that is, into the humanity of Christ, by the act of appropriation. The refractoriness of the ideas of revelation and time, consummation and becoming, cannot be overcome logically. Revelation enters into time, not only apparently but in reality, and in doing so bursts the time-form asunder. If, however, we sought for this reason to understand revelation only as a beginning (potentiality) and not as at the same time consummation (reality), we should be depriving God's revelation of its decisive quality: the fact that his Word has become history.

In order to carry out the temporal building of the church as his community, God reveals himself as the Holy Spirit. The will of God which brings individual human beings together in the church, maintains it, and is effectual only within it, is the Holy Spirit; and only by being personally appropriated by the Holy Spirit, by standing in the actual church, do we experience our election in the church, which is based on Christ.

Thus our study falls naturally into the following parts: first, we have to inquire into the consummated church established in Christ through God's action, the church of God; or, as we expressed it earlier, into the life-principle of the new basic relationships of social existence. We have therefore to discuss the analogy with the basic relationships established in Adam, and their abolition. The new relationships are completely established in Christ, not ideally but in reality. Humanity is new in Christ, that is, new when seen in the light of eternity, but it also becomes new in time. Thus the second part will be the study of the action of the Holy Spirit as the will of God for the historical actualization of the church of Jesus Christ. Only we must take strict note that the opposition here is not between actualization by the Holy Spirit and the potentiality in Christ, but between the actualization by the Holy Spirit and the reality in the revelation in Christ. That is the basis for the whole understanding of the problem of the church. The 'possibility' that the church will not be made actual by the Holy Spirit simply no longer exists. But it is the church which is completely established in Christ as a reality which is necessarily made actual. It is a great temptation to apply here the category of potentiality in Christ. But this category destroys the character of redemption as real; the reconciliation and justification of the world is, with regard to revelation, really based on Christ — for the faith which, admittedly, is possible only within the actualized church.

The church is not first made real by assuming empirical form, when the Holy Spirit does his work; but the reality of the church of the Holy Spirit is one which is founded on revelation, and it is a matter merely of believing in that revealed reality in its empirical form. As Christ and the new humanity now necessarily belong together, so the Holy Spirit too is to be seen as effectual only within this humanity. This makes evident the misunderstanding which consists in regarding the objective action of the Spirit as independent of the church. The Holy Spirit is solely in the church and the church is solely in the Spirit. And yet Troeltsch thought it necessary to maintain that in the Protestant conception of the church it was not a question of the congregation, but solely of the Word, that is, of the objective action of the Holy Spirit; that where the Word is, there the church is, even in the complete absence of hearers. This is a complete misunderstanding of the Protestant tenet of the significance of the Word, of which we have yet to speak.

It will then, thirdly, be necessary to determine the relation between the Holy Spirit ruling over the church and the human spirit of the community which the action of the Holy Spirit brings about. This raises the problem of the empirical church. In this connection the difference between the Idealist and the Christian concept of objective spirit will become plain. (*SC: 103-5*)

1. *The church established in and through Christ — its realization*

The reality of sin, we found, places the individual in the utmost loneliness, in a state of radical separation from God and man. It places him in the isolated position of one who confesses that he committed the 'first' sin, that in him the whole of humanity fell. But at the same time it brings him both objectively and subjectively into the closest bond with the rest of humanity, precisely through the guilt involved, which, while it cannot, it is true, take on empirical form as a bond of guilt, is nevertheless experienced in every concrete bond. Now since in the individual act of guilt it is precisely the humanity of man which is affirmed, humanity itself must be regarded as a community. As such it is at the same time a collective person, which, however, has the same nature as each of its members. In Christ this tension between being isolated and being bound to others is really abolished. The thread between God and man which the first Adam severed is joined anew by God, by his revealing his love in Christ. He no longer demands and summons, approaching humanity purely as Thou; but gives himself as an I, opening his heart. The church is grounded in the revelation of the heart of God. But as, when the primal communion with God was rent asunder, human community was rent too, so likewise when God restores the communion of humanity with himself, the community of men with each other is also re-established, in accordance with our proposition about the essential connection between man's communion with God and with his fellow-man.

In Christ humanity is really drawn into communion with God, just as in Adam humanity fell. And yet in the one Adam there are many Adams; but there is only one Christ. For Adam is 'man', but Christ is the Lord of his new humanity. Thus each man becomes guilty through his own strength and guilt, because he himself is Adam; but each man is reconciled without his own strength and merit because he himself is not Christ. Whereas the old humanity consists of countless isolated units of Adams which are conceived as a unified entity only through each individual, the new humanity is completely drawn together into the one single historical point, into Jesus Christ, and only in him is it comprehended as a whole; for in him as the foundation and body of the building of his church the work of God is accomplished and consummated. And in this work Christ has a function which sheds clear light on the difference in principle between Adam and Christ; his function as vicarious representative (*Funktion als Stellvertreter*). Adam's action is not deliberately vicarious but is on the contrary extremely egocentric. The fact that its effect looks very similar to that of a deliberately vicarious action must not deceive us as to its completely different basis from that of the action of Christ. With the old humanity it is as if humanity falls anew each time one man incurs guilt, whereas in Christ humanity is placed — and this is the very essence of real vicarious action — once and for all in communion with God.

As history begins with death, which is the wages of sin (Rom. 6.23), so life lived in love breaks the continuity of history, not empirically but in reality. Death can indeed still fully separate past and future for our eyes, but it cannot any longer separate them for the life lived in the love of Christ. That is why the principle of vicarious action can become fundamental for the church of God in and through Christ. Not 'solidarity', which is never possible between Christ and man, but vicarious action, is the life-principle of the new humanity. I know, certainly, that I am in a state of solidarity with the other man's guilt, but my dealings with him take place on the basis of the life-principle of vicarious action.

Since now Christ bears within him the new life-principle of his church, he is at the same time established as the Lord of the church, that is, his relation to it is that with a 'community' and that of a 'ruler'.

But because the whole of the new humanity is really established in Jesus Christ, he represents the whole history of humanity in his historical life. His history is qualified by the fact that in it the humanity of Adam is transformed into the humanity of Christ, by the fact that, as Jesus Christ's human body became the resurrection-body, so the *corpus Adae* became the *corpus Christi*. Each equally leads through death and resurrection; the human body, the *corpus Adae*, must be broken, so that the resurrection-body, the *corpus Christi*, might be created. The history of Jesus Christ is, however, closed to us without his Word. Only if we take both together shall we be able to read humanity's past and future in that history. (*SC: 106-8*)

*

The relation of Christ to the church can now be stated as follows: essentially Jesus Christ was no more a founder of the Christian religious community than he was the founder of a religion. The credit for both these things belongs to the primitive church, that is, to the apostles. That is why the question whether Christ founded a church is so ambiguous. He brought, established and proclaimed the reality of the new humanity. The circle of disciples about him was not a church; but they simply sketched out the church's inner dialectic. This was not a new religion seeking adherents, which is a picture drawn by a later time. But God established the reality of the church, of humanity pardoned in Jesus Christ. Not religion, but revelation, not a religious community, but the church: that is what the reality of Jesus Christ means. And yet there is a necessary connection between revelation and religion, as there is between religious community and the church. (*SC: 111-112*)

*

Thus the church is established in and through Christ in the three basic sociological relationships already known to us: his death isolates the individuals, each bears his own guilt, each has his own conscience; in the light of the resurrection the church of the cross is vindicated and sanctified as one in Christ. The new humanity is focused together in one point, in Jesus Christ; and as the love of God through Christ's vicarious action restores communion between God and man, so the human community too once again becomes a living reality in love. (*SC: 114*)

*

2. *The Holy Spirit and the church of Jesus Christ —*
the actualization of the essential church

The church is established in reality in and through Christ — not in such a way that we can think of the church without Christ himself, but he himself 'is' the church. He does not represent it, for only what is not present can be represented. But in God's eyes the church is present in Christ. Christ did not make the church possible, but he realized it for eternity. If this is so, Christ must be accorded central significance in the temporal actualization of the church. This place is given him through the Word, impelled by the Spirit, of the crucified and risen Lord of the church. The Spirit is capable of operating only through this Word. If there were an unmediated operation of the Spirit then the idea of the church would be individualistic, and thus be dissolved at its very source. In the Word, however, the most profound social relationships are established from the outset. The Word is socially determined not only in its origin, but equally in its aim. The linking of the Spirit with the Word expresses that the Word is intended for a plurality of hearers, and a visible sign is set up, by which the actualization is to be brought about.

The Word, however, is qualified by being the Word of Christ himself, brought by the Spirit to the hearts of the hearers as an active force. Christ himself is in the Word; the Christ in whom the church is consummated seeks through his Spirit to win man's heart, in order to fit it into the actualized church of Christ. But in the word of Christ the actualized church is also present, just as every Word of Christ comes from the church and exists only in it. If anyone should ask how the actualized church could be present at the time of the first preaching of the Word of Christ, before the individuals who were moved by that Word joined together to form a church, he would be forgetting the ideas we previously presented: that the Spirit is solely the Spirit of the church, of the community, and that there were thus no individuals moved by the Spirit before there was a community.

(*SC: 115*)

*

In the Word the Holy Spirit brings the love of God which has been revealed in Christ's crucifixion and resurrection to the hearts of men. He places them within the divine community. The church is based, however, on Christ himself. If Christ comes 'into' man through the Holy Spirit, then the church comes 'into' him too. But the Holy Spirit moves man in such a way that in putting Christ into his heart he (the

71

Spirit) creates faith and love. The faith in Christ which the Spirit effects, however, involves faith in the church in which he reigns; but love, as the love or heart of Christ in man, is given to man as a new heart, as the will for good. Faith recognizes and receives God's lordship; love makes the kingdom of God actual. Thus it is a question of love making concrete not the metaphysical but the moral social relationship, which we saw could be perceived in the sinful state only as a broken relationship, but one which could be shown actually to exist in the fact of moral personality and sin, having its basis, as a dogmatic testament, in the doctrine of the primal state. In every human socialisation there is an actualizing of the metaphysical social relationships. What is peculiar to the actualizing effect of the Holy Spirit is that it links both basic relationships. In every previous formation of a social unit the basic moral relationships remained broken. Here, by their renewal and actualization, a concrete form of community is established. The man living in the fellowship of the I-Thou relation is given the certainty that he is loved, and through his faith in Christ receives the strength to be able to love in return, in that he, who in Christ is already in the church, is led into the church. He no longer sees the other members of the church essentially as a claim, but as a gift, as a revelation of his love, that is, of God's love, and of his heart, that is, of God's heart, so that the Thou is to the I no longer law but gospel, and hence an object of love. The fact that my claim is fulfilled for me by the other I who loves me — which means, in fact, by Christ — humbles me, frees me from the bonds of my I and lets me love the other — once again, indeed, in virtue of faith in Christ — lets me give and reveal myself entirely to him.

This makes it certain that new social relationships have been created, and that the rift of sin has been closed, but both things have come about through the revelation of the divine heart in Christ, through God's putting his heart, will and Spirit into man in order to realize his purpose for the formation of the church.   (*SC: 118-119*)

*

ACT AND BEING

Act and Being (Akt und Sein) *was Bonhoeffer's habilitation thesis which enabled him to become a lecturer in theology at the University of Berlin in 1930. It was written in 1929 and first published in German in 1931. The English edition was translated by Bernard Noble and published by Collins in 1962. We have retranslated certain phrases where the English is obscure, and, in particular, we have translated* Gemeinde *by 'congregation' and not 'communion'. By* Gemeinde *Bonhoeffer meant, however, the 'congregation', not as an entity in itself, but a community of persons representative of the new humanity established in and through Jesus Christ.* Act and Being *is a closely argued and well-structured theological and philosophical treatise, and like* Sanctorum Communio *it needs to be read as a whole.*

Part A The Problem of Act and Being, Treated as the Epistemological Problem in Philosophy's Understanding of Dasein

1. *The Transcendental Endeavour*
2. *The Ontological Endeavour*

Part B The Act-Being Problem in Revelation, and the Church as its Solution

1. *Revelation in terms of Act*
2. *Revelation in terms of Being*
3. *The Church as a Unity of Act and Being*

Part C The Act-Being Problem in the Concrete Doctrine of Man 'in Adam' or 'in Christ'

1. *Being in Adam*
2. *Being in Christ*

Our selections, which are taken from Part B, chapters 1 and 3, show Bonhoeffer's disagreement with Karl Barth on the nature of the 'freedom of God', and how his resolution of the problem of act and being is in continuity with the conclusion reached in Sanctorum Communio, *viz. 'Christ exists as the congregation'.*

PART B

1   REVELATION IN TERMS OF THE ACT

The contingency of revelation

The proposition that man cannot place himself into truth is not self-evident in the sense of entitling or obliging one to postulate *thenceforth* a revelation capable of supplying truth. On the contrary, the untruth of human self-understanding is obvious only from the viewpoint of revelation and *its* truth, once it has taken place and been accepted in belief. Were it not so, revelation, as the final postulate of human thought, would itself be ensnared in the falsehood of self-understanding, with the result that man, from the postulates of his own existence, would enter the position of adjudging himself right and placing himself into truth — which nevertheless the revelation he postulates, if fully intended as real, is alone able to do for him. Consequently, only the person already placed in truth can understand himself as in truth. For from within truth he can, in his potential reproduction of his 'being known' by God understand or recognize that he is situated in truth, i.e. re-created from untruth into truth. But only from within truth, i.e. in revelation, which is to say, whether judged or pardoned, in Christ. This is what yields the theological concept of existence: existence is envisaged in reference to revelation, as encountered or not encountered by revelation. There is no longer any inherent potentiality of being encountered: existence either is or is not actually encountered by revelation, and this happens to it, as a concrete, psychophysical whole, on the 'borderline' which no longer passes through man as such, or can be drawn by him, but is Christ himself.

It is in this frame of reference that one should envisage the agenda of all theology, which ever since Duns Scotus and William of Occam has laid special stress on the contingency of revelation; but in the contingency of revelation is asserted its transcendence of reason, i.e. its absolute freedom in relation to reason, likewise to all possibilities deployable, so to speak, by an existence understood as potentiality. Revelation, which places the I into truth, i.e. gives understanding of God and self, is a contingent occurrence which can only be welcomed or rejected in its positivity — that is to say, received as a reality — but not elicited from speculations about human existence as such. It is an occurrence with its basis in the freedom of God, whether positively, as his self-giving, or negatively, as his withholding of himself.

The proposition of God's freedom in revelation admits a double interpretation. First, a formal one: God is free inasmuch as bound by nothing, not even by the manipulable 'entity' of his 'historical' Word. The Word as truly God's is free. God can give and withdraw himself absolutely according to his pleasure; in either action he remains free. He is never at man's discretion; it is his honour and glory* to remain

---

* But cf. Luther, W. A., 23, 157: 'It is the honour and glory of our God (*unseres Gottes Ehre*), however, that, giving himself for our sake in deepest condescension, he passes into the flesh, the bread, our hearts, mouths, entrails, and suffers also for our sake that he be dishonourably (*unehrlich*) handled, on the altar as on the Cross.'

utterly free and unconditional in relation to everything given and conditional. 'Now it would follow that the relationship between God and man in which God's revelation may truly be imparted to me, a man, must be a free, not a static relationship, in the sense that its very constancy may never mean anything other than constancy in a transaction not only continuous but at every moment beginning, in all seriousness, at the beginning. It may never be conceived as already given, already obtaining, nor even as analogous to a natural law or mathematical function; instead, one must always think of it as *actwise* (*aktuell*) — i.e. with all the instability of a deed in course of execution' (Barth). Revelation is interpreted purely in terms of the act. It is something happening to receptive man, but within God's freedom to suspend the connection at any moment. How could it be otherwise, since it is 'God's pleasure, majestically free' (Barth) which initiates the connection and remains its master. God is understood as pure act. God's freedom is the possibility — but with all that *possibility* implies — comprehended in the concrete act.

Inevitably, exception must be taken from the first to the fact that the God-man relationship should be resolved in terms of pure act-subjects in the very context where revelation's transcendence of consciousness is unequivocally asserted. And the suspicion therefrom arising, that transcendentalism is lurking here somewhere, receives confirmation. God reveals himself only in acts freely initiated by himself. 'Man is touched with grace when, and from the fact that, the Word of God comes to him, no sooner, no later, and not otherwise. So far as is known, the heavenly manna in the wilderness could not be put into storage' (Barth). God's Word has no being in independence of his self-revelation to man and its being heard and believed by man. This, however, is where we may recognize the transcendental thesis. Because God himself creates the hearing and belief, and is indeed himself hearing and believing, in man, 'God's Word is only in the act of belief, never in that abstraction from the strictly occasional event, at God's sole discretion, which we call grace' (Barth). God's being is solely act, is consequently in man only as act, and that in such a way that any reflexion on the accomplished act has *ipso facto* lost contact with the act itself, with the result that the act can never be grasped in conceptual form and cannot therefore be enlisted into systematic thought. It follows that although Barth has no hesitation in making use of temporal categories (moment, here and now, before, after, etc.) his concept of the act must not be regarded as temporal. The freedom of God and the act of belief are essentially supratemporal; if Barth nevertheless stresses the act which, recurrently 'beginning at the beginning', is at all times free, so that there can be no inference from one act to the next, we must understand that he is endeavouring to translate the transcendental concept of the act into terms of the *geschichtlich*. However, this attempt is bound to come to grief against the fact that (according to Barth) no 'historical' moment is *capax infiniti*, so that the empirical action of man — 'belief', 'obedience' — becomes at most a pointer to God's activity and can never, *in* its historicality, be faith and obedience themselves.

Thus the problem of transcendental philosophy, which we discovered at the beginning, presents itself afresh. God recedes into the non-objective, the non-available. That is a necessary consequence of the formal conception of his freedom, which might be traced without difficulty to the combination of nominalism and the idea of contingency in the closing stages of medievalism.

God remains always the master, always the subject, so that if any man should think he has God as an object, it is no longer *God* whom he 'has'; God is always the 'coming', not the 'existing' deity (Barth).

It was inevitable that this formal understanding of God's contingent activity should lead Barth to develop his idea of the 'dialectical'. 'God's Word is not bound, and never will be bound. Theological dialectic is genuine dialectic to the extent that it is open to this idea, to the extent — in fact — that it will subserve this idea, subserve the freedom of the Word of God'. The freedom of God's Word cannot be pinned down by unequivocal theological statements. It snaps their pronouncement in twain: thus there are only theological statements under 'critical reservation'.* All Barth's theological propositions are rooted in the necessity of saying *not-God* when I speak of God (because *I* speak of *him*), and *not-I* when I speak of the believing I; thus due regard is paid to the idea that genuinely theological concepts do not fit into an undialectical system — if it were otherwise, concepts of an act-character would have petrified, within the system, into fixed ontological abstractions, and the concept of contingency would be excluded: the 'coming' changed to the 'existing' God. Revelation would have sunk to rest in the theological system. This is countered by the critical reservation. But it is not as if the 'systematic' formula for a theology of revelation had at last been found in a dialectical theology; no, 'for theology too, there is a justification only by

---

* R. Bultmann derives his concept of dialectic from the historicality of existence, and I feel this entitles one to say, while acknowledging the difference between their concepts of existence, that on this point there is no fundamental difference between him and Barth.

faith'. The reservation made by dialectical theology is not a logical one, such as might be suspended in the antithesis, but one real and recurrent in view of predestination; however, as such no theological idea can ever seize God: it remains, 'strictly speaking, a testimony from the devil' (Barth). God remains free, non-objective, pure act, but he can, if he chooses to do so, make use of a theology in order to attest himself therein. That does not lie within the power of the theology but, again, within the freedom of God. Thought is a cohesive whole, incapable of radical self-disturbance; of this Barth is conscious — that even dialectical theology is no way to catch God. How could it be otherwise, since before all thought stands unfathomable predestination?   *(AB: 79-86)*

*

If the knowledge of God and self divinely implanted in man is considered purely as act, any being is of course wholly excluded. The act is always inaccessible to reflexion; it fulfils itself always in 'direct consciousness'. That follows from the formal understanding of God's freedom. In this way theological thought seems condemned to remain in principle profane; it can only, in the event, stand 'under the sign of God' (thus Barth). But the following objection has to be made: what can it mean to say that theology requires a justification by faith, when it can only be a question of justifying the theologian who thinks the theology? Indeed it is open to doubt whether the existence of the theologian, placed in truth, serves to distinguish his systematic thought from profane thought, whether there is any such possibility at all (if so, on what basis?). Seen from the viewpoint of a formalistic understanding of God's freedom, the theory of revelation as pure act can only serve to deny the possibility of a distinction between profane and theological or — if we may anticipate — ecclesiastical thought.

The whole situation impels one to ask whether a formalistic understanding of God's freedom in contingent revelation, conceived wholly in terms of the act, is really the proper groundwork for theology. In revelation it is a question less of God's freedom on the far side from us, i.e. his eternal isolation and aseity, than of his forth-proceeding, his *given* Word, his bond in which he has bound himself, of his freedom as it is most strongly attested in his having freely bound himself to historical man, having placed himself at man's disposal. God is not free *of* man but *for* man. Christ is the Word of his freedom. God *is there*, which is to say: not in eternal non-objectivity but 'haveable', graspable in his Word within the church. Here a substantial comes to supplant the formal understanding of God's freedom. *(AB: 89-91)*

*

PART B

3   THE CHURCH AS A UNITY OF ACT AND BEING

Revelation's mode of being within the church

Revelation should be envisaged only with reference to the church, where the church is regarded as constituted by the present annunciation, within the congregation, for the congregation, of Christ's death and resurrection. 'Present', because it is only in this annunciation that the event of revelation is realized in and for the congregation and because, secondly, this is the only way in which its contingent (i.e. extrinsic) character makes itself known — for contingency is only in presence, viz. the present. What is past, as 'having' happened, is 'background', unless the annunciation 'coming to' us in the future should raise it to 'presence'.* In the concept of contingency as happening which is 'coming to' us from outside, the present is determined by the future; in the system, inasmuch as the (in principle) 'beforeness' of the rational background obtains, the present is determined by the past. At all events the present is determined by one or the other or both; it is never *per se*. But the decision lies with man. Of the Christian revelation it may be said that the annunciation of cross and resurrection, determined by eschatology and predestination, together with the event effective within it, serves even to raise the past to the present and, paradoxically, to something future, yet 'to come'. It follows, therefore, that we may not interpret the Christian revelation as 'having happened', that for man living in the church, in the present, this unique occurrence is qualified as future. Conversely, for the very reason that the Christian revelation, in its special qualification of the unique event of cross and resurrection, is always 'yet to come', it must happen in the present: that is to say, it must be considered within the church, for the church is the Christ of the present, 'Christ existing as congregation'. *(AB: 119-120)*

*

* Bonhoeffer stresses the literal sense of *Zukunft* ('future') — 'to-coming'. German *Gegenwart*, means 'the present' and 'presence' alike.

This is why the Protestant idea of the church is conceived in personal terms. God reveals himself as a person in the church. The Christian congregation is God's final revelation: God as 'Christ existing as congregation', ordained for the rest of time until the end of the world and the return of Christ. It is here that Christ has come the very nearest to humanity, here given himself to his new humanity, so that his person enfolds in itself all whom he has won, binding itself in duty to them, and them reciprocally in duty to him. The 'church' therefore has not the meaning of a human community to which Christ is or is not self-super-added, nor of a union among such as individually seek or think to have Christ and wish to cultivate this common 'possession'; no, it is a congregation created by Christ and founded upon him, one in which Christ reveals himself as the δεύτερος ἄνϑρωπος, the new man — or rather, the new humanity itself.

This is where the question of explaining revelation in terms of act or being assumes an entirely new aspect. God gives himself in Christ to his congregation, and to each individual as member of that congregation. This he does in such a way that the active subject in the congregation, of both the annunciation and the believing of the Word, is Christ. It is in the personal congregation, and only there, that the gospel can truly be declared and believed. There, it follows, revelation is in some way secured or possessed. God's freedom has bound itself, woven itself into the personal congregation, and it is precisely that which proves it God's freedom — that he should bind himself to men. The congregation genuinely has at its disposal the Word of forgiveness; in the congregation may not only be said, existentially, 'I have been forgiven', but also — by the Christian church as such, in preaching and sacrament — 'thou art forgiven'; furthermore, every member of the church may and should 'become a Christ' to every other in so proclaiming the gospel.

Revelation, then, happens within the congregation; it demands primarily a Christian sociology of its own. The distinction between thinking of revelation individualistically and thinking of it in relation to community is fundamental. All the problematics we have examined so far have had an individualistic orientation. Both the transcendental essay at act-subjectivism and the ontological attempt to establish the continuity of the I envisaged consistently the individual man, and he was the rock on which they both foundered. They overlooked, in searching for 'reality', that man in reality is never *only* the single unit, not even the *one* 'claimed by the Thou', but invariably finds himself in some community, whether in 'Adam' or in 'Christ'. The Word of God is given to humanity, the gospel to the communion of Christ. When the sociological category is thus introduced, the problem of act and being — and also the problem of knowledge — is presented in a wholly fresh light.

The being of revelation does not lie in a unique occurrence of the past, in an entity which in principle is at my disposal and has no direct connection with my old or my new existence, neither can the being of revelation be conceived solely as the ever-free, pure and non-objective act which at certain times impinges on the existence of individuals. No, the being of revelation 'is' the being of the community of persons, constituted and embraced by the person of Christ, wherein the individual finds himself to be already in his new existence. This ensures three considerations: 1. the being of revelation can be envisaged in continuity; 2. the existence of man is critically involved; 3. it is impossible to regard the being of revelation as entity, as objective, or on the other hand as non-entity, as non-objective.

1. The continuity of revelation means that it is constantly present (in the sense of the *futurum*, the yet 'to come'). To-day, therefore, it can only be a question of the Christ preached in the church, his death and resurrection. If the individual as such were the hearer of the preaching, the continuity would still be endangered, but it is the church itself which hears the church's Word, even if 'I' were heedless on such and such an occasion. Thus preaching is always heard. It is outside 'me' that the gospel is proclaimed and heard, that Christ 'is' in his community. And so it is not in man that the continuity lies: it is supra-personally guaranteed through a community of persons. Instead of the institutional Catholic Church we have the community as the trans-subjective pledge of revelation's continuity and extrinsicality — the 'from outside'.

2. But the existence of the individual man, hearing the Word on concrete occasions, is vitally affected by this community, inasmuch as, drawn into it, he finds himself already there and as one placed into the truth of his old and new existence. This fact derives from the personal quality of the Christian congregation, in that its subject is Christ. For only through persons, and only through the person of Christ can the existence of man be affected, placed into truth and transplanted into a new manner of existing. Since moreover the person of Christ has revealed itself in the congregation, the existence of man can only be so affected through the congregation. It is only from the person of Christ that other persons acquire for man the character of personhood. In this way they even become Christ for us in what they both demand and pro-

mise, in their existential impositions upon us from without. At the same time they become, as such, the pledge of revelation's continuity. If the existence of man were unaffected by revelation within the congregation, all we have said about the being of revelation in the congregation would be pointless. Continuity which does not also impinge on existence is not the continuity of the Christian revelation, not present being, but bygone entity. In other words, the congregation guarantees the continuity of revelation only by the fact that I know and believe myself to be in this congregation. Here the problem of act and being receives its final clarification by taking the shape of the dialectic of faith and church.

3. If the being of revelation is fixed in entity, it remains past, existentially impotent; if it is volatilized into the non-objective, its continuity is lost. And so the being of revelation must enjoy a mode of being which satisfies both claims, embodying both the continuity proper to being and the existential significance of the act. It is as such a mode of being that we understand the person and the community. Here the possibility of existential impact is bound up with genuine objectivity in the sense of a concrete standing-over-against: this lets itself be drawn into the power of the I because it itself imposes a constraint on existence, because it is *the* extrinsicality.

The community in question is concretely visible, is the Christian church which hears and believes the preaching of the Word. The Word of this community is preaching and sacrament, its conduct is believing and loving. It is in this concretion that one must think of the being of revelation, in 'Christ existing as congregation'. Only thus, in the concretion of the mode of being of a true (i.e. Christ-founded) community of persons, can one observe and preserve the hovering between entity and non-entity.   (*AB: 121-125*)

*

[All this] is only comprehensible to the man who *is* placed in truth, the man for whom, through the person of Christ, his neighbour has become genuinely a person. For the man in untruth revelation remains, as 'person' remains, an entity or thing which 'there is' (*es gibt*): towards this one's relation and attitude are neutral in the sense that the existence of man is not critically involved. It is only within the congregation itself that revelation can be conceived in its real existential being. And so we come to require an account of the being of man in revelation.   (*AB: 126*)

*

Man's mode of being within the church

The being of revelation, the community of Christ (*Gemeinde*), is only in faith. Faith knows that revelation is independent of it. These two propositions must combine to make a third: only in faith does man know that the being of revelation, his own being in the church of Christ, is independent of faith. There is continuity of revelation, continuity of existence, only in faith, but there again in such a way that faith *qua* believing is suspended only in 'faith' *qua* 'being in the congregation'. If here faith were understood wholly as an act, the continuity of being would be disrupted by the discontinuity of acts. Since however faith as an act knows itself as the mode of being of its being in the church, the continuity is indeed only 'in the believing' but thereby is really preserved as being in the church.   (*AB: 128*)

*

In accordance with the being of revelation, the being of man should be conceived neither frozen as entity nor spirited into non-entity. In either of these cases the total existence of man would, in the end, stay unaffected. No; the man we must consider is the historical man who knows himself transplanted from the old into the new humanity and who is, by membership of the new, a person re-created by Christ, a person who 'is' only in the act-reference to Christ and whose being 'with reference to' Christ is based on being in Christ and his congregation in such a way that the act is 'suspended' in the being, while the being itself 'is' not in the absence of the act. The person, as a synthesis of act and being, is always two in one: *individual* and *humanity*. The concept of the absolute individual is an abstraction with no corresponding reality. It is not merely in his general psychology but in his very existentiality that man is tied to society. When his existence is touched (in judgment and mercy) he knows that he is being directed towards humanity. He has himself committed the sin of the old humanity, yet he knows at the same time that humanity drew him into its sin and guilt when he was powerless to resist. He is the bearer of the new humanity in his faith, prayer and affirmation, yet knows that he is borne in all his actions by the congregation, by Christ.

Man as individual and man as humanity, man one in these two inseparable aspects, is but another way of saying man as act and being. He is never one alone. It might be supposed that man's humanity-being could be understood as an abstraction without the slightest effect on existence, but such a supposition collapses against the historical reality of Christ's congregation and my membership thereof. In *reality* I hear another man declare the gospel to me, see him offer me the sacrament: 'thou art forgiven', see and hear him and the congregation praying for me; at the same time *I* hear the gospel, I join in the prayer and I know myself joined into the Word, sacrament and prayer of the congregation of Christ, the new humanity now as then, here as elsewhere; I bear it upon me and am borne of it. Here I, the historically whole man, individual and humanity together, am encountered, affected. I believe; that is, I know myself borne: I am borne (*pati*), therefore I am (*esse*), therefore I believe (*agere*). The circle closes. For even *agere* is *pati* here; but the I always remains the historical One — though in faith the New One. Needless to say, *as* historical it is a member of the new humanity which 'here' or 'there' takes the shape of empirical communities of individuals — though retaining the mode of being of revelation.

Is not the continuity of the I destroyed by the fact that the I, as historical, falls apart into religious life and profane life? What are we to make of the fact of everydayness? Even if we refrain from describing historicity, everydayness, as a divine punishment, the difficulty obtains only from a standpoint of unbelieving reflexion. Religious acts are simply not identical with faith, otherwise the being of faith would once again be explicable as 'entity'. The unity of the I 'is' 'only in faith'. Everything points to that conclusion. If it were possible for unbelief to discover being in continuity (e.g. as everyday psychical datum), the evangelical understanding of faith would be at fault and being would be entity.

But what is meant by the unity of the historical I 'in faith' is — unity in community, in the historical community which I believe to be the congregation of Christ. Because the humanity wherein I stand, which I myself also am, prays for me, forgives sins (in preaching and sacrament) independently of me, being always the whole humanity wherever I am, just because I am its member, my everydayness is overcome within the congregation: only there am I embraced both as individual and as humanity, in existentiality and continuity — but of course only 'in faith', which knows itself possible by virtue of the communion and is abolished within it.

(*AB: 130-132*)

*

The problem of knowledge and the idea of the church

To the being of revelation, defined as that of the Christ-person in the congregation of persons called the church, defined therefore in sociological terms, there must correspond a concept of knowledge envisaged in a sociological category. In understanding this we first need to distinguish between three ways of knowing, hence three concepts, which correspond to distinct sociological functions of the church: knowing as a *believer*, knowing in *preaching* and *theological* knowledge, of which the first may be called *existential* and the others *ecclesiastical* cognition:

Knowing as a *believer* is a question of fundamental sociological epistemology. It means knowing oneself overcome and blessed with grace by the person of Christ through the preached Word. Whether such cognition is possible is a senseless question here, since it derives, as framed, from the isolation of unbelief, whence it can only be answered with an Impossible! (*incapax!*). The asking of such a question postulates a concept of existence as potentiality. But faith is a God-given *reality:* one may question its manner of being or becoming, its How, but not the actual fact of its being. Its object is the person of Christ which is preached within the congregation. This is an object which resists inclusion in a transcendental I, or any non-objectification: it stands as person over against man as person. The person is a unity which overrides the bifurcation of 'entity' and non-entity; it is objective, i.e. knowable, yet by virtue of its genuine *ob*-jectivity, its freedom from the knower, freedom *not* to be, it never falls into the power of the knowing I. It gives itself through the Word to the I in the act of faith, which for its part acknowledges the freedom of the self-giving person and testifies thus to its absolute extrinsicality. (*AB: 137-8*)

*

Through the person of Christ the I's fellow-man is also rescued from the world of things, to which he of course continues to belong *qua* entity, and drawn into the social sphere of persons. Only through Christ does my neighbour confront me as making some form of absolute claim on me from a position outside my own existence. Only here is reality sheer first-hand decision. Without Christ my very neighbour is no more than my possibility of self-assertion through 'sustaining his claim' (Grisebach). (*AB: 139*)

*

Now we have found that in our sociological category we have the point of union of the transcendental and the ontological epistemologies. The person 'is' only in the self-giving act. And yet the person 'is' in independence of that to which it gives itself. It is through the person of Christ that we acquire this understanding of the person, which applies only to the Christ-based personal community of the Christian church. The Christ preached in the congregation gives himself to the member of the congregation. Faith means knowing that one has reference to this. In faith I 'have' Christ in his personal objectivity, i.e. as my Lord who has power over me, atones for me, redeems me. In faith there is no not-knowing, for there Christ is his own witness and confirmation.

In faith Christ is the creator of my new personal being and at the same time the Lord 'with reference to' which — $εἰς$ $αὐτόν$ — the person is created; thus existence is determined both prospectively and retrospectively in relation to transcendence: it 'is' between transcendent poles. In the act of belief, which Christ himself creates within me, inasmuch as he gives me the Holy Spirit who hears and believes within me, he also proves himself the free Lord of my existence. Christ 'is' only 'in' faith, yet he is master of my faith.

(AB: 140-1)

*

THE THEOLOGY OF CRISIS AND ITS ATTITUDE TOWARD PHILOSOPHY AND SCIENCE

Whereas the readings from Act and Being *demonstrate where Bonhoeffer differed from the 'early' Karl Barth, his seminar paper on 'The Theology of Crisis and its Attitude Toward Philosophy and Science' is in many respects an apologia for Barth's theology within a critical North American context. It shows the extent to which he was under the influence of Barth and Reformation theology, and is as much an exposition of his own theology as it is of Barth's. The paper was originally written in English and presented to Professor John Baillie's seminar on philosophical theology at Union Theological Seminary in 1931. It was later published, and translated into German, in* Gesammelte Schriften, III, 110-126.

There is a difference of method, when in examining a candidate one either asks him about things which he probably will know, or finds out the limits of his knowledge by asking him questions which he very likely cannot answer quite as well. The more modern and, for the examinee by far the more pleasant educational principle at least is the first way of asking. However, Barth today is supposed to be the victim of the other type of examination, and it is not merely his fault if the result of his examination is not going to be as satisfactory as it could have been. Barth has never prepared himself for an examination in science or in philosophy, but has always prepared himself for a quite different and distinct field, namely, for Christian theology. That is to say, Barth has been all the time thinking exclusively and intensively about the Λόγος Θεοῦ, and he found — perhaps strangely enough for our all-inclusive and extensive kind of thinking — in this subject such manifold and most important problems, that he did not feel very much attracted by the variety of countless other problems before he had explored the richness of his proper field of theology in its strict sense. Now theology does not answer every question in the whole world, but since it tries to answer at least one question, namely, the question about God, it takes up a certain attitude towards all other questions. This must be admitted, although it will be seen that the essential possibility of this attitude, as well as its concrete character, is a problem of exceeding difficulty. In order not to confuse your impression, I will give you in this paper mainly the position of the founder and the most original thinker of the theology of crisis: Karl Barth. The differences between him and Fr. Gogarten and Emil Brunner will be better explained briefly in the course of the discussion.

Since Barth has never published any comprehensive treatment of our problem, we will have to use some single utterances of his and try to show the lines of connection with his whole thinking, which sometimes Barth himself did not show. Coming to a man like K. Barth after half a year of consideration of the problem of the relation between cosmology, philosophy and theology, I confess that I do not see any other possible way for you to get into real contact with his thinking than by forgetting at least for this one hour everything you have learned before concerning this problem. We have in Barth's theology not one of the countless variations of the solution to this problem from the scholastics via Kant to Bergson or Dewey, but here we stand on an entirely different and new point of departure of the whole problem. We stand in the tradition of Paul, Luther, Kierkegaard, in the tradition of genuine Christian thinking. We do injustice to Karl Barth if we take him as a philosopher; he is not and does not claim to be one; he is just a Christian theologian. This at least must be clear, what we intend to be: Christian theologians or philosophers. To be unclear on this point means that we in any case are not Christian theologians. For the Christian theologian must know the proper and stable premise of his whole thinking which the philosopher does not recognize: the premise of the revelation of God in Christ, or, on the subjective side, the faith in this revelation.

Two questions arise: 1. What is the meaning of the premise according to K. Barth? 2. What makes such a premise necessary? Firstly, the meaning of the proper presupposition of Christian theology is that God entered history in Jesus Christ and made himself known to the world in this revelation. The word or the will of God — God himself — was made flesh. But the revelation of God in Christ was a revelation of his judgment as well as of his grace. Christ's cross is the judgment of God upon the world, Christ's resurrection is his grace. That is to say, the revelation of God in Christ is not a revelation of a new morality, of new ethical values, a revelation of a new imperative, but a revelation of God's real acting for humanity in history, a revelation of a new indicative. It is not a new 'you ought' but 'you are'. In other words the revelation of God is executed not in the realm of ideas, but in the realm of reality. The importance of this difference will be explained later. The fact that God himself comes into the world convinces the world of the impossibility of its coming to God by itself; the fact that God's way in the world leads to the cross, that Christ must die condemned as a sinner on the cross, convinces the world that the impossibility of its coming to God is its condemnation, its sin and its guilt. The fact of Christ's resurrection proves to the world that only God is righteous and powerful, that the last word is his, that by an act of his will alone the world can be renewed. Finally, the fact that the Holy Spirit still comes to man and moves men's hearts with the message of Christ's death and resurrection convinces the world that God is still God and the world still the world, that God's word in Christ is God's word forever. In short, the fact of God's coming into the world in Christ, makes the world see that here in the life of Jesus of Nazareth God is acting towards humanity in an eternal way, that through his life the decision is taken about the world and that in this decision God does everything, man nothing.

Yet it is exactly the fact that God really entered history which makes him invisible for human eyes. If the revelation were a revelation of new ideas, new moral imperatives, then it would be a revelation which everybody could recognize as such by virtue of his own ideal or ethical presuppositions. Then it would have its place in the world of general truth, which is self-evident for the human mind by its generality. This is the conception of revelation in other religions and in our modern liberal thought. The objects of revelation are ideas which are supposed to be compatible with our deepest essence, to the good in man. The Christian idea of revelation is the strict opposite of this view; it is revelation not in ideas, but in historical facts; not in imperatives, but in indicatives; not in generality, but in once-ness. It is revelation because it is not compatible with our own deepest essence, but entirely beyond our whole existence, for would it otherwise have had to be revealed, if it had been potentially in us before? The fact of God's incarnation in Christ, the fact of Christ's suffering and death and the fact of his resurrection are the revelation of God.

But, of course, who is willing to see in these facts God's word? Who is not offended by the foolishness of such a claim? God revealed in the poor life of a suffering man; God revealed on the cross; God revealed in the depth of history, in sin and death — is this a message worth hearing by a wise man, who really would be able to invent a nobler and prouder God? Karl Barth finds the Bible full of the testimony of the awkwardness and foolishness of God's revelation. 'Blessed is he, whosoever shall not be offended in me', says Jesus; and Paul: 'The cross to them is foolishness. . . . It pleased God by the foolishness of preaching to save them that believe. . . . We preach Christ crucified, unto the Jews a stumbling-block and unto the Greeks foolishness. . . . The foolishness of God is wiser than men, and the weakness of God is stronger than men. . . . God has chosen the foolish things of the world . . . that no flesh should glory in his presence.' Mt 11,6; 1. Cor 1.

All that means that God's revelation in Christ is revelation in concealment, secrecy. All other so-called revelation is revelation in openness. But who, then can see the revelation in concealment? Nobody but those to whom God himself reveals this most secret mystery of his revelation in weakness. Nobody but those to whom God gives the faith, which is not offended, but which sees God's judgment and grace in the midst of human weakness, sin and death, where otherwise man can see only godlessness; faith which sees God coming most closely to man where a man hanging on the cross dies in despair with the loud cry: 'my God, my God, why hast thou forsaken me?' Mk 15, 34. And the centurion, who stood over against him and saw that he so cried out and gave up the ghost, said: 'Truly this man was the Son of God'. Mk 15, 39. This is the real world of biblical faith, which sees God's work not on the top, but in the depth of humanity. And because faith sees God in Christ, it sees God, the same God of Christ, in man's own life, in man's own sin, weakness and death as judgment and as grace. It is God's own work that lets man see into these secrets of his revelation; as Christ says to Peter after his confession: 'Flesh and blood hath not revealed it unto thee, but my Father which is in heaven'. Mt 16, 17. So everything points back to God's own decree, to his free predestination. He comes where he wants to come, and he *renounces* whenever he pleases. For he is unconditioned and free.

This is the way Barth tries to make living the world of biblical thinking. He sees that everything in the Bible refers to God's sole truth, righteousness, freedom, judgment, grace. This precisely is the logic of the Bible, God's coming which destroys all human attempts to come, which condemns all morality and religion, by means of which man tries to make superfluous God's revelation. God's sole truth and word, which has to be spoken anew again and again. God coming not to the most seriously moral and pious group of Pharisees and Scribes, but to those who were entangled in public sin. 'Verily I say unto you, that the publicans and harlots go into the Kingdom of God before you'. Mt 21, 31. Here all human order and ranking is subverted, for God's new order has been established, which is contrary to and beyond all human understanding.

It convicts man of his godlessness in his bad and his good deeds. God's coming in Christ is the proof by God himself that man cannot come to God; that is to say, God's coming in Christ must be the judgment upon humanity, in other words, it shows to man his limitations which lie exactly there where God's work begins. Therefore, God's work with man does not begin as a continuation and perfection of man's highest, although, as every decent man will admit, imperfect enterprises, such as religion and morality, but on the contrary, it begins as the irrefragable limitation of man. It begins at man's limits, that is to say, in sin and death. This act of limiting man is God's judgment and grace *in one*. The limited man is the judged man, and at the same time the limited man who gives all righteousness and glory to God is thus justified by God's work and grace alone. The acknowledgment of one's limits before God is faith, not as a possible act of man, but only as an act of God, who sets and shows these limits to man. This is the message of justification by grace or by faith alone. But the revelation of God in the justification by faith and grace implies that man's continuity is always continuity in sin, that he by himself can never get outside of the circle of sin. Otherwise grace would not be grace and justification would not be necessary. Revelation in Christ, justification, means breaking through the circle of sin. Thus God's first word is the radical breaking of all continuity with man in his radical judgment upon man as sinner, and his act of grace is the creation of a new man, with whom God remains in continuity. Since only the revelation in Christ claims to constitute the real outside of man, it implies that it is the only criterion of any revelation. Since this claim puts itself essentially beyond all proof, it demands to be taken as a presupposition of thinking or to be refused altogether. It is perhaps too obvious to mention that as a consequence of this notion of revelation the question of grounds for belief in God is superfluous, because it involves a contradiction. For what better ground does one need, and is possible, than God's word itself? Any theology that is ashamed of this *petitio principii* cannot escape being ashamed of him who gives it whatever meaning it possesses.

Herewith I think we have the chief presuppositions which are indispensible for an understanding of Barth's attitude towards all other problems. The category which Barth tries to introduce into theology in its strict sense and which is so refractory to all general thinking and especially religious thinking is the category of the word of God, of the revelation straight from above, from *outside* of man, according to the justification of the sinner by grace. Theology is the scientific consideration of this category. But exactly here the difficulty comes in. Scientific consideration is based upon general, formal presuppositions of thinking. Since these presuppositions cannot be taken from the object of theological thinking — just because it never actually becomes an object, but always remains subject — and since, on the other hand, they must be taken from this subject-object, if they are to be at all adequate, the deepest contradiction in the task of theology becomes obvious. It is, in the final analysis, the great antithesis of the word of God and the word of man, of grace and religion, of a pure Christian category and a general religious category, of reality and interpretation. In every theological statement we cannot but use certain general forms of thinking. Theology has these forms in common with philosophy. Thus our next problem will be to consider the relation between theology and philosophy with regard to the use of forms of general philosophical thinking in theology.

Let us take the following example. Theological thinking which is based upon the general notion of substance and accidence (and it seems to me that our Western thinking at least will never be able to overcome completely this basic presupposition for this, if for no other reason, namely: the grammatical construction of our languages) — this type of thinking, I say, will conceive of sin, for instance, as substance in man or as accidens. Both in their pure form seemed inadequate to express to orthodox dogmatics the notion of sin. The consequence is either to express the real fact of sin in rather contradictory terms of the type of substantial thinking as it was done after the famous struggle with Flacius Illyricus by orthodox proponents, or to look for different presuppositional forms of thinking — for example, for a dynamic voluntaristic thinking, if that can be considered as a genuine form of thinking at all. The history of theology is to a large extent a permanent seeking for more adequate forms of thinking in order to express the facts of the revelation. Two great Christian churches have definitely settled their forms of thinking in a long history of exceedingly keen and serious thinking; both of them are based upon the scheme of substance and accidence, the Greek Church more in the Platonic, the Roman Church more in the Aristotelian interpretation. (Quite recently, it seems that a movement in the Benedictine order is trying to modify this old form of thinking; this becomes specially obvious in the modern Catholic theories of the sacrifice in the holy communion.)

Luther recognized the insufficiency of the scholastic form of thinking for an interpretation of the facts of revelation. He sees in the notion of substance a great danger in making revelation static and depriving it of its actual livingness. Luther sees this static character attributed to grace in the Catholic Church, which gives grace into the disposal of man. Thus the whole misinterpretation of the doctrine of justification in the Catholic Church is deeply connected with this basic presuppositional form of thinking. Luther himself has not developed his own philosophical terminology. Without doubt his form of thought is essentially dynamic-voluntaristic, herewith accepting a tradition which came to him from Paul via Augustine and the mystics. Yet very often he himself falls back into the substantial form of thinking (for example, in his christology). And it must be confessed even now that Protestantism lacks its own proper philosophical terminology.

Orthodox Protestantism took up the old substantial form of thinking, and it was Kant who showed its impossibility and substituted for it a transcendental philosophy. Theological language from the nineteenth century until our present day has been based not so much upon Kant as upon idealistic philosophy, even where the respective theologians were not conscious of the fact. Ritschl, on whose theology I was brought up in Berlin, could not succeed in his attempt to free theology from the wrong metaphysical premises because he had not thought out the Christian category of revelation — as it becomes obvious in his christology, his doctrine of sin and of justification.

There is finally a realistic philosophy which could offer its services to theology. Now Karl Barth is faced with this situation when he looks for a philosophical terminology for his theology. He is well aware of the fact, though, that in accepting a certain philosophical terminology theology becomes indissolubly connected with a whole philosophy. In his Römerbrief and his later writings Barth uses the philosophical terminology of Kant and the Neokantians in Marburg, and he is conscious of this fact. Like everything in Barth's thought, this also is in the closest connection with the doctrine of justification by faith and by grace alone. But we shall have to explain that. Three questions have to be answered: 1. What is for Barth the task of philosophy in general? 2. What kind of philosophy is adequate for the Christian idea of justification by faith? 3. What is true philosophy from a theological point of view?

1. The task of philosophy has always been an interpretation of the general principles of the universe according to some principles which have been considered as true. Philosophical interpretation claims to be true, even if it is sceptical. More accurately: the predicate 'true' can essentially be referred only to the *interpretation*, and *all* philosophy *is* interpretation, whether it is idealistic or realistic. The statement: here is a table, is by no means self-interpretive for philosophical thinking. What does 'here', what does 'is', what does 'table' mean? Idealism, as well as critical realism and even behaviorism as I understand it, recognizes that only 'naive realism' tries to ignore the complexity of the problem and can hardly be considered a philosophical position. But even critical realism still has to prove its logical consistency over against the superlogical rights of idealism. As long as philosophy has to do with the sheer question of truth and not with some arbitrary statements, logical consistency is an essential predication of every relevant philosophy. Barth's theology from the very beginning was connected with an energetic atack against idealism. Here the ego is found as not only a reflecting, but even a creative ego. It creates its world itself. The ego stands in the centre of the world, which is created, ruled, overpowered by the ego. The identification of the ego with the ground of everything which has been called God is inevitable. There are no limits for the ego; its power and its claim are boundless; it is its own standard. Here all transcendence is pulled into the circle of the creative ego (which of course must not be confused with the empirical ego). Man knows himself immediately by the act of the coming of the ego to itself, and knows through himself essentially everything, even God. God is in man; God is man himself. Barth and his friends discovered in this philosophy the most radical, most honest and

most consistent expression of the philosophical enterprise as such.

Although realism claims to leave room for transcendent reality, it still owes us the proof, which of course it never will be able to bring, that its definition of reality is not its own interpretation of it. As long as realism fails here, transcendent reality has to be referred to the interpreting ego, which constitutes reality and which, even though it denies it, remains the centre of reality. The ego knows reality and it knows itself. It is essentially autonomous. At the basis of all thinking lies the necessity of a system. Thinking is essentially systematic thinking, because it rests upon itself, it is the last ground and criterion of itself. System means the interpretation of the whole through the one which is its ground and its centre, the thinking ego. Idealism saw and affirmed this as the proof of the autonomy and the freedom of man. Realism tries to escape this consequence and fails. There is only one philosophy which recognizes this fact and states it as the definite and essential limit of man. This according to Barth and his friends is the essence of the Kantian philosophy. (It should be strictly noted that Barth and his friends do not care here so much for a complete presentation of the manifold sides of Kant's philosophy, but rather they try to pick out what seems to them the most important trend in Kant's thought.) Kant did not want to be called an idealist nor a dogmatist; he considers both positions equally untenable.

His philosophy is critical philosophy or transcendental philosophy. 'Transcendental' means for Kant, as it has been clearly shown by Knittermeyer and others, not involving transcendence, but referring to transcendence. Thinking is not an act which ever involves transcendence, but refers to it. The transcendence itself does not enter thinking. The ego never knows itself in coming to itself, but it always remains transcendent to itself because it never is static-objective, but always acting. Likewise, thinking does not reach the transcendence of the object, but is always directed to it, because transcendence can never be 'object'. This is the deep meaning of the *Ding an sich* and the transcendental apperception for Kant. Thinking is limited and put into the midst between two transcendences, to which it refers, but which always remain transcendent. In the very moment when the idealists pushed away the *Ding an sich*, Kant's critical philosophy was destroyed. The philosophy of the pure act turned out to be a new ontology, a fact which Hegel clearly recognized. Kant had tried to limit human thinking in order to establish it anew. But Hegel saw that limits can only be set from beyond these limits. This means, applied to Kant, that his attempt to limit reason by reason presupposes that reason must have already passed beyond the limits before it sets them. So Kant's critical philosophy presents itself as the attempt of man to set up limits for himself in order to avoid the boundlessness of his claim, but the fact is that thinking never can limit itself. In limiting itself it establishes itself. Thinking as such is boundless; it pulls all transcendent reality into its circle.

The last consequence of this knowledge has been drawn by E. Grisebach (and from another side by M. Heidegger). Grisebach's question is the question of reality. He sees that thinking, as essentially systematic thinking, does violence to reality in pulling it into the circle of egocentricity. Systematic thinking remains far from reality. Reality is given only in the concrete situation of the ethical meeting of man with man. Thus thinking has to remove itself in order to give room to reality. Grisebach's philosophy is the ultimate possible critique of thinking toward itself, but even here thinking remains dominant and constitutive of the world of reality. For the limit of thinking is a thought limit. This is the inevitable circle of all philosophy. Here at the limits, where philosophy tries to remove itself and cannot but establish itself, and where philosophy comes to its own crisis, here we are ready for our second question, namely, what philosophical terminology could be adequate for a theology of revelation, of justification by faith, for the theology of Barth?

2. Barth sees in the essential boundlessness of thinking, in its claim to be a closed system, in its egocentricity, a philosophical affirmation of the theological insight of the Reformers, which they expressed in terms of *cor curvum in se, corruptio mentis.* Man in *status corruptionis* is indeed alone, he is his own creator and lord, he is indeed the centre of his world of sin. He made himself God and God his creature. The fact that the basic question of philosophy necessarily leads into this situation proves the deepest godlessness of man, even in his profoundest philosophical ideas of God. Man remains with himself in his thinking no less than in his ethical and religious attempts. The world of man is the world of egocentricity, of godlessness. The fact that philosophy essentially gives its sanction to this situation of making man inevitably the God of his world, even if it denies it, shows the impossibility for philosophy to interpret the situation rightly. It shows philosophy as well to be the most dangerous grasping after God, in order to be like God, and thus to justify man by his own power — that is in goldlessness.

We ask: can man then do anything in order to overcome this fatal situation? Kant still believed that critical philosophy could make room for faith by means of limiting reason by reason. But he failed. Barth sees there is no way out. Man must die in his sin in spite of philosophy. He must remain alone in his overpowered and misinterpreted world. But now the Christian message comes: entirely from outside of the world of sin God himself came in Jesus Christ. As the Holy Spirit he breaks into the circle of man, not as a new idea, a new value by virtue of which man could save himself. But in concreteness as judgment and forgiveness of sin, the promise of eschatological salvation. God makes himself known to man who is a sinner in his whole existence. The whole existence of man in his egocentric world has to be shaken before man can see God as really outside of himself. Therefore there is no spectator-knowledge of God but only man in the act of despair of himself can know God by faith. Idealistic and realistic philosophy fail to give the terms for describing these facts. And yet Barth discovers in both of them elements which could be used by theology. Idealism sees God as eternal subject, realism sees reality as transcendent object. Barth can express his idea of the transcendent God in terms of God's essential subjectivity and his idea of God's coming to man in history in terms of God's most objective reality. But he knows that both these terms are essentially inadequate, since they derive from a godless philosophy. Barth's own writings are based upon a Kantian terminology. Here he finds expressed the critique of thinking upon thinking; here he sees man considered not in his full possession of transcendence, but in the eternal act of referring to transcendence, man not in boundlessness, but in limitation. Although Barth knows that even this philosophy remains in boundlessness, he sees here the attempt of philosophy to criticize itself basically and takes from here the terminology in order to express the eternal crisis of man, which is brought upon him by God in Christ and which is beyond all philosophical grasp. Barth sees that there is no Christian philosophy nor philosophical terminology at all. So he can say it does not make very much difference what philosophy a theologian has, but everything depends on how strongly he keeps his eyes on the category of the word of God, on the fact of revelation, of justification by faith.

3. Now our third question can be answered: what according to Barth and his friends ought to be the task of philosophy? Barth himself has not answered this question sufficiently, but his friends have thought a great deal about the problem. Philosophy remains profane science; there *is* no Christian philosophy. But philosophy has to be critical philosophy, not systematic. And yet since even critical philosophy is bound to be systematic (as we have seen before), philosophy must work in view of this fate. It must try to think truth with regard to the real existence

of man and must see that it is itself an expression of the real existence of man and that by its own power it not only cannot save man, but it cannot even be the crisis of man. By doing so it gives room, as far as it can, for God's revelation, which indeed makes room for itself by itself. The deepest antimony seems to me to be the antimony between pure act and reflection — as the old dogmatics said, *actus directus* and *reflectus*. God is known only in the pure act of referring to God. Theology and philosophy are executed in reflection, into which God does not enter. Philosophy essentially remains in reflection; man knows himself and God only in reflection. Theology at least knows of an act of God, which tears man out of this reflection in an *actus directus* toward God. Here man knows himself and God not by looking into himself, but by looking to the word of God, which tells him that he is sinner and justified, which he never could understand before. So as Luther said: *pecca fortiter, sed crede fortius*, Barth could say: *reflecte fortiter, sed crede fortius*.

Not very much has to be added concerning science. As far as science is a discovery of happening facts, theology is not touched (because theology is concerned only with a certain interpretation of facts). If science itself gives its own interpretation of the world, then it belongs to philosophy and is subjected to the critique of theology. The attempt of cosmology, that is, of a genetical interpretation of the world on the basis of natural science, can never reach beyond the limits of human thinking. Cosmology may come to the assumption of a last ground of the world and may call that 'God'; all we can say in the name of Christian theology is that this God is not the God of revelation and not the creator. Two reasons are to be given in the first place, I do not know God as creator without the revelation in Christ. God's being the creator means being the judge and the saviour too; and I know all that only in Christ. In the second place, creation means creation by absolute freedom, creation out of nothing. So the relationship of God to the world is completely free. It has been set and is always set anew ('*creatio continua*') by God. This God is not the first cause, the ultimate ground of the world, but its free Lord and creator. As such he is not to be discovered by any cosmologist, but he reveals himself in sovereign freedom wherever and whenever he wants. The world is fallen away from God. Therefore it is the world of sin and evil and death. No human atempt can unify what has been broken asunder, no thinking, no moral action, no religion. Only an act of God himself can do what no man can do. God has unified the broken and contradictory world. In Christ death and evil and sin are overcome by an act of God visible for faith. At the end of everything God will show his power over death and sin to everybody. He will solve this problem of death and evil and sin by an act of his power.

Our thinking in terms of theodicy tries to justify God in the world. But for Christian thinking God justifies the world, and that has been done in Christ. Thus only through Christ do we see the Creator and the preserver and the Lord *of* the world *and in* the world. Only through Christ do we see the world in God's hands. Away from Christ we live in our own overpowered and egocentric world, which is not the world of God.

Here at the end we stand again where we stood in the beginning, and that cannot be otherwise. For *everything* is included in God's revelation in Christ, in the justification of the sinner by faith and grace alone. And must not the solution of *everything* be there, where *God himself* is?

In the following discussion we shall not be able to do justice to Barth if we do not refer every thought to its theological premise of the justification by faith.

CHRISTOLOGY AND REALITY[*]

A THEOLOGICAL BASIS FOR THE WORLD ALLIANCE

Bonhoeffer's important address on 'A Theological Basis for the World Alliance' was presented at the ecumenical Youth Conference in Czecho-slovakia on 26 July 1932. Published in Gesammelte Schriften *I, 140-58, and in English in* No Rusty Swords, *153-169. The essays in NRS, edited by Edwin Robertson and translated together with John Bowden, were revised by John Bowden for the Fontana edition, 1970. We have generally followed the revised edition, and the page numbers refer to that edition.*

There is still no theology of the ecumenical movement. As often in history as the church of Christ has reached a new understanding of its nature it has produced a new theology, appropriate to this self-understanding. A change in the church's understanding of itself is proved authentic by the production of a theology. For theology is the church's self-understanding of its own nature on the basis of its under-standing of the revelation of God in Christ, and this self-understanding of necessity always begins where there is a new trend in the church's understanding of itself. If the ecumenical movement stems from a new self-understanding of the church of Christ, it must and will produce a theology. If it does not succeed in this, that will be evidence that it is nothing but a new and up to date improvement in church organization. No one requires a theology of such an organization, but simply quite definite concrete action in a concrete task. There is no theology of the 'Midnight Mission'.[†] But it is very important to see that in comparison the ecumenical movement is something completely different.

It would be wrong to say that it was the task of the Faith and Order conference at Lausanne[§] to produce a theology of the ecumenical

---

[*] See also above pp. 13-19.

[†] This was a branch of the so-called 'Inner Mission', the great social achievement of the nineteenth-century German church. The 'Midnight Mission' did specialized work among tramps and prostitutes in the big German cities.

[§] The first World Conference on Faith and Order, held in 1927.

movement. We must rather ask even here: on what basis did the conference at Lausanne do its theological work together? Was this in itself an expression of the church's new self-understanding or was it in the last resort a work of expediency aimed at the better understanding of differing theological terminologies? Depending on the answer we will know what we may and what we may not expect of Lausanne. Without doubt ecumenical work is here most closely bound up with practical work. As a result, until now a large group of men experienced in practical work have looked with some disregard on the work of theology. 'Thank God we don't have to bother about theology here. We are at last free from those problems which so hamper Christian action.' That is what they have been saying. But just this attitude has become dangerous and demands our fullest protest; for it has had as its most perceptible consequence the exposing of ecumenical work to politically determined trends. Because there is no theology of the ecumenical movement, ecumenical thought has become powerless and meaningless among German youth at present because of the political upsurge of nationalism. And the situation is scarcely different in other countries. There is no theological anchorage which holds while the waves dash in vain from right and left. Now there is great helplessness, and the confusion of concepts is boundless. Anyone engaged in ecumenical work must suffer the charges of being unconcerned with the Fatherland and unconcerned with the truth, and any attempt at a rejoinder is quickly cried down. And why is all this? Only because we have neglected to work out clear theological lines at the right time, lines along which ecumenical work should progress. I have nothing against the practical contribution of the church in ecumenical work! Here we have every occasion for thankfulness and respect. But what is it that has emerged time and time again with rudimentary force at the international youth conferences of recent times? What gave these conferences so little 'practical' character, what put them against the traditional form of resolutions? It is the recognition of the deep helplessness that there is precisely in those questions which should be the *basis* of our being together. What is this Christianity which we always hear mentioned? Is it essentially the content of the Sermon on the Mount, or is it the message of the reconciliation in the cross and the resurrection of our Lord? What significance does the Sermon on the Mount have for our actions? And what is the significance of the message of the cross? What is the relationship between the forms of our modern life and the Christian proclamation? What has the state, business, our social life to do with Christianity? It is undeniable that here we must all still confess our ignorance; and it is equally undeniable that we should recognize this our ignorance as our fault. We really *should* know more here. We have neglected to think clearly and decisively and to take up a firm attitude. And only now, when we are in the middle of the lake, do we notice that the ice on which we are standing is breaking up.

For us, this clearly means that the position that has been recognized here must not be concealed again. This must not be allowed to happen again. No good at all can come from acting before the world and one's self as though we knew the truth, when in reality we do not. This truth is too important for that, and it would be a betrayal of the truth if the church were to hide itself behind resolutions and pious so-called Christian principles, when it is called to look the truth in the face and once and for all confess its guilt and its ignorance. Indeed, some resolutions can have nothing complete, nothing clear about them unless the full seriousness of the whole Christian truth, as the church knows it or confesses that it does not know it, stands behind them. Qualified silence might perhaps be more appropriate for the church today than talk which is possibly very unqualified. That means protest against any form of the church which does not honour the question of truth above all things. And the next thing is the demand that this question now be put again in all seriousness. The concern of youth deeply involved in ecumenical work is this: How does our ecumenical work, or the work of the World Alliance, look in the mirror of the truth of the gospel? And we feel that we cannot approach such questions in any other way than by new, strict theological work on the biblical and Reformation basis of our ecumenical understanding of the church, in complete seriousness and without regard for its consequences or its success. We ask for a responsible theoolgy of the ecumenical movement for the sake of the truth and the certainty of our cause.

What follows is intended as an attempt to show the outlines of some of the basic theological questions which particularly concern our work in the World Alliance and to demonstrate their theological significance. We are unreservedly concerned with the questions which are put from within, not from outside, from the place of an onlooker. But to those who nevertheless consider these questions to be questions 'from outside', let it be said that it is just these questions which *today* are being put from within.

Our work in the World Alliance is based — consciously or unconsciously — on a quite definite view of the church. The church as the one community of the Lord Jesus Christ, who is Lord of the world, has the commission to say his Word to the whole world. The territory of the one church of Christ is the whole world. Each individual church has geographical limits drawn to its own preaching, but the *one* church has no limits. And the churches of the World Alliance have associated themselves together the better to be able to express this their claim to the whole world, or rather this claim of their Lord's to the whole world. They understand it as the task of the church to make the claim of Jesus Christ clear to the whole world. And this includes the repudiation of the idea that there are divinely willed, autonomous spheres of life which are removed from the Lordship of Jesus Christ, which need not hear this word. It is not a holy sacred part of the world which belongs to Christ, but the whole world.

Now the first question which must be asked is this: *With whose authority does the church speak when it declares this claim of Christ to the whole world?* With the authority in which alone the church can speak, with the authority of the Christ living and present in it. The church is the presence of Christ on earth, the church is the *Christus praesens.* For this reason alone its word has authority. The word of the church is the word of the present Christ, it is gospel and commandment. It would be the retrogression of the church to the synagogue if its proclamation were commandment alone, and it would be the lapse of the church into libertinism should it want to deny the commandment of God for the sake of the gospel.

Because of the *Christus praesens,* the word of the church here and now must be a valid, binding word. Someone can only speak to me with authority if a word from the deepest knowledge of my humanity encounters me here and now in all my reality. Any other word is impotent. The word of the church to the world must therefore encounter the world in all its present reality from the deepest knowledge of the world, if it is to be authoritative. The church must be able to say the Word of God, the word of authority, here and now, in the most concrete way possible, from knowledge of the situation. The church may not therefore preach timeless principles, however true, but only commandments which are true today. God is 'always' *God* to us '*today*'.

How can the gospel and how can the commandment of the church be preached with authority, i.e. in quite concrete form? Here lies a problem of the utmost difficulty and magnitude. Can the church preach the commandment of God with the same certainty with which it preaches the gospel? Can the church say 'We need a socialist ordering of the economic system', or 'Do not engage in war' with the same certainty as it can say 'Thy sins be forgiven thee'? Evidently both gospel and commandment will only be preached with authority where they are spoken in a quite concrete way. Otherwise things remain in the sphere of what is generally known, human, impotent, false. Where does this principle of concretion lie in the case of the gospel? Where does it lie in the case of the commandment? This is where the question must be decided. *The gospel becomes concrete in the hearers, the commandment becomes concrete through those who preach it.* The phrase 'Thy sins be forgiven thee' is, as the word spoken to the community in proclamation in the sermon, in the eucharist, framed in such a way that it encounters the hearer in concrete form. In contrast to this, the commandment needs to be given concrete content by the person who preaches it; the commandment 'Thou shalt love thy neighbour as thyself' is in itself so general that it needs to be made as concrete as possible if I am to hear what it means for me here and now. And only as a concrete saying is it the Word of God to me. The preacher must therefore be concerned so to incorporate the contemporary situation in his shaping of the commandment that the commandment is itself relevant to the real situation. In the event of taking up a stand about a war the church cannot just say, 'There should really be no war, but there are necessary wars' and leave the application of this principle to each individual; it should be able to say quite definitely: 'Engage in this war' or 'Do not engage in this war'. Or in social questions: the last word of the church should not be to say 'It is wrong for one man to have too much while another goes hungry, but personal property is God-willed and may not be appropriated', and once again leave the application to the individual. But, if the church really has a commandment of God, it must proclaim it in the most definite form possible, from the fullest knowledge of the matter, and it must utter a summons to obedience. A commandment must be definite, otherwise it is not a commandment. God's commandment now requires something quite definite from us. And the church should proclaim this to the community.

But at this point a tremendous difficulty arises. If the church must know all the details of the situation before it can command, if the validity of its commandment is dependent on its detailed knowledge of a matter, be it war, disarmamemt, minorities, social questions, the church always runs the danger of having overlooked this or that relevant point of view in its commandment or simply of having underestimated it. This again will make the church completely uncertain in its commandment. Thus the competence of the church in a matter on which it issues a command is on the one hand a prerequisite for a real command-ment, and on the other hand continually makes each of its command-ments uncertain because of this dependence on a complete knowledge of the situation. There are, in principle, two positions which may be adopted in view of this insoluble dilemma: first, there is that of evasion and keeping to general principles. That is the way the churches have almost always gone. Or alternatively, we can look at the difficulty squarely and then despite all the dangers we can venture to do some-thing *either* by keeping a qualified and intentional silence of ignorance *or* by daring to put the commandment, definitely, exclusively and radi-cally. In that case the church will dare to say, 'Do not engage in this war', 'Be Socialists today', uttering this commandment as the commandment *of God* in the clear recognition that this can be so. In so doing the church will recognize that it is blaspheming the name of God, erring and sin-ning, but it may speak thus in faith in the promise of the forgiveness of sins which applies also to the church. Thus the preaching of the commandment is grounded in the preaching of the forgiveness of sins. The church cannot command without itself standing in faith in the forgiveness of sins and without indicating this in its preaching of the forgiveness of sins to all those whom it commands. The preaching of the forgiveness of sins is the guarantee of the validity of the preaching of the commandment. Now does this preaching of the forgiveness of sins itself in its turn need a guarantee of its validity? The guarantee of the validity of the preaching of the forgiveness of sins is the sacrament. Here the general saying, 'Thy sins be forgiven thee', is bound up with water, wine and bread, here it comes to be put in all its own distinctness, which is understood as the concrete here and now of the Word of God only by those who hear it in faith. What the sacrament is for the preaching of the gospel, the knowledge of firm reality is for the preaching of the com-mandment. *Reality is the sacrament of command.* Just as the sacraments of Baptism and Communion are the sole forms of the first reality of crea-tion in this age, and just as they are sacraments because of this their rela-tion to the original creation, so the 'ethical sacrament' of reality is to be described as a sacrament only insofar as this reality is itself wholly grounded in its relationship to the reality of creation. Thus just as the fallen world and fallen reality only exist in their relationship to the created world and created reality, so the commandment rests on the for-giveness of sins.

The church preaches the gospel and the commandment with authority. Now as far as the task which the World Alliance has set itself is concerned, we are involved here in the question of giving a definite divine commandment to the world. We saw that this commandment can only be given on the basis of a belief in the forgiveness of sins. But it must be given, as long as the world is not the church.

Whence does the church know God's commandment for the moment? For it is evidently by no means obvious. 'We know not what to do' (II Chron. 20. 12), 'O hide not thy commandments from me' (Ps. 119. 19). The recognition of God's command is an act of God's revelation. Where does the church receive this revelation? The *first answer* could be '*The Biblical Law, the Sermon on the Mount* is the absolute norm for our action'. We have simply to take the Sermon on the Mount seriously, and to realize it. That is our obedience towards God's commandment. To this we must say: Even the Sermon on the Mount may not become the letter of the law to us. In its commandments it is the demonstration of what God's commandment can be, not what it is, today, for us. No one can hear that except ourselves, and God must say it to us today. The commandment is not there once and for all, but it is given afresh, again and again. Only in this way are we free from the law, which interposes itself between us and God; only in this way do we hear God.

The *second answer* would find God's commandment in the *orders of creation*. Because certain orders are evident in creation, one should not rebel against them, but simply accept them. One can then argue: Because the nations have been created different, each one is obliged to preserve and develop its characteristics. That is obedience towards the Creator. And if this obedience leads one to struggles and to war, these too must be regarded as belonging to the order of creation. Here too, the commandment of God is thought of as something which has been given once and for all, in definite ordinances which permit of discovery. Now there is a special danger in this argument; and because it is the one most used at the moment, it must be given special attention. The danger of the argument lies in the fact that just about everything can be defended by it. One need only hold out something to be God-willed and God-created for it to be vindicated for ever, the division of man into nations, national struggles, war, class struggle, the exploitation of the weak by the strong, the cut-throat competition of economics. Nothing simpler than to describe all this — because it is there — as God-willed and therefore to sanction it. But the mistake lies in the fact that in the solution of this apparently so simple equation the great unknown factor is overlooked, the factor which makes this solution impossible. It is not realized in all seriousness that the world is fallen and that now sin prevails and that creation and sin are so bound up together that no human eye can any longer separate the one from the other, that each human order is an order of the fallen world and not an order of creation. There is no longer any possibility of regarding any features *per se* as orders of creation and of perceiving the will of God *directly* in them. The so-called orders of creation are no longer *per se* revelations of the divine commandment, they are concealed and invisible. Thus the concept of orders of creation must be rejected as a basis for the knowledge of the commandment of God. Hence, neither the Biblical law as such nor the so-called orders of creation as such are for us the divine commandment which we perceive today.

The commandment cannot stem from anywhere but the origin of promise and fulfilment, from Christ. From Christ alone must we know what we should do. But not from him as the preaching prophet of the Sermon on the Mount, but from him as the one who gives us life and forgiveness, as the one who has fulfilled the commandment of God in our place, as the one who brings and promises the new world. We can only perceive the commandment where the law is fulfilled, where the new world of the new order of God is established. Thus we are completely directed towards Christ. Now with this we also understand the whole world order of fallen creation as directed solely towards Christ, towards the new creation. What has hitherto been dark and obscured from our sight comes into a new light. It is not as though we now knew all at once from Jesus Christ what features we should regard as orders of creation and what not, but that we know that *all* the orders of the world only exist in that they are directed towards Christ; they *all* stand under the preservation of God as long as they are still open for Christ, they are *orders of preservation*, not orders of creation. They obtain their value wholly from outside themselves, from Christ, from the new creation. Their value does not rest in themselves, in other words they are not to be regarded as orders of creation which *per se* are 'very good', but they are God's orders of preservation, which only exist as long as they are open for the revelation in Christ. Preservation is God's act with the fallen world, through which he guarantees the possibility of the new creation. Orders of preservation are forms of working against sin in the direction of the gospel. *Any order* — however ancient and sacred it may be — *can be dissolved*, and must be dissolved when it closes itself up in itself, grows rigid and no longer permits the proclamation of revelation. From this standpoint the church of Christ has to pass its verdict on the orders of the world. And it is from this standpoint that the commandment of God must be heard. In the historical change of the orders of the world it has to keep in mind only one thing: Which orders can best restrain this radical falling of the world into death and sin and hold the way open for the gospel? The church hears the commandment only from Christ, not from any fixed law or from any eternal order, and it hears it in the orders of preservation. The commandment of Christ is therefore quite simply the critical and radical commandment, which is limited by nothing else, by no so-called 'orders of creation'. It can demand the most radical destruction simply for the sake of the one who builds up. For the church to venture a decision for or against an order of preservation would be an impossibility if it did not happen in faith in the God who in Christ forgives even the church its sins. But in this faith the decision must be ventured.

The churches included in the World Alliance think that they recognize a quite definite order as commanded for us by God today. Today God's commandment for us is the order of *international peace*. To say this is to express a quite definite recognition of the will of God for our time. This recognition should now be analyzed and interpreted in the light of what has so far been said. What can the church say as God's commandment about international peace? So runs the question. First, like anyone who utters God's command, it exposes itself to the suspicion of being fanatical and of preaching dreams, that is, of speaking from the flesh and not from the spirit. It cannot 'qualify' its word as God's commandment through anything but continued, monotonous, sober reference to this commandment. It will attempt in vain to resist the scandal of pacifist humanitarianism where the commandment of peace is not already itself seen as the commandment of God. The church must know this and resist any attempt at a justification of God's commandment. It gives the commandment, but no more.

Under the predominant influence of Anglo-Saxon theological thought in the World Alliance, the peace envisaged here has been previously understood as the reality of the gospel, we may almost say, as part of the kingdom of God on earth. From this standpoint the ideal of peace is made absolute, i.e. it is no longer regarded as something expedient, as an order of preservation, but as a final order of perfection, valid in itself, as the penetration of another order into the fallen world. External peace is a 'very good' condition in itself. It is thus an order of creation and of the kingdom of God and as such must be preserved unconditionally. But this conception must be repudiated as unbalanced, and therefore untrue to the gospel. International peace is not a reality of the gospel, not a part of the kingdom of God, but a command of the angry God, an order for the preservation of the world in the light of Christ. International peace is therefore no ideal state, but an order which is directed towards something else and is not valid in itself. The making of such an order of preservation can of course become a matter of absolute urgency, but never for its own sake; but always for the sake of him towards whom it is directed, namely for the sake of the receiver of the revelation. The broken character of the order of peace is expressed in the fact that the peace commanded by God has two limits, first the truth and secondly justice. There can only be a community of peace when it does not rest on *lies* and on *injustice*. Where a community of peace endangers or chokes truth and justice, the community of peace must be broken and battle joined. If the battle is then on both sides really waged for truth and for justice, the community of peace, though outwardly destroyed, is made all the deeper and stronger in the battle over this same cause. But should it become clear that one of the combatants is only fighting for his own selfish ends, should even this form of the community of peace be broken, there is revealed that reality which is the ultimate and only tolerable ground of any community of peace, the forgiveness of sins. There is a community of peace for Christians only because one will forgive the other his sins. The forgiveness of sins still remains the sole ground of all peace, even where the order of external peace remains preserved in truth and justice. It is therefore also the ultimate ground on which all ecumenical work rests, precisely where the cleavage appears hopeless.

For Anglo-Saxon thought, truth and justice remain constantly subordinate to the ideal of peace. Indeed, the existence of peace is virtually itself the proof that truth and justice have been preserved; because the order of peace is a reality of the gospel, of the kingdom of God, truth and justice can never be contrary to it. But it has become clear that precisely this conception is illusory. The reality of the gospel is not the external order of peace, nor even the peace of the battle for the same cause, but only the peace of God, which brings about forgiveness of sins, the reality in which truth and justice are both preserved. Neither a static concept of peace (Anglo-Saxon thought) nor even a static concept of truth (the interpretation put forward by Hirsch and Althaus) comprehends the gospel concept of peace in its troubled relationship to the concepts of truth and righteousness.

If the ordering of eternal peace is not timelessly valid, but penetrable at any time, simply because the complete oppression of truth and justice would threaten to make the hearing of the revelation in Christ impossible, then *struggle* is made comprehensible in principle as a possibility of action in the light of Christ. Struggle is not an order of creation, but it can be an order of preservation for Christ's new creation. Struggle can in some cases guarantee openness for the revelation in Christ better than external peace, in that it breaks apart the hardened, self-enclosed order.

There is, however, a very widespread, extremely dangerous error about today that the *justification of struggle* already contains the justification of war, affirms war in principle. The right of war can be derived from the right of struggle as little as the use of torture may be derived from the necessity of legal procedures in human society. Anyone who has seriously studied the history of the concept of war from Luther to Fichte and Bismarck and then on to the present, knows that while the word has remained the same, its content has become something absolutely incomparable. War in our day no longer falls under the concept of struggle because it is the certain self-annihilation of both combatants. It is in no way to be regarded as an order of preservation in the light of revelation, simply because it is so destructive. The power of annihilation extends both to the inner and the outer man. War today destroys both soul and body. Now because we can in no way understand war as one of God's orders of preservation and thus as the commandment of God, and because on the other hand war needs idealizing and idolizing to be able to live, war today, and therefore the next war, must be utterly *rejected* by the church. No word of condemnation of past deeds even in the last war — that is not permitted to us, 'thou shalt not judge' — but all the power of resistance, of refusal, of rejection of the next war. Not from the fanatical erection of one commandment — perhaps the sixth — over the others, but from obedience towards the commandment of God which is directed towards us today, that war shall be no more, because it takes away the possibility of seeing revelation. Nor should we be afraid of the word pacifism today. As certainly as we leave the making of the last peace to God, so certainly should we also make peace to overcome war. It is obvious that struggle as such will not be driven out of the world in this way. But here we are concerned with a quite definite means of struggle which today stands under God's prohibition. And understood in this way, the protest of the World Alliance could be a real hearing of God's present commandment.

The will of God is directed not only to the new creating of men but also to the new creating of conditions. It is wrong to say that only the will can be good. Conditions too can be good; God's creation was *per se* 'very good'. Conditions can be good even in the fallen world, but never in themselves, and always only in the light of the action of God for his new creation. We cannot restore the creation, but under God's commandment we should create such conditions — and here we have all the hardness of the divine commandment — as are good in respect of what the God who commands today will himself do, in respect of the new creation by Christ. Conditions are good only 'in respect of' something else. But in this they are good. And as such, the peace which overcomes war is 'good'.

Now the World Alliance thinks that it can guarantee this peace by working for 'understanding'. We would ask: How is such *understanding* conceivable and obtainable *in a Christian way*? The original Anglo-Saxon view of the World Alliance, without doubt still prevailing today, is 'Understanding by personal acquaintance'. Indispensable as this first step is, it is by no means the only one or the most important one. Socialism has succeeded in setting itself up on an international basis not because the German worker knows the French and the English worker, but because they have a common ideal. Similarly, Christians too will only learn to think internationally when they have a great, common message. We need today more than anything else in the ecumenical movement the one great reconciling message. Let us not deceive ourselves, we do not have this message yet. The language of the ecumenical movement is — in spite of everything — weak. But this message will only come together with a theology. Thus here, at the end, we are led back to our first concern. Understanding in the best and truest sense comes only through present preaching and theology. There is such a tremendous danger that at international conferences we shall find friendship, 'good fellowship' with one another, and nothing else. But 'even the heathen and the tax-gatherers do that'. We are concerned with something else, with a new knowledge and a new will. And where each conference does not move towards this goal with the utmost seriousness, time is lost and gossiped away. And anyone who has been to international conferences with this aim will know that it demands hard work and a hard struggle. But that is what such conferences are for.

Now, in conclusion, two short questions: To whom does the church speak? And what is this church, to speak in this way?

The church which comes together in the World Alliance speaks to Christendom, telling it to hear its word as the commandment of God, as it stems from the forgiveness of sins. But it speaks also to the world, telling it to alter its conditions. The world cannot hear the true voice of the church, nor can the state. The voice of the church cannot be authoritative towards it, but the state finds in the church a critical limit to its possibilities and thus will have to take notice of it as a critic of its action.

What is this church? The church of the gospel, the church which proclaims the gospel in accordance with the truth. And here now at last a fearful need arises. It is the question of truth, which threatens to annul everything which has been said so far. The churches included in the World Alliance have no common recognition of the truth. It is precisely here that they are most deeply divided. When they say 'Christ' or 'Gospel', they mean something different. That is at present our most pressing problem in ecumenical work. We can only speak as the church, which proclaims the truth of the gospel. But the truth is divided. And that must make our word powerless, indeed false. But almost more fearful than this fact is the way in which we gladly set ourselves above it. We may not play with the truth, or else it will destroy us. Here we are on the edge of the abyss. If only we would open our eyes! But of course that will not do away with the fact of the division of the one true church, which alone would be in a position to speak. And now I will not end with an emphatic assertion which would remove this difficulty. I know of no solution here. I can only point to one thing, namely that where the church recognizes the guilt of its division and where it feels it must still speak under the commandment of God, the forgiveness of sins is held out and promised to the humble. Of course this cannot be a *solution* of our need, but only the expression of the waiting of the whole church for *redemption*. The last message that can be given here is that the church should remain humble in its need and live from forgiveness alone.

*

THE IMAGE OF GOD ON EARTH

Bonhoeffer presented his lectures on 'Creation and Sin' at the University of Berlin in 1931. They were subsequently published as Schopfung und Fall *in 1937 by Chr. Kaiser Verlag. Our selection is from the English translation,* Creation and Fall *(translated by John C. Fletcher and revised by SCM, London, 1959), pp. 33-38.*

Then God said, 'Let us make man in our image, after our likeness; and let them have dominion over the fish of the sea, and over the birds of the air, and over the cattle, and over all the earth, and over every creeping thing that creeps upon the earth.' So God created man in his own image, in the image of God he created him; male and female he created them.

(Genesis: 1.26 f)

God loves his work, he loves it in its own being, for the creature honours the Creator. But still God does not recognize himself in his work; he sees his work but he does not see himself. 'To see oneself' means as it were 'to behold one's face in a mirror', 'to see oneself in a likeness'. How shall this come to pass? God remains totally the Creator. His work lies at his feet. How shall he find himself in his work? The work does not resemble the Creator, it is not his image. It is the form of his command. The decisive point is that the work, at the moment when the Creator has brought it forth, is already torn away from the Creator and strange to him; it is no longer the Creator himself. Even in its aliveness the work is dead, because it is an event that has happened, because, while it comes out of freedom, it is itself not free but determined. Only that which is itself free is not dead, is not strange, is not torn away as an event that has happened. Only in something that is itself free can the One who is free, the Creator, see himself. But how can the creation be free? The creation is fixed, bound in law, determined and not free. If the Creator wills to create his own image, he must create it in freedom; and only this image in freedom would fully praise him and fully proclaim the honour of its Creator.

And now the narrative is about us; it is about the creation of man. The Bible expresses the difference of this act from all God's previous creating by the way in which it introduces it. The Hebrew plural is the way in which it shows the significance and sublimity of the Creator's action. We must observe, too, that God does not simply call man forth out of non-being as he has called forth everything else. We become drawn into God's plan, as it were, and by this we become attentive to the fact that something new, something that has never yet been, something quite extraordinary is about to happen.

Then God said, '*Let us make man in our image, after our likeness*'.

Man shall proceed from God as his ultimate, his new work, and as the image of God in his creation. There is no transition here from somewhere or other, there is new creation. This has nothing to do with Darwinism: quite independently of this man remains the new, free undetermined work of God. We have no wish at all to deny man's connection with the animal world: on the contrary. But we are very anxious not to lose the peculiar relationship of man and God in the process. In our concern with the origin and nature of man, it is hopeless to attempt to make a gigantic leap back into the world of the lost beginning. It is hopeless to want to know for ourselves what man was originally, to identify here man's ideal with the creational reality of God, not to understand that we can know about the man of the beginning only if we start from Christ. This attempt, as hopeless as it is understandable, has again and again delivered the church up to free speculation at this dangerous point. Only in the middle, as those who live from Christ, do we know of the beginning.

In man God creates his image on earth. This means that man is like the Creator in that he is free. Actually he is free only by God's creation, by means of the Word of God; he is free for the worship of the Creator. In the language of the Bible, freedom is not something man has for himself but something he has for others. No man is free 'as such', that is, in a vacuum, in the way that he may be musical, intelligent or blind as such. Freedom is not a quality of man, nor is it an ability, a capacity, a kind of being that somehow flares up in him. Anyone investigating man to discover freedom finds nothing of it. Why? because freedom is not a quality which can be revealed — it is not a possession, a presence, an object, nor is it a form for existence — but a relationship and nothing else. In truth, freedom is a relationship between two persons. Being free means 'being free for the other', because the other has bound me to him. Only in relationship with the other am I free.

No substantial or individualistic concept of freedom can conceive of freedom. I have no control over freedom as over a property. It is simply the event that happens to me through the other. We can ask how we know this, or whether this is not just again speculation about the beginning resulting from being in the middle. The answer is that it is the message of the gospel that God's freedom has bound us to itself, that his free grace only becomes real in this relation to us, and that God does not will to be free for himself but for man. God in Christ is free for man. Because he does not retain his freedom for himself the concept of freedom only exists for us as 'being free for'. For us who live in the middle through Christ and know our humanity in his resurrection, that God is free has no meaning except that we are free for God. The freedom of the Creator is proved by the fact that he allows us to be free for him, and that means nothing except that he creates his image on earth. The paradox of created freedom cannot be eliminated. Indeed it must be made as obvious as possible. Here created *freedom* means — and it is this that goes beyond all previous deeds of God, the unique *par excellence* — that God himself enters into his creation.

Now God does not only command and his Word comes to pass, he himself enters into creation and thus creates freedom. Man differs from the other creatures in that God himself is in him, in that he is God's image in which the free Creator views himself. The old dogmatists meant this when they spoke of the inherence of the Trinity in Adam. In the free creature the Holy Spirit worships the Creator, uncreated freedom praises itself in created freedom. The creature loves the Creator, because the Creator loves the creature. Created *freedom* is freedom in the Holy Spirit, but as *created* freedom it is the freedom of *man* himself. How does this created being of free man express itself? In what way does the freedom of the Creator differ from the freedom of the created? How is the created free?

Man is free by the fact that creature is related to creature. Man is free for man, *Male and female he created them.* Man is not alone, he is in duality and it is in this dependence on the other that his creatureliness consists. Man's creatureliness is not a quality, something that exists, something that is, any more than his freedom. It can only be defined in man's being over against the other, with the other and dependent upon the other. The 'image . . . after our likeness' is consequently not an *analogia entis* in which man, in his being *per se* and *a se*,* in the likeness of the being of God. There is no such analogy between God and man, if only because God — the only One existing in and for himself in his underived being, yet at the same time existing for his creatures, binding and giving his freedom to man — must not be thought of as being alone, inasmuch as he is the God who in Christ bears witness to his 'being for man'. The likeness, the analogy of man to God, is not *analogia entis* but *analogia relationis*. This means that even the relation between man and God is not a part of man; it is not a capacity, a possibility, or a structure of his being but a given, set relationship: *justitia passiva.* And in this given relation freedom is given. From this it follows secondly, that this analogy must not be understood as though man in some way had this likeness in his possession, at his disposal. The analogy, the likeness must be understood strictly as follows: the likeness has its likeness *only* from the original. It always refers us only to the original, and is 'like' *only* in this way. *Analogia relationis* is therefore the relation given by God himself and is analogy only in this relation given by God. The relation of creature with creature is a God-given relation because it exists in freedom and freedom originates from God.

* The German reads 'an und für sich'.

Man in duality — man and woman — is brought into the world of the fixed and the living in his likeness to God. And just as his freedom over against man consisted in the fact that he was to be free *for* him, his freedom over against the rest of the created world is to be free *from* it. That means that he is its master, he has command over it, he rules it. And here is the other side of man's created likeness to god. Man is to rule — of course as over God's creation, as one who receives the commission and power of his dominion from God. Being free from created things is not the ideal freedom of the spirit from nature. This freedom of dominion directly includes our tie to the creatures who are ruled. The soil and the animals whose Lord I am are the world in which I live, without which I am not. It is my world, my earth, over which I rule. I am not free from it in the sense that my real being, my spirit requires nothing of nature, foreign to the spirit though it may be. On the contrary, in my total being, in my creatureliness, I belong to this world completely. It bears me, nourishes me, and holds me. But my freedom from it consists in the fact that this world, to which I am bound as a lord to his servant, as the peasant to his soil, is subjected to me, that I am to *rule* over the earth which is and remains my earth, and the more strongly I rule it the more it is *my* earth. It is by no other commissioned authority except that given by the Word of God to man — which thus uniquely binds and sets him over against the other creatures.

This we are told, we who in the middle know nothing of all this any more, to whom all this is pious myth or a lost world. We also try to rule, but it is the same here as on Walpurgis Night: we think we are pushing and we are being pushed. We do not rule, we are ruled. The thing, the world, rules man. Man is a prisoner, a slave of the world, and his rule is illusion. Technology is the power with which the earth grips man and subdues him. And because we rule no more, we lose the ground, and then the earth is no longer *our* earth, and then we become strangers on earth. We do not rule because we do not know the world as God's creation, and because we do not receive our dominion as God-given but grasp it for ourselves. There is no 'being-free-from' without 'being-free-for'. There is no dominion without serving God. With the one, man necessarily loses the other. Without God, without his brother, man loses the earth. In his sentimental backing away from dominion over the earth man has always lost God and his brother. God, our brother, and the earth belong together. But for those who have lost the earth for us men in the middle there is no way back to the earth except the way to God and to our brother. From the beginning the way of man to the earth has only been possible as God's way to man. Only where God and man's brother come to man can man find the way back to the earth. Man's being-free-for God and the other person and his being-free-from the creature in his dominion over it is the image of God in the first man.

*

CHRISTOLOGY

With the exception of Creation and Fall, *none of the manuscripts of Bonhoeffer's lectures at Berlin University (1931-33) remain. However, some, like those on the church (*Das Wesen der Kirche*) and the series on* Christologie, *have been reconstructed from the notes of his students. The lectures on Christology were first compiled and edited by Eberhard Bethge and published in* Gesammelte Schriften *III, in 1960. The lectures were divided into three parts:*

Part One: The Present Christ — Pro Me
Part Two: The Historical Christ
Part Three: The Eternal Christ

No manuscript of Part Three has been preserved. Our extracts, from Part Two, are from the new English translation by Edwin Robertson, published as Christology *by Collins, London, in 1978. The 1966 English translation has some serious errors.*

POSITIVE CHRISTOLOGY

1. *The Incarnate One*

The question may not run, 'How is the incarnate one thinkable?', but, 'Who is he?' He is not the one adopted by God, he is not the one clothed in human characteristics. He is God who became man, as we became man. He lacks nothing belonging to man. There is no gift of this world or of man that he has not received. This protest against *enhypostasis* must remain. Jesus Christ had his own human, individual *hypostasis* and his own human mode of existence. The man whom I am, Jesus has also been. Of him only is it valid to say that nothing human was alien to him. Of this man, we say: 'This is God for us'.

Two points of denial must be carefully made:
a) We do not mean that we knew something before about what and who God was, apart from Jesus Christ, and then applied it to Christ. No, this is a direct statement of identity; all that we are here able to say about God, we have gained by a glance at him, or better, this man compels us.

b) We do not mean that the statement, 'This man is God', adds anything to his humanity. That is the essential point. Against that it could be argued that something was added to this man Jesus, which we do not have, namely his deity. That is true, but we must be careful here. We are not to think of God and man in Christ being joined together by a concept of nature (being, *ousia*). Being God is not for Jesus an extension of his being man. It is also not a continuity of his being as man, which he goes on to achieve. Rather, it is a statement which comes upon this man from above. It takes nothing from him and it adds nothing to him, but it qualifies this whole man Jesus as God. It is the judgment and Word of God on this man. This qualification, this judgment and Word of God, which 'comes from above', must not however be thought of as something added. Rather than something added, this Word coming down from God is that man Jesus Christ himself. And therefore, because Jesus Christ *is* also God's judgment on himself, he points, at one and the same time, to both God and to himself.

Thereby what is avoided is the idea of two isolated given entities being united with each other. Jesus the man is believed in as God. And that, as man, not despite his humanity, nor over the top of it. In the man Jesus, faith is kindled in the Word. Jesus Christ is not God in a divine nature, *ousia*, substance, being, nor is he God in a way that can be demonstrated or described, he is God in faith. There is no such thing as this divine being. If Jesus Christ is to be described as God, we may not speak of this divine being, nor of his omnipotence, nor his omniscience; but we must speak of this weak man among sinners, of his manger and his cross. If we are to deal with the deity of Jesus, we must speak of his weakness. In christology, one looks at the whole historical man Jesus and says of him, that he is God. One does not first look at a human nature and then beyond it to a divine nature, but one has to do with the one man Jesus Christ, who is wholly God.

The accounts of the birth and of the baptism of Jesus stand side by side. In the birth story, we are directed totally towards Jesus himself. In the story of the baptism, we are directed towards the Holy Spirit who comes from above. The reason why we find it difficult to take the two stories together is because of the doctrine of the two natures. The two stories are not teaching two natures. If we put this doctrine aside, we see that the one story concerns the being of the Word of God in Jesus, while the other concerns the coming of the Word of God upon Jesus. The child in the manger is wholly God: note Luther's christology in the Christmas hymns. The call at the baptism is confirmation of the first happening, there is no adoptionism in it. The manger directs our attention to the man, who is God; the baptism directs our attention, as we look at Jesus, to the God who calls.

If we speak of Jesus Christ as God, we may not say of him that he is the representative of an idea of God, which possesses the characteristics of omniscience and omnipotence (there is no such thing as this abstract divine nature!); rather, we must speak of his weakness, his manger, his cross. This man is no abstract God.

Strictly speaking we should not talk of the incarnation, but of the incarnate one. The former interest arises out of the question, 'How?' The question, 'How?', for example, underlies the hypothesis of the virgin birth. Both historically and dogmatically it can be questioned. The biblical witness is ambiguous. If the biblical witness gave clear evidence of the fact, then the dogmatic obscurity might not have been so important. The doctrine of the virgin birth is meant to express the incarnation of God, not only the fact of the incarnate one. But does it not fail at the decisive point of the incarnation, namely that in it Jesus has not become man just like us? The question remains open, as and because it is already open in the Bible.

The incarnate one is the glorified God: 'The Word was made flesh and we beheld his glory'. God glorifies himself in man. That is the ultimate secret of the Trinity. The humanity is taken up into the Trinity. Not from all eternity, but 'from now on even unto eternity'; the trinitarian God is seen as the incarnate one. The glorification of god in the flesh is now at the same time, the glorification of man, who shall have life through eternity with the trinitarian God. This does not mean that we should see the incarnation of God as God's judgment on man. God remains the incarnate one even in the Last Judgment. The incarnation is the message of the glorification of God, who sees his honour in becoming man. It must be noted that the incarnation is first and foremost true revelation, of the Creator in the creature, and not veiled revelation. Jesus Christ is the unveiled image of god.

The incarnation of God may not be thought of as derived from an idea of God, in which something of humanity already belongs to the idea of God — as in Hegel. Here we speak of the biblical witness, 'We saw his glory'. If the incarnation is thus spoken of as the glorification of God, it is not permissible to slip in once again a speculative idea of God, which derives the incarnation from the necessity of an idea of God. A speculative basis for the doctrine of the incarnation in an idea of God would change the free relationship between Creator and creature into a logical necessity. The incarnation is contingent. God binds himself freely to the creature and freely glorifies himself in the incarnate one.

Why does that sound strange and improbable? Because the revelation of the incarnation in Jesus Christ is not visibly a glorification of God. Because this incarnate one is also the crucified.

The Humiliated One and the Exalted One

When we look at the humiliation and the exaltation, we do not ask about the divine and human natures, but about the modes of existence as man. We do not know a deity or a humanity in its own nature. We are concerned about the modes of existence of the one who has become man. Humiliation does not signify that the incarnate one is more man and less God, that there is thus a shrinking of the state of God — and exaltation does not signify that in it he is more God and less man. In humiliation and in exaltation, Jesus remains wholly man and wholly God. The statement, 'This is God', must be made in exactly the same way about the humiliated one as about the exalted one.

Of the humiliated one we say, 'This is God'. He makes none of the divine properties evident in his death. On the contrary, we see a man doubting God as he dies. But of this man we say, 'This is God'. He who cannot do that does not know what it means for God to become man. In the incarnation God reveals himself without concealment. In the way he exists as the humiliated one he is not the Logos, the deity, nor the humanity of Christ, but the whole person of the God-Man. He is veiled in the hiddenness of this stumbling block. The principle of the humiliation is not the humanity of Christ, but the *homoioma sarkos* (Romans 8:3, 'the likeness of sinful flesh'). With the exaltation this is done away, but the humanity of Christ remains eternally.

The question is no longer, '*How* can God be the humiliated man?', but rather, '*Who* is the humiliated God-Man?' The doctrine of the incarnation and the doctrine of the humiliation must be strictly distinguished from each other. The mode of existence of the humiliation is an act of the incarnate one. Of course, that does not mean that one can separate him temporally from the act of incarnation. Rather, the God-Man in history is always and already the humiliated God-Man from the manger to the cross.

In what way does this special mode of existence of the humiliation express itself? In this way, that Christ takes sinful flesh. The humiliation is necessitated by the world under the curse. The incarnation is related to the first creation; the humiliation is related to the fallen creation. In the humiliation, Christ, of his own free will, enters the world of sin and death. He enters it in such a way as to hide himself in it in weakness and not to be recognized as God-Man. He does not enter in kingly robes of a *morphe theou* (Greek, 'form of God'). His claim, which he as God-Man raises in this form, must provoke contradiction and hostility. He goes incognito, as a beggar among beggars, as an outcast among outcasts, as despairing among the despairing, as dying among the dying. He also goes as sinner among sinners, yet how truly as the *peccator pessimus* (Luther, Latin, 'the worst sinner'), as sinless among sinners. And here lies the central problem of christology.

The doctrine of the sinlessness of Jesus is not one *locus* (Latin, 'position') among others. It is a central point at which all that is said is decided. The question is: Has Jesus as the humiliated God-Man entered fully into human sin? Was he man with sin as we are? If not, has he then really become man? If not, can he then really help? And if he has, how can he help us out of our trouble, while he is set in the same trouble?

Here it is necessary to understand what the *homoioma sarkos* can mean. What is meant is the real image of human flesh. His *sarx* is our *sarx*. It is of the very nature of our *sarx* that we are tempted to sin and self-will. Christ has taken upon him all that flesh is heir to. But to what extent does he differ from us? First, not at all. He is man as we are, he is tempted in all points like as we are, yet much more dangerously than we are. Also in his flesh was the law which is contrary to God's will. He was not the perfect good. At all times he stood in conflict. He did things which, at least from outside, looked like sin. He became angry, he was harsh to his mother, he escaped from his enemies, he broke the Law of his people, he stirred up revolt against the rulers and religious men of his country. He must have appeared a sinner in the eyes of men. Beyond recognition, he stepped into man's sinful way of existence.

But all depends upon the fact that it was *he* who assumed the flesh with its tendency to sin and self-will. It was *he* who did the things that seemed to the onlooker to be sin and failure and must be evaluated as such. But because it is *he* who does this, these statements appear in a different light. It is really human flesh that he carries — but because *he* carries it, this flesh is robbed of its rights. He pronounces the judgment on his doings. He has anguish as we do, but it is *his* anguish; he is tempted as we are, but it is *his* temptation; he is condemned as we are, but because it is *he* who is condemned, we are saved through him. Because of this '*he*', the hardest and most scandalous statements must be risked against this humiliated God-Man and be borne. He is really made sin for us and as the *peccator pessimus* he is crucified. Luther says, 'He is himself thief, murderer, adulterer, as we are, because he bears our sins'. With that, Luther describes the basic foundation of all christological statements. And as such, the one who bears our sins, and none other, he is the sinless one, the holy, the eternal, the Lord, the Son of the Father.

Here we can have no balancing of the two statements of sinner and sinless, as though by this means we may keep away the humiliated one from the *homoioma sarkos*. He is wholly man and gives the law its due and is judged, and he robs sin of its power. He is wholly in the *homoioma sarkos* and condemned as we are, and he yet is without sin. The *homoioma sarkos* is also fastened upon him with its realm of sin, but it is fastened upon *him*, who yet is without sin. Without trying to balance, we have to say, it is *he*, not the *homoioma sarkos*, who is without sin — but he will not be separated from this *homoioma sarkos*. Christology cannot by-pass this paradox.

Simply stating the sinlessness of Jesus fails if it is based upon the observable acts of Jesus. His acts take place in the *homoioma sarkos*. They are not sinless, but ambiguous. One can and should see both good and failure in them. When a person wishes to be incognito, one wrongs him by saying, 'I have both seen you and seen through you' (Kierkegaard). We should not therefore deduce the sinlessness of Jesus out of his deeds. The assertion of the sinlessness of Jesus in his deeds is not an evident moral judgment, but an assertion of faith, that it is *he*, who performs these ambiguous actions, *he* it is who is in eternity without sin. Faith confesses that the one who is tempted is the victor, the one who struggles is perfected, the unrighteous one is righteous, the one who is rejected is the holy one. Even the sinlessness of Jesus is incognito: 'Blessed is he who is not offended in me' (Matthew 11.6).

The humiliated God-Man is the stumbling block for the Jews, i.e. for religious, upright men. The historical ambiguity is offensive to them. The way *he* acts is a way that is not the way of the upright and the righteous. The claim which this man makes that he is not only upright, but that he is the Son of God, is incomprehensible to the upright, because it breaks through every law. 'You have heard it said of old, but — .' The authority he assumes is incomprehensible, 'but I say unto you' (Matthew 5.21), and, 'Your sins are forgiven you' (Matthew 9.2). That is the core of the stumbling block. If Jesus had not been wholly man, but had taken a divine nature, one might well have accepted his claim. If he had done the signs which were asked of him for proof, they might well have believed in him. But when it came to signs and wonders, he went back into his incognito and refused to give any visible evidence for faith. Thus he created the stumbling block. But now everything depended upon this. If he had answered the question put to him about his authority with an evident miracle, then it would not be true to say that he has become wholly man like us. Then at the decisive moment, for the question about Christ, an exception would be made. For this reason, the nearer the revelation, the thicker must be the disguise; the more penetrating the question of Christ becomes, the more impenetrable must be the incognito.

When that is said, the form of the stumbling block must be such that it makes possible faith in Christ. Expressed in another way, this means that the form of the humiliated one is the form of Christ *pro nobis* ('for us'). In this form he purposes and wills us to be in freedom. If Christ had proved himself by miracles, we would have believed in the visible *theophany* of deity, but that would not have been faith in Christ *pro me*. It would not have been inner conversion, but simply acknowledgement. Belief in miracles is no more than believing the evidence of one's eyes in visible Epiphany. When I acknowledge a miracle nothing happens to me. But faith is there when a man so surrenders himself to the humiliated God-Man that he bets his life on him, even when this seems against all sense. Faith is when the search for certainty out of visible evidence is given up. Then it is faith in God and not in the world. The only assurance which faith accepts is the Word itself, which comes to me through Christ.

Whoever seeks signs to establish his faith remains with himself. Nothing is changed. Whoever recognizes the Son through the stumbling block is a believer in the sense of the New Testament. He sees the Christ *pro nobis*, he is reconciled and become new. The stumbling block which the incognito presents and the ambiguous form of the Christ *pro nobis* pose at the same time the continuing challenge to faith. Yet, this challenge teaches us to pay attention to the Word (Isaiah 28.19). And from the Word comes faith.

How then are we to understand the fact that Jesus does in fact do miracles? Are they not a breaking of the incognito? If the incognito falls but once, is the game not up? Should we go along with liberal theology and see the miracles as superstitions of the time? Or must we not at last go back to the doctrine of the two natures, recognize a *genus majestaticum*? The miracles do not break the incognito. The world of the ancient religions was full of miracle workers and saviours. In that, Jesus does not stand alone. The realm of miracle is not identical with the realm of God.

121

The miracles may well rise above the everyday happenings, but they are only one step up within the created world. The concept associated with miracle is not that of God, but of magic. Magic remains within this world. When Jesus does miracles, he thus preserves his incognito within the magical picture of the world. It is not because of miracles that he is accepted as the Son of God in the New Testament. On the contrary, his power is declared to be demonic.

Only the believing community recognizes in the miracles of Jesus, the approach of the kingdom. It does not see in them only magic and false claims. But the incognito is not lifted for the unbeliever by these miracles. The unbeliever sees magic and an ambiguous world. The believer calls it, 'kingdom of God'. Our age no longer sees the world as a magical world, but it still tends to regard the miraculous as an unequivocal manifestation of the divine. When it happens, the miracle remains ambiguous, and it requires an explanation. It has its explanation both from the believer and from the unbeliever. The believer sees in it signs of what is to be done by God at the end of the world. He sees, bound to the incognito, something of the glory of God: 'We saw his glory' (John 1.14). But the unbeliever sees nothing.

The humiliated one is present for us as the risen and exalted one. That in the incognito we have to deal with the God-Man is known to us only through the resurrection and the exaltation. The incognito has already been lifted for those of us who are believers. We have the child in the manger, as the eternally present; the guilt-laden, as the sinless. But the contrary must also be said. We have not avoided the stumbling block by the resurrection. We have seen the exalted one, only as the crucified; the sinless one, only as the guilt-laden; the risen one, only as the humiliated. If it were not so, the *pro nobis* would be destroyed and there would be no faith. Even the resurrection does not break through the incognito. Even the resurrection is ambiguous. It is only believed in where the stumbling block of Jesus has not been discarded. Only the disciples see the risen one. Only blind faith has sight here. As those who do not see, they believe and in such faith, they see: 'Blessed are those who have not seen and yet believe' (John 20.29).

Between humiliation and exaltation lies oppressively the stark historical fact of the empty tomb. What is the meaning of the news of the empty tomb, before the news of the resurrection? Is it the deciding fact of christology? Was it really empty? Is it the visible evidence, penetrating the incognito, of the Sonship of Jesus, open to everyone and therefore making faith superfluous? If it was not empty, is then Christ not risen and our faith futile? It looks as though our faith in the resurrection were bound up with the news of the empty tomb. Is our faith then ultimately only faith in the empty tomb?

This is and remains, a final stumbling block, which the believer in Christ must learn to live with in one way or another. Empty or not empty, it remains a stumbling block. We cannot be sure of its historicity. The Bible itself shows this stumbling block, when it makes clear how hard it was to prove that the disciples had not stolen the body. Even here we cannot escape the realm of ambiguity. We cannot find a way round it. Even in the testimony of Scripture, Jesus enters in a form which is a stumbling block. Even as the risen one he does not lift his incognito. He will lift it only when he returns in glory. Then the incarnate one will no longer be the humiliated one. Then the decision over faith or unbelief is already taken. Then the humanity of God is really and now only the glorifying of God.

All that we know today only through the encounter with the humiliated one. It is with this humiliated one that the church goes its own way of humiliation. It cannot strive after visible confirmation of its way while he renounces it with every step. But neither can it, as the humble church, look upon itself with futile self-complacency, as though its very lowliness were visible proof that Christ is present in it. Humiliation is no proof, or at least one cannot call upon it as proof! There is here no law or principle which the church has to follow, but simply a fact — put bluntly, it is God's way with the church. As Paul says of himself that he can be exalted or lowly, so long as it happens for the sake of Christ, so the church also can be exalted or lowly, so long as in both cases it is the way of Christ with it. This way is the enemy of pride, whether it is wrapped in the purple robe or the crown of martyrdom is set upon it. The church gazes always only at the humiliated Christ, whether it itself is exalted or made low.

It is not good when the church is anxious to praise itself too readily for its humble state. Equally, it is not good for it to boast of its power and its influence too soon. It is only good when the church humbly confesses its sins, allows itself to be forgiven and confesses its Lord. Daily must it receive the will of God from Christ anew. It receives it because of the presence of the incarnate, the humiliated and the exalted one. Daily, this Christ becomes a stumbling block to its own hopes and wishes. Daily, it stumbles at the words afresh, 'You will all be offended because of me' (Matthew 26.31). And daily it holds anew to the promise, 'Blessed is he who is not offended in me' (Matthew 11.6). (*C: 102-113*)

123

3

CONFESSING CHRIST CONCRETELY*

THE CHURCH AND THE JEWISH QUESTION

Bonhoeffer was the first Evangelical theologian and pastor to attack Hitler's notorious anti-semitic legislation contained in the Aryan Clause promulgated on 7 April 1933. He did so in his essay entitled 'The Church and the Jewish Question'. Subsequently published in Gesammelte Schriften, *II, 45-53; ET in* No Rusty Swords, *217-225.*

Luther 1546: 'We would still show them the Christian doctrine and ask them to turn and accept the Lord whom they should by rights have honoured before we did.' . . . 'Where they repent, leave their usury, and accept Christ, we would gladly regard them as our brothers.'

Luther 1523: 'If the Apostles, who also were Jews, had dealt with us Gentiles as we Gentiles deal with the Jews, there would have been no Christians among the Gentiles. But seeing that they have acted in such a brotherly way towards us, we in turn should act in a brotherly way towards the Jews in case we might convert some. For we ourselves are still not yet fully their equals, much less their superiors. . . . But now we use force against them . . . what good will we do them with that? Similarly, how will we benefit them by forbidding them to live and work and have other human fellowship with us, thus driving them to practise usury?'

The fact, unique in history, that the Jew has been made subject to special laws by the state solely because of the race to which he belongs and quite apart from his religious beliefs, raises two new problems for the theologian, which must be examined separately. What is the church's attitude to this action by the state? And what should the church do as a result of it? That is one question. The other is, what attitude should the church take to its members who are baptized Jews? Both questions can only be answered in the light of a true concept of the church.

---

* See also above, pp. 19-30.

Without doubt, the church of the Reformation has no right to address the state directly in its specifically political actions. It has neither to praise nor to censure the laws of the state, but must rather affirm the state to be God's order of preservation in a godless world; it has to recognize the state's ordinances, good or bad as they appear from a humanitarian point of view, and to understand that they are based on the sustaining will of God amidst the chaotic godlessness of the world. This view of the state's action on the part of the church is far removed beyond any form of moralism and is distinct from humanitarianism of any shade through the radical nature of the gulf between the standpoint of the gospel and the standpoint of the Law. The action of the state remains free from the church's intervention. There are no piqued or pedantic comments from the church here. History is made not by the church, but by the state; but of course only the church, which bears witness to the coming of God in history, knows what history, and therefore what the state, is. And precisely because of this knowledge, it alone testifies to the penetration of history by God in Christ and lets the state continue to make history. Without doubt the Jewish question is one of the historical problems which our state must deal with, and without doubt the state is justified in adopting new methods here. It remains the concern of humanitarian associations and individual Christians who feel themselves called to the task, to remind the state of the moral side of any of its measures, i.e. on occasions to accuse the state of offences against morality. Any strong state needs such associations and such individuals, and will to some extent take good care of them. It is an insight into the finer arts of statesmanship which knows how to make use of these spokesmen in their relative significance. In the same way, a church which is essentially regarded as a cultural function of the state must at times contact the state with such reminders, and must do so all the more strongly as the state takes the church to itself, i.e. ascribes to it essentially moral and pedagogic tasks.

The true church of Christ, however, which lives solely from the gospel and realizes the character of the state's actions, will never intervene in the state in such a way as to criticize its history-making actions, from the standpoint of some humanitarian ideal. It recognizes the absolute necessity of the use of force in this world and also the 'moral' injustice of certain concrete acts of the state which are necessarily bound up with the use of force. The church cannot in the first place exert direct

125

political action, for the church does not pretend to have any knowledge of the necessary course of history. Thus even today, in the Jewish question, it cannot address the state directly and demand of it some definite action of a different nature. But that does not mean that it lets political action slip by disinterestedly; it can and should, precisely because it does not moralize in individual instances, continually ask the state whether its action can be justified as legitimate action of the state, i.e. as action which leads to law and order, and not to lawlessness and disorder. It is called to put this question with great emphasis where the state appears to be threatened precisely in its nature as the state, i.e. in its function of creating law and order by means of force. It will have to put this question quite clearly today in the matter of the Jewish question. In so doing it does not encroach on the state's sphere of responsibility, but on the contrary fathers upon the state itself the whole weight of the responsibility for its own particular actions. In this way it frees the state from any charge of moralizing and shows precisely thus its appointed function as the preserver of the world. As long as the state continues to create law and order by its acts, even if it be a new law and new order, the church of the Creator, the Mediator and the Redeemer cannot engage in direct political action against it. It may not of course prevent the individual Christian, who knows himself called to the task, from calling the state 'inhuman' on occasion, but *qua* church it will only ask whether the state is bringing about law and order or not.

Now here, of course, the state sees itself to be limited in two respects. Both too much law and order and too little law and order compel the church to speak. There is too little law and order where a group of men becomes lawless, though in real life it is sometimes extraordinarily difficult to distinguish real lawlessness from a formally permitted minimum of law. Even in slavery a minimum of law and order was preserved, and yet a re-introduction of slavery would mean real lawlessness. It is nevertheless worth noting that Christian churches tolerated slavery for eighteen centuries and that a new law was made only at a time when the Christian substance of the church could at least be put in question, with the help of the churches (but not essentially or even solely by them). However, for the church, a step back in this direction would be the expression of a lawless state. It follows that the concept of law is subject to historical change, and this in its turn once again confirms the state in its characteristic history-making law. It is not the church, but the state, which makes and changes the law.

Too little law and order stands in contrast to too much law and order.

That means that the state develops its power to such an extent that it deprives Christian preaching and Christian faith (not freedom of conscience — that would be the humanitarian illusion, which is illusory because any life in a state constrains the so-called 'free conscience') of their rights — a grotesque situation, as the state only receives its peculiar rights from this proclamation and from this faith, and enthrones itself by means of them. The church must reject this encroachment of the order of the state precisely because of its better knowledge of the state and of the limitations of its action. The state which endangers the Christian proclamation negates itself.

All this means that there are three possible ways in which the church can act towards the state: in the first place, as has been said, it can ask the state whether its actions are legitimate and in accordance with its character as state, i.e. it can throw the state back on its responsibilities. Secondly, it can aid the victims of state action. The church has an unconditional obligation to the victims of any ordering of society, even if they do not belong to the Christian community. 'Do good to all men.' In both these courses of action, the church serves the free state in its free way, and at times when laws are changed the church may in no way withdraw itself from these two tasks. The third possibility is not just to bandage the victims under the wheel, but to put a spoke in the wheel itself. Such action would be direct political action, and is only possible and required when the church sees the state fail in its function of creating law and order, i.e. when it sees the state unrestrainedly bring about too much or too little law and order. In both these cases it must see the existence of the state, and with it its own existence, threatened. There would be too little law if any group of subjects were deprived of their rights, too much where the state intervened in the character of the church and its proclamation, e.g. in the forced exclusion of baptized Jews from our Christian congregations or in the prohibition of our mission to the Jews. Here the Christian church would find itself *in statu confessionis* and here the state would be in the act of negating itself. A state which includes within itself a terrorized church has lost its most faithful servant. But even this third action of the church, which on occasion leads to conflict with the existing state, is only the paradoxical expression of its ultimate recognition of the state; indeed, the church itself knows itself to be called here to protect the state *qua* state from itself and to preserve it. In the Jewish problem the first two possibilities will be the compelling demands of the hour. The necessity of direct political action by the church is, on the other hand, to be decided at any time by an 'Evangelical Council' and cannot therefore ever by casuistically decided before-hand.

Now the measures of the state towards Judaism in addition stand in a quite special context for the church. The church of Christ has never lost sight of the thought that the 'chosen people', who nailed the redeemer of the world to the cross, must bear the curse for its action through a long history of suffering. 'Jews are the poorest people among all nations upon earth, they are tossed to and fro, they are scattered here and there in all lands, they have no certain place where they could remain safely and must always be afraid that they will be driven out . . .' (Luther, *Table Talk*). But the history of the suffering of this people, loved and punished by God, stands under the sign of the final homecoming of the people of Israel to its God. And this home-coming happens in the conversion of Israel to Christ. 'When the time comes that this people humbles itself and penitently departs from the sins of its fathers to which it has clung with fearful stubbornness to this day, and calls down upon itself the blood of the Crucified One for reconciliation, then the world will wonder at the miracle that God works, that he works with this people! And then the overweening Philistines will be like dung on the streets and like chaff on the rooftops. Then he will gather this people from all nations and bring it back to Canaan. O Israel, who is like thee? Happy the people whose God is the Lord!' (S. Menken, 1795). The conversion of Israel, that is to be the end of the people's period of suffering. From here the Christian church sees the history of the people of Israel with trembling as God's own, free, fearful way with his people. It knows that no nation of the world can be finished with this mysterious people, because God is not yet finished with it. Each new attempt to 'solve the Jewish problem' comes to nothing on the saving-historical significance of this people; nevertheless, such attempts must continually be made. This consciousness on the part of the church of the curse that bears down upon this people, raises it far above any cheap moralizing; instead, as it looks at the rejected people, it humbly recognizes itself as a church continually unfaithful to its Lord and looks full of hope to those of the people of Israel who have come home, to those who have come to believe in the one true God in Christ, and knows itself to be bound to them in brotherhood. Thus we have reached the second question.

II

The church cannot allow its actions towards its members to be prescribed by the state. The baptized Jew is a member of our church. Thus the Jewish problem is not the same for the church as it is for the state.

From the point of view of the church of Christ, Judaism is never a racial concept but a religious one. What is meant is not the biologically questionable entity of the Jewish race, but the 'people of Israel'. Now the 'people' of Israel is constituted by the law of God; a man can thus become a Jew by taking the Law upon himself. But no one can become a Jew by race. In the time of the great Jewish mission to the Gentile world there were different stages of membership of Judaism (Schürer, III 3.4 1909, pp. 150 ff.). In the same way, the concept of Jewish Christianity has religious, not biological content. The Jewish-Christian mission also stretched to Gentile territory (Paul's opponents in the Epistle to the Galatians). There were Gentile Jewish-Christians and Jewish Gentile-Christians.

Thus from the point of view of the church it is not baptized Christians of Jewish race who are Jewish Christians; in the church's view the Jewish Christian is the man who lets membership of the people of God, of the church of Christ, be determined by the observance of a divine law. In contrast, the Gentile Christian knows no presupposition for membership of the people of God, the church of Christ, but the call of God by his Word in Christ.

This difference in the understanding of the appearance of Christ and of the gospel alone led to the first division of the church of Christ into Jewish Christianity and Gentile Christianity (Apostolic Council!). This cleavage was regarded on both sides partly as intolerable heresy, partly as tolerable schism.

There would be an analogous situation today where a church group within the Reformation Church allowed membership of the church to be determined by the observance of a divine law, for example the racial unity of the members of the community. The Jewish-Christian type materialises where this demand is put irrespectively of whether its proponents belong to the Jewish race or not. Then there is the further possibility that the modern Jewish-Christian type withdraws from the Gentile-Christian community and founds its own church community based on the law. But it is in that case impossible for the church to exclude from the community that part of the community which belongs to the Jewish race because it destroys the legalistic, Jewish-Christian claim. For that would be to demand that the Gentile-Christian community be made Jewish-Christian, and that is a claim which it must rightly refuse.

The exclusion of Jews by race from our German church would bring this latter into the Jewish-Christian category. Such an exclusion thus remains impossible for the church.

The only permissible conclusion from the fact of the presence of foreign French, English, etc. communities in Germany is that there is nothing to hinder a voluntary association of Christians of Jewish race in one church (as happened, say, in London in the Jewish-Christian alliance of 1925). But the forced expulsion of Gentile-Christian Jews from Gentile-Christian congregations of German race is in no case permissible, quite apart from the difficulty of demonstrating that these Jews are not Germans (cf. Stöcker's thesis that the Jew becomes a German through his baptism). Such a forced ejection — even if it did not have a corporate, organized character — would still represent a real split in the church, simply because it would raise the racial unity of the church to the status of a law which would have to be fulfilled as a presupposition for church membership. In doing this the church community which did the excluding would constitute itself a Jewish-Christian community.

What is at stake is by no means the question whether our German members of congregations can still tolerate church fellowship with the Jews. It is rather the task of Christian preaching to say: here is the church, where Jew and German stand together under the Word of God; here is the proof whether a church is still the church or not. No one who feels unable to tolerate church fellowship with Christians of Jewish race can be prevented from separating himself from this church fellowship. But it must then be made clear to him with the utmost seriousness that he is thus loosing himself from the place on which the church of Christ stands and that he is thus bringing to reality the Jewish-Christian idea of a religion based on law, i.e. is falling into modern Jewish Christianity. It then still always remains an open question whether such a separation can or cannot be regarded as a tolerable schism. But one must have an extraordinarily restricted view not to see that any attitude of our church towards the baptized Jews among our church people, other than that described above would meet with widespread misunderstanding.

Luther on Psalm 110.3: There is no other rule or test for who is a member of the people of God or the church of Christ than this: where there is a little band of those who accept this word of the Lord, teach it purely and confess against those who persecute it, and for that reason suffer what is their due.

*

THE CHURCH AND THE PEOPLES OF THE WORLD

At the crucial ecumenical conference of 'Life and Work' held at Fanö in Denmark, 22-30 August 1934, Bonhoeffer delivered a paper, in English, on 'The Church and the Peoples of the World'. It focused on the 'Peace Question' and addressed the two questions posed by the organizers of the conference: '(1) From what basis and with what legitimation does the church have a particular responsibility to speak regarding international problems? What does the mutual relationship between ecumenicity and internationalism imply for the task of the church? (2) What are the particular means and limits of the church's cooperation in the international field?' (Reprinted in Gesammelte Schriften, *I, p. 446.) Bonhoeffer's address is published in English in* Gesammelte Schriften, *I, 447-449, and in* No Rusty Swords, *284-287. Bethge's German transcript is published in* Gesammelte Schriften, *I, 216-219.*

'I will hear what God the Lord will speak: for he will speak peace unto his people, and to his saints' (Psalm 85.8). Between the twin crags of nationalism and internationalism ecumenical Christendom calls upon her Lord and asks his guidance. Nationalism and internationalism have to do with political necessities and possibilities. The ecumenical church, however, does not concern itself with these things, but with the commandments of God, and regardless of consequences it transmits these commandments to the world.

Our task as theologians, accordingly, consists only in accepting this commandment as a binding one, not as a question open to discussion. Peace on earth is not a problem, but a commandment given at Christ's coming. There are two ways of reacting to this command from God: the unconditional, blind obedience of action, or the hypocritical question of the Serpent: 'Yea, hath God said . . .?' This question is the mortal enemy of obedience, and therefore the mortal enemy of all real peace. 'Has God not said? Has God not understood human nature well enough to know that wars must occur in this world, like laws of nature? Must God not have meant that we should talk about peace, to be sure, but that it is not to be literally translated into action? Must God not really have said that we should work for peace, of course, but also make ready tanks and poison gas for security?' And then perhaps the most serious question: 'Did God say you should not protect your own people? Did God say you should leave your own a prey to the enemy?'

No, God did not say all that. What he has said is that there shall be peace among men — that we shall obey him without further question, that is what he means. He who questions the commandment of God before obeying has already denied him.

There shall be peace because of the church of Christ, for the sake of which the world exists. And this church of Christ lives at one and the same time in all peoples, yet beyond all boundaries, whether national, political, social, or racial. And the brothers who make up this church are bound together, through the commandment of the one Lord Christ, whose Word they hear, more inseparably than men are bound by all the ties of common history, of blood, of class and of language. All these ties, which are part of our world, are valid ties, not indifferent; but in the presence of Christ they are not ultimate bonds. For the members of the ecumenical church, in so far as they hold to Christ, his word, his commandment of peace is more holy, more inviolable than the most revered words and works of the natural world. For they know that whoso is not able to hate father and mother for his sake is not worthy of him, and lies if he calls himself after Christ's name. These brothers in Christ obey his word; they do not doubt or question, but keep his commandment of peace. They are not ashamed, in defiance of the world, even to speak of eternal peace. They cannot take up arms against Christ himself — yet this is what they do if they take up arms against one another! Even in anguish and distress of conscience there is for them no escape from the commandment of Christ that there shall be peace.

How does peace come about? Through a system of political treaties? Through the investment of international capital in different countries? Through the big banks, through money? Or through universal peaceful rearmament in order to guarantee peace? Through none of these, for the single reason that in all of them peace is confused with safety. There is no way to peace along the way of safety. For peace must be dared. It is the great venture. It can never be safe. Peace is the opposite of security. To demand guarantees is to mistrust, and this mistrust in turn brings forth war. To look for guarantees is to want to protect oneself. Peace means to give oneself altogether to the law of God, wanting no security, but in faith and obedience laying the destiny of the nations in the hand of Almighty God, not trying to direct it for selfish purposes. Battles are won, not with weapons, but with God. They are won where the way leads to the cross. Which of us can say he knows what it might mean for the world if one nation should meet the aggressor, not with weapons in hand, but praying, defenceless, and for that very reason protected by 'a bulwark never failing'?

Once again, how will peace come? Who will call us to peace so that the world will hear, will have to hear, so that all peoples may rejoice? The individual Christian cannot do it. When all around are silent, he can indeed raise his voice and bear witness, but the powers of this world stride over him without a word. The individual church, too, can witness and suffer — oh, if it only would! — but it also is suffocated by the power of hate. Only the one great Ecumenical Council of the holy church of Christ over all the world can speak out so that the world, though it gnash its teeth, will have to hear, so that the peoples will rejoice because the church of Christ in the name of Christ has taken the weapons from the hands of their sons, forbidden war, proclaimed the peace of Christ against the raging world.

Why do we fear the fury of the world powers? Why don't we take the power from them and give it back to Christ? We can still do it today. The Ecumenical Council is in session; it can send out to all believers this radical call to peace. The nations are waiting for it in the East and in the West. Must we be put to shame by non-Christian people in the East? Shall we desert the individuals who are risking their lives for this message? The hour is late. The world is choked with weapons, and dreadful is the distrust which looks out of all men's eyes. The trumpets of war may blow tomorrow. For what are we waiting? Do we want to become involved in this guilt as never before?

> What use to me are crown, land, folk and fame?
> They cannot cheer my breast.
> War's in the land, alas, and on my name
> I pray no guilt may rest.   *M. Claudius*

We want to give the world a whole word, not a half word — a courageous word, a Christian word. We want to pray that this word may be given us today. Who knows if we shall see each other again another year?

*

THE CONFESSING CHURCH AND THE
ECUMENICAL MOVEMENT

Perhaps Bonhoeffer's most significant theological contribution to the ecumenical movement was his article 'The Confessing Church and the Ecumenical Movement' written at Finkenwalde in July 1935. It was published the following month in Evangelische Theologie *vol. 7. (Reprinted in* Gesammelte Schriften *I, 240-261; ET in* No Rusty Swords, *321-339).*

Preliminary observation: From the beginning, the struggle of the Confessing Church has been of deep concern to Christian churches outside Germany. This has often been noted with suspicion and condemned both by churchmen and by politicians. It is understandable that this should have been a surprise for the politicians, and one that could give rise to false interpretations, for the evangelical ecumenical world had never been so much in evidence on the occasion of a church dispute as in the past two years, and the position of ecumenical Christianity on a matter of faith has never been so clear and unambiguous as here. The German church struggle marks the second great stage in the history of the ecumenical movement and will in a decisive way be normative for its future. It was less understandable, on the other hand, that in our church people should on the whole have been so unprepared and so nonplussed at this turn of events that they were almost ashamed at the voices of our foreign brethren and felt them to be painful, instead of rejoicing at their fellowship and their testimony. The anxiety and confusion called forth by the outlawry of the political concept of internationalism in church circles had made them blind to something completely new which had begun to thrust itself forward, the evangelical ecumenical world. Under the onslaught of new nationalism, the fact that the church of Christ does not stop at national and racial boundaries but reaches beyond them, so powerfully attested in the New Testament and in the confessional writings, has been far too easily forgotten and denied. Even where it was found impossible to make a theoretical refutation, voices have never ceased to declare emphatically that of course a conversation with foreign Christians about so-called internal German church matters was unthinkable, and that a judgment or even an open attitude towards these things was impossible and reprehensible. Attempts have been made on a number of sides to convince the ecumenical organizations that nothing but scandal would attach itself to such goings-on. Ecumenical relationships have been largely regarded from the viewpoint of church-political tactics. In this, a sin has been committed against the seriousness of the ecumenicity of the Evangelical Church. It is just an expression of the true power of ecumenical thought that, despite all the fear, despite all the inner defences, despite all the attempts, honest and dishonest, to disinterest the ecumenical movement, the ecumenical movement has shared in the struggle and the suffering of German Protestantism, that it has raised its voice again and again: when the Bishop of Chichester, as President of the Ecumenical Council, wrote his letter to the National Bishop in which he implored him to remain mindful of his position as guardian of evangelical Christianity in Germany, when he then in his Ascension message of 1934 drew the attention of all Christian churches to the seriousness of the position of the church in Germany and invited them to a council session, and when finally in the memorable conference at Fanö in August 1934, the ecumenical movement framed its clear and brotherly resolution on the German church dispute and at the same time elected the President of the Confessing Synod, Dr Koch, to the Ecumenical Council. It was in those days that many leading churchmen for the first time came to see the reality of the ecumenical movement.

In all this, the spokesmen of the ecumenical movement have begun from two recognitions: first, that the struggle of the Confessing Church is bound up with the whole preaching of the gospel, and secondly, that the struggle has been brought to a head and undergone by the Confessing Church vicariously for all Christianity, and particularly for western Christianity. This recognition of necessity led to a twofold attitude. First, the natural inward and outward concern, which could not be prevented by any sort of objection, in this struggle regarded as a common cause. Prayers have been offered in countless foreign churches for the pastors of the Confessing Church, numerous conventions of clergy have sent messages to the Confessing Church to assure it of their inward concern, and in theological seminaries young students have thought every day in their prayers of the Confessing Church and its struggles. Secondly, such concern can only consist in the churches' firm attitude of brotherly help and common attention to the gospel and the right of its being preached throughout the world without hindrance or intimidation.

Because this support was governed by a sense of the responsibility of the church and not by any arbitrariness, on the one hand all attempts to make a church-political business here by confusing and muddling the situation had of necessity to fail from the start. On the other hand, for the same reason, the spokesmen of the ecumenical movement could preserve the moderate and pastoral bounds of their task and continue their way unerringly.

The ecumenical movement and the Confessing Church have made an encounter. The ecumenical movement has stood sponsor at the coming-to-be of the Confessing Church, in prayer for her and in commitment towards her. That is a fact, even if it is an extremely remarkable fact, which is most offensive to some people. It is extremely remarkable, because an understanding of ecumenical work might *a priori* have been least expected in the circles of the Confessing Church, and an interest in the theological questioning of the Confessing Church might *a priori* have been least expected in ecumenical circles. It is offensive, because it is vexatious to the German nationalist for once to have to see his church from the outside and to have to allow it to be seen from the outside, because no one gladly shows his wounds to a stranger. But it is not only a remarkable and an offensive fact, it is still more a tremendously promising fact, because in this encounter the ecumenical movement and the Confessing Church ask each other the reason for their existence. The ecumenical movement must vindicate itself before the Confessing Church and the Confessing Church must vindicate itself before the ecumenical movement, and just as the ecumenical movement is led to a serious inward concern and crisis by the Confessing Church, so too the Confessing Church is led to a serious inward concern and crisis by the ecumenical movement. This reciprocal questioning must now be developed.

I

The Confessing Church represents a genuine question for the ecumenical movement insofar as it confronts the latter in all its totality with the question of the confession. The Confessing Church is the church which would be exclusively governed in all its totality by the confession. It is fundamentally impossible to enter into conversation with this church at any point without immediately raising the question of the confession. Because the Confessing Church has learnt in the church struggle that from the preaching of the gospel to the taxing of the churches the church must be governed by the confession and the confession alone, because there is no neutral ground, divorced from the confession, within her, she immediately confronts any partner in conversation with the question of the confession. There is no other approach to the Confessing Church than through the question of the confession. There is no possibility of common tactical action outside of the question of the confession. Here the Confessing Church seals herself off hermetically against any political, social or humanitarian inroads. The confession occupies her whole sphere.

To this confession as it has been *authoritatively* expounded in the decisions of the Synods of Barmen and Dahlem, there is only a Yes or a No. Thus here too neutrality is impossible, here too an assent to this or that point outside the question of the confession remains excluded. No, the Confessing Church must insist that in any responsible church discussion it is taken seriously enough for this claim to be recognized and accepted. It must further insist that in any conversation with it the solidarity of the churches be shown by the partner in the conversations not entering into discussions with it and with the churches which it accuses of heresy at one and the same time, indeed that even for the ecumenical partner in the conversations the conversations be finally broken off where in its responsibility as a church it declares that they are broken off.

This is an unheard-of claim. But this is the only way in which the Confessing Church can enter ecumenical conversations. And this must be known if the Confessing Church is to be understood and its remarks rightly interpreted. If the Confessing Church departed from this claim, the church struggle in Germany (and with it the struggle for Christendom) would already have been decided against her. Seeing that the ecumenical movement has taken up conversations with the Confessing Church, it has consciously or unconsciously heard this claim, and the Confessing Church may gratefully start from this presupposition. At the same time, however, the ecumenical movement has by this allowed itself to be driven into a severe internal crisis, as the characteristic claim of the Confessing Church remains at the same time precisely within the sphere of the ecumenical movement. The questions of the Confessing Church, which the ecumenical movement declares that it has already heard, stand open there and can no longer be suppressed.

II

Is the ecumenical movement, in its visible representation, a church? Or to put it the other way round: Has the real ecumenicity of the church as witnessed in the New Testament found visible and appropriate expression in the ecumenical organization? This question is generally put today with great emphasis by the younger generations of theologians who take part in ecumenical work. And the importance of the question is immediately clear. It is the question of the authority with which the ecumenical movement speaks and acts. With what authority doest thou that? they ask. This question of authority is decisive, and it is not without the most serious internal damage to the work that it remains unanswered. If the ecumenical movement claims to be the church of Christ, it is as imperishable as the church of Christ itself; in that case its work has ultimate importance and ultimate authority; in that case there is fulfilled in it either the old hope of evangelical Christianity for the one true church of Christ among all the nations of the earth *or* the titanic and anti-Christian attempt of man to make visible what God would hide from our eyes. In that case, the unity of this ecumenical church is either obedience to the promise of Jesus Christ that there should be one flock and one shepherd or it is the kingdom of false peace and false unity built on the lies of the devil in angelic form. In that case, the ecumenical movement stands in this dilemma, in which any church stands.

It is indeed understandable, if there have been long-continued attempts to avoid answering this question; it is indeed more pious to confess ignorance where one knows nothing of these matters than to say a false word. But now this question has been raised afresh by the Confessing Church and demands clarity. Now it can no longer be left open in *docta ignorantia*. Now it threatens every word and every deed of the ecumenical movement, and in this lies the first service of the Confessing Church to the ecumenical movement.

There is evidently the possibility of not understanding the ecumenical movement in its present visible form as a church; it could indeed be an association of Christian men of whom each was rooted in his own church and who now assemble either for common tactical and practical action or for unauthoritative theological conversation with one another, leaving the question of the result and the theological possibility of such action and such conversation to their doubtful and unexplained end. A beginning might at least be said to have been made, and it would remain for God to do what he would with it. This action might have only a neutral character, not involving any confession, and this conversation might only have the informative character of a discussion, without including a judgment or even a decision on this or that doctrine, or even church.

The internal progress of ecumenical work over recent years lies in the fact that a breakthrough of the purely tactical-practical front of theological questioning has been achieved, a breakthrough for which the Research Division in Geneva and a man like Dr Oldham deserve especial thanks. Ecumenical work thus now has largely the character of theological conversation. This is a contribution by the work of recent years which is not to be underestimated. But one should not labour under the delusion that the construction of ecumenical thought which might be called 'theological conversation' is *in the first place* based upon specifically theological presuppositions which are generally accepted, and *in the second place* surmounts the present crisis of the ecumenical movement.

In the first place: theological conversations are said to be carried on between 'Christian personalities'. But where do we get the criterion for judging what a Christian personality is, or even for judging what an un-Christian personality is? Is not the judgment and the verdict which is so much avoided in decisions of church doctrine here expressed at a much more dangerous point, namely in a verdict on individual people and their Christianity? And is not a verdict at this particular point something which the Bible forbids, whereas it demands a decision on the true or false teaching of the church? Does not the unavoidable law under which ecumenical work stands rear its head here, namely that of testing and separating the spirits, and would it not be more humble to effect this separation on the level of the doctrine of the church than to descend as judge into the hidden and ambiguous depths of personality? There can be no serious conversation without mutual clarity about the character and authority of the discussion. Now if, as is happening from the most responsible ecumenical positions, the lack of authority in this conversation is stressed still more strongly, by the most important factors being regarded no longer as Christian personality but only as mutual interest and the ability to contribute something to the debate, then in principle the non-Christian is accorded the same rights in questions of the church of Christ as the Christian, and it remains doubtful how far the word 'ecumenical' is being used rightly, and how far the matter is relevant to the church.

In the second place: there is the very great danger, which has already become acute, as any expert knows, that just this theological conversation, necessary as it is in itself, will be used to obscure the real situation. Theological conversation will then become a bad joke by concealing the fact that it is properly concerned not with unauthoritative discussion, but with responsible, legitimate decisions of the church. With the question of the Confessing Church we have already gone beyond the stage, necessary in itself, of theological conversation. The Confessing Church knows of the fatal ambivalence of any theological conversation and presses for a clear church decision. That is the real situation.

The question of the authority of the ecumenical movement takes all constructions of this nature to their logical conclusion and tears them apart from within. Either the necessity of a separation of the spirits will be recognized as a presupposition of ecumenical work, in which case the character of this separation will have to be discussed and it will have to be taken with real seriousness, or such a separation will be rejected as a false and invalid presupposition, in which case the concept of ecumenicity in the New Testament sense and in that of the Reformation confessions is destroyed from the start. The group against which this part of the discussion is directed has its representatives in a large number of German, English and American ecumenical theologians and finds wide acceptance in ecumenical working groups.

The strongest argument of this group lies in the presupposition that ecumenical work would collapse the moment the question of its character in terms of the church were seriously put, i.e. where any claims had to be made in matters of judgment or in doctrinal decisions. This is to say that ecumenical work up till now has been carried on with an intentional shelving of the question of the confession and that it could only continue to be carried on in this way. During recent years, particularly since August 1931, and thanks to the Geneva Research Division, we have seen the fundamental theological questions emerge again and again at all the ecumenical conferences, and it is clear that the internal development of ecumenical work itself presses towards this clarification; the words and actions of the ecumenical movement are underlined. But this development can now no longer be held up by the entry of the Confessing Church. It is no use making other attempts at saving the situation. There is only one way of safety for ecumenical work, and that is for it to take up this question boldly, just as it is put, and to leave everything else in obedience to the Lord of the church. Who knows whether simply because of this task of breaking the peace the ecumenical movement will not come out of the struggle strengthened and more powerful? — And even if it must go through a severe collapse, are not the commandment and the promise of God strong enough to bring the church through, and is not this commandment more sure than false rest and illusory unity, which one day must come to grief? Historical speculations have an end in the commandment of God.

And the ecumenical movement has not withdrawn itself. At the conference in Fanö it spoke the true word of the church and therefore a word of judgment, albeit with hesitations and inward doubts, by condemning the doctrine and actions of the German Christian régime on quite definite points and by taking the side of the Confessing Church. This word arose simply from the needs of the situation and in responsible obedience to God's commandment. With the Fanö conference the ecumenical movement entered on a new era. It caught sight of its commission as a church at a quite definite point, and that is its permanent significance.

Thus the question is raised and waits for an answer, not today or tomorrow, but it waits: Is the ecumenical movement a church or is it not?

III

How can the ecumenical movement be a church and base its claim on this? That is the next question the Confessing Church has for the ecumenical movement. There can only be a church as a Confessing Church, i.e. as a church which confesses itself to be for its Lord and against his enemies. A church without a confession or free from one is not a church, but a sect, and makes itself master of the Bible and the Word of God. A confession is the church's formulated answer to the Word of God in Holy Scripture, expressed in its own words. Now unity of confession is a part of the true unity of the church. How then can the ecumenical movement be a church?

It seems that only a unity of confession, say of world Lutheranism, opens up this possibility. But from this point of view, what is to be our verdict, say, on relations with the Church of England or even Eastern Orthodoxy? How can churches which stand on such different confessional foundations be *one* church and say a common, authoritative Word?

Almost the only help towards this problem in ecumenical circles is as follows:

According to Scripture, there is one holy, ecumenical church; the existing churches are each in themselves a special shape and form of the same. Just as twigs sprout from the roots and trunk of a tree and it is only all these things together which make up the whole tree, as only the body with all its members is a whole body, so too only the community of all the churches of the world is the true ecumenical church. The significance of ecumenical work is, then, the representation of the riches and the harmony of Christendom. None has a claim to sole validity, each brings its own special gift and does its own special service for the whole; truth lies only in unity.

The attraction exercised throughout the whole Christian world by this idea, which is drawn from a great variety of spiritual sources, is quite astonishing. It is as it were the dogma of the ecumenical movement, and it is hard to say it nay.

Yet this is the construction which the Confessing Church must destroy, as it serves to obscure the seriousness of the ecumenical problem and that of the church as a whole.

True and biblical though this statement that there is only truth in unity may be, the statement that unity is possible only in the truth is equally true and biblical. Where one church by itself seeks unity with another church, leaving aside any claim to truth, the truth is denied and the church has surrendered itself. Truth bears within itself the power to divide or it is itself surrendered. But where truth stands against truth, there is no longer harmony and organism, men can no longer entrench themselves behind the general insufficiency of human knowledge, and they stand on the borders of anathema. The romantic, aesthetic, liberal idea of the ecumenical movement does not take the truth seriously and thus offers no possibility of making the ecumenical movement comprehensible as a church.

Now the question of the truth is none other than the question of the confession in its positive and limiting sense, the question of the *confitemur* and the *damnamus*. It would be wise for the Christian churches of the West not to want to overlook this experience of the Confessing Church, that a church without a confession is an unprotected and a lost church, and that a confessing church has the only weapon which does not shatter.

Thus the ecumenical movement is being driven to a last crisis on which it threatens to founder; for how will unity be possible where claims to final truth are uttered on every side? It is understandable that after previous, often by no means simple, conferences, people have been unwilling to take this step, to allow themselves to be driven into such a hopeless situation. The conversation, hardly begun, would, they say, be broken off all too quickly.

On this it must first of all most emphatically be said that there is in fact a situation in which a conversation between churches must be regarded as having been broken off. The Confessing Church knows about this situation at the moment perhaps better than any other church in the world. The conversation between the German Christian church and the Confessing Church has finally been broken off. That is a fact which cannot be denied. It is at the same time no reflection on Christian or un-

Christian personalities, but it is a verdict on the spirit of a church which has been recognized and condemned as being anti-Christian. It is an understandable consequence that such a conversation, once broken off, cannot be continued on any other ground, say that of an ecumenical conference. The representatives of the Confessing Church and the German Christians could not be partners in conversation at an ecumenical conference. The ecumenical movement must understand that and did understand it at Fanö. It was one of the great moments of the conference when Bishop Ammundsen raised his episcopal voice for the absent representatives of the Confessing Church immediately after the German Christians. It was not a matter of personalities here, but of churches; it was a matter of Christ and Antichrist — there was no neutral ground. The ecumenical movement would offend against its own task and against the Confessing Church were it to wish to evade so clear a decision.

Now it is pure doctrinairism to wish to conclude from this that such an attitude would make it equally impossible to sit together with say, representatives of Anglicanism or of a semi-Pelagian Free Church theology. Such talk knows nothing of the significance of the living confession, but regards the confession as a dead system which is from time to time applied schematically as a standard against other churches. The Confessing Church does not confess *in abstracto*; it does not confess against Anglicans or Free-churchmen, it does not even confess at this moment against Rome; still less does the Lutheran today confess against the member of the Reformed Church. It confesses *in concretissimo* against the German Christian church and against the neo-pagan divinization of the creature; for the Confessing Church, Antichrist sits not in Rome, or even in Geneva, but in the government of the National Church in Berlin. The church confesses against this because it is from here, and not from Rome, Geneva or London, that the Christian church in Germany is threatened with death, because it is here that the will for destruction is at work. The songs of the Psalter against the godless and the prayers that God himself will wage war against his enemies here take on new life. The living confession remains our only weapon.

Living confession does not mean the putting of one dogmatic thesis up against another, but it means a confession in which it is really a matter of life or death. A naturally formulated, clear, theologically based, true confession. But theology itself is not the fighting part here; it stands wholly at the service of the living, confessing and struggling church.

It is clear that despite all theological analogies the ecumenical situation is fundamentally different from this. The Confessing Church does not face the churches alien to a confession as though they were deadly enemies, which sought its life, but in the encounter it helps to bear the guilt for the brokenness of Christianity; it shares in this guilt and in all the false theology it may encounter recognizes first of all its own guilt, the want of power in its own preaching. It recognizes God's incomprehensible ways with his church, it shudders before the gravity of a cleavage in the church and before the burden which it is laying upon subsequent generations, and it hears at this point the call and the admonition to responsibility and to repentance. In the face of this picture it will experience afresh the whole need of its own decision and in this situation its confession will be first a *confession of sin.*

IV

With this the page turns, and the Confessing Church no longer stands, does not stand at all, as the one who enquires and demands, but stands as the party being questioned by the ecumenical movement, as the church put in question — and now the surprising thing is this, that after hearing the questions of the Confessing Church, the ecumenical movement throws back the selfsame questions at the Confessing Church itself. The weapon used against the ecumenical movement is now turned against the Confessing Church. How can the confession 'Christ alone, grace alone, Scripture alone', how can the confession of justification by faith alone be true in any other way than in that the confession of the Confessing Church is in the first place a confession of sin, a confession that this church with all its theology and cultus and order lives solely from the grace of God and Jesus Christ and is in need of justification? The confession of the Confessing Church becomes serious only *in actu,* i.e. here in the confession of sins, in repentance. Does the Confessing Church therefore know that the confession of the Fathers and the confession against the enemies of Jesus Christ is only credible and authoritative where the confession has first gone out against its own front? Is this the presupposition on which the Confessing Church will enter the ecumenical community?

These questions are put to the Confessing Church by the ecumenical movement *first of all* by its existence. The mere fact that the Christian churches of the whole world — with the exception of the Roman Church — have met to engage in conversation with one another and to make common decisions is there, whether the Confessing Church says Yes or

No to it. It is a fact that a shattered Christianity is coming together in unanimous acknowledgement of its needs and in unanimous prayer for the promised unity of the church of Jesus Christ, indeed that services are being held together, sermons being heard, even Eucharists being celebrated together and that there is still, or again, a possibility of ecumenical Christianity, and that all is being done calling upon the name of Jesus Christ and asking for the support of the Holy Spirit. In view of this fact, can we simply set up against it a pathetic 'Impossible', is it really right *a priori* to call down the anathema over all such actions? Is not this witness of all Christian churches at least a fact which first of all requires a moment's pause and reflection? It must indeed be openly and clearly recognized that the actual existence of the ecumenical movement constitutes no proof of its truth or of its Christian legitimacy. But if it cannot be a proof, cannot it be at least an indication of the promise which God means to lay upon this action? Is there still honest prayer for the unity of the church where anyone *a priori* excludes himself from this community? Should it not be the church, which is seriously concerned about truth, which should first of all be questioned about this truth? Should it not be a church within the confines of Germany, that finds it so difficult to cast its eyes beyond its own borders, which should take notice here? Should it not be a church that is fighting for its very existence, which is thankful and watchful for the prayers and the fellowship of all Christendom? Of course it remains the fact that all this can never be a proof, but it is an indication of the promise of God and as such it is to be taken seriously and carefully examined. It is to be examined of course in no other way than through the question of the confession, through the test of Scripture. It would not be good if the Confessing Church were to act as though it had first to call the ecumenical movement to life, but it will befit its humility to recognize that here is something, outside it, independent of its Yes or No, which it has encountered on its way and by which it knows itself to be asked and summoned; the Confessing Church must encounter the ecumenical movement in repentance. It would indeed be a bad theology which prohibited the Confessing Church from taking these things very seriously.

But with this the last word has not been said. A place must be found in the foundations of the Confessing Church *qua* church from which ecumenical work becomes an ultimate obligation. This work must be a theological necessity, as well as a practical one.

Secondly: It is understandable that the ecumenical movement should lay great stress on just this question of innermost necessity. For on this depends whether the intentions of the Confessing Church towards the ecumenical movement are chance, possibly merely utilitarian, or whether they are necessary, and therefore permanent. Thus the question which the ecumenical movement returns to the Confessing Church comes to a head: Should the Confessing Church so isolate itself in its claim of a confession that its confession leaves no more room for ecumenical thought? The question should be asked with all seriousness, whether there is still a church of Christ in the Confessing Church. Where the claim of a confession sets itself up so absolutely that it declares that conversations with any church without a confession are broken off from the start, if in its blind zeal it can look upon all the other churches only as a mission field, if the mere readiness to hear is already branded as a betrayal of the gospel, if orthodoxy in unlimited self-glorification remains wholly with itself, and if, finally, only the western belief in progress is detected in the continual protests of the ecumenical movement against unrighteousness and oppression — then the moment has come when it must seriously be asked whether the place of Jesus Christ over his church has not been taken by human dominion, that of the grace of God by human ordinances, and that of Christ by Antichrist. And if — and thus the questions come full circle — it is precisely such a church which asks the ecumenical movement whether it is itself a church, the ecumenical movement will be right in seeing only the insane claim to rule of a self-divinizing church and will have to keep itself from giving this voice a hearing.

The question of the church has been returned to the Confessing Church. The Confessing Church must say where the limits of the claims of its confession lie.

The Confessing Church gives its answer first by taking a practical part in ecumenical work, sharing in it in prayer and worship, in theological and in practical work. It does this because it is called to it and because it takes this call seriously. It leaves to God what he will make out of the encounter, and waits for him to work.

The Confessing Church takes the call of the ecumenical movement seriously because it knows itself to be bound to its members by the sacrament of holy baptism. It knows that the sum total of the baptized is still not the church. It knows that despite the one baptism the churches are divided, and it does not forget its own origin. But it recognizes in baptism the grace and the promise of the one church which is alone gathered by the Holy Spirit through his word. The Reformation churches recognized the baptism, for example, of the Roman Church, not thereby to weaken the seriousness of the division in the church — the fact that the churches must still excommunicate each other despite the one baptism makes this division still more acute — but rather to raise the claim of desiring to be nothing but the purified Catholic Church itself, the heritage of the church of Rome, and to advance their own claim to catholicity. With this at the same time the grace of God is put *above* church doctrine, once again not in such a way that the division of the church ceases to be serious and can be revoked by us, but so that it may thus be felt to be all the more fearful. In coming together on the basis of their common baptism, the Reformed churches of the ecumenical movement thereby consciously claim the heritage of the original Catholic Church, and only now does the question of the right and the legitimacy of this claim, i.e. of the scriptural purity of these churches, arise.

The Confessing Church is the church which lives not by its purity but in its impurity — the church of sinners, the church of repentance and grace, the church which can live only through Christ, through grace and through faith. As such a church, which daily stands penitent, it is a church which confesses its guilt in the division of Christendom and which knows itself to be directed at every moment to the gift of the grace of God. It therefore exists only as a listening church; it is free for listening to the other, which calls it to repentance. Thus in its recognition of the gospel as the sole grace of God through Jesus Christ, brother and Lord, lies the necessity and the possibility of listening and of ecumenical encounter. Because this church receives its life not from itself, but from without, it therefore already exists in each word that it says from the ecumenical movement. That is its innermost compulsion to ecumenical work.

The Confessing Church takes the recognition of the gospel given to it by God through holy Scripture in the confession of the Fathers and given afresh today with infinite seriousness. It has learnt that this truth alone is its weapon in the struggle for life and death. It cannot depart from this truth in the slightest degree, but with this truth it knows itself to be called not to rule, but to serve and to listen, and it will exercise this its unrestricted service in the ecumenical movement.

The Confessing Church takes part in ecumenical work as *a church*. Its word is intended to be heard as a word of the church, simply because it does not mean to attest its own word, but the authoritative word of God. It means to speak as a church to churches. Therefore it compels a decision with its word.

147

The Confessing Church will recognize the right of the ecumenical movement to brotherly help, brotherly admonition and brotherly remonstrance at any time, and will thereby testify that the unity of Christendom and love for Jesus Christ breaks through all bounds. *It will never be ashamed of the voice of its brothers*, but will give and will seek to secure for it a grateful hearing.

The question has been raised. The future of the ecumenical movement and of the Confessing Church depends on its being taken up. There can be no qualifications. No one knows the crises into which all this will lead the ecumenical movement and the Confessing Church. What remains, as a positive 'programme'? Nothing, except that this question, now raised, be not allowed to rest. Because it has within it the real power of the church, we commit ourselves to it.

Whether the hopes laid on the Ecumenical Council of Evangelical Christendom will be fulfilled, whether such a council will not only bear witness to the truth and the unity of the church of Christ with authority but also be able to bear witness against the enemies of Christianity throughout the world, whether it will speak a word of judgment about war, race hatred and social exploitation, whether through such true ecumenical unity of all evangelical Christians among all nations war itself will become impossible, whether the witness of such a council will find ears to hear — all this depends on our obedience towards the question which has been put to us and on the way in which God will use our obedience. What is set up is not an ideal, but a command and a promise — what is demanded is not our own realization of our own aims, but obedience. The question has been raised.

*

THE QUESTION OF THE BOUNDARIES OF THE CHURCH AND CHURCH UNION

Bonhoeffer's lecture to his students at Finkenwalde on 'The Question of the Boundaries of the Church and Church Union' in April 1936 provoked much controversy. It was first published in Evangelische Theologie in June 1936, and is now in Gesammelte Schriften, II, 217-241; ET by E. H. Robertson and John Bowden in The Way to Freedom, 75-96. The background to the paper was the way in which the leadership of the Confessing Church was beginning to backtrack on the decisions made at the Synods of Barmen (1934) and Dahlem (1935), especially with regard to church order and the rejection of the official state church government. Bonhoeffer's lecture has contributed significantly to the ongoing ecumenical debate on the true nature of the church and the problem of heresy. (See Duchrow, Conflict over the Ecumenical Movement, pp. 20 ff.)

The Reformation set free the question of the nature of the church from the question of who belongs to it. This was a decisive stage. Roman Catholicism and the pre-Reformation Church had thought that the question of the nature of the church could be answered by a definition of its extent. The Reformation, and particularly the Lutheran concept, first says what the church is and leaves the question of its boundaries open. Its first concern is not the unveiling of the divine mystery of who belongs to the church and who does not, the question of election and rejection, it is not aimed first and foremost at judging and distinguishing men; the most important thing is that the manifest saving act of God, the present Christ, his Word and his sacrament, should be seen and adored. There are no theoretical statements about the saved and the lost, there is no verdict 'This man belongs to the church, that man does not', but simply the joyful cry of those who have been granted a share in a great, astonishing gift, 'Here is the gospel!' 'Here are the pure sacraments!' 'Here is the church!' 'Come here!' *(WF: 75)*

*

There is a decisive difference in whether false teaching moves against the true church with a manifest intent to annihilate it or whether it stands alongside the church without a struggle. In the first instance true and false churches stand over against each other, each with the intention of being the death of the other. Here there is a life and death struggle. Here there is no communion. Here the true church recognizes anti-Christ. In the other instance, the true church knows of erring churches which have no will to destroy the true church, which themselves contribute to the mystery of the brokenness of the church, with which therefore the true church stands in a common confession of guilt. Here unity can again be sought in connection with the common confessional material. This is roughly the situation in ecumenical work. We learn from it that even church union, like the boundary of the church, has different forms. From the full communion in Word and sacrament which finds expression in an agreed confession, to a communion which is sought in faith on the ground of a common possession. It would be as false to reject and deny this communion *a limine* as it would be to equate it with full church union. It is on the one hand a fact of the church, on the other hand a state of emergency, a transition which must lead either to full communion or to separation. But because the church is not able to declare *a priori* where such communion or definitive separation exists it must take seriously the situation at any given time and leave it to God to make of it what pleases him, waiting on the hour of decision.

If it is clear that the question of church union can be answered only by the decision of the church, it must now be said that this decision of the church can in no case remain pending. It will accompany the church struggle step by step. True, it will always remain the 'strange work' of the church. But it must be made because otherwise the church's proper work can no longer be done. The church's decision on its boundary is in the last resort a merciful act both to its members and to those outside. It is the last, the 'strange', possibility of making the call to salvation audible.

The Confessing Synod of Barmen has repudiated the teaching of the German Christians in its decisive points as false teaching. This repudiation means that this false teaching has no place in the church of Jesus Christ. The Confessing Synod of Dahlem took it upon itself to declare that the government of the National Church has separated itself from the Christian church by teaching and by action. It did not bring about any exclusion from the church, but stated a *fait accompli*. At the same time it formed its own church government and claimed to represent the true church of Jesus Christ in Germany. Since then the Confessing Church has recognized that it has the responsibility of being and the commission to be the one true church of Jesus Christ in Germany. That is a fact of church history.

What does this mean? What does it express? Everything in the Confessing Church centres on this question. To make the inevitably vain and never conclusive attempt of asking about the views of those who were responsible for this decision of the synod is no sufficient answer. If we take this statement of the Synod at all seriously we will recognize that God the Lord himself wills to be responsible for it. But in that case the statement must be received as it was issued and we must look for the will of God in it. So on the presupposition that here in all human weakness and differences of opinion, through all kinds of human moods, anxieties and hastiness, the Word of the Lord became clear to the church when the Synod declared that the government of the National Church had cut itself off from the church of Jesus Christ, we must ask what this statement means. Anyone who does not share this presupposition does not speak of Barmen and Dahlem as Christian Synods, and does not share the presuppositions of the Confessing Church. Things are really in a bad way if today in large circles of the Confessing Church there is wilful and undisciplined talk, more among the clergy than among the laity. We can no longer go back behind Barmen and Dahlem not because they are historical facts of our church to which we must show due reverence, but because we can no longer go back behind the Word of God.

The question then is: What did God say about his church when he spoke through Barmen and Dahlem? The government of the National Church has cut itself off from the Christian church. The Confessing Church is the true church of Jesus Christ in Germany. What does that mean? It undoubtedly means that a definitive boundary has been recognized and confirmed between the government of the National Church and the true church of Christ. The government of the National Church is heretical. But does that mean that the man in office who continues to offer obedience to this repudiated church government falls under the same verdict? Has each German Christian pastor cut himself off from the church of Jesus? Furthermore: must we also regard the German Christians among members of the congregations and those parishes which accept their German Christian pastor without protest as cut off from the Christian church? Can the pastor of the Confessing Church claim the German Christian members of the congregation as members of his congregation? Is he permitted to exercise his office without distinction both to members of the Confessing Church and to German Christians? Where are the boundaries of the congregation for the pastor of the Confessing Church? Is there here a difference in principle between church government and congregation? And in addition: what is the position of the so-called neutrals? Finally: Does anyone engaged in common church work or even church government with the German Christians share in their sin of destroying the church? Does the Dahlem verdict also apply to the church committees? Does it apply to all those who obey the church committees? To sum up: must the division which has grown up between the government of the National Church and the Confessing Church now extend consistently to all these others just mentioned? An answer must be given. The congregation must know to whom they may listen and to whom not. The pastor must know how he is to understand his office rightly. Pastors and congregations largely do not know this today, and they cannot know it because they have not been told.

It would certainly be the easiest solution either to draw all the above-mentioned consequences neck and crop or to stand blindly by Dahlem and to draw no consequences at all. Both these courses are equally unchurchlike according to everything that has been said hitherto. Drawing consequences is no help at all, because the Word of God demands not consequences, but obedience. But to draw no consequences at all can be wilful disobedience towards the Word. Thus each single question must be examined and a decision must be sought step by step. In this way it is possible to reach a certain degree of clarity, for example, in the case of those who hold German Christian office. In parishes in which there are only ministers of this kind the Confessing Church has taken care that the true preaching and the true ministry is preserved. It has instituted emergency ministries and in this way demonstrated that the German Christian minister is deprived of his office. Nothing of this sort has happened in the case of the neutrals. The attitude towards the congregations is of a completely different nature. The mere fact of the institution of emergency pastorates is an expression of the full claim of the Confessing Church on the congregation. The attitude of the Confessing Church towards the committees and towards the members of the committees who belong to the Confessing Church, and also to pastors who offer allegiance to the committees, is completely obscure. This obscurity is pernicious. Before anything is said on the subject, however, we must look at the situation from yet another aspect.

Whereas on the one hand a continued process of separation is going on, on the other hand an extremely significant understanding is coming about between the churches of Lutheran and Reformed confessions. Since Barmen, Lutherans and Reformed have been speaking with one voice in Synodal declarations. Schismatic differences of confession no longer make it impossible to form a Confessing Synod, though of course the Synods are without intercommunion. This is to be taken into consideration as an actual fact. Of course disputes arise on the Confessing side. But the fact is there, and it is up to God to make what he will of it. (*WF: 85-89*)

*

At this point there is a further complication. The Confessing Church has found ecumenism. This meeting has up till now brought about two distinctive results. At Fanö, in 1934, in the presence of representatives of the Confessing Church the ecumenical movement declared the 'principles and methods' of the German Christian church government to be 'incompatible with the nature of the church of Christ'. By the election of a representative of the Confessing Church to the ecumenical council it has asked for the cooperation of the Confessing Church and has been given this church's promise. The Confessing Church has not yet, however, sent official representatives to any ecumenical conference. The reason for this must be found in the presence of representatives of the government of the National Church with whom conversation even on neutral ground is no longer possible for the Confessing Church. So while conversation with other, erring 'churches' would be possible, such a possibility no longer exists for conversation between the National Church and the Confessing Church. Doubtless it would be easy to point out the false doctrines of the German Christians in many other churches. Nevertheless the Confessing Church recognizes a qualitative difference.

All this must appear both incomprehensible and contradictory both to the orthodox and to those in principle without a confession. The orthodox does not understand how it can be possible to treat the clauses of the confession in a different way. He does not understand the openness of the Lutherans of the Confessing Church towards the Reformed or towards the ecumenical movement. Those without a confession, among them the great number of pastors under the sway of pietism and liberal theology, do not, on the other hand, understand the obstinacy in the application of the doctrinal concept against the German Christians.

The Confessing Church takes its confident way between the scylla of orthodoxy and the charybdis of confessionlessness. It bears the burden of the responsibility of being the true Church of Jesus. It proclaims 'Here is the church!' 'Come here!' In proclaiming this it comes up against both friends and enemies. Where it recognizes enemies it confirms the barriers they have drawn consistently and without compromise. Where it recognizes friends, it finds common ground and is ready for conversation in the hope of communion. The church will recognize friend or enemy by the Confession, but the Confession is not an ultimate, clear-cut measure. The church must decide where the enemy is standing. Because he can stand now on eucharistic doctrine, another time on the doctrine of justification, a third time on the doctrine of the church, the church has to decide. And in deciding it makes its confession. Orthodoxy confuses confession with a theological system. The confessionless confuse the church's confession with the testimony of piety. It would be very much easier if the Confessing Church could think in a clear-cut way here. But by so doing it would be unfaithful to its commission to give the call to salvation; in that, it is at the same time both open and bounded. (*WF: 90-91*)

*

Extra ecclesiam nulla salus. The question of church membership is the question of salvation. The boundaries of the church are the boundaries of salvation. Whoever knowingly cuts himself off from the Confessing Church in Germany cuts himself off from salvation. This is the recognition which has always forced itself upon the true church. That is its humble confession. Whoever separates the question of the Confessing Church from the question of his own salvation does not understand that the struggle of the Confessing Church is the struggle for his own salvation.

Is that not the Roman heresy of the church? In so far as Roman doctrine cannot think of salvation without the church and cannot think of the church without salvation, it is right. But in so far as the statement that there is only salvation in the church means anything but the call to the visible church, in so far then as this statement is not an existential expression of the faith of the true church but is intended as a theoretical truth about the saved and the lost, in so far as it is anything but an offer of grace, the means of salvation, it is reprehensible. For then a statement of faith is made a speculative statement. *Extra ecclesiam nulla salus* is in the strict sense a statement of faith. The believer is bound to God's saving revelation. He knows no other salvation than this in the visible church. In the light of this he is not free to look for God's salvation anywhere else than where the promise is given. He cannot in principle recognize salvation outside the church and it can therefore never become a point of doctrine for him. Salvation is recognized only in the promise. And the promise is given to the proclamation of the pure gospel.

But what if the gospel were now preached purely in a single congregation of the Roman Church or the National Church? Is not then the true church there also? There is no pure proclamation of the gospel independent of the whole church. And if someone preached the gospel as purely as the Apostle Paul and was obedient to the papacy or to the government of the National Church, he would be a false teacher and a misleader of the congregation.

But what if there are people in the other church whose piety and Christlikeness have been proved? What about the good Christians on the other side? Is it not unmerciful and un-Christian to pass judgment on them? Is it not intolerably pharisaic to put forward against them the claim of being the only true church? That is a spirit of judgment, we hear it said. There is an element of rebellion against the claim of the church in this question, and it is to be found right in the midst of the Confessing Church. It is this which tears the Confessing Church apart from within at this moment. The answer begins with the counter question:

1. Why are these Christian people with the German Christians and not with the true assembly of the faithful? Why do they not come to where the call of the true church is given? Why? Because it is not important enough to which church they belong? Because they have enough with their piety and their holiness? Is that what it means to be a good Christian?

2. How do we know who is a good Christian and who is not? Am I a judge over another's Christianity? Is this not an intolerable spirit of judgment which pretends to look into another's heart? Is not this supposed Christian love which would exclude no pious man from salvation unutterable *hybris* and the deepest hatefulness because it anticipates God's hidden judgment on the soul of the individual?

3. Who really calls the church? The Holy Spirit through his Word and sacrament? Or I myself, with my verdict on good and bad Christians? That is the fearful calumny which lies in the question of these loving Christians, that they want to found and gather together and limit the church of God themselves, and in so doing destroy and deny the true church of the Word.

It must be said again and again that for the church to deny its boundaries is no work of mercy. The true church comes up against boundaries. In recognizing them it does the work of love towards men by honouring the truth. *Extra ecclesiam nulla salus.* If this statement is indisputable, the other one must also be added which has its analogy in the doctrine of God. True, God is everywhere, 'but it is not his will that you should look for him everywhere'. There is a difference between the presence of God and the possibility of knowing him. As surely as the known God is our God and the unknown God can never be our God, so surely must this distinction be preserved precisely as an expression of faith which holds by the revealed God and in so doing celebrates the uniqueness and the wonder of the revelation. So now it can also be said of the church that it is only known where the promise of God rests, in the visible church. Not there is it our church. But the believer who has become certain of his salvation in the visible church celebrates the wonder of this salvation precisely in daring to speak of a being of the church beyond the manifest church of salvation. He can never do this to negate the sole salvation through the visible church, he can never do it even for the sake of this or that pious man who stands outside, he can never do it to judge and to discover himself where the 'church beyond' is. It remains unknown, believed in by the church of salvation so as to praise all the more highly the glory of the known revelation of salvation. Woe to those who make this, the last possibility of faith of the church which lives by faith, *extra ecclesiam nulla salus*, into a presupposition for their pious speculation on the saved and the lost. This is not our task. We must rather flee from the temptation of such questions to the manifest salvation of God in the true church.

The question of the boundaries of the church can become a temptation for faith. But it should only serve to make faith more certain. It is the cause of the church to make this continually clearer and to make the congregation more certain of its salvation in any decision about its boundaries.   (*WF: 93-96*)

*

THE COST OF DISCIPLESHIP

Bonhoeffer devoted much time and energy to biblical study while director of the Preachers' Seminary at Finkenwalde. This resulted in the publication of several exegetical works, the most famous of which is undoubtedly his Nachfolge *(Chr. Kaiser Verlag, 1937). He first became widely known in the English-speaking world largely as a result of its publication under the title* The Cost of Discipleship *(translated by Reginald Fuller, and published by SCM in 1949.) Since then the book has been reprinted several times and translated into many languages as a classic text of twentieth century Christianity.*

Bonhoeffer had been working on the themes of The Cost of Discipleship *since at least the end of 1932. The final product therefore took several years to mature, and was the drawing together of lectures, exegetical studies and expositions on the Sermon on the Mount which Bonhoeffer gave to his students at Finkenwalde.*

In the English edition the text is divided into four main sections: (1) Grace and Discipleship; (2) The Sermon on the Mount; (3) The Messengers; and (4) The Church of Jesus Christ and the Life of Discipleship. This structure is not, however, that of the German text and it obscures Bonhoeffer's intention.

The original is divided into two parts only, the first of which (1-3 in the ET) is an exposition of discipleship in the synoptic gospels and especially the Sermon on the Mount. The second part deals with the same theme, but now in terms of Pauline theology (section 4 in ET). Bonhoeffer is clearly wanting to show that following Jesus the suffering Messiah (the Synoptics) is an integral part of believing in and obeying Christ as Lord (Paul). Our readings are taken from section one, being chapter one and the first part of chapter two (in ET, pp. 35-60).

1. COSTLY GRACE

Cheap grace is the deadly enemy of our church. We are fighting today for costly grace.

Cheap grace means grace sold on the market like cheapjack's wares. The sacraments, the forgiveness of sin, and the consolations of religion are thrown away at cut prices. Grace is represented as the church's inexhaustible treasury, from which she showers blessings with generous hands, without asking questions or fixing limits. Grace without price; grace without cost! The essence of grace, we suppose, is that the account has been paid in advance; and, because it has been paid, everything can be had for nothing. Since the cost was infinite, the possibilities of using and spending it are infinite. What would grace be if it were not cheap?

Cheap grace means grace as a doctrine, a principle, a system. It means forgiveness of sins proclaimed as a general truth, the love of God taught as the Christian 'conception' of God. An intellectual assent to that idea is held to be of itself sufficient to secure remission of sins. The church which holds the correct doctrine of grace has, it is supposed, *ipso facto* a part in that grace. In such a church the world finds a cheap covering for its sins; no contrition is required, still less any real desire to be delivered from sin. Cheap grace therefore amounts to a denial of the living Word of God, in fact, a denial of the Incarnation of the Word of God.

Cheap grace means the justification of sin without the justification of the sinner. Grace alone does everything, they say, and so everything can remain as it was before. 'All for sin could not atone.' The world goes on in the same old way, and we are still sinners 'even in the best life' as Luther said. Well, then, let the Christian live like the rest of the world, let him model himself on the world's standards in every sphere of life, and not presumptuously aspire to live a different life under grace from his old life under sin. That was the heresy of the enthusiasts, the Anabaptists and their kind. Let the Christian beware of rebelling against the free and boundless grace of God and desecrating it. Let him not attempt to erect a new religion of the letter by endeavouring to live a life of obedience to the commandments of Jesus Christ! The world has been justified by grace. The Christian knows that, and takes it seriously. He knows he must not strive against this indispensable grace. Therefore — let him live like the rest of the world! Of course he would like to go and do something extraordinary, and it does demand a good deal of self-restraint to refrain from the attempt and content himself with living as the world lives. Yet it is imperative for the Christian to achieve renunciation, to practise self-effacement, to distinguish his life from the life of the world. He must let grace be grace indeed, otherwise he will destroy the world's faith in the free gift of grace. Let the Christian rest content with his worldliness and with this renunciation of any higher standard than the world. He is doing it for the sake of the world rather than for the sake of grace. Let him be comforted and rest assured in his possession of this grace — for grace alone does everything. Instead of following Christ, let the Christian enjoy the consolations of his grace! That is what we mean by cheap grace, the grace which amounts to the justification of sin without the justification of the repentant sinner who departs from sin and from whom sin departs. Cheap grace is not the kind of forgiveness of sin which frees us from the toils of sin. Cheap grace is the grace we bestow on ourselves.

Cheap grace is the preaching of forgiveness without requiring repentance, baptism without church discipline, communion without confession, absolution without personal confession. Cheap grace is grace without discipleship, grace without the cross, grace without Jesus Christ, living and incarnate.

Costly grace is the treasure hidden in the field; for the sake of it a man will gladly go and sell all that he has. It is the pearl of great price to buy which the merchant will sell all his goods. It is the kingly rule of Christ, for whose sake a man will pluck out the eye which causes him to stumble, it is the call of Jesus Christ at which the disciple leaves his nets and follows him.

Costly grace is the gospel which must be *sought* again and again, the gift which must be *asked* for, the door at which a man must *knock*.

Such grace is *costly* because it calls us to follow, and it is *grace* because it calls us to follow *Jesus Christ*. It is costly because it costs a man his life, and it is grace because it gives a man the only true life. It is costly because it condemns sin, and grace because it justifies the sinner. Above all, it is *costly* because it cost God the life of his Son: 'ye were bought at a price', and what has cost God much cannot be cheap for us. Above all, it is *grace* because God did not reckon his Son too dear a price to pay for our life, but delivered him up for us. Costly grace is the Incarnation of God.

Costly grace is the sanctuary of God; it has to be protected from the world, and not thrown to the dogs. It is therefore the living word, the Word of God, which he speaks as it pleases him. Costly grace confronts us as a gracious call to follow Jesus, it comes as a word of forgiveness to the broken spirit and the contrite heart. Grace is costly because it compels a man to submit to the yoke of Christ and follow him; it is grace because Jesus says: 'My yoke is easy and my burden is light.'

On two separate occasions Peter received the call, 'Follow me'. It was the first and last word Jesus spoke to his disciple (Mark 1.17; John 21.22). A whole life lies between these two calls. The first occasion was by the lake of Gennesareth, when Peter left his nets and his craft and followed Jesus at his word. The second occasion is when the Risen Lord finds him back again at his old trade. Once again it is by the lake of Gennesareth, and once again the call is: 'Follow me.' Between the two calls lay a whole life of discipleship in the following of Christ. Half-way between them comes Peter's confession, when he acknowledged Jesus as the Christ of God. Three times Peter hears the same proclamation that Christ is his Lord and God — at the beginning, at the end, and at Caesarea Philippi. Each time it is the same grace of Christ which calls to him 'Follow me' and which reveals itself to him in his confession of the Son of God. Three times on Peter's way did grace arrest him, the one grace proclaimed in three different ways.

This grace was certainly not self-bestowed. It was the grace of Christ himself, now prevailing upon the disciple to leave all and follow him, now working in him that confession which to the world must sound like the ultimate blasphemy, now inviting Peter to the supreme fellowship of martyrdom for the Lord he had denied, and thereby forgiving him all his sins. In the life of Peter grace and discipleship are inseparable. He had received the grace which costs.

As Christianity spread, and the church became more secularized, this realization of the costliness of grace gradually faded. The world was christianized, and grace became its common property. It was to be had at low cost. Yet the church of Rome did not altogether lose the earlier vision. It is highly significant that the church was astute enough to find room for the monastic movement, and to prevent it from lapsing into schism. Here on the outer fringe of the church was a place where the older vision was kept alive. Here men still remembered that grace costs, that grace means following Christ. Here they left all they had for Christ's sake, and endeavoured daily to practise his rigorous commands. Thus monasticism became a living protest against the secularization of Christianity and the cheapening of grace. But the church was wise enough to tolerate this protest, and to prevent it from developing to its logical conclusion. It thus succeeded in relativizing it, even using it in order to justify the secularization of its own life. Monasticism was represented as an individual achievement which the mass of the laity could not be expected to emulate. By thus limiting the application of the commandments of Jesus to a restricted group of specialists, the church evolved the fatal conception of the double standard — a maximum and a minimum standard of Christian obedience. Whenever the church was accused of being too secularized, it could always point to monasticism as an opportunity of living a higher life within the fold, and thus justify the other possibility of a lower standard of life for others. And so we get the paradoxical result that monasticism, whose mission was to preserve in the church of Rome the primitive Christian realization of the costliness of grace, afforded conclusive justification for the secularization of the church. By and large, the fatal error of monasticism lay not so much in its rigorism (though even here there was a good deal of misunderstanding of the precise content of the will of Jesus) as in the extent to which it departed from genuine Christianity by setting up itself as the individual achievement of a select few, and so claiming a special merit of its own.

When the Reformation came, the providence of God raised Martin Luther to restore the gospel of pure, costly grace. Luther passed through the cloister; he was a monk, and all this was part of the divine plan. Luther had left all to follow Christ on the path of absolute obedience. He had renounced the world in order to live the Christian life. He had learnt obedience to Christ and to his church, because only he who is obedient can believe. The call to the cloister demanded of Luther the complete surrender of his life. But God shattered all his hopes. He showed him through the Scriptures that the following of Christ is not the achievement or merit of a select few, but the divine command to all Christians without distinction. Monasticism had transformed the humble work of discipleship into the meritorious activity of the saints, and the self-renunciation of discipleship into the flagrant spiritual self-assertion of the 'religious'. The world had crept into the very heart of the monastic life, and was once more making havoc. The monk's attempt to flee from the world turned out to be a subtle form of love for the world. The bottom having thus been knocked out of the religious life, Luther laid hold upon grace. Just as the whole world of monasticism was crashing about him in ruins, he saw God in Christ stretching forth his hand to save. He grasped that hand in faith, believing that 'after all, nothing we can do is of any avail, however good a life we live'. The grace which gave itself to him was a costly grace, and it shattered his whole existence. Once more he must leave his nets and follow. The first time was when he entered the monastery, when he had left everything behind except his pious self. This time even that was taken from him. He obeyed the call, not through any merit of his own, but simply through the grace of God. Luther did not hear the word: 'Of course you have sinned, but now everything is forgiven, so you can stay as you are and enjoy the consolations of forgiveness.' No, Luther had to leave the cloister and go back to the world, not because the world in itself was good and holy, but because even the cloister was only a part of the world.

Luther's return from the cloister to the world was the worst blow the world had suffered since the days of early Christianity. The renunciation he made when he became a monk was child's play compared with that which he had to make when he returned to the world. Now came the frontal assault. The only way to follow Jesus was by living in the world. Hitherto the Christian life had been the achievement of a few choice spirits under the exceptionally favourable conditions of monasticism; now it is a duty laid on every Christian living in the world. The commandment of Jesus must be accorded perfect obedience in one's daily vocation of life. The conflict between the life of the Christian and the life of the world was thus thrown into the sharpest possible relief. It was a hand-to-hand conflict between the Christian and the world.

It is a fatal misunderstanding of Luther's action to suppose that his rediscovery of the gospel of pure grace offered a general dispensation from obedience to the command of Jesus, or that it was the great discovery of the Reformation that God's forgiving grace automatically conferred upon the world both righteousness and holiness. On the contrary, for Luther the Christian's worldly calling is sanctified only in so far as that calling registers the final, radical protest against the world. Only in so far as the Christian's secular calling is exercised in the following of Jesus does it receive from the gospel new sanction and justification. It was not the justification of sin, but the justification of the sinner that drove Luther from the cloister back into the world. The grace he had received was costly grace. It was grace, for it was like water on parched ground, comfort in tribulation, freedom from the bondage of a self-chosen way, and forgiveness of all his sins. And it was costly, for, so far from dispensing him from good works, it meant that he must take the call to discipleship more seriously than ever before. It was grace because it cost so much, and it cost so much because it was grace. That was the secret of the gospel of the Reformation — the justification of the sinner.

Yet the outcome of the Reformation was the victory, not of Luther's perception of grace in all its purity and costliness, but of the vigilant religious instinct of man for the place where grace is to be obtained at the cheapest price. All that was needed was a subtle and almost imperceptible change of emphasis, and the damage was done. Luther had taught that man cannot stand before God, however religious his works and ways may be, because at bottom he is always seeking his own interests. In the depth of his misery, Luther had grasped by faith the free and unconditional forgiveness of all his sins. That experience taught him that this grace had cost him his very life, and must continue to cost him the same price day by day. So far from dispensing him from discipleship, this grace only made him a more earnest disciple. When he spoke of grace, Luther always implied as a corollary that it cost him his own life, the life which was now for the first time subjected to the absolute obedience of Christ. Only so could he speak of grace. Luther had said that grace alone can save; his followers took up his doctrine and repeated it word for word. But they left out its invariable corollary, the obligation of discipleship. There was no need for Luther always to mention that corollary explicitly for he always spoke as one who had been led by grace to the strictest following of Christ. Judged by the standard of Luther's doctrine, that of his followers was unassailable, and yet their orthodoxy spelt the end and destruction of the Reformation as the revelation on earth of the costly grace of God. The justification of the sinner in the world degenerated into the justification of sin and the world. Costly grace was turned into cheap grace without discipleship.

Luther had said that all we can do is of no avail, however good a life we live. He had said that nothing can avail us in the sight of God but 'the grace and favour which confers the forgiveness of sin'. But he spoke as one who knew that at the very moment of his crisis he was called to leave all that he had a second time and follow Jesus. The recognition of grace was his final, radical breach with his besetting sin, but it was never the justification of that sin. By laying hold of God's forgiveness, he made the final, radical renunciation of a self-willed life, and this breach was such that it led inevitably to a serious following of Christ. He always looked upon it as the answer to a sum, but an answer which had been arrived at by God, not by man. But then his followers changed the 'answer' into the data for a calculation of their own. That was the root of the trouble. If grace is God's answer, the gift of Christian life, then we cannot for a moment dispense with following Christ. But if grace is the data for my Christian life, it means that I set out to live the Christian life, in the world with all my sins justified beforehand. I can go and sin as much as I like, and rely on this grace to forgive me, for after all the world is justified in principle by grace. I can therefore cling to my bourgeois secular existence, and remain as I was before, but with the added assurance that the grace of God will cover me. It is under the influence of this kind of 'grace' that the world has been made 'Christian', but at the cost of secularizing the Christian religion as never before. The antithesis between the Christian life and the life of bourgeois respectability is at an end. The Christian life comes to mean nothing more than living in the world and as the world, in being no different from the world, in fact, in being prohibited from being different from the world for the sake of grace. The upshot of it all is that my only duty as a Christian is to leave the world for an hour or so on a Sunday morning and go to church to be assured that my sins are all forgiven. I need no longer try to follow Christ, for cheap grace, the bitterest foe of discipleship, which true discipleship must loathe and detest, has freed me from that. Grace as the data for our calculations means grace at the cheapest price, but grace as the answer to the sum means costly grace. It is terrifying to realize what use can be made of a genuine evangelical doctrine. In both cases we have the identical formula — 'justification by faith alone'. Yet the misuse of the formula leads to the complete destruction of its very essence.

At the end of a life spent in the pursuit of knowledge Faust has to confess:

'I now do see that we can nothing know.'

That is the answer to a sum, it is the outcome of a long experience. But as Kierkegaard observed, it is quite a different thing when a freshman comes up to the university and uses the same sentiment to justify his indolence. As the answer to a sum it is perfectly true, but as the initial data it is a piece of self-deception. For acquired knowledge cannot be divorced from the existence in which it is acquired. The only man who has the right to say that he is justified by grace alone is the man who has left all to follow Christ. Such a man knows that the call of discipleship is a gift of grace, and that the call is inseparable from the grace. But those who try to use this grace as a dispensation from following Christ are simply deceiving themselves.

But, we may ask, did not Luther himself come perilously near to this perversion in the understanding of grace? What about his *Pecca fortiter, sed fortius fide et gaude in Christo* ('Sin boldly, but believe and rejoice in Christ more boldly still')? You are a sinner, anyway, and there is nothing you can do about it. Whether you are a monk or a man of the world, a religious man or a bad one, you can never escape the toils of the world or from sin. So put a bold face on it, and all the more because you can rely on the *opus operatum* of grace. Is this the proclamation of cheap grace, naked and unashamed, the *carte blanche* for sin, the end of all discipleship? Is this a blasphemous encouragement to sin boldly and rely on grace? Is there a more diabolical abuse of grace than to sin and rely on the grace which God has given? Is not the Roman Catechism quite right in denouncing this as the sin against the Holy Spirit?

If we are to understand this saying of Luther's, everything depends on applying the distinction between the data and the answer to the sum. If we make Luther's formula a premiss for our doctrine of grace, we are conjuring up the spectre of cheap grace. But Luther's formula is meant to be taken, not as the premiss, but as the conclusion, the answer to the sum, the coping-stone, his very last word on the subject. Taken as the premiss, *pecca fortiter* acquires the character of an ethical principle, a principle of grace to which the principle of *pecca fortiter* must correspond. That means the justification of sin, and it turns Luther's formula into its very opposite. For Luther 'sin boldly' could only be his very last refuge, the consolation for one whose attempts to follow Christ had taught him that he can never become sinless, who in his fear of sin despairs of the grace of God. As Luther saw it, 'sin boldly' did not happen to be a fundamental acknowledgement of his disobedient life; it was the gospel of the grace of God before which we are always and in every circumstance sinners. Yet that grace seeks us and justifies us, sinners though we are. Take courage and confess your sin, says Luther, do not try to run away from it, but believe more boldly still. You are a sinner, so be a sinner, and don't try to become what you are not. Yes, and become a sinner again and again every day, and be bold about it. But to whom can such words be addressed, except to those who from the bottom of their hearts make a daily renunciation of sin and of every barrier which hinders them from following Christ, but who nevertheless are troubled by their daily faithlessness and sin? Who can hear these words without endangering his faith but he who hears their consolation as a renewed summons to follow Christ? Interpreted in this way, these words of Luther become a testimony to the costliness of grace, the only genuine kind of grace there is.

Grace interpreted as a principle, *pecca fortiter* as a principle, grace at a low cost, is in the last resort simply a new law, which brings neither help nor freedom. Grace as a living word, *pecca fortiter* as our comfort in tribulation and as a summons to discipleship, costly grace is the only pure grace, which really forgives sins and gives freedom to the sinner.

We Lutherans have gathered like eagles round the carcase of cheap grace, and there we have drunk of the poison which has killed the life of following Christ. It is true, of course, that we have paid the doctrine of pure grace divine honours unparalleled in Christendom, in fact we have exalted that doctrine to the position of God himself. Everywhere Luther's formula has been repeated, but its truth perverted into self-deception. So long as our church holds the correct doctrine of justification, there is no doubt whatever that she is a justified church! So they said, thinking that we must vindicate our Lutheran heritage by making this grace available on the cheapest and easiest terms. To be 'Lutheran' must mean that we leave the following of Christ to legalists, Calvinists and enthusiasts — and all this for the sake of grace. We justified the world, and condemned as heretics those who tried to follow Christ. The result was that a nation became Christian and Lutheran, but at the cost of true discipleship. The price it was called upon to pay was all too cheap. Cheap grace had won the day.

But do we realize that this cheap grace has turned back upon us like a boomerang? The price we are having to pay today in the shape of the collapse of the organized church is only the inevitable consequence of our policy of making grace available to all at too low a cost. We gave away the word and sacraments wholesale, we baptized, confirmed, and absolved a whole nation unasked and without condition. Our humanitarian sentiment made us give that which was holy to the scornful and unbelieving. We poured forth unending streams of grace. But the call to follow Jesus in the narrow way was hardly ever heard. Where were those truths which impelled the early church to institute the catechumenate, which enabled a strict watch to be kept over the frontier between the church and the world, and afforded adequate protection for costly grace? What had happened to all those warnings of Luther's against preaching the gospel in such a manner as to make men rest secure in their ungodly living? Was there ever a more terrible or disastrous instance of the Christianizing of the world than this? What are those three thousand Saxons put to death by Charlemagne compared with the millions of spiritual corpses in our country today? With us it has been abundantly proved that the sins of the fathers are visited upon the children unto the third and fourth generations. Cheap grace has turned out to be utterly merciless to our Evangelical Church.

This cheap grace has been no less disastrous to our own spiritual lives. Instead of opening up the way to Christ it has closed it. Instead of calling us to follow Christ, it has hardened us in our disobedience. Perhaps we had once heard the gracious call to follow him, and had at this command even taken the first few steps along the path of discipleship in the discipline of obedience, only to find ourselves confronted by the word of cheap grace. Was that not merciless and hard? The only effect that such a word could have on us was to bar our way to progress, and seduce us to the mediocre level of the world, quenching the joy of discipleship by telling us that we were following a way of our own choosing, that we were spending our strength and disciplining ourselves in vain — all of which was not merely useless, but extremely dangerous. After all, we were told, our salvation had already been accomplished by the grace of God. The smoking flax was mercilessly extinguished. It was unkind to speak to men like this, for such a cheap offer could only leave them bewildered and tempt them from the way to which they had been called by Christ. Having laid hold on cheap grace, they were barred for ever from the knowledge of costly grace. Deceived and weakened, men felt that they were strong now that they were in possession of this cheap grace — whereas they had in fact lost the power to live the life of discipleship and obedience. The word of cheap grace has been the ruin of more Christians than any commandment of works.

In our subsequent chapters we shall try to find a message for those who are troubled by this problem, and for whom the word of grace has been emptied of all its meaning. This message must be spoken for the sake of truth, for those among us who confess that through cheap grace they have lost the following of Christ and further, with the following of Christ, have lost the understanding of costly grace. To put it quite simply, we must undertake this task because we are now ready to admit that we no longer stand in the path of true discipleship. We confess that, although our church is orthodox as far as her doctrine of grace is concerned, we are no longer sure that we are members of a church which follows its Lord. We must therefore attempt to recover a true understanding of the mutual relation between grace and discipleship. The issue can no longer be evaded. It is becoming clearer every day that the most urgent problem besetting our church is this: How can we live the Christian life in the modern world?

Happy are they who have reached the end of the road we seek to tread, who are astonished to discover the by no means self-evident truth that grace is costly just because it is the grace of God in Jesus Christ. Happy are the simple followers of Jesus Christ who have been overcome by his grace, and are able to sing the praises of the all-sufficient grace of Christ with humbleness of heart. Happy are they who, knowing that grace, can live in the world without being of it, who, by following Jesus Christ, are so assured of their heavenly citizenship that they are truly free to live their lives in this world. Happy are they who know that discipleship simply means the life which springs from grace, and that grace simply means discipleship. Happy are they who have become Christians in this sense of the word. For them the word of grace has proved a fount of mercy.

2. THE CALL TO DISCIPLESHIP

And as he passed by he saw Levi, the son of Alphæus, sitting at the place of toll, and he saith unto him, Follow me. And he arose and followed him.
(*Mark 2.14*)

The call goes forth, and is at once followed by the response of obedience. The response of the disciples is an act of obedience, not a confession of faith in Jesus. How could the call immediately evoke obedience? The story is a stumbling-block for the natural reason, and it is no wonder that frantic attempts have been made to separate the two events. By hook or by crook a bridge must be found between them. Something must have happened in between, some psychological or historical event. Thus we get the stupid question: Surely the publican must have known Jesus before, and that previous acquaintance explains his readiness to hear the Master's call. Unfortunately our text is ruthlessly silent on this point, and in fact it regards the immediate sequence of call and response as a matter of crucial importance. It displays not the slightest interest in the psychological reason for a man's religious decisions. And why? For the simple reason that the cause behind the immediate following of call by response is Jesus Christ himself. It is Jesus who calls, and because it is Jesus, Levi follows at once. This enounter is a testimony to the absolute, direct, and unaccountable authority of Jesus. There is no need of any preliminaries, and no other consequence but obedience to the call. Because Jesus is the Christ, he has the authority to call and to demand obedience to his word. Jesus summons men to follow him not as a teacher or a pattern of the good life, but as the Christ, the Son of God. In this short text Jesus Christ and his claim are proclaimed to men. Not a word of praise is given to the disciple for his decision for Christ. We are not expected to contemplate the disciple, but only him who calls, and his absolute authority. According to our text, there is no road to faith or discipleship, no other road — only obedience to the call of Jesus.

And what does the text inform us about the content of discipleship? Follow me, run along behind me! That is all. To follow in his steps is something which is void of all content. It gives us no intelligible programme for a way of life, no goal or ideal to strive after. It is not a cause which human calculation might deem worthy of our devotion, even the devotion of ourselves. What happens? At the call, Levi leaves all that he has — but not because he thinks that he might be doing something worth while, but simply for the sake of the call. Otherwise he cannot follow in the steps of Jesus. This act on Levi's part has not the slightest value in itself, it is quite devoid of significance and unworthy of consideration. The disciple simply burns his boats and goes ahead. He is called out, and has to forsake his old life in order that he may 'exist' in the strictest sense of the word. The old life is left behind, and completely surrendered. The disciple is dragged out of his relative security into a life of absolute insecurity (that is, in truth, into the absolute security and safety of the fellowship of Jesus), from a life which is observable and calculable (it is, in fact, quite incalculable) into a life where everything is unobservable and fortuitous (that is, into one which is necessary and calculable), out of the realm of finite (which is in truth the infinite) into the realm of infinite possibilities (which is the one liberating reality). Again it is no universal law. Rather is it the exact opposite of all legality. It is nothing else than bondage to Jesus Christ alone, completely breaking through every programme, every ideal, every set of laws. No other significance is possible, since Jesus is the only significance. Beside Jesus nothing has any significance. He alone matters.

When we are called to follow Christ, we are summoned to an exclusive attachment to his person. The grace of his call bursts all the bonds of legalism. It is a gracious call, a gracious commandment. It transcends the difference between the law and the gospel. Christ calls, the disciple follows; that is grace and commandment in one. 'I will walk at liberty, for I seek thy commandments' (Ps. 119.45).

Discipleship means adherence to Christ, and, because Christ is the object of that adherence, it must take the form of discipleship. An abstract Christology, a doctrinal system, a general religious knowledge on the subject of grace or on the forgiveness of sins, render discipleship superfluous, and in fact they positively exclude any idea of discipleship whatever, and are essentially inimical to the whole conception of following Christ. With an abstract idea it is possible to enter into a relation of formal knowledge, to become enthusiastic about it, and perhaps even to put it into practice; but it can never be followed in personal obedience. Christianity without the living Christ is inevitably Christianity without discipleship, and Christianity without discipleship is always Christianity without Christ. It remains an abstract idea, a myth which has a place for the Fatherhood of God, but omits Christ as the living Son. And a Christianity of that kind is nothing more nor less than the end of discipleship. In such a religion there is trust in God, but no following of Christ. Because the Son of God became Man, because he is the Mediator, for that reason alone the only true relation we can have with him is to follow him. Discipleship is bound to Christ as the Mediator, and where it is properly understood, it necessarily implies faith in the Son of God as the Mediator. Only the Mediator, the God-Man, can call men to follow him.

Discipleship without Jesus Christ is a way of our own choosing. It may be the ideal way. It may even lead to martyrdom, but it is devoid of all promise. Jesus will certainly reject it.

> And they went to another village. And as they went in the way, a certain man said unto him, I will follow thee whithersoever thou goest. And Jesus said unto him, The foxes have holes, and the birds of heaven have nests, but the Son of man hath not where to lay his head. And he said unto another, Follow me. But he said, Lord, suffer me first to go and bury my father. But he said unto him, Leave the dead to bury their dead, but go thou and publish abroad the kingdom of God. And another said, I will follow thee, Lord; but suffer me first to bid farewell to them that are at my house. But Jesus said unto him, No man, having put his hand unto the plough, and looking back, is fit for the kingdom of God. *(Luke 9.57-62)*

The first disciple offers to follow Jesus without waiting to be called. Jesus damps his ardour by warning him that he does not know what he is doing. In fact he is quite incapable of knowing. That is the meaning of Jesus' answer — he shows the would-be disciple what life with him involves. We hear the words of One who is on his way to the cross, whose whole life is summed up in the Apostles' Creed by the word 'suffered'. No man can choose such a life for himself. No man can call himself to such a destiny, says Jesus, and his word stays unanswered. The gulf between a voluntary offer to follow and genuine discipleship is clear.

But where Jesus calls, he bridges the widest gulf. The second would-be disciple wants to bury his father before he starts to follow. He is held bound by the trammels of the law. He knows what he wants and what he must do. Let him first fulfil the law, and then let him follow. A definite legal ordinance acts as a barrier between Jesus and the man he has called. But the call of Jesus is stronger than the barrier. At this critical moment nothing on earth, however sacred, must be allowed to come between Jesus and the man he has called — not even the law itself. Now, if never before, the law must be broken for the sake of Jesus; it forfeits all its rights if it acts as a barrier to discipleship. Therefore Jesus emerges at this point as the opponent of the law, and commands a man to follow him. Only the Christ can speak in this fashion. He alone has the last word. His would-be follower cannot kick against the pricks. This call, this grace, is irresistible.

The third would-be disciple, like the first, thinks that following Christ means that he must make the offer on his own initiative, as if it were a career he had mapped out for himself. There is however a difference between the first would-be disciple and the third, for the third is bold enough to stipulate his own terms. Unfortunately, however, he lands himself in a hopeless inconsistency, for although he is ready enough to throw in his lot with Jesus, he succeeds in putting up a barrier between himself and the Master. 'Suffer me first.' He wants to follow, but feels obliged to insist on his own terms. Discipleship to him is a possibility which can only be realized when certain conditions have been fulfilled. This is to reduce discipleship to the level of the human understanding. First you must do this and then you must do that. There is a right time for everything. The disciple places himself at the Master's disposal, but at the same time retains the right to dictate his own terms. But then discipleship is no longer discipleship, but a programme of our own to be arranged to suit ourselves, and to be judged in accordance with the standards of a rational ethic. The trouble about this third would-be disciple is that at the very moment he expresses his willingness to follow, he ceases to want to follow at all. By making his offer on his own terms, he alters the whole position, for discipleship can tolerate no conditions which might come between Jesus and our obedience to him. Hence the third disciple finds himself at loggerheads not only with Jesus, but also with himself. His desires conflict not only with what Jesus wants, but also with what he wants himself. He judges himself, and decides against himself, and all this by saying, 'Suffer me first.' The answer of Jesus graphically proves to him that he is at variance with himself and that excludes discipleship. 'No man, having put his hand to the plough and looking back, is fit for the kingdom of God.'

If we would follow Jesus we must take certain definite steps. The first step, which follows the call, cuts the disciple off from his previous existence. The call to follow at once produces a new situation. To stay in the old situation makes discipleship impossible. Levi must leave the receipt of custom and Peter his nets in order to follow Jesus. One would have thought that nothing so drastic was necessary at such an early stage. Could not Jesus have initiated the publican into some new religious experience, and leave them as they were before? He could have done so, had he not been the incarnate Son of God. But since he is the Christ, he must make it clear from the start that his word is not an abstract doctrine, but the re-creation of the whole life of man. The only right and proper way is quite literally to go with Jesus. The call to follow implies that there is only one way of believing in Jesus Christ, and that is by leaving all and going with the incarnate Son of God.

The first step places the disciple in the situation where faith is possible. If he refuses to follow and stays behind, he does not learn how to believe. He who is called must go out of his situation in which he cannot believe, into the situation in which, first and foremost, faith is possible. But this step is not the first stage of a career. Its sole justification is that it brings the disciple into fellowship with Jesus which will be victorious. So long as Levi sits at the receipt of custom, and Peter at his nets, they could both pursue their trade honestly and dutifully, and they might both enjoy religious experiences, old and new. But if they want to believe in God, the only way is to follow his incarnate Son.

Until that day, everything had been different. They could remain in obscurity, pursuing their work as the quiet in the land, observing the law and waiting for the coming of the Messiah. But now he has come, and his call goes forth. Faith can no longer mean sitting still and waiting — they must rise and follow him. The call frees them from all earthly ties, and binds them to Jesus Christ alone. They must burn their boats and plunge into absolute insecurity in order to learn the demand and the gift of Christ. Had Levi stayed at his post, Jesus might have been his present help in trouble, but not the Lord of his whole life. In other words Levi would never have learnt to believe. The new situation must be created, in which it is possible to believe in Jesus as God incarnate; that is the impossible situation in which everything is staked solely on the word of Jesus. Peter had to leave the ship and risk his life on the sea, in order to learn both his own weakness and the almighty power of his Lord. If Peter had not taken the risk, he would never have learnt the meaning of

171

faith. Before he can believe, the utterly impossible and ethically irresponsible situation on the waves of the sea must be displayed. The road to faith passes through obedience to the call of Jesus. Unless a definite step is demanded, the call vanishes into thin air, and if men imagine that they can follow Jesus without taking this step, they are deluding themselves like fanatics.

It is an extremely hazardous procedure to distinguish between a situation where faith is possible and one where it is not. We must first realize that there is nothing in the situation to tell us to which category it belongs. It is only the call of Jesus which makes it a situation where faith is possible. Secondly, a situation where faith is possible can never be demonstrated from the human side. Discipleship is not an offer man makes to Christ. It is only the call which creates the situation. Thirdly, this situation never possesses any intrinsic worth or merit of its own. It is only through the call that it receives its justification. Last, but not least, the situation in which faith is possible is itself only rendered possible through faith.

The idea of a situation in which faith is possible is only a way of stating the facts of a case in which the following two propositions hold good and are equally true: *only he who believes is obedient, and only he who is obedient believes.*

It is quite unbiblical to hold the first proposition without the second. We think we understand when we hear that obedience is possible only where there is faith. Does not obedience follow faith as good fruit grows on a good tree? First, faith, then obedience. If by that we mean that it is faith which justifies, and not the act of obedience, all well and good, for that is the essential and unexceptionable presupposition of all that follows. If however we make a chronological distinction between faith and obedience, and make obedience subsequent to faith, we are divorcing the one from the other — and then we get the practical question, when must obedience begin? Obedience remains separated from faith. From the point of view of justification it is necessary thus to separate them, but we must never lose sight of their essential unity. For faith is only real when there is obedience, never without it, and faith only becomes faith in the act of obedience.

Since, then, we cannot adequately speak of obedience as the consequence of faith, and since we must never forget the indisoluble unity of the two, we must place the one proposition that only he who believes is obedient alongside the other, that only he who is obedient believes. In the one case faith is the condition of obedience, and in the other obedience the condition of faith. In exactly the same way in which obedience is called the consequence of faith, it must also be called the presupposition of faith.

Only the obedient believe. If we are to believe, we must obey a concrete command. Without this preliminary step of obedience, our faith will only be pious humbug, and lead us to the grace which is not costly. Everything depends on the first step. It has a unique quality of its own. The first step of obedience makes Peter leave his nets, and later get out of the ship; it calls upon the young man to leave his riches. Only this new existence, created through obedience, can make faith possible.

This first step must be regarded to start with as an external work, which effects the change from one existence to another. It is a step within everybody's capacity, for it lies within the limits of human freedom. It is an act within the sphere of the natural law (*justitia civilis*) and in that sphere man is free. Although Peter cannot achieve his own conversion, he can leave his nets. In the gospels the very first step a man must take is an act which radically affects his whole existence. The Roman Catholic Church demanded this step as an extraordinary possibility which only monks could achieve, while the rest of the faithful must content themselves with an unconditional submission to the church and its ordinances. The Lutheran confessions also significantly recognize the first step. Having dealt effectively with the danger of Pelagianism, they find it both possible and necessary to leave room for the first external act which is the essential preliminary to faith. This step there takes the form of an invitation to come to the church where the word of salvation is proclaimed. To take this step it is not necessary to surrender one's freedom. Come to church! You can do that of your own free will. You can leave your home on a Sunday morning and come to hear the sermon. If you will not, you are of your own free will excluding yourself from the place where faith is a possibility. Thus the Lutheran confessions show their awareness of a situation where faith is a possibility, and of a situation where it is not. Admittedly they tend to soft-pedal it as though they were almost ashamed of it. But there it is, and it shows that they are just as aware as the gospels of the importance of the first external step.

Once we are sure of this point, we must add at once that this step is, and can never be more than, a purely external act and a dead work of the law, which can never of itself bring a man to Christ. As an external act the new existence is no better than the old. Even at the highest estimate it can only achieve a new law of life, a new way of living which is poles apart from the new life with Christ. If a drunkard signs the pledge, or a rich man gives all his money away, they are both of them freeing themselves from their slavery to alcohol or riches, but not from their bondage to themselves. They are still moving in their own little orbit, perhaps even more than they were before. They are still subject to the commandment of works, still as submerged in the death of the old life as they were before. Of course, the work has to be done, but of itself it can never deliver them from death, disobedience and ungodliness. If we think our first step is the pre-condition for faith and grace, we are already judged by our work, and entirely excluded from grace. Hence the term 'external work' includes everything we are accustomed to call 'disposition' or 'good intention', everything which the Roman Church means when it talks of *facere quod in se est*. If we take the first step with the deliberate intention of placing ourselves in the situation where faith is possible, even this possibility of faith will be nothing but a work. The new life it opens to us is still a life within the limits of our old existence, and therefore a complete misapprehension of the true nature of the new life. We are still in unbelief.

Nevertheless the external work must be done, for we still have to find our way into the situation where faith is possible. We must take a definite step. What does this mean? It means that we can only take this step aright if we fix our eyes not on the work we do, but on the word with which Jesus calls us to do it. Peter knows he dare not climb out of the ship in his own strength — his very first step would be his undoing. And so he cries, 'Lord, bid me come to thee upon the waters,' and Jesus answers: 'Come.' Christ must first call him, for the step can only be taken at his word. This call is his grace, which calls him out of death into the new life of obedience. But when once Christ has called him, Peter has no alternative — he must leave the ship and come to him. In the end, the first step of obedience proves to be an act of faith in the word of Christ. But we should completely misunderstand the nature of grace if we were to suppose that there was no need to take the first step, because faith was already there. Against that we must boldly assert that the step of obedience must be taken before faith can be possible. Unless he obeys, a man cannot believe.

Are you worried because you find it so hard to believe? No one should be surprised at the difficulty of faith, if there is some part of his life where he is consciously resisting or disobeying the commandment of Jesus. Is there some part of your life which you are refusing to surrender at his behest, some sinful passion, maybe, or some animosity, some hope, perhaps your ambition or your reason? If so, you must not be surprised that you have not received the Holy Spirit, that prayer is difficult, or that your request for faith remains unanswered. Go rather and be reconciled with your brother, renounce the sin which holds you fast — and then you will recover your faith! If you dismiss the word of God's command, you will not receive his word of grace. How can you hope to enter into communion with him when at some point in your life you are running away from him? The man who disobeys cannot believe, for only he who obeys can believe.

The gracious call of Jesus now becomes a stern command: Do this! Give up that! Leave the ship and come to me! When a man says he cannot obey the call of Jesus because he believes, or because he does not believe, Jesus says: 'First obey, perform the external work, renounce your attachments, give up the obstacles which separate you from the will of God. Do not say you have not got faith. You will not have it so long as you persist in disobedience and refuse to take the first step. Neither must you say that you have faith, and therefore there is no need for you to take the first step. You have not got faith so long as and because you will not take the first step but become hardened in your unbelief under the guise of humble faith.' It is a malicious subterfuge to argue like this, a sure sign of lack of faith, which leads in its turn to a lack of obedience. This is the disobedience of the 'believers'; when they are asked to obey, they simply confess their unbelief and leave it at that (Mark 9.24). You are trifling with the subject. If you believe, take the first step, it leads to Jesus Christ. If you don't believe, take the first step all the same, for you are bidden to take it. No one wants to know about your faith or unbelief, your orders are to perform the act of obedience on the spot. Then you will find yourself in the situation where faith becomes possible and where faith exists in the true sense of the word.

This situation is therefore not the consequence of our obedience, but the gift of him who commands obedience. Unless we are prepared to enter into that situation, our faith will be unreal, and we shall deceive ourselves. We cannot avoid that situation, for our supreme concern is with a right faith in Jesus Christ, and our objective is, and always will be faith, and faith alone ('from faith to faith', Rom. 1.17). If anyone rushes forward and challenges this point in an excess of Protestant zeal, let him ask himself whether he is not after all allowing himself to become an advocate of cheap grace. The truth is that so long as we hold both sides of the proposition together they contain nothing inconsistent with right belief, but as soon as one is divorced from the other, it is bound to prove a stumbling-block. 'Only those who believe obey' is what we say to that part of a believer's soul which obeys, and 'only those who obey believe' is what we say to that part of the soul of the obedient which believes. If the first half of the proposition stands alone, the believer is exposed to the danger of cheap grace, which is another word for damnation. If the second half stands alone, the believer is exposed to the danger of salvation through works, which is also another word for damnation.

At this point we may conveniently throw in a few observations of a pastoral character. In dealing with souls, it is essential for the pastor to bear in mind both sides of the proposition. When people complain, for instance, that they find it hard to believe, it is a sign of deliberate or unconscious disobedience. It is all too easy to put them off by offering the remedy of cheap grace. That only leaves the disease as bad as it was before, and makes the word of grace a sort of self-administered consolation, or a self-imparted absolution. But when this happens, the poor man can no longer find any comfort in the words of priestly absolution — he has become deaf to the Word of God. And even if he absolves himself from his sins a thousand times, he has lost all capacity of faith in the true forgiveness, just because he has never really known it. Unbelief thrives on cheap grace, for it is determined to persist in disobedience. Clergy frequently come across cases like this nowadays. The outcome is usually that self-imparted absolution confirms the man in his disobedience, and makes him plead ignorance of the kindness as well as of the commandment of God. He complains that God's commandment is uncertain, and susceptible of different interpretations. At first he was aware enough of his disobedience, but with his increasing hardness of heart that awareness grows ever fainter, and in the end he becomes so enmeshed that he loses all capacity for hearing the Word, and faith is quite impossible. One can imagine him conversing thus with his pastor: 'I have lost the faith I once had.' 'You must listen to the Word as it is spoken to you in the sermon.' 'I do; but I cannot get anything out of it, it just falls on deaf ears as far as I'm concerned.' 'The trouble is, you don't really want to listen.' 'On the contrary, I do.' And here they generally break off, because the pastor is at a loss what to say next. He only remembers the first half of the proposition: 'Only those who believe obey.' But this does not help, for faith is just what this particular man finds impossible. The pastor feels himself confronted with the ultimate riddle of predestination. Gods grants faith to some and withholds it from others. So the pastor throws up the sponge and leaves the poor man to his fate. And yet this ought to be the turning-point of the interview. It is the complete turning-point.

The pastor should give up arguing with him, and stop taking his difficulties seriously. That will really be in the man's own interest, for he is only trying to hide himself behind them. It is now time to take the bull by the horns, and say: 'Only those who obey believe.' Thus the flow of the conversation is interrupted, and the pastor can continue: 'You are disobedient, you are trying to keep some part of your life under your own control. That is what is preventing you from listening to Christ and believing in his grace. You cannot hear Christ because you are wilfully disobedient. Somewhere in your heart you are refusing to listen to his call. Your difficulty is your sins.' Christ now enters the lists again and comes to grips with the devil, who until now has been hiding under the cloak of cheap grace. It is all-important that the pastor should be ready with both sides of the proposition: 'Only those who obey can believe, and only those who believe can obey.' In the name of Christ he must exhort the man to obedience, to action, to take the first step. He must say: 'Tear yourself away from all other attachments, and follow him.' For at this stage, the first step is what matters most. The strong point which the refractory sinner had occupied must be stormed, for in it Christ cannot be heard. The truant must be dragged from the hiding-place which he has built for himself. Only then can he recover the freedom to see, hear, and believe. Of course, though it is a work, the first step entails no merit in the sight of Christ — it can never be more than a dead work. Even so Peter has to get out of the ship before he can believe.

Briefly, the position is this. Our sinner has drugged himself with cheap and easy grace by accepting the proposition that only those who believe can obey. He persists in disobedience, and seeks consolation by absolving himself. This only serves to deaden his ears to the Word of God. We cannot breach the fortress so long as we merely repeat the proposition which affords him his self-defence. So we must make for the turning point without further ado, and exhort him to obedience — 'Only those who obey can believe.'

Will that lead him astray, and encourage him to trust in his own works? Far from it. He will the more easily realize that his faith is no genuine one at all. He will be rescued from his entanglement by being compelled to come to a definite decision. In this way his ears are opened once more for the call of Jesus to faith and discipleship.

*

LIFE TOGETHER

After the closure of the Preachers' Seminary at Finkenwalde, Bonhoeffer had an opportunity to bring together his reflections on Christian community in what has now become another of his classic writings, Life Together. *It was written in Göttingen in 1938 and published under the title* Gemeinsames Leben *in 1939 by Chr. Kaiser Verlag. The ET by John Doberstein was first published by SCM, London, and Harper & Row, New York, in 1954. The ET unfortunately excludes Bonhoeffer's important Foreword. This was subsequently translated by John Godsey and included in* Bonhoeffer in a World Come of Age, *edited by Peter Vorkink II (Philadelphia: Fortress, 1968). It read as follows:*

> An essential characteristic of the subject treated here is that it can be furthered only through joint effort. Because it concerns, not an affair of private groups, but rather a task given to the church, it is likewise not a matter of more or less accidental, individual solutions, but of a common responsibility of the church. The understandable reticence in the handling of this task, which has hardly begun to be grasped, must gradually give way to a readiness in the church to lend assistance. The multiplicity of new forms of community within the church necessitates the watchful cooperation of all responsible people. The following study should not be considered as more than just one contribution to the comprehensive question and possibly also as an aid toward clarification and practice.

Our selected texts are from the first chapter on the nature of Christian community, and the opening section of chapter three on 'The Day Alone'.

CHAPTER ONE: COMMUNITY

Through and in Jesus Christ

Christianity means community through Jesus Christ and in Jesus Christ. No Christian community is more or less than this. Whether it be a brief, single encounter or the daily fellowship of years, Christian community is only this. We belong to one another only through and in Jesus Christ.

What does this mean? It means, first, that a Christian needs others because of Jesus Christ. It means, second, that a Christian comes to others only through Jesus Christ. It means, third, that in Jesus Christ we have been chosen from eternity, accepted in time, and united for eternity.

First, the Christian is the man who no longer seeks his salvation, his deliverance, his justification in himself, but in Jesus Christ alone. He knows that God's Word in Jesus Christ pronounces him guilty, even when he does not feel his guilt, and God's Word in Jesus Christ pronounces him not guilty and righteous, even when he does not feel that he is righteous at all. The Christian no longer lives of himself, by his own claims and his own justification, but by God's claims and God's justification. He lives wholly by God's Word pronounced upon him, whether that Word declares him guilty or innocent.

The death and the life of the Christian is not determined by his own resources; rather he finds both only in the Word that comes to him from the outside, in God's Word to him. The Reformers expressed it this way: Our righteousness is an 'alien righteousness', a righteousness that comes from outside of us (*extra nos*). They were saying that the Christian is dependent on the Word of God spoken to him. He is pointed outward, to the Word that comes to him. The Christian lives wholly by the truth of God's Word in Jesus Christ. If somebody asks him, Where is your salvation, your righteousness? he can never point to himself. He points to the Word of God in Jesus Christ, which assures him salvation and righteousness. He is as alert as possible to this Word. Because he daily hungers and thirsts for righteousness, he daily desires the redeeming Word. And it can come only from the outside. In himself he is destitute and dead. Help must come from the outside, and it has come and comes daily and anew in the Word of Jesus Christ, bringing redemption, righteousness, innocence, and blessedness.

But God has put this Word into the mouth of men in order that it may be communicated to other men. When one person is struck by the Word, he speaks it to others. God has willed that we should seek and find his living Word in the witness of a brother, in the mouth of man. Therefore, the Christian needs another Christian who speaks God's Word to him. He needs him again and again when he becomes uncertain and discouraged, for by himself he cannot help himself without belying the truth. He needs his brother man as a bearer and proclaimer of the divine word of salvation. He needs his brother solely because of Jesus Christ. The Christ in his own heart is weaker than the Christ in the word of his brother; his own heart is uncertain, his brother's is sure.

And that also clarifies the goal of all Christian community: they meet one another as bringers of the message of salvation. As such, God permits them to meet together and gives them community. Their fellowship is founded solely upon Jesus Christ and this 'alien righteousness'.

179

All we can say, therefore, is: the community of Christians springs solely from the biblical and Reformation message of the justification of man through grace alone; this alone is the basis of the longing of Christians for one another.

Second, a Christian comes to others only through Jesus Christ. Among men there is strife. 'He is our peace', says Paul of Jesus Christ (Eph. 2.14). Without Christ there is discord between God and man and between man and man. Christ became the Mediator and made peace with God and among men. Without Christ we should not know God, we could not call upon him, nor come to him. But without Christ we also would not know our brother, nor could we come to him. The way is blocked by our own ego. Christ opened up the way to God and to our brother. Now Christians can live with one another in peace; they can love and serve one another; they can become one. But they can continue to do so only by way of Jesus Christ. Only in Jesus Christ are we one, only through him are we bound together. To eternity he remains the one Mediator.

Third, when God's Son took on flesh, he truly and bodily took on, out of pure grace, our being, our nature, ourselves. This was the eternal counsel of the triune God. Now we are in him. Where he is, there we are too, in the incarnation, on the Cross, and in his resurrection. We belong to him because we are in him. That is why the Scriptures call us the Body of Christ. But if, before we could know and wish it, we have been chosen and accepted with the whole Church in Jesus Christ, then we also belong to him in eternity *with* one another. We who live here in fellowship with him will one day be with him in eternal fellowship. He who looks upon his brother should know that he will be eternally united with him in Jesus Christ. Christian community means community through and in Jesus Christ. On this presupposition rests everything that the Scriptures provide in the way of directions and precepts for the communal life of Christians.

'But as touching brotherly love ye need not that I write unto you: for ye yourselves are taught of God to love one another. . . . but we beseech you, brethren, that ye increase more and more' (I Thess. 4.9, 10). God himself has undertaken to teach brotherly love; all that men can add to it is to remember this divine instruction and the admonition to excel in it more and more. When God was merciful, when He revealed Jesus Christ to us as our Brother, when He won our hearts by his love, this was the beginning of our instruction in divine love. When God was merciful to us, we learned to be merciful with our brethren. When we received forgiveness instead of judgment, we, too, were made ready to forgive our brethren. What God did to us, we then owed to others. The more we received, the more we were able to give; and the more meagre our brotherly love, the less were we living by God's mercy and love. Thus God himself taught us to meet one another as God has met us in Christ. 'Wherefore receive ye one another, as Christ also received us to the glory of God' (Rom 15.7).

In this wise does one, whom God has placed in common life with other Christians, learn what it means to have brothers. 'Brethren in the Lord', Paul calls his congregation (Phil. 1.14). One is a brother to another only through Jesus Christ. I am a brother to another person through what Jesus Christ did for me and to me; the other person has become a brother to me through what Jesus Christ did for him. This fact that we are brethren only through Jesus Christ is of immeasurable significance. Not only the other person who is earnest and devout, who comes to me seeking brotherhood, must I deal with in fellowship. My brother is rather that other person who has been redeemed by Christ, delivered from his sin, and called to faith and eternal life. Not what a man is in himself as a Christian, his spirituality and piety, constitutes the basis of our community. What determines our brotherhood is what that man is by reason of Christ. Our community with one another consists solely in what Christ has done to both of us. This is true not merely at the beginning, as though in the course of time something else were to be added to our community; it remains so for all the future and to all eternity. I have community with others and I shall continue to have it only through Jesus Christ. The more genuine and the deeper our community becomes, the more will everything else between us recede, the more clearly and purely will Jesus Christ and his work become the one and only thing that is vital between us. We have one another only through Christ, but through Christ we do have one another, wholly, and for all eternity.

That dismisses once and for all every clamorous desire for something more. One who wants more than what Christ has established does not want Christian brotherhood. He is looking for some extraordinary social experience which he has not found elsewhere; he is bringing muddled and impure desires into Christian brotherhood. Just at this point Christian brotherhood is threatened most often at the very start by the greatest danger of all, the danger of being poisoned at its root, the danger of confusing Christian brotherhood with some wishful idea of religious fellowship, of confounding the natural desire of the devout heart for community with the spiritual reality of Christian brotherhood. In Christian brotherhood everything depends upon its being clear right from the beginning, *first, that Christian brotherhood is not an ideal, but a divine reality. Second, that Christian brotherhood is a spiritual and not a psychic reality.*

Not an Ideal but a Divine Reality

Innumerable times a whole Christian community has broken down because it had sprung from a wish dream. The serious Christian, set down for the first time in a Christian community, is likely to bring with him a very definite idea of what Christian life together should be and to try to realize it. But God's grace speedily shatters such dreams. Just as surely as God desires to lead us to a knowledge of genuine Christian fellowship, so surely must we be overwhelmed by a great disillusionment with others, with Christians in general, and, if we are fortunate, with ourselves.

By sheer grace, God will not permit us to live even for a brief period in a dream world. He does not abandon us to those rapturous experiences and lofty moods that come over us like a dream. God is not a God of the emotions but the God of truth. Only that fellowship which faces such disillusionment, with all its unhappy and ugly aspects, begins to be what it should be in God's sight, begins to grasp in faith the promise that is given to it. The sooner this shock of disillusionment comes to an individual and to a community the better for both. A community which cannot bear and cannot survive such a crisis, which insists upon keeping its illusion when it should be shattered, permanently loses in that moment the promise of Christian community. Sooner or later it will collapse. Every human wish dream that is injected into the Christian community is a hindrance to genuine community and must be banished if genuine community is to survive. He who loves his dream of a community more than the Christian community itself becomes a destroyer of the latter, even though his personal intentions may be ever so honest and earnest and sacrificial.

God hates visionary dreaming; it makes the dreamer proud and pretentious. The man who fashions a visionary ideal of community demands that it be realized by God, by others, and by himself. He enters the community of Christians with his demands, sets up his own law, and judges the brethren and God himself accordingly. He stands adamant, a living reproach to all others in the circle of brethren. He acts as if he is the creator of the Christian community, as if his dream binds men together. When things do not go his way, he calls the effort a failure. When his ideal picture is destroyed, he sees the community going to smash. So he becomes, first an accuser of his brethren, then an accuser of God, and finally the despairing accuser of himself.

Because God has already laid the only foundation of our fellowship, because God has bound us together in one body with other Christians in Jesus Christ, long before we entered into common life with them, we enter into that common life not as demanders but as thankful recipients. We thank God for what He has done for us. We thank God for giving us brethren who live by his call, by his forgiveness, and his promise. We do not complain of what God does not give us; we rather thank God for what He does give us daily. And is not what has been given us enough: brothers, who will go on living with us through sin and need under the blessing of His grace? Is the divine gift of Christian fellowship anything less than this, any day, even the most difficult and distressing day? Even when sin and misunderstanding burden the communal life, is not the sinning brother still a brother, with whom I, too, stand under the Word of Christ? Will not his sin be a constant occasion for me to give thanks that both of us may live in the forgiving love of God in Jesus Christ? Thus the very hour of disillusionment with my brother becomes incomparably salutary, because it so thoroughly teaches me that neither of us can ever live by our own words and deeds, but only by that one Word and Deed which really binds us together — the forgiveness of sins in Jesus Christ. When the morning mists of dreams vanish, then dawns the bright day of Christian fellowship.

In the Christian community thankfulness is just what it is anywhere else in the Christian life. Only he who gives thanks for little things receives the big things. We prevent God from giving us the great spiritual gifts He has in store for us, because we do not give thanks for daily gifts. We think we dare not be satisfied with the small measure of spiritual knowledge, experience, and love that has been given to us, and that we must constantly be looking forward eagerly for the highest good. Then we deplore the fact that we lack the deep certainty, the strong faith, and the rich experience that God has given to others, and we consider this lament to be pious. We pray for the big things and forget to give thanks for the ordinary, small (and yet really not small) gifts. How can God entrust great things to one who will not thankfully receive from him the little things? If we do not give thanks daily for the Christian fellowship in which we have been placed, even where there is no great experience, no discoverable riches, but much weakness, small faith, and difficulty; if on the contrary, we only keep complaining to God that everything is so paltry and petty, so far from what we expected, then we hinder God from letting our fellowship grow according to the measure and riches which are there for us all in Jesus Christ.

This applies in a special way to the complaints often heard from pastors and zealous members about their congregations. A pastor should not complain about his congregation, certainly never to other people, but also not to God. A congregation has not been entrusted to him in order that he should become its accuser before God and men. When a person becomes alienated from a Christian community in which he has been placed and begins to raise complaints about it, he had better examine himself first to see whether the trouble is not due to his wish dream that should be shattered by God; and if this be the case, let him thank God for leading him into this predicament. But if not, let him nevertheless guard against ever becoming an accuser of the congregation before God. Let him rather accuse himself for his unbelief. Let him pray God for an understanding of his own failure and his particular sin, and pray that he may not wrong his brethren. Let him, in the consciousness of his own guilt, make intercession for his brethren. Let him do what he is committed to do, and thank God.

Christian community is like the Christian's sanctification. It is a gift of God which we cannot claim. Only God knows the real state of our fellowship, of our sanctification. What may appear weak and trifling to us may be great and glorious to God. Just as the Christian should not be constantly feeling his spiritual pulse, so, too, the Christian community has not been given to us by God for us to be constantly taking its temperature. The more thankfully we daily receive what is given to us, the more surely and steadily will fellowship increase and grow from day to day as God pleases.

Christian brotherhood is not an ideal which we must realize; it is rather a reality created by God in Christ in which we may participate. The more clearly we learn to recognize that the ground and strength and promise of all our fellowship is in Jesus Christ alone, the more serenely shall we think of our fellowship and pray and hope for it. (*LT: 21-30*)

*

CHAPTER THREE: THE DAY ALONE

Many people seek fellowship because they are afraid to be alone. Because they cannot stand loneliness, they are driven to seek the company of other people. There are Christians, too, who cannot endure being alone, who have had some bad experiences with themselves, who hope they will gain some help in association with others. They are generally disappointed. Then they blame the fellowship for what is really their own fault. The Christian community is not a spiritual sanatorium. The person who comes into a fellowship because he is running away from himself is misusing it for the sake of diversion, no matter how spiritual this diversion may appear. He is really not seeking community at all, but only distraction which will allow him to forget his loneliness for a brief time, the very alienation that creates the deadly isolation of man. The disintegration of communication and all genuine experience, and finally resignation and spiritual death are the result of such attempts to find a cure.

Solitude and Silence

Let him who cannot be alone beware of community. He will only do harm to himself and to the community. Alone you stood before God when he called you; alone you had to answer that call; alone you had to struggle and pray; and alone you will die and give an account to God. You cannot escape from yourself; for God has singled you out. If you refuse to be alone you are rejecting Christ's call to you, and you can have no part in the community of those who are called. 'The challenge of death comes to us all, and no one can die for another. Everyone must fight his own battle with death by himself, alone. . . . I will not be with you then, nor you with me' (Luther).

But the reverse is also true: *Let him who is not in community beware of being alone.* Into the community you were called, the call was not meant for you alone; in the community of the called you bear your cross, you struggle, you pray. You are not alone, even in death, and on the Last Day you will be only one member of the great congregation of Jesus Christ. If you scorn the fellowship of the brethren, you reject the call of Jesus Christ, and thus your solitude can only be hurtful to you. 'If I die, then I am not alone in death; if I suffer they [the fellowship] suffer with me' (Luther).

We recognize, then, that only as we are within the fellowship can we be alone, and only he that is alone can live in the fellowship. Only in the fellowship do we learn to be rightly alone and only in aloneness do we learn to live rightly in the fellowship. It is not as though the one preceded the other; both begin at the same time, namely, with the call of Jesus Christ.

Each by itself has profound pitfalls and perils. One who wants fellowship without solitude plunges into the void of words and feelings, and one who seeks solitude without fellowship perishes in the abyss of vanity, self-infatuation, and despair.

Let him who cannot be alone beware of community. Let him who is not in community beware of being alone.

Along with the day of the Christian family fellowship together there goes the lonely day of the individual. This is as it should be. The day together will be unfruitful without the day alone, both for the fellowship and for the individual.

The mark of solitude is silence, as speech is the mark of community. Silence and speech have the same inner correspondence and difference as do solitude and community. One does not exist without the other. Right speech comes out of silence, and right silence comes out of speech.

Silence does not mean dumbness, as speech does not mean chatter. Dumbness does not create solitude and chatter does not create fellowship. 'Silence is the excess, the inebriation, the victim of speech. But dumbness is unholy, like a thing only maimed, not cleanly sacrificed. . . . Zacharias was speechless, instead of being silent. Had he accepted the revelation, he may perhaps have come out of the temple not dumb but silent' (Ernest Hello). The speech, the Word which establishes and binds together the fellowship, is accompanied by silence. 'There is a time to keep silence, and a time to speak' (Eccles. 3.7). As there are definite hours in the Christian's day for the Word, particularly the time of common worship and prayer, so the day also needs definite times of silence, silence under the Word and silence that comes out of the Word. These will be especially the times before and after hearing the Word. The Word comes not to the chatterer but to him who holds his tongue. The stillness of the temple is the sign of the holy presence of God in his Word.

There is an indifferent, or even negative, attitude toward silence which sees in it a disparagement of God's revelation in the Word. This is the view which misinterprets silence as a ceremonial gesture, as a mystical desire to get beyond the Word. This is to miss the essential relationship of silence to the Word. Silence is the simple stillness of the individual under the Word of God. We are silent before hearing the

Word because our thoughts are already directed to the Word, as a child is quiet when he enters his father's room. We are silent after hearing the Word because the Word is still speaking and dwelling within us. We are silent at the beginning of the day because God should have the first word, and we are silent before going to sleep because the last word also belongs to God. We keep silence solely for the sake of the Word, and therefore not in order to show disregard for the Word but rather to honour and receive it.

Silence is nothing else but waiting for God's Word and coming from God's Word with a blessing. But everybody knows that this is something that needs to be practiced and learned, in these days when talkativeness prevails. Real silence, real stillness, really holding one's tongue comes only as the sober consequence of spiritual stillness.

But this stillness before the Word will exert its influence upon the whole day. If we have learned to be silent before the Word, we shall also learn to manage our silence and our speech during the day. There is such a thing as forbidden, self-indulgent silence, a proud, offensive silence. And this means that it can never be merely silence as such. The silence of the Christian is listening silence, humble stillness, that may be interrupted at any time for the sake of humility. It is silence in conjunction with the Word. This is what Thomas à Kempis meant when he said: 'None speaketh surely but he that would gladly keep silence if he might.' There is a wonderful power of clarification, purification, and concentration upon the essential thing in being quiet. This is true as a purely secular fact. But silence before the Word leads to right hearing and thus also to right speaking of the Word of God at the right time. Much that is unnecessary remains unsaid. But the essential and the helpful thing can be said in a few words.

Where a family lives close together in a constricted space and the individual does not have the quietness he needs, regular times of quiet are absolutely necessary. After a time of quiet we meet others in a different and a fresh way. Many a household fellowship will be able to provide for the individual's need to be alone, and thus preserve the fellowship itself from injury, only by adopting a regular order.

We shall not discuss here all the wonderful benefits that can accrue to the Christian in solitude and silence. It is all too easy to go astray at this point. We could probably cite many a bad experience that has come from silence. Silence can be a dreadful ordeal with all its desolation and terrors. It can also be a false paradise of self-deception; the latter is no better than the former. Be that as it may, let none expect from silence anything but a direct encounter with the Word of God, for the sake of which he has entered into silence. But this encounter will be given to him. The Christian will not lay down any conditions as to what he expects or hopes to get from this encounter. If he will simply accept it, his silence will be richly rewarded.

There are three purposes for which the Christian needs a definite time when he can be alone during the day: Scripture meditation, prayer, and intercession. All three should have their place in the daily period of meditation. The word 'meditation' should not frighten us. It is an ancient concept of the church and of the Reformation that we are beginning to rediscover. *(LT: 76-81)*

*

THE PRESENTATION* OF NEW TESTAMENT TEXTS

As already intimated, Bonhoeffer engaged in intensive biblical exegetical studies at Finkenwalde, and as part of his responsibility was the training of preachers, he spent much of his time helping his students learn the art of biblical interpretation and homiletics. The following extract is taken from the lecture on 'The Presentation of New Testament Texts', which Bonhoeffer originally gave to pastors of the Confessing Church in Saxony in August 1935. It sets out the approach to the subject which he used throughout the Finkenwalde period. The original is published in Gesammelte Schriften, *I, 303-324, and the full ET in* No Rusty Swords, *302-312.*

1. The Right and the Wrong Meaning of Presentation

In principle, it is possible to interpret the question of the presentation of the New Testament message in two ways. The phrase means either that the biblical message must justify itself to the present age and in that way must show itself capable of being made present, or that the present age must justify itself before the biblical message and in that way the message must become present. Where the question of presentation is put with that uncanny urgency that we know so well, indeed is the central question of theology, it is always bound to serve the first purpose. The New Testament is meant to justify itself to the present age.

In this form, the question became acute for the first time in the age of the emancipation of the autonomous reason, i.e. in rationalism, and it

---

* *Vergegenwärtigung* meaning making present or relevant; i.e. hermeneutics.

has influenced theology right up to the German Christian theology. So far as rationalism was nothing but the emergence of the hitherto latent claim of man to shape his own life from the resources of the world at his disposal, the question was one that implied the human claim to autonomy. I.e., the autonomous man who wants to profess Christianity at the same time demands the justification of the Christian message before the forum of his autonomy. If this succeeds, he calls himself a *Christian*; if it does not, he calls himself a *pagan*. It does not make the slightest difference whether the forum before which the biblical message has to justify itself is called, as in the eighteenth century, reason, as in the nineteenth century, culture, or as in the twentieth century, the people, viz. the year 1933 and all that that includes; *the question is exactly the same*: 'Can Christianity make itself present to us, just as we are!' There is exactly the same urgent need of all those who would lay claim to the name of Christian on any grounds, be they those of reason, of culture, or of politics, to justify Christianity in the present age; there is *exactly the same presupposition*, namely that the Archimedean point, the firm starting point which stands beyond all doubt, has already been found (be it in reason, culture, or the idea of the people) and the movable, *questionable*, uncertain element is the Christian message; and there is *exactly the same method*, namely to go about the presentation in such a way that the biblical message is passed through the sieve of man's own knowledge — what will not go through is scorned and tossed away. The message is trimmed and cropped until it fits the frame which has been decided, and the result is that the eagle (with his clipped wings) can no longer rise and fly away to his true element but can be pointed out as a special showpiece among the other household animals. It is like a farmer who needs a horse for his fields; he leaves the fiery stallion on one side and buys the tame, broken-in horse. This is just the way men have tamed a usable Christianity for themselves, and it is only a matter of time and honest thought before they lose all interest in their creation and get rid of it. *This presentation* of the Christian message leads directly to paganism. It therefore follows that the only difference between the German Christians and the so-called neo-pagans is one of *honesty*. Secondly, however, there also follows the kind of cry, doubtless in part uttered with great passion and subjective earnestness, for the presentation of the Christian message, which went up at the beginning of the German Christian movement. This surely should not have been taken seriously either by the church or by the theologians; it was at best the terror-stricken shout of those who saw the gulf between Christianity and the world opening up beneath them, who, conscious of their complete conformity to the world, recognized that it was all up with Christianity for themselves, but were not strong enough to say a clear 'Yes' and an equally clear 'No', and cravenly pulled down Christianity with themselves in their fall into the world. The clearest indication of this is the fact that no one here found the courage to ask afresh after the *content* of the Christian message; they sought only its *presentation*, precisely — unlike Liberal theology, e.g. Naumann! — *in order to evade the content*. But where the question of presentation becomes the *theme of theology*, we can be certain that the cause has already been betrayed and sold out. We will have to be very much on our guard against letting the struggle get us entangled in false questions and false themes. The danger is always there. I need only recall theological writing of the last two years — and from our side too! (Althaus' *German Hour of the Church*, Heim, even Schlatter, *New German Characteristics in the Church*) — to make my point. This question of *presentation* all too easily acquires a false emphasis and displaces the question of *content*. What is the sense in talking about presentation when we cannot even feel completely sure about what we are presenting?

Anyone who is thirsty will drink water from any utensil, even if it is somewhat inconvenient. And it is better to take some trouble in getting the water pure than to drink polluted water out of a glass. Anyone who is thirsty has always found living water in the Bible itself or in a sermon the content of which is based on the Bible, even if it were a little out-of-date — and it is an acknowledgment of a dangerous decadence of faith if the question of the relevance of the message, as a methodological question, becomes too loud. Anyone really concerned with the salvation of his soul has found that Luther's German version of Holy Scripture still best fulfils the demand for the presentation of the Gospel in a German way. Here is Christianity which is both present and German.

That should be enough of the negative side of the definition for the moment; now the positive significance of this question of presentation can be put in the right light. The intention should be not to justify Christianity in this present age, but *to justify the present age before the Christian message*. Presentation then means that the present age is brought before the forum of the Christian message, in other words that the question is of the *content*, the 'value' (!) of the Christian message instead of being of the character of the present age, as in the false concept of presentation. True presentation lies in this question of the content. It is felt of the *content itself* that where it is really expressed it is in itself completely and utterly relevant; it therefore needs no other special act of presentation, because the presentation is achieved in the content itself. This, however, is only so because *this* content is the concern of the New Testament, because the content here is Christ and his word. Where Christ is spoken of in the word of the New Testament, presentation is achieved. *The present* is not where the present age announces its claim before Christ, but where the present age stands before the claims of Christ, for the concept of the present is determined not by a temporal definition but by the Word of Christ as the Word of God. The present is not a feeling of time, an interpretation of time, an atmosphere of time, but the Holy Spirit, and the Holy Spirit alone. The present is and begins where God himself is in his Word. The Holy Spirit is the subject of the present, not we ourselves, so the Holy Spirit is also the subject of the presentation. *The most concrete element of the Christian message* and of textual exposition is not a human act of presentation but is always God himself, it is the Holy Spirit. Because the 'content' of the New Testament is this, that Christ speaks to us through his Holy Spirit; and because this does not happen outside or alongside, but solely and exclusively *through the word* of Scripture, keeping to the content, i.e. the adherence of preaching to the Scriptures, is itself presentation — 'keeping to the content' both as a method (of which we shall soon be speaking) and as obedience and trust towards the fact of the Holy Spirit. For the matter of this content is the Holy Spirit himself, and he is the presence of both God and Christ.

Here too the *concept of the present* first comes into its own linguistically. The fact that something is 'present towards' us means that *the present is defined from without* and not from within, that it is incapable of definition by us, and is defined by what comes to us from outside, by what comes to us, by the future. The present is primarily defined not by the past, but by the *future*, and this future is Christ, it is the Holy Spirit. 'Presentation' therefore means attention to this *future*, to this that is *outside* — and it is a most fatal confusion of present and past to think that the present can be defined as that which *rests upon itself* and *carries its criterion within itself.* The criterion of the true present lies outside itself, it lies in the future, it lies in Scripture and in the word of Christ witnessed in it. Thus the *content* will consist in something outside, something 'over against', something 'future' being heard as present — the strange Gospel, not the familiar one, will be the present Gospel. A scandalous 'point of contact'!

2. Presentation as 'Method'

If we have learnt that correct presentation lies in our coming to the content and expressing that content in words, as far as method is concerned it will mean that preaching which is relevant to the present age must be essentially *exegesis*, exegesis of the Word that alone has power to make itself present, exegesis of Scripture. The act of presentation, insofar as it can be achieved by us through any method at all, is strict and exclusive reference to the word of Scripture. Thus the movement is not from the word of Scripture to the present; it goes from the present to the word of Scripture and remains there. It is thus apparently away from the present, but it is away from the false present in order to come to the true present. If this seems incomprehensible to anyone, it is because he has not yet grasped the basic supposition that there is only 'present' where Christ speaks with the Holy Spirit. This backward movement towards Scripture closely corresponds to the backward movement of Christian faith and Christian hope, namely towards the cross of Christ; and it is the historicity of the revelation of God which is expressed.

'Exegesis' is no simple concept; it must be clearly distinguished from untheological methods of presentation.

The evident presupposition of any presentation is, for the untheological understanding, that there is something in the past which is *not only past*, but projects beyond the past. Indeed, this thing which projects beyond the past is essentially, in itself, *not past* and not temporal but supra-temporal. It is therefore said that in history there is something *eternal*, in the contingent there is something necessary, in the individual instance there is general validity. This validity, this eternal can be a doctrine, it can be an ethical norm, it can be a general human feeling, it can be a myth. Presentation means *discovering* this eternal, this validity, this significance, which holds today as much as it did then. In our case it means *discovering* the eternal doctrine, or the general ethical norm, or the myth, contained in Holy Scripture and the application of this general element to the present situation of each person today.

How is such a discovery of the eternal in the temporal possible? Only by the interpreter himself having control over the eternal standard, which he discovers again in Scripture. Because like can only be recognized by like, the interpreter of Holy Scripture can on the basis of the general ideas and standards which he has within him recognize these again in Scripture and discover them. The *principle of presentation* thus lies in me; it lies in the interpreter. In the strictly logical sense I am the *subject of the presentation* and only that can be made relevant which is already to hand in me as a principle of presentation. Here Scriptural exegesis means the referring of Scripture to the eternal truths which I already know — be it an intellectual truth, an ethical principle, a general human insight, or a myth. In other words, the truth is already established before I begin to expound Scripture.

We recognize once again in this method of presentation the false understanding of presentation we discussed at the beginning. Scripture is brought before the forum of the present age and must justify itself before this forum. It must yield recognitions, norms, general truths which are given in the present. Anything which opposes this process is left in the past as being temporal; it cannot be made present, it is not eternal, divine.

Thus the interpreter makes the claim to be able to distinguish the Word of God and the word of man in Holy Scripture. He himself knows where is the Word of God and where is the word of man. So, for example, the theology of Paul is the word of man, the so-called religion of Jesus is divine; the doctrines of sin and justification are temporal and past, the struggle for the good and the pure is eternal; or, the ethical teaching of Jesus is eternal, the miracle stories are a product of their time; or, Jesus the fighter and his death are an expression of the eternal fight of light against darkness, the suffering, defenceless Jesus does not concern us; or, the doctrine of grace is eternal, the commandments of the Sermon on the Mount are no longer valid for us.

With this, the key to the exposition of Scripture is put into our hand. Just as in a secular writing we can distinguish the genuine words of the author from spurious additions, so now in the Bible we can distinguish the Word of God from the word of man and can separate the one from the other. We have the criterion for the Word of God, it is in our reason, in our conscience, or in our experience, fashioned by our nation or in any other way. The criterion for the Word of God lies outside it, in us — *the norm of presentation lies in us, the Bible is the material in which this norm finds its application.*

This sentence must now be turned round for *our* concept of exegesis and presentation to become clear: the norm for the Word of God in Scripture is the Word of God itself, and what we possess, reason, conscience, experience, are the materials to which this norm seeks to be applied. We too may say that the Word of God and the word of man are joined in Holy Scripture; but they are joined in such a way that God himself says where his Word is, and he says it through the *word of man.* The word of man does not cease to be a temporal, past word by becoming the Word of God; it is the Word of God precisely as such a historical temporal word. The distinction between the eternal and the temporal, the contingent and the necessary, in the Bible, is fundamentally false. The temporal word of Scripture itself — say perhaps Jesus' confession that he does not know the hour of his coming — or the question 'Why callest thou me good?', are precisely the Word of God in that they are words completely set in time. God alone says where his Word is, and that again means that God alone presents his Word, that the Holy Ghost is the principle of interpretation. This method of exegesis does not approach Scripture as a book in which general truths, general ethical norms, or myths can be discovered; holy Scripture is rather as a whole *the witness* of God in Christ, and it will be concerned to bring out the witnessing character of the Word in every passage. There are in principle no special places, unless we understand 'special' to refer to degree of clarity. *Presentation is achieved not by the choice of certain texts but by the demonstration of the whole of Holy Scripture as the testimony of the Word of God.* The only *method* of presentation is therefore the exegesis of the content of the text as the witness of Christ, and such exegesis has the promise of the presence of Christ.

Two questions: 1 As a preacher, must I not have a concrete application following the exegesis, must I not say the Word authoritatively to the congregation as concretely as possible, and must not the accent of eternity itself lie on this concrete thing that I say? Does not this form of presentation go substantially beyond exegesis? The text is not the general starting point, to which I would have to give a concete application for the congregation and on which I would have to let the light of eternity fall. The most concrete part of preaching is not *the application I give*, but the Holy Spirit himself, who speaks through the text of the Bible. Even the clearest application, the most distinct appeal to the congregation, is irrelevant so long as the Holy Spirit himself does not create the *concretissimum*, the present. As far as talking of the accent of eternity is concerned, it must be said that the accent of eternity has already fallen, on Christ and on his cross, and here it remains, and in any sermon the accent of eternity once again falls only on Christ and on his cross, and nowhere else. Where an accent of eternity is sought outside Christ, there men fall into sectarianism.

2 Does not the concrete situation of the congregation demand a form of presentation that goes beyond exegesis? The so-called special concrete situation of the congregation is for any congregation anywhere understandable as the general position of man before God, of man in his pride, in his unbelief, in his unbrotherliness, in his questioning. The answer is Christ, as he comes through his Word, always as one who

judges, commands and forgives. The Word for the concrete situation is not this or that concrete thing which I have to say about the so-called concrete situation, but Christ himself as the Lord, the Judge and the Saviour. The fact that I sit under the pulpit as man or woman, National Socialist or reactionary or Jew, coming from this or that field of experience, has in itself no special right or claim on the Word; my true concrete situation, which is revealed and set right for me by the sermon, is that as man or National Socialist I am an an unbeliever become sinner before God, asking for God. Where Christ himself comes to testify in the exegesis of the text, the man who beforehand took himself seriously as a man or a National Socialist or a Jew now takes himself seriously only as one who has sinned and has called and has been forgiven. Precisely because the so-called concrete situation of the congregation is *not taken with the utmost seriousness*, there is room to see the true situation of man before God. God does not ask us about our being men or women or National Socialists, he asks us about our faith in him and his forgiving love and our obedience towards his Word which is witnessed in the Bible.

It is quite strange that there is still a widespread view that there must be something more than textual exegesis, something going beyond it, more concrete. — What can be more concrete today than the exegesis of the text of certain chapters of the Apocalypse or the Prophets or the Sermon on the Mount or the parable of the Good Samaritan? Is not exegesis of the text, insofar as it really takes this text as a testimony of the living Christ, everything here? Is not this precisely the surprising thing in our time, that today we can take almost any text and only need to expound it clearly and sharply and factually and it becomes present to us? (The view has gradually developed that a sermon of the Confessing Church should always contain concrete polemic against Rosenberg, etc., and that this is the form of presentation — to say nothing against that; but a good sermon does not need it at all, not today! — The polemic lies in the exegesis of the text itself!)

*

PROTESTANTISM WITHOUT REFORMATION

Bonhoeffer's essay on 'Protestantism without Reformation' was written on his return from his second visit to the United States in 1939. It makes interesting comparison with the Report to his Church in Berlin which he submitted after his first visit as a student at Union Theological Seminary (see

No Rusty Swords, *82-87*). *'Protestantism without Reformation', originally published in* Gesammelte Schriften *I, 323-354, is published in English in* No Rusty Swords, *88-113.*

Time and again, two obstacles stand in the way of a correct assessment of a strange church and therefore of a genuine encounter with it.

First, the observer is inclined to attribute the strangeness of another church to the peculiarities of its geographical, national or social setting, in other words to have the desire to make it historically, politically, or sociologically comprehensible. Hence the great revivalist movements, the call for sanctification, Puritanism, are 'typically Anglo-Saxon', the 'social gospel' is 'typically American', while the Reformation, on the other hand, is 'typically continental', viz. German. Such an approach is as customary as it is in the last resort tedious and false. It has become customary since there has been more interest in the historical manifest-ations of Christianity than in its truth; it is tedious because it leads to a dreary and facile schematizing. It is false because from the outset it destroys the mutually compelling character of the churches in their preaching and in their doctrine; for when all is said and done, what con-cern of the Christian in Germany is something typically American, and what concern of the Christian in America is a typically continental Reformation? At the best one can take a certain aesthetic delight in the diversity of the outward forms of Christianity; one can even recognize in the other church a welcome complement of the nature of one's own; but this never leads to a serious encounter, to a binding discussion. As long as we are interested in American peculiarities, we are moving in the realm of uncommitted observation. What God is doing to and with his church, to and in America, how he is showing himself to her, and whether and in what way we recognize him again in that church, is quite another question. At this point the question of God's word, God's will and God's action is set between us. Both the Americans and ourselves are concerned with the same word, the same commandment, the same promise, the same ministry and the same community of Jesus Christ. And only this question does justice to the situation. The Reformation is not in fact to be understood as a typically German event; this just does not work out. And the same is true of the forms and histories of other churches. They simply cannot be explained from racial peculiarities. Something still remains, and that is what is at stake.

Secondly, the observer of a strange church is too easily content with the contemporary picture of the church's situation. He forgets that it is also necessary to pay serious attention to the history of this other church. God speaks to his church in different ways at different times. To the church in Germany he spoke differently, i.e. more urgently, more distinctly, more openly than at any later time, in the Reformation. Just as no one can understand the German church without the Reformation, so too American Christianity remains a closed book to those who know nothing of the beginnings of the Congregationalists in New England, of the Baptists in Rhode Island and of the 'Great Awakening' led by Jonathan Edwards. American Christianity is precisely what happened then, and it seems as unlike present American Christianity as our church at the turn of the century seemed unlike the church of the Reformation.

What is God doing to and with his church in America? What is he doing through her to us and through us to her? The following observations are intended as a contribution towards the answering of this question.

1. The unity of the church and the denominations

It has been granted to the Americans less than any other nation of the earth to realize on earth the visible unity of the church of God. It has been granted to the Americans more than any other nation of the earth to have before their eyes the multiplicity of Christian insights and communities. Statistics show over two hundred Christian denominations; about fifty of these have more than fifty thousand members. In Minneapolis, four Lutheran churches of different observances are said to stand in a single street. American Christianity has no central organization, no common creed, no common cultus, no common church history and no common ethical, social or political principles. Not only from North to South (the slave question), but also the movement from East to West (the 'frontier') means changes and divisions in the denominations. In addition there is the colour bar between blacks and whites, which is reproduced in the churches; finally, social distinctions too have had a determining influence on the form of the denomination. The 'Federal Council of Churches of Christ in America', an alliance for common public action in which twenty-nine denominations take part, is not a representation of *the* church of Jesus Christ in America, but a representation of churches.

Even the concept of 'church' is frequently suspect. The characteristic concept is that of the denomination. Many American Christians associate the church too much with clericalism, autocracy, confessional arrogance, intolerance and heresy-hunting, and excessive currying of worldly power and political favour. True, the Episcopalians, the Lutherans and the Presbyterians are consciously churches, even if in the eyes of the others they are only denominations along with the rest. The other communities understand themselves more as denominations than as churches.

The concept of the denomination is not fully clear. It is not a theological concept. It rather gives some indication of historical, political and social position. The denomination is a free association of Christians on the basis of definite common experiences which, while being Christian, are also historical, political and social. From the start it concedes the possibility of other such associations. There is a certain modesty in the way in which the denomination regards itself, in that it does not dare to claim for itself the name of the church of Jesus Christ because this name is too great, too dangerous. The church is something beyond the denominations. The concept of the invisible church cannot be far away. The denominations are the visible constituent members of the invisible church.

Deeper sources of denominational self-understanding may be demonstrated in church history. First, it is the message of the sole dominion of God on earth which has been normative in the beginnings of the formation of the Presbyterian and Congregational denominations in England. All human claims must yield before the sovereign dominion of God. So in America the denomination is the negative aspect of the dawn of the dominion of God. Secondly, responsibility must be laid on the concept of tolerance among the Congregationalist-Baptist enthusiasts, particularly as it was developed by Roger Williams in Maryland. Here the dominion of God becomes synonymous with the freedom of the individual to follow by himself the inner voice and the inner light. In this way the path is made open to the formation of a denomination without a creed. Thirdly, the denomination's understanding of itself involves a definite relationship to the state. The American denomination is not a state church, but on the other hand it is not to be compared with the English Free Church, which stands in conscious contrast to the state church. The American denomination is state-free, and knows itself despite all internal limitations *vis-à-vis* the state to be a part of the free church of God on earth. Nowhere does the denominational self-understanding approach more nearly the church's self-understanding than in the relationship to the state.

The creed is not the primary norm of the denomination. Most

denominations do not recognize a fixed credal formulation. True, the *Lutheran* and *Episcopalian Churches* require in their ordinands commitment to their creeds. The *Presbyterians* are simply content — remarkably enough — with commitment to the Scriptures, and the *Congregational* form of ordination is completely free, requiring only a confession of personal commitment to the Lord Christ in personal experience, in consciousness of a call to the ministry and in belief. But even where there are commitments to a creed, these are in a sense further qualified by the fact that among the majority of denominations in America there is a reciprocal recognition of the administration of the sacraments, of ministry and of ordination. This is the case with the Presbyterians, Methodists, Congregationalists, Reformed, United Lutherans, Northern Baptists and Evangelicals. Only the Episcopalians, the Missouri Lutherans and the Southern Baptists have opposed this to date. Doctrinal differences within the denominations (e.g. Baptists, Presbyterians) are frequently significantly stronger than those between different denominations. Denominations are not Confessing Churches, and even where the individual denomination raises this claim it is still held back as a denomination by the others. The relationship of the denominations to each other is today less than ever a struggle for the truth in preaching and doctrine.

From this state of affairs one might conclude that there must be in American Christianity particularly favourable preconditions for a right understanding of the unity of the churches of Jesus Christ. Where no struggle for truth divides the churches, the unity of the church should already have been won. The actual picture, however, is just the opposite. Precisely here, where the question of truth is not the criterion of church communion and church division, disintegration is greater than anywhere else. That is to say, precisely where the struggle for the right creed is not the factor which governs everything, the unity of the church is more distant than where the creed alone unites and divides the churches. What is the significance of this? To answer the question we must draw attention to a deeper distinction.

The *Churches of the Reformation* begin from the unity of the church of Christ. There can be only one church on earth. And this church alone is the true church, founded by Jesus Christ. Division of the church means apostasy from the church, treachery to the true church of Christ. The division of the church which took place at the Reformation can only be understood as a struggle for the real unity of the church. The churches of the Reformation therefore understand themselves as the one church on earth, and not as groups of individual Christians, driven by their personal conscience to split off from the one church; they are not individual embodiments of the one church. The Reformation was concerned with the one holy universal church of Jesus Christ on earth.

The *denominations of America* see themselves from the start faced with an immense multiplicity of Christian communities. None of them can dare to make for itself the claim of being the one church. It is felt to be only Christian humility that such a claim is not made in the face of this incredible picture of fragmentation. American Christianity has experienced the consequences of church division, but not the act of division itself. It is therefore no longer itself involved in the struggle for the one church, but stands amazed before the results of this struggle, able only to accept the situation in the deepest humility and to heal the wounds. The unity of the church of Jesus Christ is to American Christianity less something essential, originally given by God, than something required, something which ought to be. It is less origin than goal. The unity of the church therefore belongs here to the realm of sanctification.

One might point out — though of course the observation is not wholly a satisfactory one — that since the time of Occam *nominalism* has been deeply rooted in Anglo-Saxon thought. For in nominalism the individual precedes the whole, in that the individual and empirically given thing is what is real, while totality is only a concept, a *nomen*. The individual stands at the beginning, unity at the end. On the other hand, the German-continental philosophical tradition is governed by *realism* and *idealism*, for which the whole is the original reality and the individual entity only a derivative. These modes of thinking cannot, however, be regarded as being in themselves sufficient explanation for the variety of thought about the unity of the church, because they in their turn are postulates of a philosophic method based on theological insights. Nominalist and realist philosophy cannot be understood without a theological background and therefore cannot provide any axiomatic interpretation of the theological question.

Only the truth revealed in Holy Scripture can and must decide between the present differences. The churches must take counsel of each other on the basis of Holy Scripture. *The denominations in America confront the church in Germany with the question of the multiplicity of churches:* What is the significance of this fact of disintegration within the church? Is only a confessional church a true church, and may the American denominations not be a church simply because for the most part they are not confessional churches? Is only the church of a certain confession a church, in the face of which other confessional churches are false churches? Is one individual church on earth granted the measure by which it can and must measure all other churches to their vindication or their condemnation? Does a multiplicity of churches mean only apostasy? Is there here only the inexorable contrast of true and false? Is the unity of the church only given through the creed, or to what extent is church community also based on practical action in common?

On the other hand, the church of Jesus Christ in Germany confronts the denominations of America with the question of the unity of the church on earth: May one simply be resigned to the multiplicity of churches as a given and hence a God-willed fact? But can there be a unity of the church other than in the unity of faith and of the confession of the one Lord? Is not all unity in action and in organization only a self-delusion, with which the real disruption in belief is concealed? Is not indifference or resignation towards the question of truth a fault which has the consequence of tearing the church apart in disputes over organization, culture and politics? What is the significance of the fact that disintegration is at its height precisely where the question of creed is made relative? Is not the unity of the church first and foremost its origin and only then its goal?

They remind us from over there: You overrate thought, theology, dogma; it is only one of many expressions of the church, and not the most important one at that. We reply: It is not a question of thought, but of the truth of the Word of God, by which we mean to live and die. It is a question of salvation. Granted, the unity of the church does not lie in human thought, but neither does it lie in human 'Life and Work'.* It lies solely in the life and work of Jesus Christ, in which we participate through faith. Unity in thought is not superior to unity in work, but unity in faith, which is confession, breaks right through both and alone creates the preconditions for common thought and action.

It is impossible to continue this conversation here. This much, however, can be said:

First, the unity of the church is origin as much as it is goal, fulfilment as much as it is promise; it is a part of faith as much as it is a part of sanctification. Where the unity of the church is forgotten as its origin, human organizations for union take the place of unity in Jesus Christ; the feeling of the age, which is for unification, takes the place of the Holy Ghost

---

* That part of the ecumenical movement which had to do with practical cooperation. 'Faith and Order' was concerned with the theological basis of unity. The two together led to the forming of the World Council of Churches in 1948.

who alone unites in the truth, and human 'Life and Work' ousts the life and work of Jesus Christ. On the other hand, where the unity of the church is forgotten as its goal, living oppositions harden, the work of the Holy Ghost, who will fulfil the promise of the unity of the church, is no longer taken seriously, and a separatist Pharisaic claim takes the place of the divine unity of the church. But where unity is regarded equally as origin and as goal, there grows up on the basis of the life and work of Jesus Christ, in whom all unity of the church is fulfilled, the life and work of Christianity which seeks and finds the unity of the shattered church.

Secondly, the claim to be the church of Jesus Christ has nothing to do with Pharisaic arrogance; it is rather a recognition which is humbling because it leads to repentance. The church is a church of sinners and not of the righteous. There can be more self-righteousness in renouncing the claim to be a church than in the claim itself. This renunciation can conceal a false humility which desires something better, more pious, than the church which God has chosen from sinners. The denominational self-understanding is no protection from spiritual pride. On the other hand, the church's understanding of itself must always recall it to repentance and humility. And after all there remains one fact, that it is not the concept of the denomination, but that of the church, which possesses New Testament validity.

Thirdly, the unity of the church as promise, as future, as fruit of sanctification is a work of the Holy Spirit. This unity will be forced neither by theological discussion nor by common action. But we know that God lets the churches find each other both by the way of common discovery and by the way of common action, and that often common discovery is only given through common action and common action only through common discovery. There are no methods of arriving at the unity of the church except complete obedience to the Holy Spirit who leads us to common discovery, confession, action and suffering.

Fourthly, the particular difficulty of reaching an understanding between the churches of the Reformation and the American denominations consists in the fact that they cannot make an immediate encounter on the level of the credal question, because the creed is not the constituent mark of the denomination while for the churches of the Reformation it is the sole matter of any ecumenical importance. In America, culture, the liturgy, community life and organization occupy the same position as the creed in Germany. But it is for precisely this reason that this encounter is so fruitful, because it puts in question the whole existence

202

of the church and of the denomination. An enquiry directed principally and solely towards the place of the creed in the American denomination is as immaterial as one which principally and solely seeks the constitution of the churches of the Reformation or their relationship to the state. Pertinent questioning of the other, however, leads to an unsuspected enrichment of one's own church. One finds disclosed a whole wealth of religious, liturgical form, of active community life and of rich experience of the significance of church organization, while the other side is brought to see the urgency of the question of truth and the richness of Christian insights in the confession of the church. Moreover, and this is the main point, both are driven by this encounter to a humility which looks for salvation not from its own condition, but solely from the grace of God. It is a hard task for the American denominations to understand aright the struggle for a confessional church, and it is no less difficult for the churches of the Reformation to understand the way of an American denomination. But precisely because here the common ground for an encounter seems to be missing, the attention is left undistracted for the only ground on which Christians can encounter each other, the Bible.

II. Refuge of Christians

The history of the church of Jesus Christ in America is distinct from the histories of all other churches on earth by virtue of the fact that from the beginning America has been a refuge for persecuted Christians from the European continent. Since the seventeenth century, America has been the sanctuary for victims of religious intolerance, for those who wished to live in freedom for their worship. At the same time, America is consciously a 'Protestant' land. Americans have always been taken with the idea of a special providence which postponed the discovery of America until the rise of Protestantism. Thus America is the only country in which the concept of 'Protestantism' has gained significance and reality in church history; for America means to be not the country of the Lutheran or the Reformed Church, but the country of 'Protestantism' in all its denominational broadness. One might say that the American Lutherans are perhaps least representative of American Protestantism. America, the sanctuary of persecuted 'Protestants' — that is the peculiarity of the church history of America and the historical understanding of itself which is still vividly possessed by American Christianity.

The beginnings of a great number of American denominations are to be found in voluntary or forced flight and all the Christian problems which that involves.

Perseverance or flight in times of persecution have been the two Christian possibilities throughout the whole of church history since the days of the Apostles. Perseverance to the end can be necessary; flight may be permissible, even necessary. The flight of Christians in persecution does not of itself signify apostasy and disgrace; for God does not call everyone to martyrdom. Not to flee, but to disavow one's faith is sin; that is to say that there can be a situation where flight is equivalent to renunciation, just as on the other hand flight itself can be a part of martyrdom. The Protestant fugitives who came to an unknown America did not come to a paradise, but to the hardest of work. They took upon themselves the struggle of colonization so as to be able to live out their faith in freedom without a struggle. This sheds a light on the fate of the Christian fugitive. He has claimed for himself the right to forgo the final suffering in order to be able to serve God in quietness and peace. Now in the place of refuge, there is no more justification for a continuation of the struggle. Here there are Protestants of all confessions who have already waived their claim to the final struggle over their creed. In the sanctuary there is no longer a place for strife. Confessional stringency and intolerance must cease for the person who has himself shunned intolerance. With his right to flee the Christian fugitive has forfeited the right to fight. So, at any rate, the American Christian understands the matter. True, even in America the church has not always managed to avoid a struggle; even there bitter persecutions have arisen, particularly at the beginning. But the deep abhorrence which any confessional discrimination in American Christianity has always met with in the long run may be quite adequately explained from the Christian right to flee, from the character of America as a sanctuary.

For the first generation of fugitives the journey to America was a decision of faith for their whole lives. For them the renunciation of the confessional struggle was therefore a hard-fought Christian possibility. A danger arises here, however, for the subsequent generations, who are born into this battle-free situation without themselves having decided to spend their lives under these conditions. Sooner or later they must misunderstand their position. What was for their fathers a right of their Christian faith won at risk of their lives becomes for the sons a general Christian rule. The struggle over the creed, because of which the fathers took flight, has become for the sons something which is in itself unchristian. Absence of struggle becomes for them the normal and ideal state of Christianity. The descendants of the fugitives grow up into a peace which is not won, but inherited.

Thus for American Christianity the concept of *tolerance* becomes the basic principle of everything Christian. Any intolerance is in itself unchristian. They therefore muster understanding and concern not for a confessional struggle as such, but for the victims of such a struggle. This must remain unsatisfactory for the victims themselves, who are not primarily concerned with their personal fate, but with the truth of their cause. To abstain from the final settlement of the question of truth remains the hardest task for the Christian fugitive all his life. All that can be convincing for him in America is the deep earnestness and unbounded extent of the concern and the right of sanctuary in the land of his refuge. His longing for a decision for truth against its distortion remains, and must remain, unfulfilled. It is in the last resort faithfulness to its own church history which is expressed in this peculiar relativism of the question of truth in the thought and action of American Christianity.

III. Freedom

America calls herself the land of the free. Under this term today she understands the right of the individual to independent thought, speech and action. In this context, religious freedom is, for the American, an obvious possession. Church preaching and organization, the life of the communities can develop independently, without being molested. Praise of this freedom may be heard from pulpits everywhere, coupled with the sharpest condemnation of any limitation of such freedom which has taken place anywhere. Thus freedom here means possibility, the possibility of unhindered activity given by the world to the church.

Now if the freedom of the church is essentially understood as this possibility, then the concept is still unrecognized. *The freedom of the church is not where it has possibilities, but only where the Gospel really and in its own power makes room for itself on earth, even and precisely when no such possibilities are offered to it.* The essential freedom of the church is not a gift of the world to the church, but the freedom of the Word of God itself to gain a hearing. Freedom of the church is not an unbounded number of possibilities: it only exists where a 'must', a necessity, on occasion compels it against all possibilities. The praise of freedom as the possibility for existence given by the world to the church can stem precisely from an agreement entered upon with this world in which the true freedom of the Word of God is surrendered. Thus it can happen that a church which boasts of its freedom as a possibility offered to it by the world slips back into the world to a special degree, that a church which is free in this way becomes secularized more quickly than a church which does not possess freedom as possibility. The American praise of freedom is more a praise which is directed to the world, the state and society, than a statement about the church. Such freedom may be a sign that the world truly belongs to God. But whether it belongs to him in reality does not depend on any freedom as possibility, but on freedom as reality, as constraint, as actual event. Freedom as an institutional possession is not an essential mark of the church. It can be a gracious gift given to the church by the providence of God; but it can also be the great temptation to which the church succumbs in sacrificing its essential freedom to institutional freedom. Whether the churches of God are really free can only be decided by the actual preaching of the Word of God. Only where this word can be preached concretely, in the midst of historical reality, in judgment, command, forgiveness of sinners and liberation from all human institutions is there freedom of the church. But where thanks for institutional freedom must be rendered by the sacrifice of freedom of preaching, the church is in chains, even if it believes itself to be free.

IV. Church and State

Nowhere has the principle of the separation of church and state become a matter of such general, almost dogmatic significance as in American Christianity, and nowhere, on the other hand, is the participation of the churches in the political, social, economic and cultural events of public life so active and so influential as in the country where there is no state church. This appears to be a paradox, the only explanation of which is to be found in the character of the American separation of church and state.

Church and state have not always been separated. In the seventeenth century, the Congregationalists in New England, the Anglicans in Virginia and the Catholics in Maryland were all state churches. This, however, was more a case of a state controlled by the church than of a state-controlled church. *Only with the establishment of Federal Rule after the American revolution did the privileges of the state churches gradually cease;* for the Union is in principle religionless. Religious questions were left to the individual states. Just at this time the first great alliances of denominations, transcending state borders, began. In 1784 the *Methodists* formed the Methodist-Episcopal church. In 1788 the *Presbyterians* formed the General Assembly and in 1789 the *Anglicans* joined together, without of course choosing an archbishop, even to this day. These church unions corresponded to the political movement for union. With the nineteenth century the complete separation of church and state was achieved and generally recognized. Not only the Union, but also the states are religionless. There are no public statistics of religion, there is no religious instruction in state schools, there is no enquiry about religious beliefs in appointments to state posts. All this originally happened with the agreement of the denominations, for in this way competitive proselytizing in state institutions, particularly in the schools, was avoided. Moreover the denominational influence still dominated the life of Christians so completely that the help of the state could be refused. But above all, the religionlessness of the state expressed a fact which was of fundamental significance for American Christianity, namely that the state has its boundaries at the churches. The religionlessness of the state was from this point of view not a triumph of secular authority over Christianity, but quite the reverse, the victory of the church over any unbounded claim by the state.

Here lies the key to the understanding of the original significance of the American separation of church and state, and of the American constitution. Although it took place almost at the same time and was not without political connection with the French Revolution, the American Revolution is fundamentally different from it. *American democracy is founded not on humanity or on the dignity of man, but on the kingdom of God and the limitation of all earthly power.* It is significant that notable American historians can say that the Federal constitution was written by men who knew about original sin. The human authorities and also the people themselves are shown their limits because of the wickedness of the human heart and the sole sovereignty of God. This idea, deriving from *Puritanism*, is then of course associated with the other, deriving from what could be properly called *Spiritualism*, that the kingdom of God on earth cannot be built by the state, but only by the community of Jesus Christ. Thus the church is given clear pre-eminence over the state. The church proclaims the principles of social and political order, the state merely provides the technical means of putting them into effect. These originally and essentially different foundations of democracy, by Puritanism and by 'Spiritualism', run into one another almost imperceptibly, and it is the latter which is more normative than the former for the general attitude of American Christianity. 'Christians nowadays think in terms of Christian principles (the realm of the church) and of technical policies whereby they can be put into practice (the realm of the state)' (W.A. Brown).

The fundamental distinction between this relationship between church and state and that of the Reformation is immediately obvious. *The American separation of church and state does not rest on the doctrine of the two offices or the two realms*, which will remain ordained by God until the end of the world, each with its own duty fundamentally different from the other. The dignity of the state, which is developed in Reformation doctrine more strongly than anywhere else, grows weaker in American thought. The interplay of state and church becomes a subordinate relationship in which the state is merely the executive of the church. The *state* is essentially technical organization and administrative apparatus. But the dignity of the divine office of the sword 'to avenge the evil and reward the good' appears to be lost. It is the enthusiastic doctrine of the state, whose destiny it is to be taken up into the church even on this earth, which governs American thought and at the same time provides a firm Christian foundation for American democracy. We shall have to ponder why a democracy with a Christian foundation has never been successfully established on the European continent, but that democracy and Christianity have always been regarded there as in some sort of opposition, while in America democracy can be extolled as *the* form of the Christian state. In answering this question we must remember that it was by persecuting and expelling those who held to the belief in the dominance of the spiritual (the enthusiasts) that the European continent deprived itself of this possibility. The country which afforded hospitality to the enthusiasts has, however, been fruitfully influenced by them even in political thought.

It accords with the character of the relationship between church and state in America that despite the separation of the two institutions in principle, material for conflict is not entirely removed. The *church* claims for itself the right to speak and act in all matters of public life, for only so can the kingdom of God be built. Here the difference of offices is not recognized in principle. State life, like the whole of public life, stands without distinction under the judgment of the church, and there can be no significant decision in public in which the church would not have to raise its voice and state its views. Thus as often as not topical discussions of certain public events or conditions are to be heard from American pulpits. A glance at the New York church notices is sufficient to convince one of this. But it would be a mistake to assess this type of preaching simply as a manifestation of secularization. Granted, it is that too, but behind it stands the old enthusiasts' claim to be building the kingdom of God publicly and visibly. *The secularization of the church on the continent of Europe* arose from the misinterpretation of the reformers' distinction of the two realms; *American secularization* derives precisely from the imperfect distinction of the kingdoms and offices of church and state, from the enthusiastic claim of the church to universal influence on the world. That is a significant distinction. While for the churches of the Reformation the doctrine of the two realms needs a new examination and correction, the American denominations today must learn the necessity of this distinction, if they are to be rescued from complete secularization.

The lesson which we can learn from a knowledge of the nature of the American church is this: *a state-free church is no more protected against secularization than is a state church.* The world threatens to break in on the church as much because of freedom as because of association. There is no form of the church which is as such protected in principle from secularization.

The following list of decisions in the sphere of public and political life which is shown by a *Report of the General Council of the Presbyterians* is indicative of the state of affairs in America — it should at the same time be observed that in this case we are dealing not with enthusiasts, but with Presbyterians, who are reformed in their doctrine of church and state. The report begins by disputing the right of the state to limit religious freedom. The agreement of the government with Uruguay on this matter is approved. Further steps should be taken for the colonization of American blacks in Africa, a new marriage and divorce law is demanded, as is vaccination legislation and female suffrage. A stand is made against games of chance, lotteries and horse racing, and against lynch justice. The government is asked to recognize Liberia as an independent republic. Further demands are made for better race relationships, old age pensions and unemployment assistance, and for a simplification of legal procedure in civil cases. Further points generally discussed in church conferences are the International Court of Justice, disarmament, naturalization laws, and so on. A Congregational statement is in accord with this: 'We have stood resolutely for the separation of state and church but with equal insistence have we stood for the continuous impact of the church upon the state' (cited by W. A. Brown). Brown sums up the attitude of the American denominations to the state in three points:

1. All declare the separation of state and church as a basic supposition.
2. All recognize the authorities to be ordained by God.
3. All claim for themselves the unquestionable right of speaking in

social, political and economic questions in so far as these imply general ethical questions.

At this time two questions of special importance provide much cause for conflict between state and church in America. The first is the school question, the second the peace question.

The school question: The religionless state schools are today a matter of grave concern to the denominations. What was once a limitation of power allowed by the church is now beginning to become an instrument against the denominations. The more the educational tasks of the school extend today, the more the denominations feel impelled to say their word in the matter. It is now possible for an intentional attack to be made on the church in a state school, while it is impossible to speak there in the name of the church. Thus there is once again a strong trend throughout American Christianity against the religionless character of schools. Significantly enough, the Lutherans alone among the Protestants have stood out against the religionless schools from the beginning, and have run their own confessional schools. This is all the more remarkable because it is just these American Lutherans who have never appropriated the 'spiritualist' conception of the relationship between state and church and unlike any of the other great denominations have abstained from any incursion into the sphere of the state. They alone have reserved the schools to the church and still maintain their own schools today, though with double school fees.

The peace question in America particularly concerns the problem of the undertaking of military service by Christians and ministers of different denominations. Exemption from military service may now be obtained on three conditions: first, membership of a church which repudiates armed service on grounds of Christian conviction (Quakers, etc.); secondly, membership of a church which grants the 'conscientious objector' the same right (i.e. Protestant Episcopal since 1936, Methodist Episcopal since 1932, Northern Baptist since 1934, Unitarian since 1936); thirdly, appeal on grounds of personal conscience. In the case of the individual the decision depends on whether a personal interview reveals that it is really only religious or conscientious motives which are the grounds for refusal. The struggle over this question has been carried on particularly vigorously during the last ten years.

A question of less importance relates to the display of the American flag in church. This was particularly common during the war years and can still be found in many places today. Questionnaires have shown that the laity, rather than the clergy, are behind the preservation of this custom. Nevertheless, it is surprising in a land where church and state are separated.

The strongest influence of the church on the state in America is exerted not by the community and the pulpit, but by the *considerable power of the free Christian associations which are not linked with any denomination.* The picture of American Christianity is not complete without this decisive connecting link between community and public life. These are private associations, founded by individual Christians for any limited aim which may be termed working for the kingdom of God in America. Great financial contributions are made to these institutions, with which the equivalent European associations cannot compare at all in extent and influence. There are associations for evangelization, for social aims, the Y.M.C.A. and the Y.W.C.A., societies for temperance and abstinence, for the hallowing of Sunday, for prison reform, for fighting vice, for aid to the unemployed, for bettering of race relations, and especially for advancing the living conditions of blacks, and in addition an overwhelming number of peace movements and so on. It was essentially the dogged work of the Women's Christian Temperance Union, supported primarily by Methodists, and the Anti-Saloon League, which had the support of all denominations except the Lutherans and the Anglicans, which succeeded in carrying through the prohibition law in the 18th Amendment. In this connection, however, American Christianity has had a strange and perhaps highly momentous experience. It has had to recognize that the transference of Christian principles to state life has led to a catastrophic breakdown. The prohibition law gave an unprecedented impulse to crime in the large cities. A 'Christian' law meant the ruin of the state and had — with the agreement of the churches — to be repealed. This fact has given American Christians much food for thought, and it must make us think too.

V. The Black Church*

The race question has been a real problem for American Christianity from the beginning. Today about one American in ten is black. The turning aside of the newly arising generation of blacks from the faith of their elders, which, with its strong eschatological orientation, seems to them to be a hindrance to the progress of their race and their rights is one of the ominous signs of a failing of the church in past centuries and a hard

* Bonhoeffer used the phrase *Die Negerkirche.* Wherever he uses *Neger* we have used 'Black'.

problem for the future. If it has come about that today the 'black Christ' has to be led into the field against the 'white Christ' by a young black poet, then a deep cleft in the church of Jesus Christ is indicated. We may not overlook the fact that many white Christians are doing their best through influential organizations for a better relationship between the races and that discerning blacks recognize the difficulties. Nevertheless, the picture of a racially divided church is still general in the United States today. Black and white hear the Word and receive the sacrament in separation. They have no common worship. The following *historical* development lies in the background. At the time of the arrival of the first large shipments of blacks in America, who had been plundered as slaves from Africa, there was a general rejection of the idea of making the black Christian, particularly by the white slave-owners. Slavery was justified on the ground that blacks were heathen. Baptism would put in question the permissibility of slavery and would bring blacks undesirable rights and privileges. Only after a dreadful letter of reassurance from the Bishop of London, in which he promised the white masters that the external conditions of blacks need not be altered in the least by baptism, that baptism was a liberation from sin and evil desire and not from slavery or from any other external fetters, did the slave owners find themselves ready to afford the gospel an entry among blacks. Finally it was even found to have the advantage of keeping the slaves more easily under supervision than if they were left to continue their own pagan cults. So it came about that blacks became Christians and were admitted to the gallery at white services and as the last guests to the communion table. Any further participation in the life of the congregation was excluded: holding offices in the congregation and ordination remained reserved for whites. Under these circumstances worship together became more and more of a farce for blacks, and after the complete failure of all attempts to be recognized as equal members in the community of Jesus Christ, blacks began to attempt to organize themselves into their own black congregations. It was a voluntary decision which led the black to this, but one which circumstances made inevitable. A number of incidents, particularly at the time of the Civil War, which brought about the abolition of slavery, gave rise to the formation of independent black churches. Since then the great denominations have been divided, a significant example of the make-up of a denomination in the United States. The most influential contribution made by the black to American Christianity lies in the 'negro spirituals', in which the distress and delivery of the people of Israel ('Go down, Moses . . .'), the misery and consolation of the human heart ('Nobody knows the trouble I've seen'), and the love of the Redeemer and longing for the kingdom of heaven ('Swing low, sweet chariot . . .') find moving expression. Every white American knows, sings and loves these songs. It is barely understandable that great black singers can sing these songs before packed concert audiences of whites, to tumultuous applause, while at the same time these same men and women are still denied access to the white community through social discrimination. One may also say that nowhere is revival preaching still so vigorous and so widespread as among blacks, that here the gospel of Jesus Christ, the saviour of the sinner, is really preached and accepted with great welcome and visible emotion. The solution to the race problem* is one of the decisive future tasks of the white churches.

VI. Theology

After what has been said it will no longer be surprising that theology is mentioned here in last place. That is not to say that American theology is itself insignificant. It does, however, give expression to the fact that the denominations of America are not to be understood primarily from their theology, but from their practical work in the community and their public effectiveness. This is true in a similar way of almost all Anglo-Saxon churches and represents a great difficulty for us. No one does justice to these churches as long as he judges them by their theology. Such emphasis is laid here on liturgical, official and community order and tradition that even a bad theology cannot do too much damage. It is, however, not only the conservative — from the point of view of the history of thought — background which explains this strange state of affairs; at this point there opens up an almost incalculably deep opposition between the churches of the Reformation and 'Protestantism without Reformation'. We mean to speak of this at the close.

At the beginning of this year, the magazine *Christian Century* published a series of articles on the theme, 'How my mind has changed in the last decade'. *Churchmen and teachers of theology* were asked to give in brief to the Christian public *an autobiographical, theological account of their development in the last ten years.* Common to all these articles — with the exception of those by the Fundamentalists, who assert with conviction that nothing essential could have altered in their thought as they were

* Bonhoeffer uses *Negerproblem.*

then advancing the same doctrine as they are now — is a confession of a decided change in theological thought during the past ten years. Common too is the direction which this change is seen to have taken: it is a return from secularism in its different forms, such as modernism, humanitarianism and naturalism, to the great facts of revelation. Where ten years previously interest was predominantly centred in the 'social gospel', today an explicitly dogmatic interest has been aroused and is particularly perceptible in the most significant place of theological education in the country, Union Theological Seminary in New York. German theology, in so far as it has been translated into English — thus chiefly the works of Barth, Brunner, Heim, and alongside them Tillich — has left behind strong influences. Kierkegaard is beginning to be known in wider circles through new translations. Besides this, with almost stronger influence, is the new English theology with its emphatic advocacy of the need for a natural theology. Common too is the reason given for this change, namely the collapse of the old social order in America and in other countries, and the resultant criticism of the liberal, optimistic belief in progress which has hitherto dominated theology. *All*, under this influence, speak more strongly than before of sin and the judgment of God, which is manifesting itself in the present world crisis. And *all*, finally, are united in deliberate rejection of Barth's criticism of natural theology. Within these limits there are, of course, all shades of theological thought, or as many as can achieve a reconciliation of a Christian theology of revelation with the tradition of American thought.

The articles by the following writers are particularly worth reading: *W. L. Sperry* (Professor of Practical Theology at Harvard), whose remarks can be summed up in the following words: American life has been until quite recently, optimistic, once-born ... Our once-born America is changing before our eyes. *H. N. Wiemann* (Professor of Religious Philosophy in Chicago), exponent of a 'theistic naturalism', whose definition of sin is a strange mixture of Reformation insights and naturalistic anthropology, influenced by James and Whitehead: 'Therefore, he, who makes ideas supreme over his life, no matter how lofty and no matter how perfectly he may live up to them, is sinking'; the following statement about grace is equally remarkable: 'The grace of God is the good which God puts into each concrete situation over and above all that man can plan or do or imagine'; on the other hand he comes down badly in his remarks about the living Christ as the 'working of a process of history which used that human personality' (of Jesus) or as 'the growth of a community' which breaks through all natural communities; equally weak is the definition of the church as 'a new way of living'. On the other hand, again, there is another notable remark about the otherness of God: 'God alone is concrete in his working . . . man must work abstractly', leading to a special evaluation of the Apostle Paul. The neglect of christology is characteristic of the whole of contemporary American Christianity (with the exception of Fundamentalism). *Reinhold Neibuhr* (Professor at Union Theological Seminary), one of the most significant and most creative of contemporary American theologians, whose main works must be known for a survey of the theological situation (*Moral Man and Immoral Society, Interpretation of Christian Ethics, Beyond Tragedy*), the sharpest critic of contemporary American Protestantism and the present social order, has for years been making a deep impression by his strong emphasis on the cross as the midpoint and the end of history, coupled with a strongly active political theology. He sees the right way between neo-orthodoxy, for which Jesus Christ becomes the ground for human despair, and a true liberalism, for which Christ is the Lord, the norm, the ideal and the revelation of our essential being. Both are equally necessary. But even here a doctrine of the person and redemptive work of Jesus Christ is still missing. *W. M. Horton* (Professor at Oberlin College) would join together Augustine, Calvin, Barth, Wiemann and the 'Social gospel'. *E. S. Ames* (sometime professor and pastor in Chicago) is the only liberal not to acknowledge any change in his thought through recent developments and he defiantly entitles his article 'Confirmed Liberalism'. The new theology is and remains atavism, because it is unscientific. 'God is life as you love it.'(!) 'Worship as praise and adulation does not fit in with my ideas of either God or man. It tends to separate them, to exalt one too much and to debase the other too much.' It is barely conceivable how anyone with this doctrine can have been pastor of a congregation for some decades! On the other hand, this is only a candid expression of what others have thought and were thinking in past years and even today.

With few exceptions contemporary American theology presents a fairly uniform picture, at any rate for an observer who comes from a church of the Reformation. And with this we come to the last point.

God has granted American Christianity no Reformation. He has given it strong revivalist preachers, churchmen and theologians, but no Reformation of the church of Jesus Christ by the Word of God. Anything of the churches of the Reformation which has come to America either stands in conscious seclusion and detachment from the general life of the church or has fallen victim to Protestantism without Reformation. There are Americans who assert with pride and conviction that they are building on pre- and extra-Reformation foundations and see in this their characteristic nature. True, it cannot be denied that the dangers which thus threaten contemporary American Christianity are clearly seen by some leading theologians. Reinhold and Richard Neibuhr, Pauck, Miller and some others of the younger generation continue to speak in a reformed way. But they are the exceptions. American theology and the American church as a whole have never been able to understand the meaning of 'criticism' by the Word of God and all that signifies. Right to the last they do not understand that God's 'criticism' touches even religion, the Christianity of the churches and the sanctification of Christians, and that God has founded his church beyond religion and beyond ethics. A symptom of this is the general adherence to natural theology. In American theology, Christianity is still essentially religion and ethics. But because of this, the person and work of Jesus Christ must, for theology, sink into the background and in the long run remain misunderstood, because it is not recognized as the sole ground of radical judgment and radical forgiveness. The decisive task for today is the dialogue between Protestantism without Reformation and the churches of the Reformation.

*

LETTER TO THE FINKENWALDE BRETHREN, CHRISTMAS 1939

Germany invaded Poland in September 1939 and the second world war began. After his very brief second visit to the United States (2 June-27 July), Bonhoeffer was back, fulfilling his responsibilities with the collective pastorates in Köslin and Sigurdshof. Many of his students, both past and present, were called up for military service. In order to keep in touch and continue his ministry to them, Bonhoeffer started to write circular letters. The following is his Christmas letter of 1939. (Published in Gesammelte Schriften *III, 382-388; ET in* Bonhoeffer: True Patriotism, *28-33).*

Christmas 1939

No priest, no theologian stood at the cradle in Bethlehem. And yet all Christian theology has its origin in the wonders, that God became man. 'Alongside the brilliance of the holy night there burns the fire of the unfathomable mystery of theology.' *Theologia sacra* arises from those on bended knees who do homage to the mystery of the divine child in the stall. Israel had no theology. She did not know God in the flesh. Without the holy night there is no theology. 'God revealed in the flesh', the God-man Jesus Christ, is the holy mystery which theology is appointed to guard. What a mistake to think that it is the task of theology to unravel God's mystery, to bring it down to the flat, ordinary human wisdom of experience and reason! It is the task of theology solely to preserve God's wonder as wonder, to understand, to defend, to glorify God's mystery as mystery. This and nothing else was the intention of the ancient church when it fought with unflagging zeal over the mystery of the persons of the Trinity and the natures of Jesus Christ. How superficial and flippant, especially of theologians, to send theology to the knacker's yard, to make out that one is not a theologian and doesn't want to be, and in so doing to ridicule one's own ministry and ordination and in the end to have, and to advocate, a bad theology instead of a good one! But of course, where in our theological classes were we shown and taught the mystery of God in the flesh, the birth of Jesus Christ, the God-man and saviour, as the unfathomable mystery of God? Where do we hear it preached? Surely Christmas Eve can kindle in us again something like a love of sacred theology, so that, seized and compelled by the wonder of the cradle of the Son of God, we are moved to consider again, reverently, the mysteries of God. But it may well be that the glow of the divine mysteries has already been quenched, and has died in our hearts as well.

The ancient church meditated on the question of Christ for several centuries. It imprisoned reason in obedience to Jesus Christ, and in harsh, conflicting sentences gave living witness to the mystery of the person of Jesus Christ. It did not give way to the modern pretence that this mystery could only be felt or experienced, for it knew the corruption and self-deception of all human feeling and experience. Nor, of course, did it think that this mystery could be thought out logically, but by being unafraid to express the ultimate conceptual paradoxes, it bore witness to, and glorified, the mystery as a mystery against all reason. The Christology of the ancient church really arose at the cradle of Bethlehem, and the brightness of Christmas lies on its weather-beaten face. Even today, it wins the hearts of all who come to know it. So at Christmas time we should again go to school with the ancient church and seek to understand in worship what it thought and taught, to glorify and to defend belief in Christ. The hard concepts of that time are like stones from which one strikes fire.

Let us look briefly at three well-known Christological principles,

217

which survive in our Lutheran confessions, not only that we might preach them to the congregations, but to put our thought and knowledge, as preachers of the word, to work in the light of the holy night.

1. The Fathers were concerned to say that God, the Son, took upon himself *human nature*, not that he took upon himself *a man*. What does that mean? God became man by taking upon himself human nature, not by taking an individual man. This distinction was necessary to preserve the universality of the wonder of Christmas. 'Human nature', that is, the nature, essence, flesh of all men, i.e. my nature, my flesh; human nature, that is, the embodiment of all human possibilities. Perhaps we moderns might put it more simply by saying that in the birth of Jesus Christ, God took human nature, and not just an individual man. But this taking happened corporeally, and that is the unique wonder of the incarnation. The body of Jesus Christ is our flesh. He bears our flesh. Therefore, where Jesus Christ is, there we are, whether we know it or not; that is true because of the incarnation. What happens to Jesus Christ, happens to us. It really is all *our* 'poor flesh and blood' which lies there in the crib; it is *our* flesh which dies with him on the cross and is buried with him. He took human nature so that we might be eternally with him. Where the body of Jesus Christ is, there are we; indeed, we are his body. So the Christmas message for all men runs: You are accepted, God has not despised you, but he bears in his body all your flesh and blood. Look at the cradle! In the body of the little child, in the incarnate son of God, your flesh, all your distress, anxiety, temptation, indeed all your sin, is borne, forgiven and healed. If you complain, 'My nature, my whole being is beyond salvation and I must be eternally lost', the Christmas message replies, 'Your nature, your whole being is accepted; Jesus bears it, in this way he has become your saviour.' Because Christmas is the physical acceptance of all human flesh by the gracious God, we must affirm that God's son took human nature upon himself.

2. 'Two natures and one person' — the ancient church has ventured to express its knowledge of Christmas in this paradoxical dogmatic formula. 'Ventured', for it, too, knew that something inexpressible was expressed here, simply because one could not be silent about it (Augustine). People found two things in the cradle, and bore witness to them: humanity taken in the flesh and the eternal Godhead, both united in the one name Jesus Christ, human and divine nature united in the person of the Son of God. Divine nature, that is, the Godhead: the Father, Son and Holy Spirit united for ever. It is the eternal might, glory and majesty of the triune God. Wherever the Son is, he brings this divine nature with

him, for he remains true God from eternity to eternity. If the Son of God has truly become man, the divine nature is certainly also present in all its majesty; otherwise Christ would not be true God. This really is so: if Jesus Christ is not true God, how could he *help* us? If Christ is not true man, how could he help *us?* Of course, the divine nature is hidden in the cradle, and it shines through the poor rags of the human nature only here and there in the life of Jesus. But however mysteriously hidden, it is still present, hidden for us, present for us. Divine and human nature, united in Christ and still not made one; for otherwise the vast difference between Godhead and humanity would be done away with. So it may never be said that the divine nature assumed the human nature; that would imply that the father and the Holy Spirit also took flesh, and would thus mean the ultimate (modalistic, idealistic, pantheistic, Schleiermacherian) confusion of God and man. No, it means that the Son of God, the divine person of the Logos, took human nature. But Godhead and manhood, divine nature and human nature, met and united only in the *person* of the Son of God, in Jesus Christ. Nowhere else but in and through the person of Jesus Christ are Godhead and manhood united, 'without confusion, without change, without division, without separation', as the Chalcedonian definition put it in a supreme paradox, and at the same time in a most reverent preservation of the mystery of the person of the Mediator. Rarely in later ages has reason been so ready to humble and surrender itself before the miracle of God as it does in these words. But precisely because of that, reason has been made a better instrument for the glorification of the divine revelation. The Christological formula, 'Two natures, one person', at the same time has supreme soteriological significance: Godhead and humanity separated from one another before Christ came, united with each other only in the incarnation of the Son of God. Only through the person do the natures have communion with each other, i.e. only through Jesus Christ are Godhead and humanity united.

3. The contribution of the Lutheran Church, added to the ancient church's Christology, consisted in the doctrine of the *genus majestaticum* (disputed most vigorously by Reformed theologians), i.e. the doctrine of the mediation of the properties of the divine nature to the human nature which took place in the incarnation. 'For to make alive, to have all judgment and power in heaven and on earth, to have all things in his hands, to have subjected all things under his feet, to purify from sin, etc., are not created gifts, but divine, infinite properties, which according to the testimony of Scripture are still given and supplied to the *man* Christ' (For-

mula of Concord, S.D. VII 55). True, it remains incomprehensible how the human nature, which is our nature, should share the properties of the divine majesty, but this is scriptural doctrine, and it expresses the deepest and ultimate union of God with man thus, so that one can now say with Luther: 'Wherever you can say "Here is God", you must also say, "So Christ the man is also there". And if you could point to a place where there was God and not man, the person would already be divided. No, friend, where you show me God you must also show me man.' 'It is the glory of our Lord God that he condescends so deeply to the flesh'. Lutheran teaching parried the objection of the Reformed Church that the human nature was no longer taken seriously by referring to the unique miracle, and to Scripture. Indeed, only from this standpoint do we have the right understanding of the holy eucharist and the words of the Lord, 'This is my body'. If Christ speaks in this way, then he must know better than any man what his body is and may be. So incarnation and eucharist are extremely closely connected. The doctrine of the *genus majestaticum* illuminates this connection. The same God who came in the flesh for our salvation gives himself to us with his body and blood in the sacrament. 'The end of the ways of God is bodiliness' (Oetinger).

The thoughts that we have expressed here are ancient ones: they are minute fragments of the edifice of the church's Christology. But it is not a question of our marvelling at this building, but of our being led by one thought or another to read and to consider more reverently and more prayerfully the biblical witness of the mystery of the incarnation of God, and perhaps also to sing Luther's Christmas hymns more thoughtfully and more joyfully.

4

THE LIFE OF FREE RESPONSIBILITY*

ETHICS

Bonhoeffer's Ethics *was edited by Bethge after the war and published post-humously in 1949. (*Ethik, *Chr. Kaiser Verlag, ET by Neville H. Smith,* Ethics, *New York: Macmillan, 1955). As already indicated in the Introduction, what we now have is not Bonhoeffer's final work but a series of chapters for his proposed book on ethics. Some of the material is incomplete, and there has been much debate about the order in which the material was written and the structure which Bonhoeffer had in mind for putting it all together. Dissatisfied with his original thematic structure, Bethge attempted to provide a strictly chronological arrangement of the material for the sixth German edition published in 1963. This was adopted by subsequent English editions (Collins Fontana, 1964; Macmillan, 1965; and SCM, 1971). But this too has proved somewhat unsatisfactory, and those engaged in the edition of the new critical German edition, including Bethge, all agree that the sixth edition has to be revised once more (to be published as* Ethik, *Band 6, Dietrich Bonhoeffer Werke, edited by Ernst Feil, Clifford Green, Heinz Eduard Todt, and Ilse Todt). A possible new arrangement would be:*

A. Chapter 1: The Love of God and the Decay of the World
      (probably written between mid-March and summer 1940, as 'a preliminary attempt which is superseded by the second block', B)

B. Chapter 3: Ethics as Formation
      Chapter 2 The Church as the World
      Chapter 4: The Last Things and the Things before Last
      Chapter 5: Christ, Reality and Good
      Chapter 6: History and Good
      (These chapters were written between late 1940 and late 1941 at various places, including Klein-Krössin the Benedictine monastery at Ettal, and Berlin)

---

* See also above, pp. 30-35.

C.   Chapter 7: The Ethical and the Christian as a Theme
     *(Bonhoeffer was working on this chapter in Berlin when
     arrested by the Gestapo, who confiscated and later returned it.
     According to Green, it was 'inspired by Karl Barth'.)*

Our selections are from chapters 3, 4, 5 and 6.

ETHICS AS FORMATION

The theoretical ethicist and reality

Rarely perhaps has any generation shown so little interest as ours does
in any kind of theoretical or systematic ethics. The academic question
of a system of ethics seems to be of all questions the most superfluous.
The reason for this is not to be sought in any supposed ethical indifference on the part of our period. On the contrary it arises from the fact that
our period, more than any earlier period in the history of the west, is
oppressed by a superabounding reality of concrete ethical problems. It
was otherwise when the established orders of life were still so stable as
to leave room for no more than minor sins of human weakness, sins
which generally remained hidden, and when the criminal was removed
as abnormal from the horrified or pitying gaze of society. In those conditions ethics could be an interesting theoretical problem.

Today there are once more villains and saints, and they are not hidden from the public view. Instead of the uniform greyness of the rainy
day we now have the black storm-cloud and the brilliant lightning-
flash. The outlines stand out with the exaggerated sharpness. Reality
lays itself bare. Shakespeare's characters walk in our midst. But the
villain and the saint have little or nothing to do with systematic ethical
studies. They emerge from primeval depths and by their appearances
they tear open the infernal or the divine abyss from which they come and
enable us to see for a moment into mysteries of which we had never
dreamed. What is worse than doing evil is being evil. It is worse for a liar
to tell the truth than of a lover of truth to lie. It is worse when a mis-
anthropist practises brotherly love than when a philanthropist gives
way to hatred. Better than truth in the mouth of the liar is the lie. Better
than the act of brotherly love on the part of the misanthrope is hatred.
One sin, then, is not like another. They do not all have the same weight.
There are heavier sins and lighter sins. A falling away is of infinitely
greater weight than a falling down. The most shining virtues of him who

has fallen away are as black as night in comparison with the darkest of the steadfast.

If evil appears in the form of light, beneficence, loyalty and renewal, if it conforms with historical necessity and social justice, then this, if it is understood straightforwardly, is a clear additional proof of its abysmal wickedness. But the moral theorist is blinded by it. With the concepts he already has in mind he is unable to grasp what is real and still less able to come seriously to grips with that of which the essence and power are entirely unknown to him. One who is committed to an ethical programme can only waste his forces on the empty air, and even his martyrdom will not be a source of strength for his cause or a serious threat to the wicked. But, remarkably enough, it is not only the adept of an ethical theory or programme who fails to strike his opponent. The wicked adversary himself is scarcely capable of recognizing his rival for what he is. Each falls into the other's trap. It is not by astuteness, by knowing the tricks, but only by simple steadfastness in the truth of God, by training the eye upon this truth until it is simple and wise, that there comes the experience and the knowledge of the ethical reality.

One is distressed by the failure of *reasonable* people to perceive either the depths of evil or the depths of the holy. With the best of intentions they believe that a little reason will suffice them to clamp together the parting timbers of the building. They are so blind that in their desire to see justice done to both sides they are crushed between the two clashing forces and end by achieving nothing. Bitterly disappointed at the unreasonableness of the world, they see that their efforts must remain fruitless and they withdraw resignedly from the scene or yield unresistingly to the stronger party.

Still more distressing is the utter failure of all ethical *fanaticism*. The fanatic believes that he can oppose the power of evil with the purity of his will and of his principle. But since it is part of the nature of fanaticism that it loses sight of the totality of evil and rushes like a bull at the red cloth instead of at the man who holds it, the fanatic inevitably ends by tiring and admitting defeat. He aims wide of the mark. Even if his fanaticism serves the high cause of truth or justice, he will sooner or later become entangled with non-essentials and petty details and fall into the snare set by his more skilful opponent.

The man with a *conscience* fights a lonely battle against the overwhelming forces of inescapable situations which demand decisions. But he is torn apart by the extent of the conflicts in which he has to make his choice with no other aid or counsel than that which his own innermost conscience can furnish. Evil comes upon him in countless respectable and seductive disguises so that his conscience becomes timid and unsure of itself, till in the end he is satisfied if instead of a clear conscience he has a salved one, and lies to his own conscience in order to avoid despair. A man whose only support is his conscience can never understand that a bad conscience may be healthier and stronger than a conscience which he deceived.

It looks as though the way out from the confusing multiplicity of possible decisions is the *path of duty*. What is commanded is seized upon as being surest. Responsibility for the command rests upon the man who gives it and not upon him who executes it. But in this confinement within the limits of duty there can never come the bold stroke of the deed which is done on one's own free responsibility, the only kind of deed which can strike at the heart of evil and overcome it. The man of duty will end by having to fulfil his obligation even to the devil.

But if someone sets out to fight his battles in the world in his own absolute *freedom*, if he values the necessary deed more highly than the spotlessness of his own conscience and reputation, if he is prepared to sacrifice a fruitless principle to a fruitful compromise, or for that matter the fruitless wisdom of the *via media* to a fruitful radicalism, then let him beware lest precisely his supposed freedom may ultimately prove his undoing. He will easily consent to the bad, knowing full well that it is bad, in order to ward off what is worse, and in doing this he will no longer be able to see that precisely the worse which he is trying to avoid may still be the better. This is one of the underlying themes of tragedy.

Some who seek to escape from the taking a stand publicly find a place of refuge in a *private virtuousness*. Such a man does not steal. He does not commit murder. He does not commit adultery. Within the limits of his powers he does good. But in his voluntary renunciation of publicity he knows how to remain punctiliously within the permitted bounds which preserve him from involvement in conflict. He must be blind and deaf to the wrongs which surround him. It is only at the price of an act of self-deception that he can safeguard his private blamelessness against contamination through responsible action in the world. Whatever he may do, that which he omits to do will give him no peace. Either this disquiet will destroy him or he will become the most hypocritical of Pharisees.

Who would wish to pour scorn on such failures and frustrations as these? Reason, moral fanaticism, conscience, duty, free responsibility and silent virtue, these are the achievements and attitudes of a noble humanity. It is the best of men who go under in this way, with all that they can do or be. Here is the immortal figure of Don Quixote, the knight of the doleful countenance, who takes a barber's dish for a helmet and a miserable hack for a charger and who rides into endless battlers for the love of a lady who does not exist. That is how it looks when an old world ventures to take up arms against a new one and when a world of the past hazards an attack against the superior forces of the commonplace and mean. Even the deep cleft which separates the two halves of the great story is characteristic in that the story-teller himself turns against his hero in the second half, which was not written until many years later than the first, and allies himself with the mean and mocking world. It is all too easy to pour scorn on the weapons which we have inherited from our fathers, the weapons which served them to perform great feats but which in the present struggle can no longer be sufficient. It is a mean-spirited man who can read of what befell Don Quixote and not be stirred to sympathy.

Yet our business now is to replace our rusty swords with sharp ones. A man can hold his own here only if he can combine simplicity with wisdom. But what is simplicity? What is wisdom? And how are the two to be combined? To be simple is to fix one's eye solely on the simple truth of God at a time when all concepts are being confused, distorted and turned upside-down. It is to be single-hearted and not a man of two souls, an ἀνὴρ δίψυχος (Jas. 1.8). Because the simple man knows God, because God is his, he clings to the commandments, the judgments and the mercies which come from God's mouth every day afresh. Not fettered by principles, but bound by love for God, he has been set free from the problems and conflicts of ethical decision. They no longer oppress him. He belongs simply and solely to God and to the will of God. It is precisely because he looks only to God, without any sidelong glance at the world, that he is able to look at the reality of the world freely and without prejudice. And that is how simplicity becomes wisdom. The wise man is the one who sees reality as it is, and who sees into the depths of things. That is why only that man is wise who sees reality in God. To understand reality is not the same as to know about outward events. It is to perceive the essential nature of things. The best-informed man is not necessarily the wisest. Indeed there is a danger that precisely in the multiplicity of his knowledge he will lose sight of what is essential. But on the other hand knowledge of an apparently trivial detail quite often makes it possible to see into the depths of things. And so the wise man will seek to acquire the best possible knowledge about events, but always without becoming dependent upon this knowledge. To recognize the significant in the factual is wisdom. The wise man is aware of the limited receptiveness of reality for principles; for he knows that reality is not built upon principles but that it rests upon the living and creating God. He knows too, therefore, that reality cannot be helped by even the purest of principles or by even the best of wills, but only by the living God. Principles are only tools in God's hand, soon to be thrown away as unserviceable. To look in freedom at God and at reality, which rests solely upon him, this is to combine simplicity with wisdom. There is no true simplicity without wisdom and there is no wisdom without simplicity.

This may sound very theoretical, and it is theoretical until it becomes clear at what point this attitude has its basis in reality so that it can itself become real. 'Be ye wise as serpents and harmless as doves' is a saying of Jesus (Matt. 10.16) and is therefore, like all his sayings, interpreted only by Jesus himself. No man can look with undivided vision at God and at the world of reality so long as God and the world are torn asunder. Try as he may, he can only let his eyes wander distractedly from one to the other. But there is a place at which God and the cosmic reality are reconciled, a place at which God and man have become one. That and that alone is what enables man to set his eyes upon God and upon the world at the same time. This place does not lie somewhere out beyond reality in the realm of ideas. It lies in the midst of history as a divine miracle. It lies in Jesus Christ, the Reconciler of the world. As an ideal the unity of simplicity and wisdom is doomed to failure, just as is any other attempt to hold one's own against reality. It is an impossible ideal, and an extremely contradictory one. But if it is founded upon the reality of a world which is at one with God in Jesus Christ, the commandment of Jesus acquires reality and meaning. Whoever sees Jesus Christ does indeed see God and the world in one. He can henceforward no longer see God without the world or the world without God.   (*E: 64-70*)

*

Conformation

The word 'formation' (*Gestaltung*) arouses our suspicion. We are sick and tired of Christian programmes and of the thoughtless and superficial slogan of what is called 'practical' Christianity as distinct from 'dogmatic' Christianity. We have seen that the formative forces in the world do not arise from Christianity at all and that the so-called practical Christianity is at least as unavailing in the world as is the dogmatic

226

kind. The word 'formation', therefore, must be taken in quite a different sense from that to which we are accustomed. And in fact the holy Scriptures speak of formation in a sense which is at first entirely unfamiliar to us. Their primary concern is not with the forming of a world by means of plans and programmes. Whenever they speak of forming they are concerned only with the one form which has overcome the world, the form of Jesus Christ. Formation can come only from this form. But here again it is not a question of applying directly to the world the teaching of Christ or what are referred to as Christian principles, so that the world might be formed in accordance with these. On the contrary, formation comes only by being drawn in into the form of Jesus Christ. It comes only as formation in his likeness, as *conformation with the unique form of him who was made man, was crucified, and rose again.*

This is not achieved by dint of efforts 'to become like Jesus', which is the way in which we usually interpret it. It is achieved only when the form of Jesus Christ itself works upon us in such a manner that it moulds our form in its own likeness (Gal. 4.19). Christ remains the only giver of forms. It is not Christian men who shape the world with their ideas, but it is Christ who shapes men in conformity with himself. But just as we misunderstand the form of Christ if we take him to be essentially the teacher of a pious and good life, so, too, we should misunderstand the formation of man if we were to regard it as instruction in the way in which a pious and good life is to be attained. Christ is the Incarnate, Crucified and Risen One whom the Christian faith confesses. To be transformed in his image (2 Cor. 3.18, Phil. 3.10, Rom. 8.29 and 12.2) — this is what is meant by the formation of which the Bible speaks.

To be conformed with the *Incarnate* — that is to be a real man. It is man's right and duty that he should be a man. The quest for the superman, the endeavour to outgrow the man within the man, the pursuit of the heroic, the cult of the demigod, all this is not the proper concern of man, for it is untrue. The real man is not an object either for contempt or for deification, but an object of the love of God. The rich and manifold variety of God's creation suffers no violence here from the false uniformity or from the forcing of men into the pattern of an ideal or a type or a definite picture of the human character. The real man is at liberty to be his Creator's creature. To be conformed with the Incarnate is to have the right to be the man one really is. Now there is no more pretence, no more hypocrisy or self-violence, no more compulsion to be something other, better and more ideal than what one is. God loves the real man. God became a real man.

227

To be formed in the likeness of the *Crucified*— this means being a man sentenced by God. In his daily existence man carries with him God's sentence of death, the necessity of dying before God for the sake of sin. With his life he testifies that nothing can stand before God save only under God's sentence and grace. Every day man dies the death of a sinner. Humbly he bears the scars on his body and soul, the marks of the wounds which sin inflicts on him. He cannot raise himself up above any other man or set himself before him as a model, for he knows himself to be the greatest of all sinners. He can excuse the sin of another, but never his own. He bears all the suffering imposed on him, in the knowledge that it serves to enable him to die with his own will and to accept God's judgment upon him. But in surrendering himself to God's judgment upon him and against him he is himself just in the eyes of God. In the words of K. F. Harttmann's poem, 'it is in suffering that the Master imprints upon our minds and hearts his own all-valid image'.

To be conformed with the *Risen One*— that is to be a new man before God. In the midst of death he is in life. In the midst of sin he is righteous. In the midst of the world he is new. His secret remains hidden from the world. He lives because Christ lives, and lives in Christ alone. 'Christ is my life' (Phil. 1.21). So long as the glory of Christ is hidden, so long, too, does the glory of his new life remain 'hidden with Christ in God' (Col. 3.3). But he who knows espies already here and there a gleam of what is to come. The new man lives in the world like any other man. Often there is little to distinguish him from the rest. Nor does he attach importance to distinguishing himself, but only to distinguishing Christ for the sake of his brethren. Transfigured though he is in the form of the Risen One, here he bears only the sign of the cross and the judgment. By bearing it willingly he shows himself to be the one who has received the Holy Spirit and who is united with Jesus Christ in incomparable love and fellowship.

The form of Jesus Christ takes form in man. Man does not take on an independent form of his own, but what gives him form and what maintains him in the new form is always solely the form of Jesus Christ himself. It is therefore not a vain imitation or repetition of Christ's form but Christ's form itself which take form in man. And again, man is not transformed into a form which is alien to him, the form of God, but into his own form, the form which is essentially proper to him. Man becomes man because God became man. But man does not become God. It is not he, therefore, who was or is able to accomplish his own transformation, but it is God who changes his form into the form of man, so that man may become, not indeed God, but, in the eyes of God, man.

In Christ there was re-created the form of man before God. It was not an outcome of the place or the time, of the climate or the race, of the individual or the society, or of religion, or of taste, but quite simply of the life of humanity as such, that humanity at this point recognized its image and its hope. What befell Christ had befallen mankind. It is a mystery, for which there is no explanation, that only a part of humanity recognize the form of their Redeemer. The longing of the Incarnate to take form in all men is as yet still unsatisfied. He bore the form of man as a whole, and yet he can take form only in a small band. These are his church.

'Formation' consequently means in the first place Jesus's taking form in his church. What takes form here is the form of Jesus Christ himself. The New Testament states the case profoundly and clearly when it calls the church the Body of Christ. The body is the form. So the church is not a religious community of worshippers of Christ but is Christ himself who has taken form among men. The church can be called the Body of Christ because in Christ's Body man is really taken up by him, and so too, therefore, is humanity. The church, then, bears the form which is in truth the proper form of all humanity. The image in which she is formed is the image of man. What takes place in her takes place as an example and substitute for all men. But it is impossible to state clearly enough that the church, too, is not an independent form by herself, side by side with the form of Christ, and that she, too, can therefore never lay claim to an independent character, title, authority or dignity on her own account and apart from him. The church is nothing but a section of humanity in which Christ has really taken form. What we have here is utterly and completely the form of Jesus Christ and not some other form side by side with him. The church is the man in Christ, incarnate, sentenced and awakened to new life. In the first instance, therefore, she has essentially nothing whatever to do with the so-called religious functions of man, but with the whole man in his existence in the world with all its implications. What matters in the church is not religion but the form of Christ, and its taking form amidst a band of men. If we allow ourselves to lose sight of this, even for an instant, we inevitably relapse into that programme-planning for the ethical or religious shaping of the world, which was where we set out from.

We have now seen that it is only with reference to the form that we can speak of formation in a Christian and ethical sense. Formation is not an independent process or condition which can in some way or other be detached from this form. The only formation is formation by and into the form of Jesus Christ. The point of departure for Christian ethics is the body of Christ, the form of Christ in the form of the church, and formation of the church in conformity with the form of Christ. The concept of formation acquires its significance, indirectly, for all humanity only if what takes place in the church does in truth take place for all men. But this again does not mean that the church is set up, so to speak, as a model for the world. One can speak of formation and of world only if humanity is called by name in its true form, which is its own by right, which it has already received, but which it merely fails to understand and accept, namely, the form of Jesus Christ, which is proper to man, and if in this way, in anticipation as one might say, humanity is drawn in into the church. This means, then, that even when we speak in terms of the formation of the world we are referring solely to the form of Jesus Christ.

The form of Christ is one and the same at all times and in all places. And the church of Christ also is one and the same throughout all generations. And yet Christ is not a principle in accordance with which the whole world must be shaped. Christ is not a proclaimer of a system of what would be good today, here and at all times. Christ teaches no abstract ethics such as must at all costs be put into practice. Christ was not essentially a teacher and legislator, but a man, a real man like ourselves. And it is not therefore his will that we should in our time be the adherents, exponents and advocates of a definite doctrine, but that we should be men, real men before God. Christ did not, like a moralist, love a theory of good, but he loved the real man. He was not, like a philosopher, interested in the 'universally valid', but rather in that which is of help to the real and concrete human being. What worried him was not, like Kant, whether 'the maxim of an action can become a principle of general legislation', but whether my action is at this moment helping my neighbour to become a man before God. For indeed it is not written that God became an idea, a principle, a programme, a universally valid proposition or a law, but that God became man. This means that though the form of Christ certainly is and remains one and the same, yet it is willing to take form in the real man, that is to say, in quite different guises. Christ does not dispense with human reality for the sake of an idea which demands realization at the expense of the real. What Christ does is precisely to give effect to reality. He affirms reality. And indeed he is himself the real man and consequently the foundation of all human reality. And so formation in conformity with Christ has this double implication. The form of Christ remains one and the same, not as a general idea but in its own unique character as the incarnate, crucified and risen God. And precisely for the sake of Christ's form the form of the real man is preserved, and in this way the real man receives the form of Christ.

The concrete place

This leads us away from any kind of abstract ethic and towards an ethic which is entirely concrete. What can and must be said is not what is good once and for all, but the way in which Christ takes form among us here and now. The atempt to define that which is good once and for all has, in the nature of the case, always ended in failure. Either the proposition was asserted in such general and formal terms that it retained no significance as regards its contents, or else one tried to include in it and elaborate the whole immense range of conceivable contents, and thus to say in advance what would be good in every single conceivable case; this led to a caustic system so unmanageable that it could satisfy the demands neither of general validity not of concreteness. The concretely Christian ethic is beyond formalism and casuistry. Formalism and casuistry set out from the conflict between the good and the real, but the Christian ethic can take for its point of departure the reconciliation, already accomplished, of the world with God and the man Jesus Christ and the experience of the real man by God.

But the question of how Christ takes form among us here and now, or how we are conformed with his form, contains within itself still further difficult questions. What do we mean by 'among us', 'now' and 'here'? If it is impossible to establish for all times and places what is good, then the question still arises for what times and places can any answer at all be given to our enquiry. It must not remain in doubt for a single moment that any one section to which we may now turn our attention is to be regarded precisely as a section, as a part of the whole of humanity. In every section of his history man is simply and entirely the man taken upon himself by Christ. And for this reason whatever may have to be said about this section will always refer not only to this part but also to the whole. However, we must now answer the question regarding the times and places of which we are thinking when we set out to speak of formation through the form of Christ. These are in the first place quite generally the times and places which in some way concern us, those of which we have experience and which are reality for us. They are the times and places which confront us with concrete problems, set us tasks and charge us with responsibility. The 'among us', the 'now' and 'here' is therefore the region of our decisions and encounters. This region undoubtedly varies very greatly in extent according to the individual, and it might consequently be supposed that these definitions could in the end be interpreted so widely and vaguely as to make room for unrestrained individualism. What prevents this is the fact that by our history we are set objectively in a definite nexus of experiences, responsibilities and decisions from which we cannot free ourselves again except by an abstraction. We live, in fact, within the nexus, whether or not we are in every respect aware of it. Futhermore, this nexus is characterized in a quite peculiar manner by the fact that until our own days its consciously affirmed and recognized underlying basis has been the form of Christ. In our historical identity, therefore, we stand already in the midst of Christ's taking form, in a section of human history which he himself has chosen. It is consequently in this sense that we regard the west as the region for which we wish to speak and must speak, the world of the peoples of Europe and America in so far as it is already united through the form of Jesus Christ. To take a narrower view or to limit our consideration to Germany, for example, would be to lose sight of the fact that the form of Christ is the unity of the western nations and that for this reason no single one of these nations can exist by itself or even be conceived as existing by itself. And to take a wider view would be to overlook the mysterious fact of the self-containedness of the western world.

The purpose of what follows is not indeed to develop a programme for shaping or formation of the western world. What is intended is rather a discussion of the way in which in this western world the form of Christ takes form. This means that the discussion must be neither abstract nor casuistic, but entirely concrete. It must be insisted that no other form may be placed side by side with the form of Jesus Christ, for he alone is the subduer and reconciler of the world. Only this one form can help. And so whatever concrete assertion may have to be made here today about the way in which this form takes form amongst us, it must be referred quite strictly to this form of Jesus Christ. Moreover, in the incarnation of Christ the assurance is given us that Christ is willing to take form amongst us here and today.

Ethics and formation, then, means the bold endeavour to speak about the way in which the form of Jesus Christ takes form in our world, in a manner which is neither abstract nor casuistic, neither programmatic nor purely speculative. Concrete judgments and decisions will have to be ventured here. Decision and action can here no longer be delegated to the personal conscience of the individual. Here there are concrete commandments and instructions for which obedience is demanded.

Ethics as formation is possible only upon the foundation of the form of Jesus Christ which is present in his Church. 'The church is the place where Jesus Christ's taking form is proclaimed and accomplished. It is this proclamation and this event that Christian ethics is designed to serve.

(E: 80-88)

*

CHRIST, REALITY AND GOOD
CHRIST, THE CHURCH AND THE WORLD

The concept of reality

Whoever wishes to take up the problem of a Christian ethic must be confronted at once with a demand which is quite without parallel. He must from the outset discard as irrelevant the two questions which, alone, impel him to concern himself with the problem of ethics, 'How can I be good?' and 'How can I do good?', and instead of these he must ask the utterly and totally different question 'What is the will of God?' This requirement is so immensely far-reaching because it presupposes a decision with regard to the ultimate reality; it presupposes a decision of faith. If the ethical problem presents itself essentially in the form of enquiries about one's own being good and doing good, this means that it has already been decided that it is the self and the world which are the ultimate reality. The aim of all ethical reflection is, then, that I myself shall be good and that the world shall become good through my action. But the problem of ethics at once assumes a new aspect if it becomes apparent that these realities, myself and the world, themselves lie embedded in a quite different ultimate reality, namely, the reality of God, the Creator, Reconciler and Redeemer. What is of ultimate importance is now no longer that I should become good, or that the condition of the world should be made better by my action, but that the reality of God should show itself everywhere to be the ultimate reality. Where there is faith in God as the ultimate reality, all concern with ethics will have as its starting-point that God shows himself to be good, even if this involves the risk that I myself and the world are not good but thoroughly bad. All things appear distorted if they are not seen and recognized in God. All so-called data, all laws and standards, are mere abstractions so long as there is no belief in God as the ultimate reality.

But when we say that God is the ultimate reality, this is not an idea, through which the world as we have it is to be sublimated. It is not the religious rounding-off of a profane conception of the universe. It is the acceptance in faith of God's showing forth of himself, the acceptance of his revelation. If God were merely a religious idea there would be nothing to prevent us from discerning, behind this allegedly 'ultimate' reality, a still more final reality, the twilight of the gods and the death of the gods. The claim of this ultimate reality is satisfied only in so far as it is revelation, that is to say, the self-witness of the living God. When this is so, the relation to this reality determines the whole of life. The apprehension of this reality is not merely a gradual advance towards the discovery of ever more profound realities; it is the crucial turning-point in the apprehension of reality as a whole. The ultimate reality now shows itself to be at the same time the initial reality, the first and last, alpha and omega. Any perception or apprehension of things or laws without him is now abstraction, detachment from the origin and goal. Any enquiry about one's own goodness, or the goodness of the world, is now impossible unless enquiry has first been made about the goodness of God. For without God what meaning could there be in a goodness of man and a goodness of the world? But God as the ultimate reality is no other than he who shows forth, manifests and reveals himself, that is to say, God in Jesus Christ, and from this it follows that the question of good can find its answer only in Christ.

The point of departure for Christian ethics is not the reality of one's own self, or the reality of the world; nor is it the reality of standards and values. It is the reality of God as he reveals himself in Jesus Christ. It is fair to begin by demanding assent to this proposition of anyone who wishes to concern himself with the problem of a Christian ethic. It poses the ultimate and crucial question of the reality which we mean to reckon with in our lives, whether it is to be the reality of the revelational word of God or earthly imperfections, whether it is to be resurrection or death. No man can decide this question by himself, by his own choice, without deciding it wrongly, for it pre-supposes the answer given, namely that, whatever our decision may be, God has already spoken his word of revelation, and even in the false reality we cannot live otherwise than through the true reality of the word of God. Thus when we ask about the ultimate reality we are thereby at once inescapably bound by the answers to our question. For the question conveys us into the midst of its origin, the reality of the revelation of God in Jesus Christ.

The problem of Christian ethics is the realization among God's creatures of the revelational reality of God in Christ, just as the problem of dogmatics is the truth of the revelational reality of God in Christ. The place which in all other ethics is occupied by the antithesis of 'should be' and 'is', idea and accomplishment, motive and performance, is occupied in Christian ethics by the relation of reality and realization, past and present, history and event (faith), or, to replace the equivocal concept by the unambiguous name, the relation of Jesus Christ and the Holy Spirit. The question of good becomes the question of participation in the divine reality which is revealed in Christ. Good is now no longer a valuation of what is, a valuation, for example, of my own being, my outlook or my actions, or of some condition or state in the world. It is no longer a predicate that is assigned to something which is in itself in being. Good is the real itself. It is not the real in the abstract, the real which is detached from the reality of God, but the real which possesses reality only in God. There is no good without the real, for the good is not a general formula, and the real is impossible without the good. The wish to be good consists solely in the longing for what is real in God. A desire to be good for its own sake, as an end in itself, so to speak, or as a vocation in life, falls victim to the irony of unreality. The genuine striving for good now becomes the self-assertiveness of the prig. Good is not in itself an independent theme for life; if it were so it would be the craziest kind of quixotry. Only if we share in reality can we share in good.

It is a fundamentally mistaken formulation of the question that gives rise to the old dispute about whether it is only the will, the mental act or the person that can be good, or whether goodness may also be predicated of performance, achievement or success, and, if so, which of these two precedes the other and which is more important. This dispute has found its way even into theology, and there, as elsewhere, it has been the source of serious errors. It tears asunder what by its origin and essence forms a unity, namely, the good and the real, man and his work. To object that Christ, too, had this distinction between person and work in view in his saying about the good tree that brings forth good fruit (Matt. 7.17) is to distort the meaning of this saying of Jesus into its exact opposite. What is meant by this saying is not that first the person and then the work is good, but that only the two together are good or bad, in other words that the two together are to be understood as a single unit. The same holds true of the distinction which has been drawn by Reinhold Neibuhr, the American philosopher of religion, in his use of the two concepts 'moral man' and 'immoral society'. The distinction which is intended here between individual and society is a purely abstract one, just as is that between the person and work. In such a case one is tearing asunder things which are inseparable and examining separately parts which in isolation from each other, are dead. The consequence is that complete ethical aporia which nowadays goes by the name of 'social ethics'. Naturally, if good is supposed to lie in the conformity of something that is with something that should be, then the relatively more massive resistance which is offered by society to that which should be must necessarily lead to an ethical favouring of the individual at the expense of society. (And conversely it is precisely this circumstance which suggests that this concept of the ethical has its sociological origin in the age of individualism.) The question of good must not be reduced to an examination of the motives or consequences of actions by applying to them some ready-made ethical yardstick. An ethic of motives or of mental attitudes is as superficial as an ethic of practical consequences. For what right have we to stop short at the immediate motive and to regard this as the ultimate ethical phenomenon, refusing to take into account the fact that a 'good' motive may spring from a very dark background of human consciousness and unconsciousness and that a 'good attitude' may often be the source of the worst of actions? And just as the question of the motivation of action is in the end lost in the inextricable complexities of the past, so, too, does the question of its consequences finally disappear from view in the mists of the future. On both sides there are no fixed frontiers and nothing justifies us in calling a halt at some point which we ourselves have arbitrarily determined so that we may at last form a definite judgment. Whether one pursues the line of the ethic of motives or that of the ethic of consequences, it is a matter of sheer expediency, dependent on the conjunctures of the times, that in practice one always ends with some such arbitrary setting of limits. In principle neither of these has anything to commend it in preference to the other, for in both of them the question of good is posed in abstract terms and in isolation from reality. Good is not the correspondence between a criterion which is placed at our disposal by nature or grace and whatever entity I may designate as reality. Good is reality itself, reality seen and recognized in God. The question of good embraces man with his motives and purposes, with his fellow-men and with the entire creation around him; it embraces reality as a whole, as it is held in being by God. The divine words 'Behold, it was very good' (Gen. 1.31) refer to the whole of creation. The good demands the whole, not only the whole of a man's outlook but his whole work, the whole man, together with the fellow-men who are given to him. What sense would it have if only a part were to be called good, a motive perhaps, while the action is bad, or if the reverse were the case? Man is an indivisible whole, not only as an individual in his person and work but also as a member of the community of men and creatures in which he stands. This indivisible whole, this reality which is founded on God and apprehended in him, is what the question of good has in view. With respect to its origin this indivisible whole is called 'creation'. With respect to its goal it is called the 'kingdom of God'. Both of these are equally remote from us and equally close to us, for God's creation and God's kingdom are present with us solely in God's self-revelation in Jesus Christ.

Participation in the indivisible whole of the divine reality — this is the sense and the purpose of the Christian enquiry concerning good. For the sake of avoiding a misunderstanding, there is need at this point of some further clarification of what is meant here by reality.

There is a way of basing ethics upon the concept of reality which differs entirely from the Christian way. This is the positive and empirical approach, which aims at the entire elimination from ethics of the concept of norms and standards because it regards this concept as being merely the idealization of factual and practically expedient attitudes. Fundamentally, according to this view, the good is no more than what is expedient, useful and advantageous to reality. From this it follows that there is no universal good but only an infinitely varying good which is determined in each case on the basis of 'reality'. This conception is undoubtedly superior to the idealist conception in that it is 'closer to reality'. Good does not consist here in an impossible 'realization' of what is unreal, the realization of ethical ideas. It is reality itself that teaches what is good. The only question is whether the reality that is intended here is capable of satisfying this demand. It now transpires that the concept of reality which underlies the positivistic ethic is the meretricious concept of the empirically verifiable, which implies denial of the origin of this reality in the ultimate reality, in God. Reality, understood in this inadequate sense, cannot be the source of good, because all it demands is complete surrender to the contingent, the casual, the adventitous and the momentarily expedient, because it fails to recognize the ultimate reality and because in this way it destroys and abandons the unity of good.

The Christian ethic speaks in a quite different sense of the reality which is the origin of good, for it speaks of the reality of God as the ultimate reality without and within everything that is. It speaks of the reality of the world as it is, which possess reality solely through the reality of God. Christian belief deduces that the reality of God is not in itself merely an idea from the fact that this reality of God has manifested and revealed itself in the midst of the real world. In Jesus Christ the reality of God entered into the reality of this world. The place where the answer is given, both to the question concerning the reality of God and to the question concerning the reality of the world, is designated solely and alone by the name Jesus Christ. God and the world are comprised in this name. In him all things consist (Col. 1.17). Henceforward one can speak neither of God nor of the world without speaking of Jesus Christ. All concepts of reality which do not take account of him are abstractions. When good has become reality in Jesus Christ, there is no more force in any discussion of good which plays off what should be against what is and what is against what should be. Jesus Christ cannot be identified either with an ideal or standard or with things as they are. The hostility of the ideal towards things as they are, the fanatical putting into effect of an idea in the face of a resisting actuality, may be as remote from good as is the sacrifice of what should be to what is expedient. Both what should be and what is expedient acquire in Christ an entirely new meaning. The irreconcilable conflict between what is and what should be is reconciled in Christ, that is to say, in the ultimate reality. Participation in this reality is the true sense and purpose of the enquiry concerning good.

In Christ we are offered the possibility of partaking in the reality of God and in the reality of the world, but not in the one without the other. The reality of God discloses itself only by setting me entirely in the reality of the world, and when I encounter the reality of the world it is always already sustained, accepted and reconciled in the reality of God. This is the inner meaning of the revelation of God in the man Jesus Christ. Christian ethics enquires about the realization in our world of this divine and cosmic reality which is given in Christ. This does not mean that 'our world' is something outside the divine and cosmic reality which is in Christ, or that it is not already part of the world which is sustained, accepted and reconciled in Him. It does not mean that one must still begin by applying some kind of 'principle' to our situation and our time. The enquiry is directed rather towards the way in which the reality in Christ, which for a long time already has comprised us and our world within itself, is taking effect as something now present, and towards the way in which life may be conducted in this reality. Its purpose is, therefore, participation in the reality of God and of the world in Jesus Christ today, and this participation must be such that I never experience the reality of God without the reality of the world or the reality of the world without the reality of God.

Thinking in terms of two spheres

As soon as we try to advance along this path, our way is blocked by the colossal obstacle of a large part of traditional Christian ethical thought. Since the beginnings of Christian ethics after the times of the New Testament the main underlying conception in ethical thought, and the one which consciously or unconsciously has determined its whole course, has been the conception of a juxtaposition and conflict of two spheres, the one divine, holy, supernatural and Christian, and the other worldly, profane, natural and un-Christian. This view becomes dominant for the first time in the Middle Ages, and for the second time in the pseudo-Protestant thought of the period after the Reformation. Reality as a whole now falls into two parts, and the concern of ethics is with the proper relation of these two parts to each other. In the scholastic scheme of things the realm of the natural is made subordinate to the realm of grace; in the pseudo-Lutheran scheme the autonomy of the orders of this world is proclaimed in opposition to the law of Christ, and in the scheme of the Enthusiasts the congregation of the Elect takes up the struggle with a hostile world for the establishment of God's kingdom on earth. In all these schemes the cause of Christ becomes a partial and provincial matter within the limits of reality. It is assumed that there are realities which lie outside the reality that is in Christ. It follows that these realities are accessible by some way of their own, and otherwise than through Christ. However great the importance which is attached to the reality of Christ, it still always remains a partial reality amid other realities. The division of the total reality into a sacred and a profane sphere, a Christian and a secular sphere, creates the possibility of existence in a single one of these spheres, a spiritual existence which has no part in secular existence, and a secular existence which can claim autonomy for itself and can exercise this right of autonomy in its dealings with the spiritual sphere. The monk and the nineteenth-century Protestant secularist typify these two possibilities. The whole of medieval history is centred upon the theme of the predominance of the spiritual sphere over the secular sphere, the predominance of the *regnum gratiae* over the *regnum naturae*; and the modern age is characterized by an ever increasing independence of the secular in its relation with the spiritual. So long as Christ and the world are conceived as

239

two opposing and mutually repellent spheres, man will be left in the following dilemma: he abandons reality as a whole, and places himself in one or other of the two spheres. He seeks Christ without the world, or he seeks the world without Christ. In either case he is deceiving himself. Or else he tries to stand in both spaces at once and thereby becomes the man of eternal conflict, the kind of man who emerged in the period after the Reformation and who has repeatedly set himself up as representing the only form of Christian existence which is in accord with reality.

It may be difficult to break the spell of this thinking in terms of two spheres, but it is nevertheless quite certain that it is in profound contradiction to the thought of the Bible and to the thought of the Reformation, and that consequently it aims wide of reality. There are not two realities, but only one reality, and that is the reality of God, which has become manifest in Christ in the reality of the world. Sharing in Christ we stand at once in both the reality of God and the reality of the world. The reality of Christ comprises the reality of the world within itself. The world has no reality of its own, independently of the revelation of God in Christ. One is denying the revelation of God in Jesus Christ if one tries to be 'Christian' without seeing and recognizing the world in Christ. There are, therefore, not two spheres, but only the one sphere of the realization of Christ, in which the reality of God and the reality of the world are united. Thus the theme of the two spheres, which has repeatedly become the dominant factor in the history of the church, is foreign to the New Testament. The New Testament is concerned solely with the manner in which the reality of Christ assumes reality in the present world, which it has already encompassed, seized and possessed. There are not two spheres, standing side by side, competing with each other and attacking each other's frontiers. If that were so, this frontier dispute would always be the decisive problem of history. But the whole reality of the world is already drawn in into Christ and bound together in him, and the movement of history consists solely in divergence and convergence in relation to this centre.   (*E: 188-198*)

*

Ethical thinking in terms of spheres, then, is invalidated by faith in the revelation of the ultimate reality in Jesus Christ, and this means that there is no real possibility of being a Christian outside the reality of the world and that there is no real worldly existence outside the reality of Jesus Christ. There is no place to which the Christian can withdraw from the world, whether it be outwardly or in the sphere of the inner life.

Any attempt to escape from the world must sooner or later be paid for with a sinful surrender to the world. It is after all a matter of experience that when the gross sins of sex have been overcome they are succeeded by covetousness and avarice, which are equally gross sins even though the world may treat them less severely. The cultivation of a Christian inner life, untouched by the world, will generally present a somewhat tragicomical appearance to the worldly observer. For the sharp-sighted world recognizes itself most distinctly at the very point where the Christian inner life deceives itself in the belief that the world is most remote. Whoever professes to believe in the reality of Jesus Christ, and the revelation of God, must in the same breath profess his faith in both the reality of God and the reality of the world; for in Christ he finds God and the world reconciled. And for just this reason the Christian is no longer the man of eternal conflict, but, just as the reality in Christ is one, so he, too, since he shares in this reality in Christ, is himself an undivided whole. His worldliness does not divide him from Christ, and his Christianity does not divide him from the world. Belonging wholly to Christ, he stands at the same time wholly in the world. *(E: 200-201)*

*

HISTORY AND GOOD
THE STRUCTURE OF RESPONSIBLE LIFE

The structure of responsible life is conditioned by two factors; life is bound to man and to God and a man's own life is free. It is the fact that life is bound to man and to God which sets life in the freedom of a man's own life. Without this bond and without this freedom there is no responsibility. Only when it has become selfless in this obligation does a life stand in the freedom of a man's truly own life and action. The obligation assumes the form of deputyship and of correspondence with reality; freedom displays itself in the self-examination of life and of action and in the venture of a concrete decision. This gives us the arrangement for our discussion of the structure of responsible life.

*Deputyship**

The fact that responsibility is fundamentally a matter of deputyship is demonstrated most clearly in those circumstances in which a man is

---

* *Stellvertretung.*

241

directly obliged to act in the place of other men, for example as a father, as a statesman or as a teacher. The father acts for the children, working for them, caring for them, interceding, fighting and suffering for them. Thus in a real sense he is their deputy. He is not an isolated individual, but he combines in himself the selves of a number of human beings. Any attempt to live as though he were alone is a denial of the actual fact of his responsibility. He cannot evade the responsibility which is laid on him with his paternity. This reality shatters the fiction that the subject, the performer, of all ethical conduct is the isolated individual. Not the individual in isolation but the responsible man is the subject, the agent, with whom ethical reflexion must concern itself. This principle is not affected by the extent of the responsibility assumed, whether it be for a single human being, for a community or for whole groups of communities. No man can altogether escape responsibility, and this means that no man can avoid deputyship. Even the solitary lives as a deputy, and indeed quite especially so, for his life is lived in deputyship for man as man, for humanity as a whole. And, in fact, the concept of responsibility for oneself possesses a meaning only in so far as it refers to the responsibility which I bear with respect to myself as a man, that is to say, because I am a man. Responsibility for oneself is in truth responsibility with respect to the man, and that means responsibility with respect to humanity. The fact that Jesus lived without the special responsibility of a marriage, of a family or of a profession, does not by any means set him outside the field of responsibility; on the contrary, it makes all the clearer his responsibility and his deputyship for all men. Here we come already to the underlying basis of everything that has been said so far. Jesus, life, our life, lived in deputyship for us as the incarnate Son of God, and that is why through him all human life is in essence a life of deputyship. Jesus was not the individual, desiring to achieve a perfection of his own, but he lived only as the one who has taken up into himself and who bears within himself the selves of all men. All his living, his action and his dying was deputyship. In him there is fulfilled what the living, the action and the suffering of men ought to be. In this real deputyship which constitutes his human existence he is the responsible person *par excellence*. Because he is life all life is determined by him to be deputyship. Whether or not life resists, it is now always deputyship, for life or for death, just as the father is always a father, for good or for evil.

Deputyship, and therefore also responsibility, lies only in the complete surrender of one's own life to the other man. Only the selfless man lives responsibly, and this means that only the selfless man *lives*. Wherever the divine 'yes' and 'no' become one in man, there is responsible living. Selflessness in responsibility is so complete that here we may find the fulfilment of Goethe's saying about the man of action always without conscience. The life of deputyship is open to two abuses; one may set up one's own ego as an absolute, or one may set up the other man as an absolute. In the first case the relation of responsibility leads to forcible exploitation and tyranny; this springs from a failure to recognize that only the selfless man can act responsibly. In the second case what is made absolute is the welfare of the other man, the man towards whom I am responsible, and all other responsibilities are neglected. From this there arises arbitrary action which makes mock of the responsibility to God who in Jesus Christ is the God of all men. In both these cases there is a denial of the origin, the essence and the goal of responsible life in Jesus Christ, and responsibility itself is set up as a self-made abstract idol.

Responsibility, as life and action in deputyship, is essentially a relation of man to man. Christ became man, and he thereby bore responsibility and deputyship for men. There is also a responsibility for things, conditions and values, but only in conjunction with the strict observance of the original, essential and purposive determination of all things, conditions, and values through Christ (John 1.3), the incarnate God. Through Christ the world of things and of values is once more directed towards humanity as it was in the Creation. It is only within these limits that there is a legitimate sense in speaking, as is often done, about responsibility for a thing or for a cause. Beyond these limits it is dangerous, for it serves to reverse the whole order of life, making things the masters of men. There is a devotion to the cause of truth, goodness, justice and beauty which would be profaned if one were to ask what is the moral of it, and which indeed itself makes it abundantly clear that the highest values must be subservient to man. But there is also a deification of all these values which has no connexion at all with responsibility; it springs from a demonical possession which destroys the man in sacrificing him to the idol. 'Responsibility for a thing' does not mean its utilization for man and consequently the abuse of its essential nature, but it means the essential directing of it towards man. Thus that narrow pragmatism is entirely excluded which, in Schiller's words 'makes a milch-cow of the goddess' when that which has value in itself is in a direct and short-sighted manner subordinated to human utility. The world of things attains to its full liberty and depth only when it is grasped in its original, essential and purposive relevance to the world of persons; for, as St Paul expresses it, the earnest expectation of the creature waits for the manifestation of the glory of the children of God; and indeed the creature itself shall be delivered from the bondage of corruption (which also consists in its own false self-deification) into the glorious liberty of the children of God (Rom. 8.19-21).

Correspondence with Reality

The responsible man is dependent on the man who is concretely his neighbour in his concrete possibility. His conduct is not established in advance, once and for all, that is to say, as a matter of principle, but arises with the given situation. He has no principle at his disposal which possesses absolute validity and which he has to put into effect fanatically, overcoming all the resistance which is offered to it by reality, but he sees in the given situation what is necessary and what is 'right' for him to grasp and to do. For the responsible man the given situation is not simply the material on which he is to impress his idea or his programme by force, but this situation is itself drawn in into the action and shares in giving form to the deed. It is not an 'absolute good' that is to be realized; but on the contrary it is part of the self-direction of the responsible agent that he prefers what is relatively better to what is relatively worse and that he perceives that the 'absolute good' may sometimes be the very worst. The responsible man does not have to impose upon reality a law which is alien to it, but his action is in the true sense 'in accordance with reality'.

This concept of correspondence to reality certainly needs to be defined more exactly. It would be a complete and a dangerous misunderstanding if it were to be taken in the sense of that 'servile conviction in the face of the fact' that Nietzsche speaks of, a conviction which yields to every powerful pressure, which on principle justifies success, and which on every occasion chooses what is opportune as 'corresponding to reality'. 'Correspondence with reality' in this sense would be contrary of responsibility; it would be irresponsibility. But the true meaning of correspondence with reality lies neither in this servility towards the factual nor yet in a principle of opposition to the factual, a principle of revolt against the factual in the name of some higher reality. Both extremes alike are very far removed from the essence of the matter. In action which is genuinely in accordance with reality there is an indissoluble link between the acknowledgement and the contradiction of the factual. The reason for this is that reality is first and last not lifeless; but it is the real man, the incarnate God. It is from the real man, whose name is Jesus Christ, that all factual reality derives its ultimate foundation and its ultimate annulment, its justification and its ultimate contradiction, its ultimate affirmation and its ultimate negation. To attempt to understand reality without the real man is to live in an abstraction to which the responsible man must never fall victim; it is to fail to make contact with reality in life; it is to vacillate endlessly between the extremes of servility and revolt in relation to the factual. God became man; he accepted man in the body and thereby reconciled the world of man with God. The affirmation of man and of his reality took place upon the foundation of the acceptance, and not the foundation of the affirmation. It was not because man and his reality were worthy of the divine affirmation that God accepted them and that God became man, but it was because man and his reality were worthy of divine being that God accepted man and affirmed him by himself becoming man in the body and thereby taking upon himself and suffering the curse of the divine 'no' to the human character. It is from this action of God, from the real man, from Jesus Christ, that reality now receives its 'yes' and its 'no', its right and its limitations. Affirmation and contradiction are now conjoined in the concrete action of him who has recognized the real man. Neither the affirmation nor the contradiction now comes from a world which is alien to reality, from a systematic opportunism or idealism; but they come from the reality of the reconciliation of the world with God which has taken place in Jesus Christ. In Jesus Christ, the real man, the whole reality is taken up and comprised together; in him it has its origin, its essence and its goal. For that reason it is only in him, and with him as the point of departure, that there can be an action which is in accordance with reality. The origin of action which accords with reality is not the pseudo-Lutheran Christ who exists solely for the purpose of sanctioning the facts as they are, nor the Christ of radical enthusiasm whose function is to bless every revolution, but it is the incarnate God Jesus who has accepted man and who has loved, condemned and reconciled man and with him the world.

Our conclusion from this must be that action which is in accordance with Christ is action which is in accordance with reality. This proposition is not an ideal demand, but it is an assertion which springs from the knowledge of reality itself. Jesus Christ does not confront reality as one who is alien to it, but it is he who alone has borne and experienced the essence of the real in his own body, who has spoken from the standpoint of reality as no man on earth can do, who alone has fallen victim to no ideology, but who is the the truly real one, who has borne within himself and fulfilled the essence of history, and in whom the law of the life of history is embodied. He is the real one, the origin, essence and goal of all that is real, and for that reason he is himself the Lord and the Law of the real. Consequently the word of Jesus Christ is the interpretation of his existence, and it is therefore the interpretation of that reality in which history attains to its fulfilment. The words of Jesus are the divine commandment for responsible action in history in so far as this history is the reality of history as it is fulfilled in Christ, the responsibility for man as it is fulfilled in Christ alone. They are not intended to serve the ends of an abstract ethic; for an abstract ethic they are entirely incomprehensible and they lead to conflicts which can never be resolved, but they take effect in the reality of history, for it is from there that they originate. Any attempt to detach them from this origin distorts them into a feeble ideology and robs them of the power, which they possess in their attachment to their origin, of witnessing to reality.

Action which is in accordance with Christ is in accordance with reality because it allows the world to be the world; it reckons with the world as the world; and yet it never forgets that in Jesus Christ the world is loved, condemned and reconciled by God.   *(E: 224-230)*

*

The acceptance of guilt

From what has just been said it emerges that the structure of responsible action includes both readiness to accept guilt and freedom.

When we once more turn our attention to the origin of all responsibility it becomes clear to us what we are to understand by acceptance of guilt. Jesus is not concerned with the proclamation and realization of new ethical ideals; he is not concerned with himself being good (Matt. 19.17); he is concerened solely with love for the real man, and for that reason he is able to enter into the fellowship of the guilt of men and to take the burden of their guilt upon himself. Jesus does not desire to be regarded as the only perfect one at the expense of men; he does not desire to look down on mankind as the only guiltless one while humanity goes to its ruin under the weight of its guilt; he does not wish that some idea of a new man should triumph amid the wreckage of a humanity whose guilt has destroyed it. He does not wish to acquit himself of the guilt under which men die. A love which left man alone in his guilt would not be love for the real man. As one who acts responsibly in the historical existence of men Jesus becomes guilty. It must be emphasized that it is solely his love which makes him incur guilt. From his selfless love, from his freedom from sin, Jesus enters into the guilt of men and takes this guilt upon himself. Freedom from sin and the question of guilt are inseperable in him. It is as the one who is without sin that Jesus takes upon himself the guilt of his brothers, and it is under the burden of this guilt that he shows himself to be without sin. In this Jesus Christ, who is guilty without sin, lies the origin of every action of responsible deputyship. If it is responsible action, if it is action which is concerned solely and entirely with the other man, if it arises from selfless love for the real man who is our brother, then, precisely because this is so, it cannot wish to shun the fellowship of human guilt. Jesus took upon himself the guilt of all men, and for that reason every man who acts responsibly becomes guilty. If any man tries to escape guilt in responsibility he detaches himself from the ultimate reality of human existence, and what is more he cuts himself off from the redeeming mystery of Christ's bearing guilt without sin and he has no share in the divine justification which lies upon this event. He sets his own personal innocence above his responsibility for men, and he is blind to the more irredeemable guilt which he incurs precisely in this; he is blind also to the fact that real innocence shows itself precisely in a man's entering into the fellowship of guilt for the sake of other men. Through Jesus Christ it becomes an essential part of responsible action that the man who is without sin loves selflessly and for that reason incurs guilt.

Conscience

There is a reply to all this which undeniably commands respect. It comes from the high authority of conscience; for conscience is unwilling to sacrifice its integrity to any other value, and it therefore refuses to incur guilt for the sake of another man. Responsibility for our neighbour is cut short by the inviolable call of conscience. A responsibility which would oblige a man to act against his conscience would carry within it its own condemnation. In what respects is this true and in what respects is it false?

It is true that it can never be advisable to act against one's own conscience. All Christian ethics is agreed in this. But what does that mean? Conscience comes from a depth which lies beyond a man's own will and his own reason and it makes itself heard as the call of human existence to unity with itself. Conscience comes as an indictment of the loss of this unity and as a warning against the loss of one's self. Primarily it is directed not towards a particular kind of doing but towards a particular mode of being. It protests against a doing which imperils the unity of this being with itself.

So long as conscience can be formally defined in these terms it is extremely inadvisable to act against its authority; disregard for the call of conscience will necessarily entail the destruction of one's own being, not even a purposeful surrender of it; it will bring about the decline and collapse of a human existence. Action against one's own conscience runs parallel with suicidal action against one's own life, and it is not by chance that the two often go together. Responsible action which did violence to conscience in this formal sense would indeed be reprehensible.

But that is not by any means the end of the question. The call of conscience arises from the imperilling of man's unity with himself, and it is therefore now necessary to ask what constitutes this unity. The first constituent is the man's own ego in its claim to be 'like God', *sicut deus*, in the knowledge of good and evil. The call of conscience in natural man is the attempt on the part of the ego to justify itself in its knowledge of good and evil before God, before men and before itself, and to secure its own continuance in this self-justification. Finding no firm support in its own contingent individuality the ego traces its own derivation back to a universal law of good and seeks to achieve unity with itself in conformity with this law. Thus the call of conscience has its origin and its goal in the autonomy of a man's own ego. A man's purpose in obeying this call is on each occasion anew that he should himself once more realize this autonomy which has its origin beyond his own will and knowledge 'in Adam'. Thus in his conscience he continues to be bound by a law of his own finding, a law which may assume different concrete forms but which he can transgress only at the price of losing his own self.

We can now understand that the great change takes place at the moment when the unity of human existence ceases to consist in its autonomy and is found, through the miracle of faith, beyond the man's own ego and its law, in Jesus Christ. The form of this change in the point of unity has an exact analogy in the secular sphere. When the national socialist says 'My conscience is Adolf Hitler' that, too, is an attempt to find a foundation for the unity of his own ego somewhere beyond himself. The consequence of this is the surrender of one's autonomy for the sake of an unconditional heteronomy; and this in turn is possible only if the other man, the man to whom I look for the unity of my life, fulfils the function of a redeemer for me. This, then, provides an extremely direct and significant parallel to the Christian truth, and at the same time an extremely direct and significant contrast with it.

When Christ, true God and true man, has become the point of unity of my existence, conscience will indeed still formally be the call of my actual being to unity with myself, but this unity cannot now be realized by means of a return to the autonomy which I derive from the law; it must be realized in fellowship with Jesus Christ. Natural conscience, no matter how strict and rigorous it may be, is now seen to be the most ungodly self-justification, and it is overcome by the conscience which is set free in Jesus Christ and which summons me to unity with myself in Jesus Christ. Jesus Christ has become my conscience. This means that I can now find unity with myself only in the surrender of my ego to God and to men. The origin and the goal of my conscience is not a law but it is the living God and the living man as he confronts me in Jesus Christ. For the sake of God and of men Jesus became a breaker of the law. He broke the law of the Sabbath in order to keep it holy in love for God and for men. He forsook his parents in order to dwell in the house of his Father and thereby to purify his obedience towards his parents. He sat at table with sinners and outcasts; and for the love of men he came to be forsaken by God in his last hour. As the one who loved without sin, he became guilty; he wished to share in the fellowship of human guilt; he rejected the devil's accusation which was intended to divert him from this course. Thus it is Jesus Christ who sets conscience free for the service of God and of our neighbour; he sets conscience free even and especially when man enters into the fellowship of human guilt. The conscience which has been set free from the law will not be afraid to enter into the guilt of another man for the other man's sake, and indeed precisely in doing this it will show itself in its purity. The conscience which has been set free is not timid like the conscience which is bound by the law, but it stands wide open for our neighbour and for his concrete distress. And so conscience joins with the responsibility which has its foundation in Christ in bearing guilt for the sake of our neighbour. Human action is poisoned in a way which differs from essential original sin, yet as responsible action, in contrast to any self-righteously high-principled action, it nevertheless indirectly has a part in the action of Jesus Christ. For responsible action, therefore, there is a kind of relative freedom from sin, and this shows itself precisely in the responsible acceptance of the guilt of others. *(E: 240-245).*

*

However greatly responsibility and the conscience which is set free in Christ may desire to be united, they nevertheless continue to confront one another in a relation of irreducible tension. Conscience imposes two kinds of limit upon that bearing of guilt which from time to time becomes necessary in responsible action.

In the first place, the conscience which is set free in Christ is still essentially the summons to unity with myself. The acceptance of a responsibility must not destroy this unity. The surrender of the ego in selfless service must never be confused with the destruction and annihilation of this ego; for then indeed this ego would no longer be capable of assuming responsibility. The extent of the guilt which may be accepted in the pursuit of responsible action is on each occasion concretely limited by the requirement of the man's unity with himself, that is to say, by his carrying power. There are responsibilities which I cannot carry without breaking down under their weight; it may be a declaration of war, the violation of a political treaty, a revolution or merely the discharge of a single employee who thereby loses the means of supporting his family; or it may be simply a piece of advice in connexion with some personal decisions in life. Certainly the strength to bear responsible decisions can and should grow; certainly any failure to fulfil a responsibility is in itself a responsible decision; and yet in the concrete instance the summons of conscience to unity with oneself in Jesus Christ remains irresistible, and it is this which explains the infinite multiplicity of responsible decisions.

Secondly, even when it is set free in Jesus Christ conscience still confronts responsible action with the law, through obedience to which man is preserved in that unity with himself which has its foundation in Jesus Christ. Disregard for this law can give rise only to irresponsibility. This is the law of love for God and for our neighbour as it is explained in the decalogue, in the Sermon on the Mount and in the apostolic parenesis. It has been correctly observed that in the contents of its law natural conscience is in strikingly close agreement with that of the conscience which has been set free in Christ. This is due to the fact that it is upon conscience that the continuance of life itself depends; conscience, therefore, contains fundamental features of the law of life, even though these features may be distorted in detail and perverted in principle. The liberated conscience is still what it was as the natural conscience, namely the warner against transgression of the law of life. But the law is no longer the last thing; there is still Jesus Christ; for that reason, in the contest between conscience and concrete responsibility, the free decision must be given for Christ. This does not mean an everlasting conflict, but the winning of ultimate unity; for indeed the foundation, the essence and the goal of concrete responsibility is the same Jesus Christ who is the Lord of conscience. Thus responsibility is bound by conscience, but conscience is set free of responsibility. It is now clear that it is the same thing if we say that the responsible man becomes guilty without sin or if we say that only the man with a free conscience can bear responsibility.

When a man takes guilt upon himself in responsibility, and no responsible man can avoid this, he imputes this guilt to himself and to no one else; he answers for it; he accepts responsibility for it. He does not do this in the insolent presumptuousness of his own power, but he does it in the knowledge that this liberty is forced upon him and that in this liberty he is dependent on grace. Before other men the man of free responsibility is justified by necessity; before himself he is acquitted by his conscience; but before God he hopes only for mercy.

Freedom

We must therefore conclude our analysis of the structure of responsible action by speaking of freedom.

Responsibility and freedom are corresponding concepts. Factually, though not chronologically, responsibility presupposes freedom and freedom can consist only in responsibility. Responsibility is the freedom of men which is given only in the obligation to God and to our neighbour.

The responsible man acts in the freedom of his own self, without the support of men, circumstances or principles, but with a due consideration for the given human and general conditions and for the relevant questions of principle. The proof of his freedom is the fact that nothing can answer for him, nothing can exonerate him, except his own deed and his own self. It is he himself who must observe, judge, weigh up, decide and act. It is man himself who must examine the motives, the prospects, the value of the purpose of his action. But neither the purity of the motivation, nor the opportune circumstances, nor the value, nor the significant purpose of an intended undertaking can become the governing law of his action, a law to which he can withdraw, to which he can appeal as an authority, and by which he can be exculpated and acquitted. For in that case he would indeed no longer be truly free. The action of the responsible man is performed in the obligation which alone gives freedom and which gives entire freedom, the obligation to God and to our neighbour as they confront us in Jesus Christ. At the same time it is performed wholly within the domain of relativity, wholly in the twilight which the historical situation spreads over good and evil; it is performed in the midst of the innumerable perspectives in which every given phenomenon appears. It has not to decide simply between right and wrong and between good and evil, but between right and right and between wrong and wrong. As Aeschylus said, 'right strives with right'. Precisely in this respect responsible action is a free venture; it is not justified by any law; it is performed without any claim to a valid self-justification, and therefore also without any claim to an ultimate valid knowledge of good and evil. Good, as what is responsible, is performed in ignorance of good and in the surrender to God of the deed which has become necessary and which is nevertheless, or for that very reason, free; for it is God who sees the heart, who weighs up the deed, and who directs the course of history.

With this there is disclosed to us a deep secret of history in general. The man who acts in the freedom of his own most personal responsibility is precisely the man who sees his action finally committed to the guidance of God. The free deed knows itself in the end as the deed of God; the decision knows itself as guidance; the free venture knows itself as divine necessity. It is in the free abandonment of knowledge of his own good that a man performs the good of God. It is only from this last point of view that one can speak of good in historical action. We shall have to take up these considerations again later at the point at which we have left off.

Before that we still have to give some space to a crucial question which makes an essential contribution to the clarification of our problem. What is the relationship between free responsibility and obedience? It must seem at first sight as though everything we have said about free responsibility is applicable in practice only when a man finds himself in what we call a 'responsible position' in life, in other words when he has to take independent decisions on the very largest scale. What connexion can there be between responsibility and the monotonous daily work of the labourer, the factory worker, the clerk, the private soldier, the apprentice or the schoolboy? It is a different matter already with the owner-farmer, the industrial contractor, the politician or statesman, the general, the master craftsman, the teacher or the judge. But in their lives, too, how much there is of technique and duty and how little of really free decision! And so it seems that everything that we have said about responsibility can in the end apply only to a very small group of men, and even to these only in a few moments of their lives; and consequently it seems as though for the great majority of men one must speak not of responsibility but of obedience and duty. This implies one ethic for the great and the strong, for the rulers, and another for the small and the weak, the subordinates; on the one hand responsibility and on the other obedience, on the one hand freedom and on the other subservience. And indeed there can be no doubt that in our modern social order, and especially in the German one, the life of the individual is so exactly defined and regulated, and is at the same time assured of such complete security, that it is granted to only very few men to breathe the free air of the wide open spaces of great decisions and to experience the hazard of responsible action which is entirely their own. In consequence of the compulsory regulation of life in accordance with a definite course of training and vocational activity, our lives have come to be relatively free from ethical dangers; the individual who from his childhood on has had to take his assigned place in accordance with this principle is ethically emasculated; he has been robbed of the creative moral power, freedom. In this we see a deep-seated fault in the essential development of our modern social order, a fault which can be countered only with a clear exposition of the fundamental concept of responsibility. As things stand, the large-scale experimental material for the problem of responsibility must be sought for among the great political leaders, industrialists and generals; for indeed those few others who venture to act on their own free responsibility in the midst of the pressure of everyday life, are crushed by the machinery of the social order, by the general routine.

Yet it would be an error if we were to continue to look at the problem from this point of view. There is, in fact, no single life which cannot experience the situation of responsibility; every life can experience this situation in its most characteristic form, that is to say, in the encounter with other people. Even when free responsibility is more or less excluded from a man's vocational and public life, he nevertheless always stands in a responsible relation to other men; these relations extend from his family to his workmates. The fulfilment of genuine responsibility at this point affords the only sound possibility of extending the sphere of responsibility once more into vocational and public life. Where man meets man — and this includes the encounters of professional life — there arises genuine responsibility, and these responsible relationships cannot be supplanted by any general regulation or routine. That holds true, then, not only for the relation between married people, or for parents and children, but also for the master and the apprentice, the teacher and his pupil, the judge and the accused.

But we can go one step further than this. Responsibility does not only stand side by side with relationships of obedience; it has its place also within these relationships. The apprentice has a duty of obedience towards his master, but at the same time he has also a free responsibility for his work, for his achievement and, therefore, also for his master. It is the same with the schoolboy and the student, and indeed also with the employee in any kind of industrial undertaking and with the soldier in war. Obedience and responsibility are interlinked in such a way that one cannot say that responsibility begins only where obedience leaves off, but rather that obedience is rendered in responsibility. There will always be a relation of obedience and dependence; all that matters is that these should not, as they already largely do today, leave no room for responsibilities. To know himself to be responsible is more difficult for the man who is socially dependent than for the man who is socially free, but a relationship of dependence does not in any case in itself exclude free responsibility. The master and the servant, while preserving the relationship of obedience, can and should answer for each other in free responsibility.

The ultimate reason for this lies in that relation of men to God which is realized in Jesus Christ. Jesus stands before God as the one who is both obedient and free. As the obedient one he does his Father's will in blind compliance with the law which is commanded him, and as the free one he acquiesces in God's will out of his own most personal knowledge, with open eyes and a joyous heart; he recreates this will, as it were, out of himself. Obedience without freedom is slavery; freedom without obedience is arbitrary self-will. Obedience restrains freedom; and freedom ennobles obedience. Obedience binds the creature to the Creator and freedom enables the creature to stand before the Creator as one who is made in his image. Obedience shows man that he must allow himself to be told what is good and what God requires of him (Micah 6.8); and liberty enables him to do good himself. Obedience knows what is good and does it, and freedom dares to act, and abandons to God the judgment of good and evil. Obedience follows blindly and freedom has open eyes. Obedience acts without questioning and freedom asks what is the purpose. Obedience has its hands tied and freedom is creative. In obedience man adheres to the decalogue and in freedom man creates new decalogues (Luther).

In responsibility both obedience and freedom are realized. Responsibility implies tension between obedience and freedom. There would be no more responsibility if either were made independent of the other. Responsible action is subject to obligation, and yet it is creative. To make obedience independent of freedom leads only to the Kantian ethic of duty, and to make freedom independent of obedience leads only to the ethic of irresponsible genius. Both the man of duty and the genius carry their justification within themselves. The man of responsibility stands between obligation and freedom; he must dare to act under obligation and in freedom; yet he finds his justification neither in his obligation nor in his freedom but solely in him who has put him in this (humanly impossible) situation and who requires this deed of him. The responsible man delivers up himself and his deed to God.

We have tried to define the structure of responsible life in terms of deputyship, correspondence with reality, acceptance of guilt, and freedom. Now the demand for more concrete formulation brings us to the question whether it is possible to advance a more exact definition of the place, the *locus*, at which responsible life is realized. Does responsibility set me in an unlimited field of activity? Or does it confine me strictly within the limits which are implied in my daily concrete tasks? What must I know myself to be responsible for? And what does not lie within the scope of my responsibility? Is there any purpose in regarding myself as responsible for everything that takes place in the world? Or can I stand by and watch these great events as an unconcerned spectator so long as my own tiny domain is in order? Am I to wear myself out in important zeal against all the wrong and all the misery that is in the world? Or am I entitled, in self-satisfied security, to let the wicked world run its course, so long as I cannot myself do anything to change it and so long as I have done my own work? What is the place and what are the limits of my responsibility? *(E: 246-254)*

*

AFTER TEN YEARS

Although Bonhoeffer's essay 'After Ten Years' now appears in the Letters and Papers from Prison *it is, in fact, a bridging text which links Bonhoeffer's ethical reflections with those theological explorations which are expressed in his prison writings. Written at the end of 1942, 'After Ten Years' was a Christmas gift to Eberhard Bethge, and Bonhoeffer's co-conspirators Hans Oster and his brother-in-law Hans von Dohnanyi. The final unfinished paragraph provides a clue as to why Bonhoeffer has become an inspiration and a resource for contemporary theologies of liberation.*

Ten years is a long time in anyone's life. As time is the most valuable thing that we have, because it is most irrevocable, the thought of any lost time troubles us whenever we look back. Time lost is time in which we have failed to live a full human life, gain experience, learn, create, enjoy, and suffer; it is time that has not been filled up, but left empty. These last years have certainly not been like that. Our losses have been great and immeasurable, but time has not been lost. It is true that the knowledge and experience that were gained, and of which one did not become conscious till later, are only abstractions of reality, of life actually lived. But just as the capacity to forget is a gift of grace, so memory, the recalling of lessons we have learnt, is also part of responsible living. In the following pages I should like to try to give some account of what we have experienced and learnt in common during these years — not personal experiences, or anything systematically arranged, or arguments and theories, but conclusions reached more or less in common by a circle of like-minded people, and related to the business of human life, put down one after the other, the only connection between them being that of concrete experience. There is nothing new about them, for they were known long before; but it has been given to us to reach them anew by first-hand experience. One cannot write about these things without a constant sense of gratitude for the fellowship of spirit and community of life that have been proved and preserved throughout these years.

No ground under our feet

One may ask whether there have ever before in human history been people with so little ground under their feet — people to whom every available alternative seemed equally intolerable, repugnant, and futile, who looked beyond all these existing alternatives for the source of their strength so entirely in the past or in the future, and who yet, without being dreamers, were able to await the success of their cause so quietly and confidently. Or perhaps one should rather ask whether the responsible thinking people of any generation that stood at a turning-point in history did not feel much as we do, simply because something new was emerging that could not be seen in the existing alternatives.

Who stands fast?

The great masquerade of evil has played havoc with all our ethical concepts. For evil to appear disguised as light, charity, historical necessity, or social justice is quite bewildering to anyone brought up on our traditional ethical concepts, while for the Christian who bases his life on the Bible it merely confirms the fundamental wickedness of evil.

The '*reasonable*' people's failure is obvious. With the best intentions and a naïve lack of realism, they think that with a little reason they can bend back into position the framework that has got out of joint. In their lack of vision they want to do justice to all sides, and so the conflicting forces wear them down with nothing achieved. Disappointed by the world's unreasonableness, they see themselves condemned to ineffectiveness; they step aside in resignation or collapse before the stronger party.

Still more pathetic is the total collapse of moral *fanaticism.* The fanatic thinks that his single-minded principles qualify him to do battle with the powers of evil; but like a bull he rushes at the red cloak instead of the person who is holding it; he exhausts himself and is beaten. He gets entangled in non-essentials and falls into the trap set by cleverer people.

Then there is the man with a *conscience*, who fights single-handed against heavy odds in situations that call for a decision. But the scale of the conflicts in which he has to choose — with no advice or support except from his own conscience — tears him to pieces. Evil approaches him in so many respectable and seductive disguises that his conscience becomes nervous and vacillating, till at last he contents himself with a salved instead of a clear conscience, so that he lies to his own conscience in order to avoid despair; for a man whose only support is his conscience can never realize that a bad conscience may be stronger and more wholesome than a deluded one.

From the perplexingly large number of possible decisions, the way of *duty* seems to be the sure way out. Here, what is commanded is accepted as what is most certain, and the responsibility for it rests on the commander, not on the person commanded. But no one who confines himself to the limits of duty ever goes so far as to venture, on his sole responsibility, to act in the only way that makes it possible to score a direct hit on evil and defeat it. The man of duty will in the end have to do his duty by the devil too.

As to the man who asserts his complete *freedom* to stand four-square to the world, who values the necessary deed more highly than an unspoilt conscience or reputation, who is ready to sacrifice a barren principle for a fruitful compromise, or the barren wisdom of a middle course for a fruitful radicalism — let him beware lest his freedom should bring him down. He will assent to what is bad so as to ward off something worse, and in doing so he will no longer be able to realize that the worse, which he wants to avoid, might be the better. Here we have the raw material of tragedy.

Here and there people flee from the public altercation into the sanctuary of private *virtuousness*. But anyone who does this must shut his mouth and his eyes to the injustice around him. Only at the cost of self-deception can he keep himself pure from the contamination arising from the responsible action. In spite of all that he does, what he leaves undone will rob him of his peace of mind. He will either go to pieces because of this disquiet, or become the most hypocritical of Pharisees.

Who stands fast? Only the man whose final standard is not his reason, his principles, his conscience, his freedom, or his virtue, but who is ready to sacrifice all this when he is called to obedient and responsible action in faith and in exclusive allegiance to God — the responsible man, who tries to make his whole life an answer to the question and call of God. Where are these responsible people?

Civil courage?

What lies behind the complaint about the dearth of civil courage? In recent years we have seen a great deal of bravery and self-sacrifice, but civil courage hardly anywhere, even among ourselves. To attribute this simply to personal cowardice would be too facile a psychology; its background is quite different. In a long history, we Germans have had to learn the need for and the strength of obedience. In the subordination of all personal wishes and ideas to the tasks to which we have been called, we have seen the meaning and the greatness of our lives. We have looked upwards, not in servile fear, but in free trust, seeing in our tasks a call, and in our call a vocation. This readiness to follow a command from 'above' rather than our own private opinions and wishes was a sign of legitimate self-distrust. Who would deny that in obedience, in their task and calling, the Germans have again and again shown the utmost bravery and self-sacrifice? But the German has kept his freedom — and what nation has talked more passionately of freedom than the Germans, from Luther to the idealist philosophers? — by seeking deliverance from self-will through service to the community. Calling and freedom were to him two sides of the same thing. But in this he misjudged the world; he did not realize that his submissiveness and self-sacrifice could be exploited for evil ends. When that happened, the exercise of the calling itself became questionable, and all the moral principles of the German were bound to totter. The fact could not be escaped that the German still lacked something fundamental: he could not see the need for free and responsible action, even in opposition to his tasks and his calling; in its place there appeared on the one hand an irresponsbile lack of scruple, and on the other a self-tormenting punctiliousness that never led to action. Civil courage, in fact, can grow only out of the free responsibility of free men. Only now are the Germans beginning to discover the meaning of free responsibility. It depends on a God who demands responsible action in a bold venture of faith, and who promises forgiveness and consolation to the man who becomes a sinner in that venture.

Of success

Although it is certainly not true that success justifies an evil deed and shady means, it is impossible to regard success as something that is ethically quite neutral. The fact is that historical success creates a basis for the continuance of life, and it is still a moot point whether it is ethically more responsible to take the field like a Don Quixote against a new age, or to admit one's defeat, accept the new age, and agree to serve it. In the last resort success makes history; and the ruler of history repeatedly brings good out of evil over the heads of the history-makers. Simply to ignore the ethical significance of success is a short-circuit created by dogmatists who think unhistorically and irresponsibly; and it is good for us sometimes to be compelled to grapple seriously with the ethical problem of success. As long as a goodness is successful, we can afford the luxury of regarding it as having no ethical significance; it is when success is achieved by evil means that the problem arises. In the face of such a situation we find that it cannot be adequately dealt with, either by theoretical dogmatic arm-chair criticism, which means a refusal to face the facts, or by opportunism, which means giving up the struggle and surrendering to success. We will not and must not be either outraged critics or opportunists, but must take our share of responsibility for the moulding of history in every situation and at every moment, whether we are the victors or the vanquished. One who will not allow any occurrence whatever to deprive him of his responsibility for the course of history — because he knows that it has been laid on him by God — will thereafter achieve a more fruitful relation to the events of history than that of barren criticism and equally barren opportunism. To talk of going down fighting like heroes in the face of certain defeat is not really heroic at all, but merely a refusal to face the future. The ultimate question for a responsible man to ask is not how he is to extricate himself heroically from the affair, but how the coming generation is to live. It is only from this question, with its responsibility towards history, that fruitful solutions can come, even if for the time being they are very humiliating. In short, it is much easier to see a thing through from the point of view of abstract principle than from that of concrete responsibility. The rising generation will always instinctively discern which of these we make the basis of our actions, for it is their own future that is at stake.

Of folly

Folly is a more dangerous enemy to the good than evil. One can protest against evil; it can be unmasked and, if need be, prevented by force. Evil always carries the seeds of its own destruction, as it makes people, at the least, uncomfortable. Against folly we have no defence. Neither protests nor force can touch it; reasoning is no use; facts that contradict personal prejudices can simply be disbelieved — indeed, the fool can counter by criticizing them, and if they are undeniable, they can just be pushed aside as trivial exceptions. So the fool, as distinct from the scoundrel, is completely self-satisfied; in fact, he can easily become dangerous, as it does not take much to make him aggressive. A fool must therefore be treated more cautiously than a scoundrel; we shall never again try to convince a fool by reason, for it is both useless and dangerous.

If we are to deal adequately with folly, we must try to understand its nature. This much is certain, that it is a moral rather than an intellectual defect. There are people who are mentally agile but foolish, and people who are mentally slow but very far from foolish — a discovery that we make to our surprise as a result of particular situations. We thus get the impression that folly is likely to be, not a congenital defect, but one that is acquired in certain circumstances where people *make* fools of themselves or allow others to make fools of them. We notice further that this defect is less common in the unsociable and solitary than in individuals or groups that are inclined or condemned to sociability. It seems, then, that folly is a sociological rather than a psychological problem, and that it is a special form of the operation of historical circumstances on people, a psychological by-product of definite external factors. If we look more closely, we see that any violent display of power, whether political or religious, produces an outburst of folly in a large part of humanity; indeed, this seems actually to be a psychological and sociological law: the power of some needs the folly of the others. It is not that certain human capacities, intellectual capacities for instance, become stunted or destroyed, but rather that the upsurge of power makes such an overwhelming impression that men are deprived of their independent judgment, and — more or less unconsciously — give up trying to assess the new state of affairs for themselves. The fact that the fool is often stubborn must not mislead us into thinking that he is independent. One feels in fact, when talking to him, that one is dealing, not with the man himself, but with slogans, catchwords, and the like, which have taken hold of him. He is under a spell, he is blinded, his very nature is being misused and exploited. Having thus become a passive instrument, the fool will be capable of any evil and at the same time incapable of seeing that it is evil. Here lies the danger of a diabolical exploitation that can do irreparable damage to human beings.

But at this point it is quite clear, too, that folly can be overcome, not by instruction, but only by an act of liberation; and so we have come to terms with the fact that in the great majority of cases inward liberation must be preceded by outward liberation, and that until that has taken place, we may as well abandon all attempts to convince the fool. In this state of affairs we have to realize why it is no use our trying to find out what 'the people' really think, and why the question is so superfluous for the man who thinks and acts resonsibly — but always given these particular circumstances. The Bible's words that 'the fear of the Lord is the beginning of wisdom' (Ps. 111.10) tell us that a person's inward liberation to live a responsible life before God is the only real cure for folly.

But there is some consolation in these thoughts on folly: they in no way justify us in thinking that most people are fools in all circumstances. What will really matter is whether those in power expect more from people's folly than from their wisdom and independence of mind.

Contempt for humanity?

There is a very real danger of our drifting into an attitude of contempt for humanity. We know quite well that we have no right to do so, and that it would lead us into the most sterile relation to our fellow-men. The following thoughts may keep us from such a temptation. It means that we at once fall into the worst blunders of our opponents. The man who despises another will never be able to make anything of him. Nothing that we despise in the other man is entirely absent from ourselves. We often expect from others more than we are willing to do ourselves. Why have we hitherto thought so intemperately about man and his frailty and temptability? We must learn to regard people less in the light of what they do or omit to do, and more in the light of what they suffer. The only profitable relationship to others — and especially to our weaker brethren — is one of love, and that means the will to hold fellowship with them. God himself did not despise humanity, but became man for men's sake.

Immanent rightousness

It is one of the most surprising experiences, but at the same time one of the most incontrovertible, that evil — often in a surprisingly short time — proves its own folly and defeats its own object. That does not mean that punishment follows hard on the heels of every evil action; but it does mean that deliberate transgression of the divine law in the supposed interests of worldly self-preservation has exactly the opposite effect. We learn this from our own experience, and we can interpret it in various ways. At least it seems possible to infer with certainty that in social life there are laws more powerful than anything that may claim to dominate them, and that it is therefore not only wrong but unwise to disregard them. We can understand from this why Aristotelian—Thomist ethics made wisdom one of the cardinal virtues. Wisdom and folly are not ethically indifferent, as Neo-protestant motive-ethics would have it. In the fullness of the concrete situation and the possibilities which it offers, the wise man at the same time recognizes the impassable limits that are set to all action by the permanent laws of human social life; and in this knowledge the wise man acts well and the good man wisely.

It is true that all historically important action is constantly overstepping the limits set by these laws. But it makes all the difference whether such overstepping of the appointed limits is regarded in principle as the superseding of them, and is therefore given out to be a law of a special kind, or whether the overstepping is deliberately regarded as a fault which is perhaps unavoidable, justified only if the law and the limit are re-established and respected as soon as possible. It is not necessarily hypocrisy if the declared aim of political action is the restoration of the law, and not mere self-preservation. The world *is*, in fact, so ordered that a basic respect for ultimate laws and human life is also the best means of self-preservation, and that these laws may be broken only on the odd occasion in case of brief necessity, whereas anyone who turns necessity into a principle, and in so doing establishes a law of his own alongside them, is inevitably bound, sooner or later, to suffer retribution. The immanent righteousness of history rewards and punishes only men's deeds, but the eternal righteousness of God tries and judges their hearts.

A few articles of faith on the sovereignty of God in history

I believe that God can and will bring good out of evil, even out of the greatest evil. For that purpose he needs men who make the best use of everything. I believe that God will give us all the strength we need to help us to resist in all time of distress. But he never gives it in advance, lest we should rely on ourselves and not on him alone. A faith such as this should allay all our fears for the future. I believe that even our mistakes and shortcomings are turned to good account, and that it is no harder for God to deal with them than with our supposedly good deeds. I believe that God is no timeless fate, but that he waits for and answers sincere prayers and responsible actions.

Confidence

There is hardly one of us who has not known what it is to be betrayed. The figure of Judas, which we used to find so difficult to understand, is now fairly familiar to us. The air that we breathe is so polluted by mistrust that it almost chokes us. But where we have broken through the layer of mistrust, we have been able to discover a confidence hitherto undreamed of. Where we trust, we have learnt to put our very lives into the hands of others; in the face of all the different interpretations that have been put on our lives and actions, we have learnt to trust unreservedly. We now know that only such confidence, which is always a venture, though a glad and positive venture, enables us really to live and work. We know that it is most reprehensible to sow and encourage mistrust, and that our duty is rather to foster and strengthen confidence wherever we can. Trust will always be one of the greatest, rarest, and happiest blessings of our life in community, though it can emerge only on the dark background of a necessary mistrust. We have learnt never to trust a scoundrel an inch, but to give ourselves to the trustworthy without reserve.

The sense of quality

Unless we have the courage to fight for a revival of wholesome reserve between man and man, we shall perish in an anarchy of human values. The impudent contempt for such reserve is the mark of the rabble, just as inward uncertainty, haggling and cringing for the favour of insolent people, and lowering oneself to the level of the rabble are the way of becoming no better than the rabble oneself. When we forget what is due to ourselves and to others, when the feeling for human quality and the power to exercise reserve cease to exist, chaos is at the door. When we tolerate impudence for the sake of material comforts, then we abandon our self-respect, the flood-gates are opened, chaos bursts the dam that we were to defend; and we are responsible for it all. In other times it may have been the business of Christianity to champion the equality of all men; its business today will be to defend passionately human dignity and reserve. The misinterpretation that we are acting for our own interests, and the cheap insinuation that our attitude is anti-social, we shall simply have to put up with; they are the invariable protests of the rabble against decency and order. Anyone who is pliant and uncertain in this matter does not realize what is at stake, and indeed in his case the reproaches may well be justified. We are witnessing the levelling down of all ranks of society, and at the same time the birth of a new sense of nobility, which is binding together a circle of men from all former social classes. Nobility arises from and exists by sacrifice, courage, and a clear sense of duty to oneself and society, by expecting due regard for itself as a matter of course; and it shows an equally natural regard for others, whether they are of higher or lower degree. We need all along the line to recover the lost sense of quality and a social order based on quality. Quality is the greatest enemy of any kind of mass-levelling. Socially it means the renunciation of all place-hunting, a break with the cult of the 'star', an open eye both upwards and downwards, especially in the choice of one's more intimate friends, and pleasure in private life as well as courage to enter public life. Culturally it means a return from the newspaper and the radio to the book, from feverish activity to unhurried leisure, from dispersion to concentration, from sensationalism to reflection, from virtuosity to art, from snobbery to modesty, from extravagance to moderation. Quantities are competitive, qualities are complementary.

Sympathy

We must allow for the fact that most people learn wisdom only by personal experience. This explains, first, why so few people are capable of taking precautions in advance — they always fancy that they will somehow or other avoid the danger, till it is too late. Secondly, it explains their insensibility to the sufferings of others; sympathy grows in proportion to the fear of approaching disaster. There is a good deal of excuse on ethical grounds for this attitude. No one wants to meet fate head-on; inward calling and strength for action are acquired only in the actual emergency. No one is responsible for all the injustice and suffering in the world, and no one wants to set himself up as the judge of the world. Psychologically, our lack of imagination, of sensitivity, and of mental alertness is balanced by a steady composure, an ability to go on working, and a great capacity for suffering. But from a Christian point of view, none of these excuses can obscure the fact that the most important factor, large-heartedness, is lacking. Christ kept himself from suffering till his hour had come, but when it did come he met it as a free man, seized it, and mastered it. Christ, so the scriptures tell us, bore the sufferings of all humanity in his own body as if they were his own — a thought beyond our comprehension — accepting them of his own free will. We are certainly not Christ; we are not called on to redeem the world by our own deeds and sufferings, and we need not try to assume such an impossible burden. We are not lords, but instruments in the hand of the Lord of history; and we can share in other people's sufferings only to a very limited degree. We are not Christ, but if we want to be Christians, we must have some share in Christ's large-heartedness by acting with responsibility and in freedom when the hour of danger comes, and by showing a real sympathy that springs, not from fear, but from the liberating and redeeming love of Christ for all who suffer. Mere waiting and looking on is not Christian behaviour. The Christian is called to sympathy and action, not in the first place by his own sufferings, but by the sufferings of his brethren, for whose sake Christ suffered.

Of suffering

It is infinitely easier to suffer in obedience to a human command than in the freedom of one's own responsibility. It is infinitely easier to suffer with others than to suffer alone. It is infinitely easier to suffer publicly and honourably than apart and ignominiously. It is infinitely easier to suffer through staking one's life than to suffer spiritually. Christ suffered as a free man alone, apart and in ignominy, in body and spirit; and since then many Christians have suffered with him.

Present and future

We used to think that one of the inalienable rights of man was that he should be able to plan both his professional and private life. That is a thing of the past. The force of circumstances has brought us into a situation where we have to give up being 'anxious about tomorrow' (Matt. 6.34). But it makes all the difference whether we accept this willingly and in faith (as the Sermon on the Mount intends), or under continual constraint. For most people, the compulsory abandonment of planning for the future means that they are forced back into living just for the moment, irresponsibly, frivolously, or resignedly; some few dream longingly of better things to come, and try to forget the present. We find both these courses equally impossible, and there remains for us only the very narrow way, often extremely difficult to find, of living every day as if it were our last, and yet living in faith and responsibility as though there were to be a great future: 'Houses and fields and vineyards shall again be bought in the land' proclaims Jeremiah (32.15), in paradoxical contrasts to his prophecies of woe, just before the destruction of the holy city. It is a sign from God and a pledge of a fresh start and a great future, just when all seems black. Thinking and acting for the sake of the coming generation, but being ready to go any day without fear or anxiety — that, in practice, is the spirit in which we are forced to live. It is not easy to be brave and keep that spirit alive, but it is imperative.

Optimism

It is wiser to be pessimistic; it is a way of avoiding disappointment and ridicule, and so wise people condemn optimism. The essence of optimism is not its view of the present, but the fact that it is the inspiration of life and hope when others give in; it enables a man to hold his head high when everything seems to be going wrong; it gives him strength to sustain reserves and yet to claim the future for himself instead of abandoning it to his opponent. It is true that there is a silly, cowardly kind of optimism, which we must condemn. But the optimism that is will for the future should never be despised, even if it is proved wrong a hundred times; it is health and vitality, and the sick man has no business to impugn it. There are people who regard it as frivolous, and some Christians think it impious for anyone to hope and prepare for a better earthly future. They think that the meaning of present events is chaos, disorder, and catastrophe; and in resignation or pious escapism they surrender all responsibility for reconstruction and for future generations. It may be that the day of judgment will dawn tomorrow; in that case, we shall gladly stop working for a better future. But not before.

Insecurity and death

In recent years we have become increasingly familiar with the thought of death. We surprise ourselves by the calmness with which we hear of the death of one of our contemporaries. We cannot hate it as we used to, for we have discovered some good in it, and have almost come to terms with it. Fundamentally we feel that we really belong to death already, and that every new day is a miracle. It would probably not be true to say that we welcome death (although we all know that weariness which we ought to avoid like the plague); we are too inquisitive for that — or, to put it more seriously, we should like to see something more of the meaning of our life's broken fragments. Nor do we try to romanticize death, for life is too great and too precious. Still less do we suppose that danger is the meaning of life — we are not desperate enough for that, and we know too much about the good things that life has to offer, though on the other hand we are only too familiar with life's anxieties and with all the other destructive effects of prolonged personal insecurity. We still love life, but I do not think that death can take us by surprise now. After what we have been through during the war, we hardly dare admit that we should like death to come to us, not accidentally and suddenly through some trivial cause, but in the fullness of life and with everything at stake. It is we ourselves, and not outward circumstances, who make death what it can be, a death freely and voluntarily accepted.

Are we still of any use?

We have been silent witnesses of evil deeds; we have been drenched by many storms; we have learnt the arts of equivocation and pretence; experience has made us suspicious of others and kept us from being truthful and open; intolerable conflicts have worn us down and even made us cynical. Are we still of any use? What we shall need is not geniuses, or cynics, or misanthropes, or clever tacticians, but plain, honest, straightforward men. Will our inward power of resistance be strong enough, and our honesty with ourselves remorseless enough, for us to find our way back to simplicity and straightforwardness?

The view from below

There remains an experience of incomparable value. We have for once learnt to see the great events of world history from below, from the perspective of the outcast, the suspects, the maltreated, the powerless, the oppressed, the reviled — in short, from the perspective of those who suffer. The important thing is that neither bitterness nor envy should have gnawed at the heart during this time, that we should have come to look with new eyes at matters great and small, sorrow and joy, strength and weakness, that our perception of generosity, humanity, justice and mercy should have become clearer, freer, less corruptible. We have to learn that personal suffering is a more effective key, a more rewarding principle for exploring the world in thought and action than personal good fortune. This perspective from below must not become the partisan possession of those who are eternally dissatisfied; rather, we must do justice to life in all its dimensions from a higher satisfaction, whose foundation is beyond any talk of 'from below' or 'from above'. This is the way in which we may affirm it.

5

CHRIST IN A WORLD COME OF AGE[*]

Bonhoeffer's Fiction from Prison, *edited by Eberhard and Renate Bethge, was only published in 1978 (*Fragmente aus Tegel. Drama und Roman, Chr. Kaiser Verlag), *and the English edition, translated by Ursula Hoffmann, edited and introduced by Clifford Green, in 1981 (Fortress Press). The volume contains two lengthy fragments, a drama and a novel, the first written in the spring and early summer of 1943, and the latter in the summer and winter of the same year. They therefore predate those letters from prison which include Bonhoeffer's theological reflections. The Bethge's hesitated to publish these fragments earlier because of their autobiographical rather than theological content. But as we have indicated, there are interesting theological elements in the texts, understandably enough if we remember the autobiographical character of Bonhoeffer's theology. Both in the drama and the novel, Christoph represents Bonhoeffer himself. Our extract from the novel describes Christoph in conversation with his friend Ulrich, a discussion which turns to 'unconscious Christianity'.*

UNCONSCIOUS CHRISTIANITY

'And whose fault is this calamity?' Christoph continued. 'It's the fault of none other than the fashionable people, the so-called upper class that everyone envies and watches to learn how to live with success. And this upper class itself is largely composed of rotten, pushy people, with the souls of lackeys, who mix flattery for superiors with brutality for inferiors, grand phrases for the outside with decay on the inside. And the few decent people and families who might count for something withdraw into themselves in disgust with this hollow, conceited society. Ulrich, that's where the whole problem lies. We need a genuine upper class again, but how can we get it? You yourself say it's always up to the few big wheels, then the rest topples over. That simply means, doesn't it, that Ulrich Karstensen and Christoph Brake, not Archibald Meyer, must set the tone? We can't get around it, and false modesty is out of place in this matter.'

---

* See also above, pp. 35-41.

Ulrich had sat up during these statements and was watching Christoph. He enjoyed listening to Christoph developing his ideas with such assurance and passion, and although he was happy to be caught up by them and agreed with Christoph's line of thought, he still kept his own clear perspective and sometimes saw matters more simply but also more profoundly than Christoph.

'You are right, Christoph, it simply depends on us. But are we really immune to the poisons of vanity and pushiness that infect people nowadays? Look, I often have to think of my mother in this context. She surely is a simple woman; and a village organist, as my father was, certainly isn't part of the upper class. Nevertheless, I have never found in my mother a trace of false ambition or anxieties while in contact with superiors. With all her modesty, she moves with total freedom and assurance wherever she goes without wanting to be something different from what she is. She knows precisely, of course, what it means for me to be in your house and I really don't think she is depressed about being unable to return the favour to your parents. And yet I can sense how she fears that, because of my contact with you, I might some day aspire to be more than I am by birth and by environment, and that someday I would have to be unhappy if I realized the unbridgeable gap between your origins and mine. What I mean to say is — Mother is as free of the modern disease of pushiness as one can be. And if I wonder where she gets that, then there is only one very clear answer: from her Christian piety; that is what makes her so assured and so modest simultaneously. And now I often think that everything has come to the state it is in today because most people no longer have what Mother has. Do you understand? And Christoph, if it is ever going to change, if someday, as you say, there is to be a new, genuine, and responsible upper class — don't you think that then such people must again have what Mother has? Or else they'll immediately revert to their previous state.'

Ulrich never found putting his thoughts into words as easy as Christoph did and this difficulty always pained him somewhat. But his warmth, his personal manner, and his great inner modesty always lent a quality to his speech that was winning and engaged one's attention. While Christoph enjoyed presenting the same idea in ever new variations of phrase and illustration and had at his disposal a great facility for expression, Ulrich always stated his thoughts just once, and then left it to Christoph to assimilate and integrate them into his own train of thought and give them a form in which they could become effective. That was why Ulrich was usually the listener and also gave the impression to others that, essentially, he was the echo of Christoph's views. In reality, those views were often Ulrich's thoughts, observations, and feelings, which he had stated briefly and often clumsily; Christoph presented them in brilliant form and with the most personal conviction. Ulrich felt profound joy and satisfaction in having found in Christoph such an appreciative and persuasive interpreter of his own thoughts.

What Ulrich had just said had never been voiced yet between the two friends, not because Ulrich might have been ashamed of these thoughts in some fashion — that simply didn't exist between the two — but because Ulrich always took a long time letting obscurely felt matters work themselves up to the clarity of consciousness and word. Christoph was surprised and sensed immediately that something had been said that was quite decisive and new for them both. This had happened to him several times before with Ulrich, and what Christoph had just said about the necessity of the upper class had, itself, grown on the soil of some similarly startling ideas of Ulrich's.

Christoph looked at Ulrich. 'So you think we would have to have more religion if we want to occupy a responsible position someday?'

'I think, Christoph — rather, I wonder — no, I think we would have to be Christians.'

Christoph looked toward the lake, saw young Martin paddling along on his raft in complete absorption. He looked toward the forest, toward the wide sky.

'A damned old-fashioned thought!' he said.

Ulrich didn't answer.

'And just as uncomfortable.'

Ulrich remained silent. A long silence reigned.

'You spoke about your mother, Ulrich', Christoph started in again, 'and you know how much I like her — excuse that dumb expression! But I am thinking now of Papa and Mama. One probably can't call them Christians, at least not in the usual sense of the word. They don't go to church. We say grace at table only because of Little Brother. And yet they are just as little infected as your mother by the spirit of false ambition, careerism, titles, and medals. They prefer a good labourer or artisan a hundred times over some conceited person with the title of "Excellency". Why is that?'

Ulrich pondered. 'That is because, without knowing, and at any rate without saying so, in reality they still live in Christianity — an unconscious Christianity.'

Christoph became restless; he got up and walked, barefoot, back and forth in the thick grass.

'You are a funny character, Ulrich, the way you say that all of a sudden, so assuredly and calmly, as though it were quite certain.'

Ulrich sat without moving, his arms around his drawn up knees. Suddenly he laughed. 'You needn't worry, Christoph. I didn't kneel on the Salvation Army's repentance stool, and I didn't join any sect.'

Christoph, too, had to laugh at this idea. What would Ulrich have had to confess? A grotesque idea! No, that's not quite what he had meant. Christoph continued pacing, pondering, then he stopped before Ulrich. 'Something seems to be wrong, Ulrich,' he said. 'As far as I know Christ didn't differentiate between the good and the bad, the just and the sinners, the decent and the mean. In my opinion the so-called publicans were lousy traitors to their people and the prostitutes belonged to them, as now, together with the Archibald Meyers. And from the confirmation classes with the odious Pastor Schönrock I remember Paul's words: "There is neither Jew nor Greek, there is neither slave nor free, there is neither male nor female." So according to the Christian doctrine all people are supposed to be equal and [illegible]; "God hath chosen the weak and base things of the world," or even, "The weaker and poorer, the better." That's the exact opposite, after all, of what both of us experience and think and want every day. How then should Christianity of all things be able to help form a new upper class, an elite? That would only lead to hopeless equalization.'

Ulrich was silent again. He had to think of old Frau Karoline Brake.

'And your grandmother, Christoph? I am sure she is serious about Christianity and probably knows more about it than most ministers. Do you think she doesn't differentiate between people? Doesn't she think, just as we do, that there must be a top and a bottom and that everything depends on the right people being on top?'

Christoph hesitated. 'I don't understand it. Somewhere there must be a contradiction,' he said.   (*FFP: 74-77*)

*

OUTLINE FOR A BOOK

Bonhoeffer's Letters and Papers from Prison *were edited by Eberhard Bethge, the recipient of many of them, and first published in German in 1951 as* Widerstand und Ergebung. *The first English edition, translated by Reginald Fuller, was published in 1953 (London: SCM). A new and enlarged edition of* Widerstand und Ergebung *was prepared by Bethge and published in 1970. The following year it appeared in English (SCM and Macmillan), and in every respect, not least the accuracy of the translation, it is a superior volume to its predecessors. This version contains many of the letters which were sent to Bonhoeffer as well as a great deal more of his own writing in prison, and thus enables us to see more clearly the human narrative within which his theological reflections unfolded. Bonhoeffer's theological reflections, contained in his letters, need to be read in relation to the outline for his proposed book on which he was working in prison.*

I should like to write a book of not more than 100 pages, divided into three chapters:

1. A stocktaking of Christianity.
2. The real meaning of Christian faith.
3. Conclusions.

Chapter 1 to deal with:

(*a*) The coming of age of humanity (as already indicated). The safeguarding of life against 'accidents' and 'blows of fate'; even if these cannot be eliminated, the danger can be reduced. Insurance (which, although it lives on 'accidents', seeks to mitigate their effects) as a western phenomenon. The aim: to be independent of nature. Nature was formerly conquered by spiritual means, with us by technical organization of all kinds. Our immediate environment is not nature, as formerly, but organization. But with this protection from nature's menace there arises a new one — through organization itself.

But the spiritual force is lacking. The question is: What protects us against the menace of organization? Man is again thrown back on himself. He has managed to deal with everything, only not with himself. He can insure against everything, only not against man. In the last resort it all turns on man.

(*b*) The religionessness of man who has come of age. 'God' as a working hypothesis, as a stop-gap for our embarrassment, has become superfluous (as already indicated).

(*c*) The Protestant church: Pietism as a last attempt to maintain evangelical Christianity as a religion; Lutheran orthodoxy, the attempt to rescue the church as an institution for salvation; the Confessing Church: the theology of revelation; a δός μοι πού στῶ over against the world, involving a 'factual' interest in Christianity; art and science searching for their origin. Generally in the Confessing Church: stand-

273

ing up for the church's 'cause', but little personal faith in Christ. 'Jesus' is disappearing from sight. Sociologically: no effect on the masses — interest confined to the upper and lower middle classes. A heavy incubus of difficult traditional ideas. The decisive factor: the church on the defensive. No taking risks for others.

(*d*) Public morals — as shown by sexual behaviour.

Chapter 2

(*a*) God and the secular.

(*b*) Who is God? Not in the first place an abstract belief in God, in his omnipotence, etc. That is not a genuine experience of God, but a partial extension of the world. Encounter with Jesus Christ. The experience that a transformation of all human life is given in the fact that 'Jesus is there only for others'. His 'being there for others' is the experience of transcendence. It is only this 'being there for others', maintained till death, that is the ground of his omnipotence, omniscience, and omnipresence. Faith is participation in this being of Jesus (incarnation, cross, and resurrection). Our relation to God is not a 'religious' relationship to the highest, most powerful, and best Being imaginable — that is not authentic transcendence — but our relation to God is a new life in 'existence for others', through participation in the being of Jesus. The transcendental is not infinite and unattainable tasks, but the neighbour who is within reach in any given situation. God in human form — not, as in oriental religions, in animal form, monstrous, chaotic, remote, and terrifying, nor in the conceptual forms of the absolute, metaphysical, infinite, etc., nor yet in the Greek divine-human form of 'man in himself', but 'the man for others', and therefore the Crucified, the man who lives out of the transcendent.

(*c*) Interpretation of biblical concepts on this basis. (Creation, fall, atonement, repentance, faith, the new life, the last things.)

(*d*) Cultus. (Details to follow later, in particular on cultus and 'religion'.)

(*e*) What do we really believe? I mean, believe in such a way that we stake our lives on it? The problem of the Apostles' Creed? 'What *must* I believe?' is the wrong question; antiquated controversies, especially those between the different sects; the Lutheran versus Reformed, and to some extent the Roman Catholic versus Protestant, are now unreal. They may at any time be revived with passion, but they no longer carry conviction. There is no proof of this, and we must simply take it that it is so. All that we can prove is that the faith of the Bible and Christianity does not stand or fall by these issues. Karl Barth and the Confessing Church have encouraged us to entrench ourselves persistently behind the 'faith of the church', and evade the honest question as to what we ourselves really believe. That is why the air is not quite fresh, even in the Confessing Church. To say that it is the church's business, not mine, may be a clerical evasion, and outsiders always regard it as such. It is much the same with the dialectical assertion that I do not control my own faith, and that it is therefore not for me to say what my faith is. There may be a place for all these considerations, but they do not absolve us from the duty of being honest with ourselves. We cannot, like the Roman Catholics, simply identify ourselves with the church. (This, incidentally, explains the popular opinion about Roman Catholics' insincerity.) Well then, what do we really believe? Answer: see (*b*), (*c*), and (*d*).

Chapter 3
Conclusions:

The church is the church only when it exists for others. To make a start, it should give away all its property to those in need. The clergy must live solely on the free-will offerings of their congregations, or possibly engage in some secular calling. The church must share in the secular problems of ordinary human life, not dominating, but helping and serving. It must tell men of every calling what it means to live in Christ, to exist for others. In particular, our own church will have to take the field against the vices of *hubris*, power-worship, envy, and humbug, as the roots of all evil. It will have to speak of moderation, purity, trust, loyalty, constancy, patience, discipline, humility, contentment, and modesty. It must not under-estimate the importance of human example (which has its origin in the humanity of Jesus and is so important in Paul's teaching); it is not abstract argument, but example, that gives its word emphasis and power. (I hope to take up later this subject of 'example' and its place in the New Testament; it is something that we have almost entirely forgotten.) Further: the question of revising the creeds (the Apostles' Creed); revision of Christian apologetics; reform of the training for the ministry and the pattern of clerical life.

All this is very crude and condensed, but there are certain things that I'm anxious to say simply and clearly — things that we so often like to shirk. Whether I shall succeed is another matter, especially if I cannot discuss it with you. I hope it may be of some help for the church's future.

*   (*LPP: 380-383*)

LETTERS FROM PRISON

The letters which follow, including the extracts from Bonhoeffer's sermon on the occasion of the baptism of Eberhard and Renate (Bonhoeffer's niece) Bethge's son, contain the key passages in which Bonhoeffer discusses the theological ideas which were exercising his mind in prison. The letters were all addressed to Bethge. The material has been substantially edited to include mainly those sections of the letters which deal with his theological thoughts, and they are published here in chronological order in order to show their development. The first letter, that of 30 April 1944, provided the initial intimation that Bonhoeffer was involved in breaking new ground.

[Tegel] 30 April 1944

Dear Eberhard,

Another month gone. Does time fly as fast with you as it does with me here? I'm often surprised at it myself — and when will the month come when you and Renate, I and Maria,* and we two can meet again? I have such a strong feeling that great events are moving the world every day and could change all our personal relationships, that I should like to write to you much oftener, partly because I don't know how much longer I shall be able to, and even more because we want to share everything with each other as often and as long as we can. I'm firmly convinced that, by the time you get this letter, great decisions will already be setting things moving on all fronts. During the coming weeks we shall have to keep a stout heart, and that is what I wish you. We shall have to keep all our wits about us, so as to let nothing scare us. In view of what is coming, I'm almost inclined to quote the biblical δεῖ, and I feel that I 'long to look', like the angels in 1 Peter 1.12, to see how God is going to solve the apparently insoluble. I think God is about to accomplish something that, even if we take part in it either outwardly or inwardly, we can only receive with the greatest wonder and awe. Somehow it will be clear — for those who have eyes to see — that Ps. 58.11b and Ps. 9.19f are true; and we shall have to repeat Jer. 45.5 to ourselves every day. It's harder for you to go through this separated from Renate and your boy than it is for me, so I will think of you especially, as I am already doing now.

How good it would seem to me, for both of us, if we could go through

* Maria von Wedemeyer, Bonhoeffer's fiancée.

this time together, helping each other. But it's probably 'better' for it not to be so, but for each of us to have to go through it alone. I find it hard not to be able to help you in anything — except by thinking of you every morning and evening when I read the Bible, and often during the day as well. You've no need to worry about me at all, as I'm getting on uncommonly well — you would be surprised, if you came to see me. People here keep on telling me (as you can see, I feel very flattered by it) that I'm 'radiating so much peace around me', and that I'm 'always so cheerful', — so that the feelings that I sometimes have to the contrary must, I suppose, rest on an illusion (not that I really believe that at all!). You would be surprised, and perhaps even worried, by my theological thoughts and the conclusions that they lead to; and this is where I miss you most of all, because I don't know anyone else with whom I could so well discuss them to have my thinking clarified. What is bothering me incessantly is the question what Christianity really is, or indeed who Christ really is, for us today. The time when people could be told everything by means of words, whether theological or pious, is over, and so is the time of inwardness and conscience — and that means the time of religion in general. We are moving towards a completely religionless time; people as they are now simply cannot be religious any more. Even those who honestly describe themselves as 'religious' do not in the least act up to it, and so they presumably mean something quite different by 'religious'.

Our whole nineteen-hundred-year-old Christian preaching and theology rest on the 'religious *a priori*' of humanity. 'Christianity' has always been a form — perhaps the true form — of 'religion'. But if one day it becomes clear that this *a priori* does not exist at all, but was a historically conditioned and transient form of human self-expression, and if therefore man becomes radically religionless — and I think that that is already more or less the case (else how is it, for example, that this war, in contrast to all previous ones, is not calling forth any 'religious' reaction?) — what does that mean for 'Christianity'? It means that the foundation is taken away from the whole of what has up to now been our 'Christianity', and that there remain only a few 'last survivors of the age of chivalry', or a few intellectually dishonest people, on whom we can descend as 'religious'. Are they to be the chosen few? Is it on this dubious group of people that we are to pounce in fervour, pique, or indignation, in order to sell them our goods? Are we to fall upon a few unfortunate people in their hour of need and exercise a sort of religious compulsion on them? If we don't want to do all that, if our final judgment must be that the western form of Christianity, too, was only a preliminary stage to a complete absence of religion, what kind of situation emerges for us, for the church? How can Christ become the Lord of the religionless as well? Are there religionless Christians? If religion is only a garment of Christianity — and even this garment has looked very different at different times — then what is a religionless Christianity?

Barth, who is the only one to have started along this line of thought, did not carry it to completion, but arrived at a positivism of revelation, which in the last analysis is essentially a restoration. For the religionless working man (or any other man) nothing decisive is gained here. The question to be answered would surely be: What do a church, a community, a sermon, a liturgy, a Christian life mean in a religionless world? How do we speak of God — without religion, i.e. without the temporally conditioned presuppositions of metaphysics, inwardness, and so on? How do we speak (or perhaps we cannot now even 'speak' as we used to) in a 'secular' way about 'God'? In what way are we 'religionless-secular' Christians, in what way are we the ἐκ-κλησία, those who are called forth, not regarding ourselves from a religious point of view as specially favoured, but rather as belonging wholly to the world? In that case Christ is no longer an object of religion, but something quite different, really the Lord of the world. But what does that mean? What is the place of worship and prayer in a religionless situation? Does the secret discipline, or alternatively the difference (which I have suggested to you before) between penultimate and ultimate, take on a new importance here?

I must break off for today, so that the letter can go straight away. I'll write to you again about it in two days' time. I hope you see more or less what I mean, and that it doesn't bore you. Goodbye for the present. It's not easy always to write without an echo, and you must excuse me if that makes it something of a monologue.

I'm thinking of you very much.   Your Dietrich

I find, after all, that I can write a little more. — The Pauline question whether περιτομή [circumcision] is a condition of justification seems to me in present-day terms to be whether religion is a condition of salvation. Freedom from περιτομή is also freedom from religion. I often ask myself why a 'Christian instinct' often draws me more to the religionless people than to the religious, by which I don't in the least mean with any evangelizing intention, but, I might almost say, 'in brotherhood'. While I'm often reluctant to mention God by name to religious people —

because that name somehow seems to me here not to ring true, and I feel myself to be slightly dishonest (it's particularly bad when others start to talk in religious jargon; I then dry up almost completely and feel awkward and uncomfortable) — to people with no religion I can on occasion mention him by name quite calmly and as a matter of course. Religious people speak of God when human knowledge (perhaps simply because they are too lazy to think) has come to an end, or when human resources fail — in fact it is always the *deus ex machina* that they bring on to the scene, either for the apparent solution of insoluble problems, or as strength in human failure — always, that is to say, exploring human weakness or human boundaries. Of necessity, that can go on only till people can by their own strength push these boundaries somewhat further out, so that God becomes superfluous as a *deus ex machina*. I've come to be doubtful of talking about any human boundaries (is even death, which people now hardly fear, and is sin, which they now hardly understand, still a genuine boundary today?) It always seems to me that we are trying anxiously in this way to reserve some space for God: I should like to speak of God not on the boundaries but at the centre, not in weaknesses but in strength; and therefore not in death and guilt but in man's life and goodness. As to the boundaries, it seems to me better to be silent and leave the insoluble unsolved. Belief in the resurrection is *not* the 'solution' of the problem of death. God's 'beyond' is not the beyond of our cognitive faculties. The transcendence of epistemological theory has nothing to do with the transcendence of God. God is beyond in the midst of our life. The church stands, not at the boundaries where human powers give out, but in the middle of the village. That is how it is in the Old Testament, and in this sense we still read the New Testament far too little in the light of the Old. How this religionless Christianity looks, what form it takes, is something that I'm thinking about a great deal, and I shall be writing to you again about it soon. It may be that on us in particular, midway between East and West, there will fall a heavy responsibility.

Now I really must stop. It would be fine to have a word from you about all this; it would mean a great deal to me — probably more than you can imagine. Some time, just read Prov. 22.11, 12, there is something that will bar the way to any escapism disguised as piety.

All the very best.

Your Dietrich
(LPP: 278-282)

*

[Tegel] 5 May 1944

Dear Eberhard,

A few more words about 'religionlessness'. I expect you remember
Bultmann's essay on the 'demythologizing' of the New Testament? My
view of it today would be, not that he went 'too far', as most people
thought, but that he didn't go far enough. It's not only the 'mythological'
concepts, such as miracle, ascension, and so on (which are not in principle separable from the concepts of God, faith, etc.), but 'religious'
concepts generally, which are problematic. You can't, as Bultmann
supposes, separate God and miracle, but you must be able to interpret
and proclaim *both* in a 'non-religious' sense. Bultmann's approach is
fundamentally still a liberal one (i.e. abridging the gospel), whereas I'm
trying to think theologically.

What does it mean to 'interpret in a religious sense'? I think it means
to speak on the one hand metaphysically, and on the other hand individualistically. Neither of these is relevant to the biblical message or to
the man of today. Hasn't the individualistic question about personal
salvation almost completely left us all? Aren't we really under the
impression that there are more important things than that question
(perhaps not more important than the *matter* itself, but more important
than the *question*!)? I know it sounds pretty monstrous to say that. But,
fundamentally, isn't this in fact biblical? Does the question about saving
one's soul appear in the Old Testament at all? Aren't righteousness and
the Kingdom of God on earth the focus of everything, and isn't it true
that Rom. 3.24ff. is not an individualistic doctrine of salvation, but the
culmination of the view that God alone is righteous? It is not with the
beyond that we are concerned, but with this world as created and
preserved, subjected to laws, reconciled, and restored. What is
above this world is, in the gospel, intended to exist *for* this world;
I mean that, not in the anthropocentric sense of liberal, mystic
pietistic, ethical theology, but in the biblical sense of the creation
and of the incarnation, crucifixion, and resurrection of Jesus Christ.

Barth was the first theologian to begin the criticism of religion,
and that remains his really great merit; but he put in its place a positivist
doctrine of revelation which says, in effect, 'Like it or lump it': virgin
birth, Trinity, or anything else; each is an equally significant and
necessary part of the whole, which must simply be swallowed as a whole
or not at all. That isn't biblical. There are degrees of knowledge and
degrees of significance; that means that a secret discipline must be re-

stored whereby the *mysteries* of the Christian faith are protected against profanation. The positivism of revelation makes it too easy for itself, by setting up, as it does in the last analysis, a law of faith, and so mutilates what is — by Christ's incarnation! — a gift for us. In the place of religion there now stands the church — that is in itself biblical — but the world is in some degree made to depend on itself and left to its own devices, and that's the mistake.

I'm thinking about how we can reinterpret in a 'worldly' sense — in the sense of the Old Testament and of John 1.14 — the concepts of repentance, faith, justification, rebirth, and sanctification. I shall be writing to you about it again.   (*LPP: 285-287*)

*

[Tegel] 29 May 1944

Dear Eberhard,

I hope that, in spite of the alerts, you are enjoying to the full the peace and beauty of these warm, summer-like Whitsuntide days. One gradually learns to acquire an inner detachment from life's menaces — although 'acquire detachment' seems too negative, formal, artificial, and stoical; and it's perhaps more accurate to say that we assimilate these menaces into our life as a whole. I notice repeatedly here how few people there are who can harbour conflicting emotions at the same time. When bombers come, they are all fear; when there is something nice to eat, they are all greed; when they are disappointed, they are all despair; when they are successful, they can think of nothing else. They miss the fullness of life and the wholeness of an independent existence: everything objective and subjective is dissolved for them into fragments. By contrast, Christianity puts us into many different dimensions of life at the same time; we make room in ourselves, to some extent, for God and the whole world. We rejoice with those who rejoice, and weep with those who weep; we are anxious (— I was again interrupted just then by the alert, and am now sitting out of doors enjoying the sun —) about our life, but at the same time we must think about things much more important to us than life itself. When the alert goes, for instance: as soon as we turn our minds from worrying about our own safety to the task of helping other people to keep calm, the situation is completely changed; life isn't pushed back into a single dimension, but is kept multi-dimensional and polyphonous. What a deliverance it is to be able to *think*, and thereby remain multi-dimensional. I've almost made it a

281

rule here, simply to tell people who are trembling under an air raid that it would be much worse for a small town. We have to get people out of their one-track minds; that is a kind of 'preparation' for faith, or something that makes faith possible, although really it's only faith itself that can make possible a multi-dimensional life, and so enable us to keep this Whitsuntide, too, in spite of the alarms.

At first I was a bit disconcerted, and perhaps even saddened, not to have a letter from anyone this Whitsuntide. Then I told myself that it was perhaps a good sign, as it meant that no one was worrying about me. It's a strange human characteristic that we like other people to be anxious about us — at least just a trifle anxious.

Weizsäcker's book *The World-View of Physics* is still keeping me very busy. It has again brought home to me quite clearly how wrong it is to use God as a stop-gap for the incompleteness of our knowledge. If in fact the frontiers of knowledge are being pushed further and further back (and that is bound to be the case), then God is being pushed back with them, and is therefore continually in retreat. We are to find God in what we know, not in what we don't know; God wants us to realize his presence, not in unsolved problems but in those that are solved. That is true of the relationship between God and scientific knowledge, but it is also true of the wider human problems of death, suffering, and guilt. It is now possible to find, even for these questions, human answers that take no account whatever of God. In point of fact, people deal with these questions without God (it has always been so), and it is simply not true to say that only Christianity has the answers to them. As to the idea of 'solving' problems, it may be that the Christian answers are just as unconvincing — or convincing — as any others. Here again, God is no stop-gap; he must be recognized at the centre of life, not when we are at the end of our resources; it is his will to be recognized in life, and not only when death comes; in health and vigour, and not only in suffering; in our activities, and not only in sin. The ground for this lies in the revelation of God in Jesus Christ. He is the centre of life, and he certainly didn't 'come' to answer our unsolved problems. From the centre of life certain questions, and their answers, are seen to be wholly irrelevant (I'm thinking of the judgment pronounced on Job's friends). In Christ there are no 'Christian problems'. — Enough of this; I've just been disturbed again.

(LPP: 310-312)

*

[Tegel] 8 June 1944

Dear Eberhard,

You now ask so many important questions on the subjects that have been occupying me lately, that I should be happy if I could answer them myself. But it's all very much in the early stages; and, as usual, I'm being led on more by an instinctive feeling for questions that will arise later than by any conclusions that I've already reached about them. I'll try to define my position from the historical angle.

The movement that began about the thirteenth century (I'm not going to get involved in any argument about the exact date) towards the autonomy of man (in which I should include the discovery of the laws by which the world lives and deals with itself in science, social and political matters, art, ethics, and religion) has in our time reached an undoubted completion. Man has learnt to deal with himself in all questions of importance without recourse to the 'working hypothesis' called 'God'. In questions of science, art, and ethics this has become an understood thing at which one now hardly dares to tilt. But for the last hundred years or so it has also become increasingly true of religious questions; it is becoming evident that everything gets along without 'God' — and, in fact, just as well as before. As in the scientific field, so in human affairs generally, 'God' is being pushed more and more out of life, losing more and more ground.

Roman Catholic and Protestant historians agree that it is in this development that the great defection from God, from Christ, is to be seen; and the more they claim and play off God and Christ against it, the more the development considers itself to be anti-Christian. The world that has become conscious of itself and the laws that govern its own existence has grown self-confident in what seems to us to be an uncanny way. False developments and failures do not make the world doubt the necessity of the course that it is taking, or of its development; they are accepted with fortitude and detachment as part of the bargain, and even an event like the present war is no exception. Christian apologetic has taken the most varied forms of opposition to this self-assurance. Efforts are made to prove to a world thus come of age that it cannot live without the tutelage of 'God'. Even though there has been surrender on all secular problems, there still remain the so-called 'ultimate questions' — death, guilt — to which only 'God' can give an answer, and because of which we need God and the church and the pastor. So we live, in some degree, on these so-called ultimate questions of humanity. But what if one day they no longer exist as such, if they too can be answered 'without God'? Of course, we now have the secularized offshoots of Christian theology, namely existentialist philosophy and the psychotherapists, who demonstrate to secure, contented, and happy humanity that it is really unhappy and desperate and simply unwilling to admit that it is in a predicament about which it knows nothing, and from which only they can rescue it. Wherever there is health, strength, security, simplicity, they scent luscious fruit to gnaw at or to lay their pernicious eggs in. They set themselves to drive people to inward despair, and then the game is in their hands. That is secularized methodism. And whom does it touch? A small number of intellectuals, of degenerates, of people who regard themselves as the most important thing in the world, and who therefore like to busy themselves with themselves. The ordinary man, who spends his everyday life at work and with his family, and of course with all kinds of diversions, is not affected. He has neither the time nor the inclination to concern himself with his existential despair, or to regard his perhaps modest share of happiness as a trial, a trouble, or a calamity.

The attack by Christian apologetic on the adulthood of the world I consider to be in the first place pointless, in the second place ignoble, and in the third place unchristian. Pointless, because it seems to me like an attempt to put a grown-up man back into adolescence, i.e. to make him dependent on things on which he is, in fact, no longer dependent, and thrusting him into problems that are, in fact, no longer problems to him. Ignoble, because it amounts to an attempt to exploit man's weakness for purposes that are alien to him and to which he has not freely assented. Unchristian, because it confuses Christ with one particular stage in man's religiousness, i.e. with a human law. More about this later.

But first, a little more about the historical position. The question is: Christ and the world that has come of age. The weakness of liberal theology was that it conceded to the world the right to determine Christ's place in the world; in the conflict between the church and the world it accepted the comparatively easy terms of peace that the world dictated. Its strength was that it did not try to put the clock back, and that it genuinely accepted the battle (Troeltsch), even though this ended with its defeat.

Defeat was followed by surrender, and by an attempt to make a completely fresh start based on the fundamentals of the Bible and the Reformation. Heim sought, along pietist and methodist lines, to convince the individual man that he was faced with the alternative 'despair or Jesus'. He gained 'hearts'. Althaus (carrying forward the modern and positive line with a strong confessional emphasis) tried to wring from the world a place for Lutheran teaching (ministry) and Lutheran worship, and otherwise left the world to its own devices. Tillich set out to interpret the evolution of the world (against its will) in a religious sense — to give it its shape through religion. That was very brave of him, but the world unseated him and went on by itself; he, too, sought to understand the world better than it understood itself; but it felt that it was completely misunderstood, and rejected the imputation. (Of course, the world *must* be understood better than it understands itself, but not 'religiously' as the religious socialists wanted.)

Barth was the first to realize the mistake that all these attempts (which were all, in fact, still sailing, though unintentionally, in the channel of liberal theology) were making in leaving clear a space for religion in the world or against the world. He brought in against religion the God of Jesus Christ, *'pneuma* against *sarx'.* That remains his greatest service (his *Epistle to the Romans,* second edition, in spite of all the neo-Kantian egg-shells). Through his later dogmatics, he enabled the church to effect this distinction, in principle, all along the line. It was not in ethics, as is often said, that he subsequently failed — his ethical observations, as far as they exist, are just as important as his dogmatic ones —; it was that in the non-religious interpretation of theological concepts he gave no concrete guidance, either in dogmatics or in ethics. There lies his limitation, and because of it his theology of revelation has become positivist, a 'positivism of revelation', as I put it.

The Confessing Church has now largely forgotten all about the Barthian approach, and has lapsed from positivism into conservative restoration. The important thing about that church is that it carries on the great concepts of Christian theology; but it seems as if doing this is gradually just about exhausting it. It is true that there are in those concepts the elements of genuine prophecy (among them two things that you mention: the claim to truth, and mercy) and of genuine worship; and to that extent the Confessing Church gets only attention, hearing, and rejection. But both of them remain undeveloped and remote, because there is no interpretation of them. Those who, like e.g. Schültz or the Oxford Group or the Berneucheners, miss the 'movement' and the 'life', are dangerous reactionaries; they are reactionary because they go right back behind the approach of the theology of revelation and seek for 'religious' renewal. They simply haven't understood the problem at all yet, and their talk is entirely beside the point. There is no future for them (though the Oxford Group would have the best chance if they were not so completely without biblical substance).

Bultmann seems to have somehow felt Barth's limitations, but he misconstrues them in the sense of liberal theology, and so goes off into the typical liberal process of reduction — the 'mythological' elements of Christianity are dropped, and Christianity is reduced to its 'essence'. — My view is that the full content, including the 'mythological' concepts, must be kept — the New Testament is not a mythological clothing of a universal truth; this mythological (resurrection etc.) is the thing itself — but the concepts must be interpreted in such a way as not to make religion a precondition of faith (cf. Paul and circumcision). Only in that way, I think, will liberal theology be overcome (and even Barth is still influenced by it, though negatively) and at the same time its question be genuinely taken up and answered (as is *not* the case in the Confessing Church's positivism of revelation!). Thus the world's coming of age is no longer an occasion for polemics and apologetics, but is now really better understood than it understands itself, namely on the basis of the gospel and in the light of Christ.

Now for your question whether there is any 'ground' left for the church, or whether that ground has gone for good; and the other question, whether Jesus didn't use men's 'distress' as a point of contact with them, and whether therefore the 'methodism' that I criticized earlier isn't right. *(LCP: 325-329)*

*

[Tegel] 9 June [1944]

. . . .

Now I will try to go on with the theological reflections that I broke off not long since. I had been saying that God is being increasingly pushed out of a world that has come of age, out of the spheres of our knowledge and life, and that since Kant he has been relegated to a realm beyond the world of experience. Theology has on the one hand resisted this development with apologetics, and has taken up arms — in vain — against Darwinism, etc. On the other hand, it has accommodated itself to the development by restricting God to the so-called ultimate question as a *deus ex machina*; that means that he becomes the answer to life's problems, and the solution of its needs and conflicts. So if anyone has no such difficulties, or if he refuses to go into these things, to allow others to pity him, then either he cannot be open to God; or else he must be shown that he is, in fact, deeply involved in such problems, needs, and conflicts, without admitting or knowing it. If that can be done — and existentialist philosophy and psychotherapy have worked out some quite ingenious methods in that direction — then this man can now be claimed for God, and methodism can celebrate its triumph. But if he cannot be brought to see and admit that his happiness is really an evil, his health sickness, and his vigour despair, the theologian is at his wits' end. It's a case of having to do either with a hardened sinner of a particularly ugly type, or with a man of 'bourgeois complacency', and the one is as far from salvation as the other.

You see, that is the attitude that I am contending against. When Jesus blessed sinners, they were real sinners, but Jesus did not make everyone a sinner first. He called them away from their sin, not into their sin. It is true that encounter with Jesus meant the reversal of all human values. So it was in the conversion of Paul, though in his case the encounter with Jesus preceded the realization of sin. It is true that Jesus cared about people on the fringe of human society, such as harlots and tax-collectors, but never about them alone, for he sought to care about man as such. Never did he question a man's health, vigour, or happiness, regarded in themselves, or regard them as evil fruits; else why should he heal the sick and restore strength to the weak? Jesus claims for himself and the Kingdom of God the whole of human life in all its manifestations.

Of course I have to be interrupted just now! Let me just summarize briefly what I'm concerned about — the claim of a world that has come of age by Jesus Christ.

I can't write any more today, or else the letter will be kept here another week, and I don't want that to happen. So: To be continued!

(LPP: 341-2)

*

[Tegel] 8 July [1944]

Dear Eberhard,

. . . .

Now for a few more thoughts on our theme. Marshalling the biblical evidence needs more lucidity and concentration than I can command at present. Wait a few more days, till it gets cooler! I haven't forgotten, either, that I owe you something about the non-religious interpretation of biblical concepts. But for today, here are a few preliminary remarks:

The displacement of God from the world, and from the public part of human life, led to the attempt to keep his place secure at least in the sphere of the 'personal', the 'inner', and the 'private'. And as every man still has a private sphere somewhere, that is where he was thought to be the most vulnerable. The secrets known to a man's valet — that is, to put it crudely, the range of his intimate life, from prayer to his sexual life — have become the hunting-ground of modern pastoral workers. In that way they resemble (though with quite different intentions) the dirtiest gutter journalists — do you remember the *Wahrheit* and the *Glocke*, which made public the most intimate details about prominent people? In the one case it's social, financial, or political blackmail and in the other, religious blackmail. Forgive me, but I can't put it more mildly.

From the sociological point of view this is a revolution from below, a revolt of inferiority. Just as the vulgar mind isn't satisfied till it has seen some highly placed personage 'in his bath', or in other embarrassing situations, so it is here. There is a kind of evil satisfaction in knowing that everyone has his failings and weak spots. In my contacts with the 'outcasts' of society, its 'pariahs', I've noticed repeatedly that mistrust is the dominant motive in their judgment of other people. Every action, even the most unselfish, of a person of high repute is suspected from the outset. These 'outcasts' are to be found in all grades of society. In a flower-garden they grub around only for the dung on which the flowers grow. The more isolated a man's life, the more easily he falls a victim to this attitude.

There is also a parallel isolation among the clergy, in what one might call the 'clerical' sniffing-around-after-people's-sins in order to catch them out. It's as if you couldn't know a fine house till you had found a cobweb in the furthest cellar, or as if you couldn't adequately appreciate a good play till you had seen how the actors behave off-stage. It's the same kind of thing that you find in the novels of the last fifty years, which do not think they have depicted their characters properly till they have described them in their marriage-bed, or in films where undressing scenes are thought necessary. Anything clothed, veiled, pure, and chaste is presumed to be deceitful, disguised, and impure; people here simply show their own impurity. A basic anti-social attitude of mistrust and suspicion is the revolt of inferiority.

Regarded theologically, the error is twofold. First, it is thought that a man can be addressed as a sinner only after his weaknesses and mean-nesses have been spied out. Secondly, it is thought that a man's essential

288

nature consists of his inmost and most intimate background; that is defined as his 'inner life', and it is precisely in those secret human places that God is to have his domain!

On the first point it is to be said that man is certainly a sinner, but is far from being mean or common on that account. To put it rather tritely, were Goethe and Napoleon sinners because they weren't always faithful husbands? It's not the sins of weakness, but the sins of strength, which matter here. It's not in the least necessary to spy out things; the Bible never does so. (Sins of strength: in the genius, *hubris*; in the peasant, the breaking of the order of life — is the decalogue a peasant ethic?—; in the bourgeois, fear of free responsibility. Is this correct?)

On the second point: the Bible does not recognize our distincion between the outward and the inward. Why should it? It is always concerned with *anthrōpos teleios*, the *whole* man, even where, as in the Sermon on the Mount, the decalogue is pressed home to refer to 'inward disposition'. That a good 'disposition' can take the place of total goodness is quite unbiblical. The discovery of the so-called inner life dates from the Renaissance, probably from Petrarch. The 'heart' in the biblical sense is not the inner life, but the whole man in relation to God. But as a man lives just as much from 'outwards' to 'inwards' as from 'inwards' to 'outwards', the view that his essential nature can be understood only from his intimate spiritual background is wholly erroneous.

I therefore want to start from the premise that God shouldn't be smuggled into some last secret place, but that we should frankly recognize that the world, and people, have come of age, that we shouldn't run man down in his worldliness, but confront him with God at his strongest point, that we should give up all our clerical tricks, and not regard psychotherapy and existentialist philosophy as God's pioneers. The importunity of all these people is far too unaristocratic for the Word of God to ally itself with them. The Word of God is far removed from this revolt of mistrust, this revolt from below. On the contrary, it reigns.

Well, it's time to say something concrete about the secular interpretation of biblical concepts; but it's too hot! *(LPP: 344-346)*

*

[Tegel] 16 July [1944]

. . . .

If you have to preach in the near future, I should suggest taking some such text as Ps. 62.1; 119-94a; 42.5; Jer. 31.3; Isa. 41.10; 43.1; Matt.

28.20b; I should confine myself to a few simple but vital thoughts. One has to live for some time in a community to understand how Christ is 'formed' in it (Gal. 4.19); and that is especially true of the kind of community that you would have. If I can help in any way, I should be glad to.

Now for a few more thoughts on our theme. I'm only gradually working my way to the non-religious interpretation of biblical concepts; the job is too big for me to finish just yet.

On the historical side: There is one great development that leads to the world's autonomy. In theology one sees it first in Lord Herbert of Cherbury, who maintains that reason is sufficient for religious knowledge. In ethics it appears in Montaigne and Bodin with their substitution of rules of life for the commandments. In politics Machiavelli detaches politics from morality in general and founds the doctrine of 'reasons of state'. Later, and very differently from Machiavelli, but tending like him towards the autonomy of human society, comes Grotius, setting up his natural law as international law, which is valid *etsi deus non daretur*, 'even if there were no God'. The philosophers provide the finishing touches: on the one hand we have the deism of Descartes, who holds that the world is a mechanism, running by itself with no interference from God; and on the other hand the pantheism of Spinoza, who says that God is nature. In the last resort, Kant is a deist, and Fichte and Hegel are pantheists. Everywhere the thinking is directed towards the autonomy of man and the world.

(It seems that in the natural sciences the process begins with Nicolas of Cusa and Giordano Bruno and the 'heretical' doctrine of the infinity of the universe. The classical *cosmos* was finite, like the created world of the Middle Ages. An infinite universe, however it may be conceived, is self-subsisting, *etsi deus non daretur*. It is true that modern physics is not as sure as it was about the infinity of the universe, but it has not gone back on the earlier conceptions of its finitude.)

God as a working hypothesis in morals, politics, or science, has been surmounted and abolished; and the same thing has happened in philosophy and religion (Feuerbach!). For the sake of intellectual honesty, that working hypothesis should be dropped, or as far as possible eliminated. A scientist or physician who sets out to edify is a hybrid.

Anxious souls will ask what room there is left for God now; and as they know of no answer to the question, they condemn the whole development that has brought them to such straits. I wrote to you before about the various emergency exits that have been contrived; and we ought to add to them the *salto mortale* [death-leap] back into the Middle

Ages. But the principle of the Middle Ages is heteronomy in the form of clericalism; a return to that can be a counsel of despair, and it would be at the cost of intellectual honesty. It's a dream that reminds one of the song *O wüsst' ich doch den Weg zurück, den weiten Weg ins Kinderland*. There is no such way — at any rate not if it means deliberately abandoning our mental integrity; the only way is that of Matt. 18.3, i.e. through repentance, through *ultimate* honesty.

And we cannot be honest unless we recognize that we have to live in the world *etsi deus non daretur*. And this is just what we do recognize — before God! God himself compels us to recognize it. So our coming of age leads us to a true recognition of our situation before God. God would have us know that we must live as men who manage our lives without him. The God who is with us is the God who forsakes us (Mark 15:34). The God who lets us live in the world without the working hypothesis of God is the God before whom we stand continually. Before God and with God we live without God. God lets himself be pushed out of the world on to the cross. He is weak and powerless in the world, and that is precisely the way, the only way, in which he is with us and helps us. Matt. 8.17 makes it quite clear that Christ helps us, not by virtue of his omnipotence, but by virtue of his weakness and suffering.

Here is the decisive difference between Christianity and all religions. Man's religiosity makes him look in his distress to the power of God in the world: God is the *deus ex machina*. The Bible directs man to God's powerlessness and suffering; only the suffering God can help. To that extent we may say that the development towards the world's coming of age outlined above, which has done away with a false conception of God, opens up a way of seeing the God of the Bible, who wins power and space in the world by his weakness. This will probably be the starting-point for our 'secular interpretation'.   *(LPP: 359-361)*

*

[Tegel] 18 July [1944]

I wonder whether any letters have been lost in the raids on Munich. Did you get the one with the two poems? It was just sent off that evening, and it also contained a few introductory remarks on our theological theme. The poem about Christians and pagans contains an idea that you will recognize: 'Christians stand by God in his hour of grieving'; that is what distinguishes Christians from pagans. Jesus asked in Gethsemane, 'Could you not watch with me one hour?' That is a reversal of what the religious man expects from God. Man is summoned to share in God's sufferings at the hands of a godless world.

He must therefore really live in the godless world, without attempting to gloss over or explain its ungodliness in some religious way or other. He must live a 'secular' life, and thereby share in God's sufferings. He *may* live a 'secular' life (as one who has been freed from false religious obligations and inhibitions). To be a Christian does not mean to be religious in a particular way, to make something of oneself (a sinner, a penitent, or a saint) on the basis of some method or other, but to be a man — not a type of man, but the man that Christ creates in us. It is not the religious act that makes the Christian, but participation in the sufferings of God in the secular life. That is *metanoia*: not in the first place thinking about one's own needs, problems, sins, and fears, but allowing oneself to be caught up in the way of Jesus Christ, into the messianic event, thus fulfilling Isa. 53. Therefore 'believe in the gospel', or, in the words of John the Baptist, 'Behold, the Lamb of God, who takes away the sin of the world' (John 1.29). (By the way, Jeremias has recently asserted that the Aramaic word for 'lamb' may also be translated 'servant': very appropriate in view of Isa. 53!)

This being caught up into the messianic sufferings of God in Jesus Christ takes a variety of forms in the New Testament. It appears in the call to discipleship, in Jesus' table-fellowship with sinners, in 'conversions' in the narrower sense of the word (e.g. Zacchaeus), in the act of the woman who was a sinner (Luke 7) — an act that she performed without any confession of sin, in the healing of the sick (Matt. 8.17; see above), in Jesus' acceptance of children. The shepherds, like the wise men from the East, stand at the crib, not as 'converted sinners', but simply because they are drawn to the crib by the star just as they are. The centurion of Capernaum (who makes no confession of sin) is held up as a model of faith (cf. Jairus). Jesus 'loved' the rich young man. The eunuch (Acts 8) and Cornelius (Acts 10) are not standing at the edge of an abyss. Nathanial is 'an Israelite indeed, in whom there is no guile' (John 1.47). Finally, Joseph of Arimathea and the women at the tomb. The only thing that is common to all these is their sharing in the suffering of God in Christ. That is their 'faith'. There is nothing of religious method here. The 'religious act' is always something partial; faith is something whole, involving the whole of one's life. Jesus calls men, not to a new religion, but to life.

But what does this life look like, this participation in the powerlessness of God in the world? I will write about that next time, I hope. Just one more point for today. When we speak of God in a 'non-religious' way, we must speak of him in such a way that the godlessness of the world is not in some way concealed, but rather revealed, and thus exposed to an unexpected light. The world that has come of age is more godless, and perhaps for that very reason nearer to God, than the world before its coming of age. Forgive me for still putting it all so terribly clumsily and badly, as I really feel I am. But perhaps you will help me again to make things clearer and simpler, even if only by my being able to talk about them with you and to hear you, so to speak, keep asking and answering.   *(LPP 361-362)*

*

[Tegel] 21 July [1944]

Dear Eberhard,
All I want to do today is to send you a short greeting. I expect you are often with us here in your thoughts and are always glad of any sign of life, even if the theological discussion stops for a moment. These theological thoughts are, in fact, always occupying my mind, but there are times when I am just content to live the life of faith without worrying about its problems. At those times I simply take pleasure in the days' readings — in particular those of yesterday and today; and I'm always glad to go back to Paul Gerhardt's beautiful hymns.

During the last year or so I've come to know and understand more and more the profound this-worldliness of Christianity. The Christian is not a *homo religiosus,* but simply a man, as Jesus was a man — in contrast, shall we say, to John the Baptist. I don't mean the shallow and banal this-worldliness of the enlightened, the busy, the comfortable, or the lascivious, but the profound this-worldliness, characterized by discipline and the constant knowledge of death and resurrection. I think Luther lived a this-worldly life in this sense.

I remember a conversation that I had in America thirteen years ago with a young French pastor. We were asking ourselves quite simply what we wanted to do with our lives. He said he would like to become a saint (and I think it's quite likely that he did become one). At the time I was very impressed, but I disagreed with him, and said, in effect, that I should like to learn to have faith. For a long time I didn't realize the depth of the contrast. I thought I could acquire faith by trying to live a holy life, or something like it. I suppose I wrote *The Cost of Discipleship* at the end of that path. Today I can see the dangers of that book, though I still stand by what I wrote.

I discovered later, and I'm still discovering right up to this moment, that it is only by living completely in this world that one learns to have faith. One must completely abandon any attempt to make something of oneself, whether it be a saint, or a converted sinner, or a churchman (a so-called priestly type!), a righteous man or an unrighteous one, a sick man or a healthy one. By this-worldliness I mean living unreservedly in life's duties, problems, successes and failures, experiences and perplexities. In so doing we throw ourselves completely into the arms of God, taking seriously, not our own sufferings, but those of God in the world — watching with Christ in Gethsemane. That, I think, is faith; that is *metanoia*; and that is how one becomes a man and a Christian (cf. Jer. 45!). How can success make us arrogant, or failure lead us astray, when we share in God's sufferings through a life of this kind?

I think you see what I mean, even though I put it so briefly. I'm glad to have been able to learn this, and I know I've been able to do so only along the road that I've travelled. So I'm grateful for the past and present, and content with them.

You may be surprised at such a personal letter; but if for once I want to say this kind of thing, to whom should I say it? Perhaps the time will come one day when I can talk to Maria like this; I very much hope so. But I can't expect it of her yet.

May God in his mercy lead us through these times; but above all, may he lead us to himself.

I was delighted to hear from you, and am glad you're not finding it too hot. There must be a good number of letters from me on the way. Didn't we go more or less along that way in 1936?

Goodbye. Keep well, and don't lose hope that we shall all meet again soon. I always think of you in faithfulness and gratitude.

Your Dietrich
(*LPP: 369-370*)

*

THOUGHTS ON THE DAY OF BAPTISM OF DIETRICH WILHELM RÜDGER BETHGE, MAY 1944

We have grown up with the experience of our parents and grandparents that a man can and must plan, develop, and shape his own life, and that life has a purpose, about which a man must make up his mind, and which he must then pursue with all his strength. But we have learnt by experience that we cannot plan even for the coming day, that what we have built up is being destroyed overnight, and that our life, in contrast to that of our parents, has become formless or even fragmentary. In spite of that, I can only say that I have no wish to live in any other time than our own, even though it is so inconsiderate of our outward well-being. We realize more clearly than formerly that the world lies under the wrath and grace of God. We read in Jer. 45: 'Thus says the Lord: Behold, what I have built I am breaking down, and what I have planted I am plucking up . . . And do you seek great things for yourself? Seek them not; for, behold, I am bringing evil upon all flesh; . . . but I will give your life as a prize of war in all places to which you may go.' If we can save our souls unscathed out of the wreckage of our material possessions, let us be satisfied with that. If the Creator destroys his own handiwork, what right have we to lament the destruction of ours? It will be the task of our generation, not to 'seek great things', but to save and preserve our souls out of the chaos, and to realize that it is the only thing we can carry as a 'prize' from the burning building. 'Keep your heart with all vigilance; for from it flows the spring of life' (Prov. 4.23). We shall have to keep our lives rather than shape them, to hope rather than plan, to hold out rather than march forward. But we do want to preserve for you, the rising generation, what will make it possible for you to plan, build up, and shape a new and better life.

We have spent too much time in thinking, supposing that if we weigh in advance the possibilities of any action, it will happen automatically. We have learnt, rather too late, that action comes, not from thought but from a readiness for responsibility. For you thought and action will enter on a new relationship; your thinking will be confined to your responsibilities in action. With us thought was often the luxury of the onlooker; with you it will be entirely subordinated to action. 'Not every one who *says* to me, "Lord, Lord", shall enter the kingdom of heaven, but he who *does* the will of my Father who is in heaven', said Jesus (Matt. 7.21).

For the greater part of our lives pain was a stranger to us. To be as free as possible from pain was unconsciously one of our guiding principles. Niceties of feeling, sensitive to our own and other people's pain are at once the strength and the weakness of our way of life. From its early days your generation will be tougher and closer to real life, for you will have had to endure privation and pain, and your patience will have been greatly tried. 'It is good for a man that he bear the yoke in his youth' (Lam. 3.27).

We thought we could make our way in life with reason and justice, and when both failed, we felt that we were at the end of our tether. We have constantly exaggerated the importance of reason and justice in the course of history. You, who are growing up in a world war which ninety per cent of mankind did not want, but for which they have to risk losing their goods and their lives, are learning from childhood that the world is controlled by forces against which reason can do nothing; and so you will be able to cope with those forces more successfully. In our lives the 'enemy' did not really exist. You know that you have enemies and friends, and you know what they can mean in your life. You are learning very early in life ways (which we did not know) of fighting an enemy, and also the value of unreserved trust in a friend. 'Has not man a hard service upon earth?' (Job 7.1.) 'Blessed be the Lord, my rock, who trains my hands for war, and my fingers for battle; my rock and my fortress, my stronghold and my deliverer, my shield and he in whom I take refuge' (Ps. 144.1f). 'There is a friend who sticks closer than a brother' (Prov. 18.24).

Are we moving towards an age of colossal organizations and collective institutions, or will the desire of innumerable people for small, manageable personal relationships be satisfied? Must they be mutually exclusive? Might it not be that world organizations themselves, with their wide meshes, will allow more scope for personal interests? Similarly with the question whether we are moving towards an age of the selection of the fittest, i.e. an aristocratic society, or to uniformity in all material and spiritual aspects of human life. Although there has been a very far-reaching equalization here, the sensitiveness in all ranks of society for the human values of justice, achievement, and courage could create a new selection of people who will be allowed the right to provide strong leadership. It will not be difficult for us to renounce our privileges, recognizing the justice of history. We may have to face events and changes that take no account of our wishes and our rights. But if so, we shall not give way to embittered and barren pride, but consciously submit to divine judgment, and so prove ourselves worthy to survive by identifying ourselves generously and unselfishly with the life of the community and the sufferings of our fellow-men. 'But any nation which will bring its neck under the yoke of the king of Babylon and serve him, I will leave on its own land, to till it and dwell there, says the Lord' (Jer. 27.11). 'Seek the welfare of the city . . . and pray to the Lord on its behalf' (Jer. 29.7). 'Come, my people, enter your chambers, and shut your doors behind you; hide yourselves for a little while until the wrath is past' (Isa. 26.20). 'For his anger is but for a moment, and his favour is for a lifetime. Weeping may tarry for the night, but joy comes with the morning' (Ps. 30.5).

Today you will be baptized a Christian. All those great ancient words of the Christian proclamation will be spoken over you, and the command of Jesus Christ to baptize will be carried out on you, without your knowing anything about it. But we are once again being driven right back to the beginnings of our understanding. Reconciliation and redemption, regeneration and the Holy Spirit, love of our enemies, cross and resurrection, life in Christ and Christian discipleship — all these things are so difficult and so remote that we hardly venture any more to speak of them. In the traditional words and acts we suspect that there may be something quite new and revolutionary, though we cannot as yet grasp or express it. That is our own fault. Our church, which has been fighting in these years only for its self-preservation, as though that were an end in itself, is incapable of taking the word of reconciliation and redemption to mankind and the world. Our earlier words are therefore bound to lose their force and cease, and our being Christians today will be limited to two things: prayer and righteous action among men. All Christian thinking, speaking, and organizing must be born anew out of this prayer and action. By the time you have grown up, the church's form will have changed greatly. We are not yet out of the melting-pot, and any attempt to help the church prematurely to a new expansion of its organization will merely delay its conversion and purification. It is not for us to prophesy the day (though the day will come) when men will once more be called so to utter the word of God that the world will be changed and renewed by it. It will be a new language, perhaps quite non-religious, but liberating and redeeming — as was Jesus' language; it will shock people and yet overcome them by its power; it will be the language of a new righteousness and truth, proclaiming God's peace with men and the coming of his kingdom. 'They shall fear and tremble because of all the good and all the prosperity I provide for it' (Jer. 33.9). Till then the Christian cause will be a silent and hidden affair, but there will be those who pray and do right and wait for God's own time. May you be one of them, and may it be said of you one day, 'The path of the righteous is like the light of dawn, which shines brighter and brighter till full day' (Prov. 4.18).   *(LPP: 297-300)*

SELECTED BIBLIOGRAPHY

BONHOEFFER'S WORKS IN ENGLISH TRANSLATION

Sanctorum Communio. A Dogmatic Inquiry into the Sociology of the Church. London: Collins, 1963.

Act and Being. London: Collins; New York: Harper & Row, 1962.

Creation and Fall. A Theological Interpretation of Genesis 1-3. London: SCM; New York: Macmillan, 1959.

Christology. London: Collins, 1966. Title in the U.S., *Christ the Center.* New York: Harper & Row, 1966. Revised edition, 1978.

Spiritual Care. Philadelphia: Fortress Press, 1985.

The Cost of Discipleship. London: SCM, 1959; New York: Macmillan, 1963.

Temptation. London: SCM; New York: Macmillan, 1955.

Life Together. London: SCM; New York: Harper & Row, 1954.

Psalms. The Prayer Book of the Bible. Minneapolis: Augsburg, 1970.

Ethics. London: Collins (Fontana Books), 1964; New York: Macmillan (paperback), 1965.

Letters and Papers from Prison. London: SCM, 1971; New York: Macmillan Paperbacks, 1972.

Fiction from Prison. Gathering up the Past. Edited by Renate and Eberhard Bethge with Clifford Green (in the English Edition). Philadelphia: Fortress Press, 1981.

The following volumes contain extracts from *Dietrich Bonhoeffer Gesammelte Schriften* I-VI (1958-74) ed. E. Bethge. Münich: Chr. Kaiser Verlag.

No Rusty Swords. Letters, Lectures and Notes, 1928-1936, from the Collected Works of Dietrich Bonhoeffer, volume I. Edited and introduced by Edwin H. Robertson. London: Collins; New York: Harper & Row, 1965. Revised by John Bowden, Fontana edition, 1970.

The Way to Freedom, Letters, Lectures and Notes, 1935-1939, from the Collected Works of Dietrich Bonhoeffer, volume II. Edited and introduced by Edwin H. Robertson. London: Collins; New York: Harper & Row, 1966.

True Patriotism. Letters, Lectures and Notes, 1939-1945, from the Collected Works of Dietrich Bonhoeffer, volume III. Edited and introduced by Edwin H. Robertson. London: Collins; New York: Harper & Row, 1973.

SECONDARY LITERATURE IN ENGLISH

Bethge, Eberhard. *Bonhoeffer, Exile and Martyr.* Edited and with an Essay by John W. de Gruchy. London: Collins, 1975.

Bethge, Eberhard. 'The Challenge of Dietrich Bonhoeffer's Life and Theology.' *The Chicago Theological Seminary Register* Vol. 51, No. 2 (February, 1961).

Bethge, Eberhard. *Dietrich Bonhoeffer. Theologian, Christian, Contemporary.* London: Collins; New York: Harper & Row, 1970.

Bethge, Eberhard. *Bonhoeffer. An Illustrated Introduction.* London: Collins (Fount Paperbacks), 1979; New York: Harper and Row, 1979, with the title *Costly Grace. An Illustrated Introduction to Dietrich Bonhoeffer.*

Bosanquet, Mary. *The Life and Death of Dietrich Bonhoeffer.* Hodder & Stoughton, 1968; New York: Harper & Row, 1969.

Burtness, James. *Shaping The Future. The Ethics of Dietrich Bonhoeffer.* Philadelphia: Fortress Press, 1985.

Clements, Keith W. *A Patriotism For Today: Dialogue with Dietrich Bonhoeffer.* Bristol: Bristol Baptist College, 1984. London: Collins, 1986.

Day, Thomas, I. *Dietrich Bonhoeffer on Christian Community and Common Sense.* Lewiston, NY: Mellen Press, 1982.

de Gruchy, John W. *Bonhoeffer and South Africa.* Grand Rapids: Eerdmans; London: Paternoster, 1984.

Dumas, André. *Dietrich Bonhoeffer. Theologian of Reality.* New York: Macmillan, 1971.

Fant, Clyde E. *Bonhoeffer: Wordly Preaching.* Nashville and New York: Thomas Nelson, 1975.

Feil, Ernst. *The Theology of Dietrich Bonhoeffer.* Philadelphia: Fortress Press, 1985.

Godsey, John D. *Preface to Bonhoeffer: The Man and Two of His Shorter Writings.* Philadelphia: Fortress, 1965.

Godsey, John D. 'Reading Bonhoeffer in English translation: Some Difficulties'. *USQR* XXIII.1 (Fall, 1967), 79-90.

Godsey, John D. *The Theology of Dietrich Bonhoeffer.* Philadelphia: Westminster; London: SCM, 1960.

Godsey, John D. and Geffrey B. Kelly, eds. *Ethical Responsibility: Bonhoeffer's Legacy to the Churches.* New York and Toronto: The Edwin Mellen Press, 1981.

Green, Clifford James. *The Sociality of Christ and Humanity. Dietrich Bonhoeffer's Early Theology, 1927-1933.* Missoula, Montana: Scholars Press, 1975.

Hamilton, Kenneth. *Life in One's Stride. A Short Study in Dietrich Bonhoeffer.* Grand Rapids, Michigan: Eerdmans, 1968.

Hopper, David H. *A Dissent on Bonhoeffer.* Philadelphia: Westminster, 1975.

Kelly, Geffrey B. *Liberating Faith. Bonhoeffer's Message for Today.* Minneapolis: Augsburg Publishing House, 1984.

Klassen, A.J. *A Bonhoeffer Legacy.* Grand Rapids: William B. Eerdmans, 1981.

Kuhns, William. *In Pursuit of Dietrich Bonhoeffer.* London: Burnes and Oates, 1968; paperback edition, New York: Doubleday, 1969.

Lovin, Robin W. *Christian Faith and Public Choices: The Social Ethics of Barth, Brunner and Bonhoeffer.* Philadelphia: Fortress Press, 1984.

Marty, Martin E. ed. *The Place of Bonhoeffer. Problems and Possibilities in His Thought.* New York: Associated Press, 1962; London: SCM, 1963.

Moltmann, Jürgen and Jürgen Weissbach. *Two Studies in the Theology of Bonhoeffer.* New York: Charles Schribner and Sons, 1967.

Ott, Heinrich. *Reality and Faith.* London: Lutterworth Press, 1971.

Peck, William J. ed. *New Studies in Bonhoeffer's Ethics.* New York: Edwin Mellen Press, 1987.

Phillips, John A. *Christ for Us in the Theology of Dietrich Bonhoeffer.* New York: Harper, 1967. British title: *The Form of Christ in the World: A Study of Bonhoeffer's Christology.* London: Collins, 1967.

Rasmussen, Larry. *Dietrich Bonhoeffer. Reality and Resistance.* Nashville: Abingdon, 1972.

Reist, Benjamin A. *The Promise of Bonhoeffer.* Philadelphia: Lippincott, 1969.

Smith, Ronald Gregor, ed. *World Come of Age.* London: Collins, 1967.

Vorkink, Peter, II. ed. *Bonhoeffer in a World Come of Age.* Philadelphia: Fortress, 1968.

Woelfel, James W. *Bonhoeffer's Theology. Classical and Revolutionary.* Nashville: Abingdon, 1970.

Zerner, Ruth. 'Dietrich Bonhoeffer and the Jews: Thoughts and Actions, 1933-1945.' *Jewish Social Studies* 37.3-4 (Summer—Fall 1975).

Zerner, Ruth. 'Dietrich Bonhoeffer's American Experiences: People, Letters, and Papers from Union Seminary'. *USQR* Vol. XXXI No. 4 Summer, 1976.

Zimmermann, Wolf-Dieter and Ronald Gregor Smith eds. *I Knew Dietrich Bonhoeffer. Reminiscences by his Friends.* London: Collins; New York: Harper, 1966.

For a Comprehensive Biography see:

Clifford J. Green & Wayne W. Floyd, Jr., *Bonhoeffer Bibliography: Primary and Secondary Sources in English.* Published by The International Bonhoeffer Society, 1986.

NOTES TO THE INTRODUCTION

[1] *Dietrich Bonhoeffer Werke*, Munchen: Chr. Kaiser Verlag, 1986-. This new German critical edition of Bonhoeffer's works will comprise sixteen volumes.

[2] Eberhard Bethge, *Bonhoeffer: Exile & Martyr*, London: Collins, 1975, pp. 155f.

[3] See Hans Pfeifer et al., eds., *Dietrich Bonhoeffer: Jugend und Studium, 1918-1927*, DBW, Band 9, 1986, p. 640.

[4] Thomas Day, *Dietrich Bonhoeffer on Christian Community and Common Sense*, Toronto: Edwin Mellen Press, 1982, p. 9.

[5] Day, *ibid.*

[6] Karl Barth, *CD*, IV/2, p. 641.

[7] Clifford Green, *Bonhoeffer: The Sociality of Christ and Humanity*, Missoula: Scholars Press, 1975, p. 53

[8] John A. Phillips, *The Form of Christ in the World*, London: Collins, 1967, p. 54.

[9] Ernst Feil, *The Theology of Dietrich Bonhoeffer*, Philadelphia: Fortress, 1985, p. 63.

[10] See Regin Prenter, 'Dietrich Bonhoeffer and Karl Barth's Positivism of Revelation', in R. G. Smith, ed., *World Come of Age*, London: Collins, 1967.

[11] Ruth Zerner, 'Dietrich Bonhoeffer's American Experiences: People, Letters, and Papers from Union Seminary', in *Union Seminary Quarterly Review*, vol. xxxi, no. 4, Summer, 1976, p. 276.

[12] On Bonhoeffer's pacifism see, inter alia, Larry L. Rasmussen, *Dietrich Bonhoeffer: Reality and Resistance*, Nashville: Abingdon, 1972, p. 94ff.

[13] Barth, *CD*, III/1, p. 194f.

[14] See Walter Harrelson, 'Bonhoeffer and the Bible', in Marty, *The Place of Bonhoeffer*, New York: Association Press, 1962, pp. 115ff.

[15] See Martin Kuske, *The Old Testament as the Book of Christ: An Appraisal of Bonhoeffer's Interpretation*, Philadelphia: Westminster, 1976, p. 132ff.

[16] See also his lecture 'The Church is Dead', given at an Ecumenical Conference in Gland, August 1932. NRS, revised edition, p. 178ff.

[17] See Martin Kahler, *The So-Called Historical Jesus and the Historic, Biblical Christ*, Philadelphia, Fortress, 1964.

[18] Several years later in his essay 'Rechtfertigung und Recht' (1938), Barth developed the same theme. See *Community, State and Church*, New York: Doubleday, 1960, pp. 101ff.

[19] Guenter Lewy, *The Catholic Church and Nazi Germany*, New York: McGraw Hill, 1964.

[20] See the correspondence between Bonhoeffer and Barth of September 1933, *NRS*, pp. 226f.

[21] On Barmen and the Church Struggle see Arthur C. Cochrane, *The Church's Confession under Hitler*, Philadelphia: Westminster, 1962; John S. Conway, *The Nazi Persecution of the Churches*, New York: Basic Books, 1968.

[22] See David Gill, ed., *Gathered for Life: Official Report of the Sixth Assembly of the World Council of Churches*, Geneva, WCC, 1983, p. 183.

[23] See Ulrich Duchrow, *Conflict Over the Ecumenical Movement*, Geneva: WCC, 1981.

[24] See Helmut Gollwitzer's response in *WF*, pp. 97-106, and Bonhoeffer's summing up of the debate, pp. 106-114.

[25] *CD*, IV/2, pp. 533ff.

[26] Day, *op. cit.*, p. 99.

[27] Jay C. Rochelle, *Spiritual Care*, Philadelphia: Fortress Press, 1985.

[28] David H. Hopper, *A Dissent on Bonhoeffer*, Philadelphia: Westminster, 1975.

[29] Clifford Green, in William J. Peck, ed., *New Studies in Bonhoeffer's Ethics*, Lewiston, New York: Edwin Mellen Press, 1987, p. 12.

[30] Robin Lovin, *Christian Faith and Public Choices: the Social Ethics of Barth, Brunner, and Bonhoeffer*, Philadelphia: Fortress, 1984, p. 127.

[31] See Larry L. Rasmussen, *Dietrich Bonhoeffer: Reality and Resistance*, Nashville: Abingdon, 1972, p. 40.

[32] *ibid.*, p. 50.

[33] Barth, *Fragments Grave and Gray*, Collins Fontana, 1971, p. 121.

[34] See 'The New Theology, An Essay' in *DB*, pp. 757ff.

[35] Bethge, 'The Editing and Publishing of the Bonhoeffer Papers', in *The Andover Newton Bulletin*, vol. lii, no. 2, December 1959, p. 3.

[36] See Bethge, *Bonhoeffer: Exile & Martyr*, p. 63.

[37] See Henry Mottu, 'Feuerbach and Bonhoeffer: Criticism of Religion and the Last Period of Bonhoeffer's Thought', in *USQR*, vol. xxv, no. 1, Fall, 1969

[38] Notably H. Müller, *Von der Kirche zur Welt*, Hamburg-Bergstedt: Herbert Reich Ev. Verlag, 1961.

[39] See Gerhard Krause, 'Dietrich Bonhoeffer and Rudolf Bultmann', in James M. Robinson, ed., *The Future of our Religious Past: Essays in Honour of Rudolf Bultmann*, New York: Harper and Row, 1971.

[40] Ruth Zerner, 'Dietrich Bonhoeffer's Prison Fiction: A Prison Commentary', in *FFP*, p. 154.

[41] Geffrey B. Kelly, *Liberating Faith: Bonhoeffer's Message for Today*, Minneapolis: Augsburg, 1984, p. 16.

INDEX OF NAMES

INDEX OF PLACES AND SUBJECTS